COCHRANE

COCHRANE

The Real Master and Commander

DAVID CORDINGLY

BLOOMSBURY

Published by Bloomsbury USA, New York
Distributed to the trade by Holtzbrinck Publishers

All papers used by Bloomsbury USA are natural, recyclable products made from wood
grown in well-managed forests. The manufacturing processes conform to the
environmental regulations of the country of origin.

LIBRARY OF CONGRESS CATALOGING-IN-PUBLICATION DATA HAS BEEN APPLIED FOR

ISBN-10 1-58234-534-1
ISBN-13 978-1-58234-534-5

First U.S. Edition 2007

1 3 5 7 9 10 8 6 4 2

Typeset by Hewer Text UK Ltd, Edinburgh
Printed in the United States of America by Quebecor World Fairfield

For Bill Swainson

'He was tall and commanding in person, lively and winning in manner, prompt in counsel, and daring but cool in action. Endowed by nature both with strength of character and military genius, versed in naval science both by study and experience, and acquainted with seamen in every clime and country, nothing but an untimely restlessness of disposition, and a too strongly expressed contempt for mediocrity and conventional rules, prevented his becoming one of Britain's naval heroes.'

Description of Lord Cochrane in Greece
at the age of fifty-two, by George Finlay

'Cool calculation would make it appear that the attempt to take Valdivia is madness. This is one reason why the Spaniards will hardly believe us in earnest, even when we commence; and you will see that a bold onset, and a little perseverance afterwards, will give a complete triumph; for operations unexpected by the enemy are, when well executed, almost certain to succeed, whatever may be the odds; and success will preserve the enterprise from the imputation of rashness.'

Lord Cochrane to Major Miller before the taking
of the fortified naval base of Valdivia in Chile

'A British nobleman is a free man, capable of judging between right and wrong, and at liberty to adopt a country and a cause which aim at restoring the rights of oppressed human nature.'

Lord Cochrane to Don Joaquim de la Pezuela,
the Spanish Viceroy of Peru

CONTENTS

ACKNOWLEDGEMENTS

This book is based to a large extent on the Admiralty collections in the National Archives at Kew, and on the Dundonald papers in the National Archives of Scotland. I am grateful to Douglas, Earl of Dundonald, for granting me access to the family papers, for the loan of colour transparencies of many of the family pictures, and for helpful discussions about his famous ancestor whose turbulent life he views with a keen but notably impartial interest. I am also indebted to some of the earlier biographies of Cochrane, particularly those by Christopher Lloyd, Ian Grimble and Donald Thomas. Grimble helped the fourteenth earl to catalogue the family papers and his book is a valuable source of quotations which he patiently extracted from the mass of often scarcely legible letters.

My greatest debt is to two more recent biographers. I am most grateful to John Sugden for his help and advice and for his masterly Ph.D. thesis, which covers Cochrane's life up to 1818 and is a model of detailed research and sober analysis. I have also been heavily reliant on Brian Vale's pioneering publications on Cochrane's activities in South America and would like to thank him for sharing his thoughts and for lending me some of his unpublished material. I am also indebted to the Rt. Hon. Sir Anthony Evans, former Lord Justice of Appeal, who has examined the papers relating to the Stock Exchange fraud of 1814 and has given me the benefit of his legal opinion on the controversial trial which caused such a stir at the time and has continued to provoke dissenting opinions to this day. My thanks to him and his wife Caroline for their kindness and hospitality on many occasions. Thanks also to my friend John English, who invited me to sail with him two summers ago and with whom I spent an enjoyable week sailing from Majorca around the island of Minorca to the great harbour of Port Mahon – the starting point for Cochrane's (and Jack Aubrey's) first cruise as master and commander.

I would also like to thank John Batchelor for his excellent cutaway drawing of the *Imperieuse*, Norman Swales for drawing up the lines of the *Speedy* so beautifully, John Gilkes for his fine maps, and all those people who have answered my queries and supplied me with information or whose books I have plundered for information, especially Ian Cashmore, Robert Gardiner, Brian Lavery, Pieter van der Merwe, Roger Knight and Richard Woodman, as well as the staff of the British Library, the Essex Record Office, the Guildhall Library, the London Library, the National Archives of Scotland, the National Library of Scotland, the National Maritime Museum and the Newspaper Library at Colindale. I am most grateful to Nicholas Blake for painstakingly checking my draft text for historical and maritime errors but would stress that I am responsible for any errors that remain.

The staff of Bloomsbury, my publishers, have been unfailingly helpful and a pleasure to work with: I am particularly grateful to Bill Swainson for his constant support and wise advice but would also like to thank Emily Sweet and Polly Napper, both of whom have contributed to producing a book which, in my view at least, is an extremely handsome production. Above all my thanks go to my wife Shirley, who has helped me sort out my thoughts on numerous occasions, has once again put other things on hold while the writing was in progress, and has accompanied me on travels which have taken us from Edinburgh and Hampshire to Chile and Brazil in the tracks of Lord Cochrane.

And finally two notes on unrelated matters. Previous biographers have persisted in calling Cochrane's wife Kitty. I have been unable to find any evidence for this and the current earl believes that it was a later member of the family who was called Kitty and not the woman that Cochrane himself invariably called Kate. Lastly I must acknowledge my debt to G. A. Henty, that once popular author of patriotic stories for boys. Fans of Henty will note that I have borrowed part of the title of one of his historical novels for the title of this book.

D.C.

Brighton, Sussex. April 2007

LIST OF ILLUSTRATIONS

First colour plates

William Cochrane, the first Earl of Dundonald. (*Courtesy of the Earl of Dundonald*)

Thomas Cochrane's father Archibald, the ninth Earl of Dundonald. (*Courtesy of the Earl of Dundonald*)

Thomas Cochrane as a boy. (*Courtesy of the Earl of Dundonald*)

The confluence of the Thames and Medway, 1808, by J.M.W. Turner. (© *Tate, London, 2007*)

The harbour and town of Lerwick, by J. C. Schetky. (© *National Maritime Museum, London*)

A British squadron off Valetta during the blockade of Malta, by Rev. Cooper Willyams. (© *National Maritime Museum, London*)

Lord St Vincent as First Lord of the Admiralty. (© *National Maritime Museum, London*)

A portrait of Admiral Lord Keith by William Owen. (© *National Maritime Museum, London*)

The Rock of Gibraltar viewed from the ruins of Fort St Philip. (© *National Maritime Museum, London*)

The capture of the Spanish *El Gamo* by the British sloop *Speedy*, 6 May 1801, by Clarkson Stanfield. (*V&A Images, Victoria and Albert Museum*)

A detail from a panoramic view of the royal dockyard at Plymouth, by Nicholas Pocock. (© *National Maritime Museum, London*)

A watercolour by J.M.W. Turner of Plymouth, looking across the shipping in the Cattewater towards the Citadel. (*V&A Images, Victoria and Albert Museum*)

Black and white plates

The boarding and taking of the Spanish xebec frigate *El Gamo* by His Majesty's sloop *Speedy*. Engraving after the picture by Nicholas Pocock. (© *National Maritime Museum, London*)

Second colour plates

The rock of Lisbon, by J. C. Schetky. (© *National Maritime Museum, London*)

Crowds gathered around the hustings at Covent Garden, from Akermann's Micorcosm of London. (*By permission of The British Library*)

Lord Cochrane, the naval hero, by Stroehling. (© *National Maritime Museum, London*)

Lord Cochrane, the Radical politician, by Adam Buck. (© *National Maritime Museum, London*)

A watercolour by Lieutenant William Innes Pocock identifying seven types of Mediterranean vessel. (© *National Maritime Museum, London*)

Sir Francis Burdett, watercolour by Adam Buck. (© *National Portrait Gallery, London*)

William Cobbett, writer and journalist. (© *National Portrait Gallery, London*)

The House of Commons as it would have looked in Cochrane's day, from Ackermann's *Microcosm of London*. (*By permission of the British Library*)

Cochrane's wife Kate with their daughter Elisabeth, by Sir George Hayter. (*Courtesy of the Earl of Dundonald*)

Portrait by Sir Thomas Lawrence of Maria Graham. (© *National Portrait Gallery, London*)

General Bernardo O'Higgins, Supreme Director of Chile. (*Courtesy of Earl of Dundonald*)

A view of the Bay of Guanabara, Brazil, by George L. Hall. (*Private collection*)

A portrait of Cochrane in his fifties by Sir George Hayter. (*Courtesy of Earl of Dundonald*)

Images in the text

Lord Cochrane as a civilian in his early forties, by W. Walton. (*National Portrait Gallery, London*)

Culross in the late seventeenth century, viewed across the Firth of Forth. (*By permission of the British Library*)

The south front of Culross Abbey House as it looked in the 1780s. (*By permission of the British Library*)

Shipping off Leith Roads with the city of Edinburgh in the distance, by J. C. Schetky. (© *National Maritime Museum, London*)

A plan and elevation of His Majesty's dockyard at Sheerness. (© *National Maritime Museum, London*)

A watercolour by George Tobin depicting the *Thetis* aground on the coast of North Carolina. (© *National Maritime Museum, London*)

A warship entering the harbour of Port Mahon, Minorca. (© *National Maritime Museum, London*)

The wreckage of the *Queen Charlotte* at Leghorn in March 1800. (© *National Maritime Museum, London*)

A detail from a watercolour by Nicholas Pocock showing the brig sloop *Childers*. (© *National Maritime Museum, London*)

The *Speedy*, under the command of Captain Jahleel Brenton, attacked by enemy gunboats off Gibraltar. (© *National Maritime Museum, London*)

MAPS

Map of Scotland showing places connected with Cochrane's domestic life and the places he visited during his cruises in the *Thetis* and the *Arab*.

Map of the English Channel and Atlantic coast of France showing the ports, naval bases and anchorages associated with Cochrane's various cruises.

Map of the Mediterranean showing naval bases and anchorages as well as the harbours and coastal towns attacked by the *Speedy* and the *Imperieuse*.

A plan of the fireship attack on the French fleet anchored in Aix Roads on the evening of 11 April 1809. The time is around 9 p.m. The explosion vessels are approaching the floating boom and are followed by the fireships.

A plan of Aix Roads showing the British ships attacking the grounded French ships around 4 p.m. on 12 April 1809. Cochrane's *Imperieuse* has been joined by the bomb vessel *Aetna*, a brig sloop, three gun brigs, five frigates and two 74-gun ships.

A map of South America showing the places associated with Cochrane's cruises and naval campaigns.

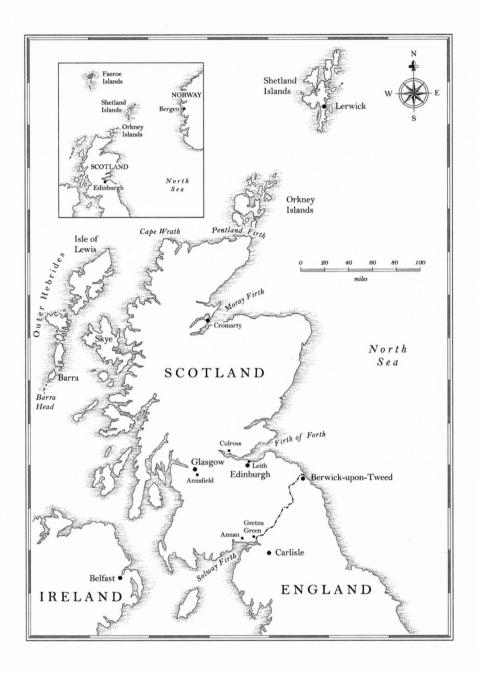

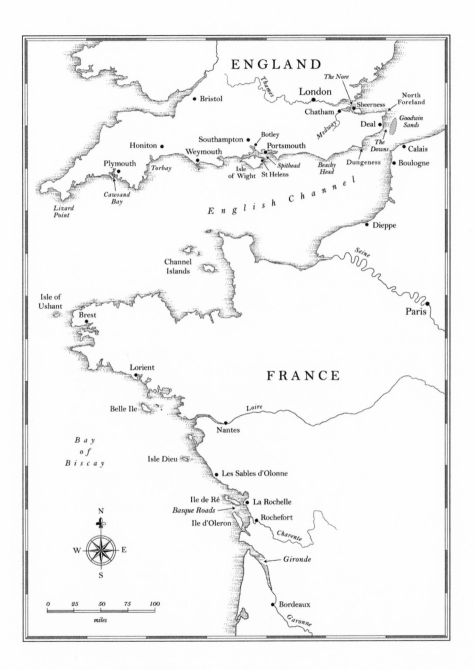

ENGLAND

Bristol

Thames

The Nore

London

Sheerness

Chatham

Medway

Deal

North
Foreland

Goodwin
Sands

Honiton

Southampton

Botley

Weymouth

Portsmouth

The
Downs

Calais

Plymouth

Torbay

Isle
of Wight

Spithead

St Helens

Beachy
Head

Dungeness

Boulogne

Cawsand
Bay

Lizard
Point

English Channel

Dieppe

Seine

Channel
Islands

Isle of
Ushant

Brest

Paris

Lorient

FRANCE

Belle Ile

Loire

Nantes

Bay
of
Biscay

Isle Dieu

Les Sables d'Olonne

Ile de Ré

La Rochelle

Basque Roads

Rochefort

Ile d'Oleron

Charente

N

W   E

S

Gironde

Bordeaux

Garonne

0   25   50   75   100

miles

Isle of Ushant

Brest

Paris

Lorient

*Atlantic
Ocean*

*Bay of
Biscay*

Basque
Roads

La Rochelle
Rochefort

Bordeaux

La Coruna

FRANCE

Vigo

Montpellier
Sete
Narbonne
Marseilles
Ciotat
Port Vendres
Palamos
Blanes
Mongat
Barcelona
Bay of Rosas
Tarragona

PORTUGAL

SPAIN

Madrid

Lisbon

Peniscola

Valencia

MINORCA

Cape St Vincent

Sevilla

Alicante
Cartagena

IBIZA

MAJORCA

Malaga
Almeria

Cape de Palos

Cadiz
Gibraltar

M e d i t e r r a n e a

Tangier

Tetouan

MOROCCO

Algiers

ALGERIA

Bay of Cadiz

Cadiz

SPAIN

*Cape de
Formentor*

MINORCA

MAJORCA

*Bay of
Alcudia*

Port
Mah

Isla Dragonera

Palma

IBIZA

Cape Trafalgar

Algeciras

Gibraltar

*Europa
Point*

Strait of Gibraltar

Cape de Salinas

CABRERA

20 miles

Tangier

MOROCCO

FORMENTERA

50 miles

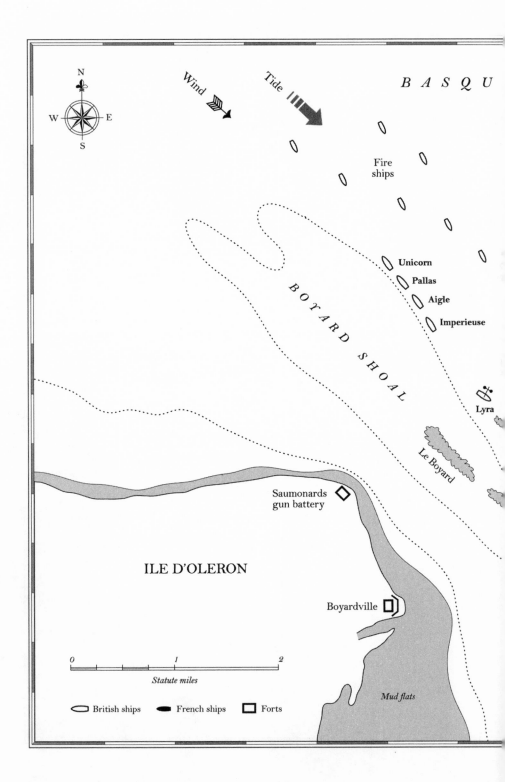

N

W · E

S

Wind

Tide

B A S Q U

Fire
ships

Unicorn

Pallas

Aigle

Imperieuse

B O Y A R D   S H O A L

Lyra

Le Boyard

Saumonards
gun battery

ILE D'OLERON

Boyardville

0   1   2

Statute miles

🡒 British ships   ● French ships   ▭ Forts

Mud flats

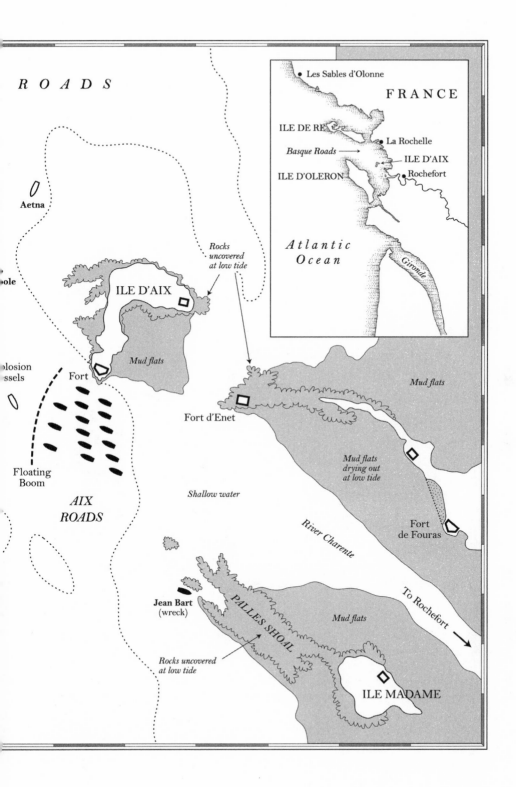

R O A D S

Aetna

ole

losion
ssels

Fort

Floating
Boom

*AIX
ROADS*

ILE D'AIX

Mud flats

Rocks
uncovered
at low tide

Fort d'Enet

Mud flats

*Mud flats
drying out
at low tide*

Shallow water

River Charente

Fort
de Fouras

Jean Bart
(wreck)

PALLES SHOAL

Rocks uncovered
at low tide

Mud flats

To Rochefort

ILE MADAME

Les Sables d'Olonne

FRANCE

ILE DE RE

La Rochelle

Basque Roads

ILE D'AIX

Rochefort

ILE D'OLERON

*Atlantic
Ocean*

Gironde

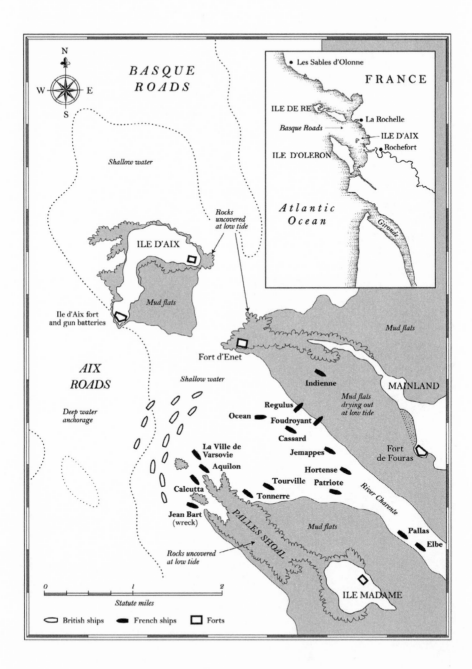

N
W ⊕ E
S

BASQUE
ROADS

Shallow water

*Rocks
uncovered
at low tide*

ILE D'AIX

Mud flats

Ile d'Aix fort
and gun batteries

AIX
ROADS

*Deep water
anchorage*

Shallow water

Fort d'Enet

Indienne

Regulus

Ocean   Foudroyant

Cassard

La Ville de
Varsovie   Jemappes

Aquilon   Hortense

Tourville   Patriote

Calcutta   Tonnerre

Jean Bart
(wreck)

*Rocks uncovered
at low tide*

PALLES SHOAL

Mud flats

Mud flats

MAINLAND

*Mud flats
drying out
at low tide*

Fort
de Fouras

River Charente

Pallas

Elbe

ILE MADAME

0   1   2
Statute miles

⬭ British ships   ⬛ French ships   ☐ Forts

Les Sables d'Olonne

FRANCE

ILE DE RE

La Rochelle

Basque Roads →

ILE D'AIX

Rochefort

ILE D'OLERON

*Atlantic
Ocean*

Gironde

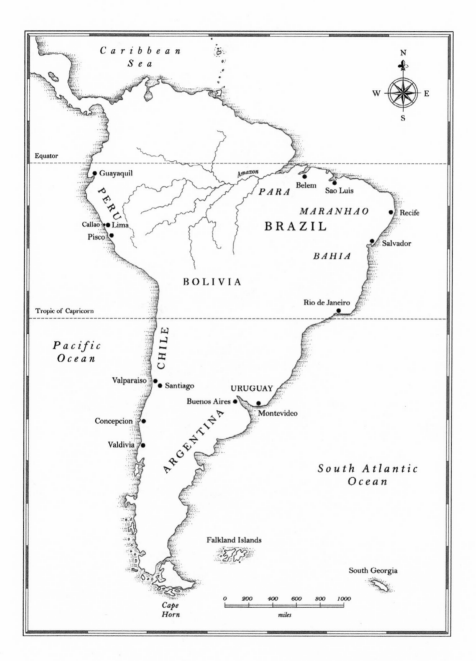

Caribbean
Sea

N
W E
S

Equator

Guayaquil

PERU

Amazon

PARA

Belem

Sao Luis

MARANHAO

BRAZIL

Recife

Callao Lima
Pisco

Salvador

BAHIA

BOLIVIA

Tropic of Capricorn

Rio de Janeiro

Pacific
Ocean

CHILE

Valparaiso Santiago

URUGUAY

Buenos Aires

Montevideo

Concepcion

ARGENTINA

Valdivia

South Atlantic
Ocean

Falkland Islands

South Georgia

0 200 400 600 800 1000

Cape
Horn

miles

Lord Cochrane as a civilian in his early forties before he departed for South America. Engraving published in 1819 after a picture by W. Walton.

PROLOGUE

Thomas Cochrane, the tenth Earl of Dundonald, was a man of outstanding courage and determination. He had a brilliant record as a frigate captain but he was also a fearless fighter for radical causes, a friend of the oppressed and a champion of liberty. When Lord Byron learnt of his arrival in the capital of Peru following the liberation of that country from the colonial rule of Spain he wrote, 'there is no man I envy so much as Lord Cochrane. His entry into Lima, which I see in today's paper, is one of the great events of the day.' Sir Walter Scott was so impressed by the standing ovation which Cochrane and his wife received in an Edinburgh theatre on their return from South America that he was inspired to write a poem in their honour. William Cobbett, the outspoken campaigner against corruption in public life, and Sir Francis Burdett, the leading spokesman for parliamentary reform, were among Cochrane's closest friends and supporters. When he died in 1860 *The Times* noted that he had outlived envy and malice, had suffered much, and triumphed at last. 'History can produce few examples of such a man or of such achievements. There have been greater heroes because there have been heroes with greater opportunities, but no soldier or sailor of modern times ever displayed a more extraordinary capacity than the man who now lies dead.'[1]

In an age which saw the rise and fall of Napoleon and the upsurge in poetry, literature and painting of the Romantic movement, Cochrane was the very epitome of the Romantic hero. His life has an epic quality and was marked by a dramatic succession of ups and downs. Remarkable triumphs were all too often followed by disappointment and recriminations. Like so many heroes he was a flawed character with a temperament which led him into conflict and disputes. He imagined

enemies where there were none and made enemies of people who
should have been his friends. He was frequently out of step with his
times and lacked the insight and the humility to understand why this
should be and to adapt to it. His most damaging fault was his pursuit
of money and his relentless determination to make his fortune. Many
naval officers were motivated by the lure of prize money – the reward
for the capture and subsequent sale of an enemy warship or merchant
vessel. But with Cochrane it became an obsession. When he arrived in
Chile he told his brother William, 'I have every prospect of making the
largest fortune which has been made in our days, save that of the Duke
of Wellington.'[2] There were good reasons for his mercenary attitude,
as we shall see, but it was to cause trouble in his lifetime and in recent
years has tarnished his once glittering reputation.

Cochrane's autobiographies have also been responsible for the
conflicting views about him. The first of these appeared in 1859
and was entitled *Narrative of Services in the Liberation of Chili, Peru, and
Brazil from Spanish and Portuguese Domination*. The second, which was
simply called *The Autobiography of a Seaman*, was a racy account of
Cochrane's career in the Royal Navy and was published shortly before
his death in 1860. It was widely read at the time and has since become
one of the classics of naval literature. Both biographies were compiled
when Cochrane was in his eighties and were based on his memories of
distant events as well as letters, logbooks, journals, newspaper cuttings and the memoirs of those who had known him. Neither book was
written by Cochrane but by a professional author called George Butler
Earp. Both contain vivid accounts of his naval actions but the South
American volume is marred by the excessive amount of space devoted
to arguments about pay and prize money, and *The Autobiography of a
Seaman* is a platform for Cochrane's embittered views of the Basque
Roads action, the court martial of Admiral Lord Gambier, and the
Stock Exchange trial of 1814.

Cochrane used the biographies to settle old scores and it was not
long before his attacks on leading figures of his day produced a
backlash from their families and supporters. The first shots came
from Lady Chatterton who published a biography of Gambier, com-

mander-in-chief at the time of Cochrane's fireship attack on the
anchored French fleet at Basque Roads. She strongly defended Gambier's actions and pointed out a number of errors in Cochrane's
account.[3] Far more damaging were two books which set out to defend
Lord Ellenborough, the formidable judge who had presided over the
Stock Exchange trial which had led to Cochrane's imprisonment and
disgrace. The first book, by J. B. Atlay, an Oxford scholar and a
barrister, was published in 1897 and was a meticulous examination of
the background to the trial, the evidence presented and the arguments
for the defence and the prosecution. Atlay not only set out a convincing case for the guilty verdict on Cochrane but was dismissive of
the autobiography. 'No naval biography is more entertaining,' he
wrote. 'Yet this popular book has been compiled in so extraordinary a
manner as to have little claim to be considered anything more than a
historical romance.'[4] The second book, *The Guilt of Lord Cochrane in
1814*, which was written by Lord Ellenborough's grandson, underlined Atlay's verdict on the trial and concluded, 'The so-called
"Autobiography of a Seaman" has been a fraud on the boyhood of
England for over fifty years. It is not an autobiography, it was not even
written by a seaman.'[5]

The doubts cast on Cochrane's character and on the reliability of
the biographies did nothing to stem the interest in his life. The heroic
and dramatic nature of so many of his exploits proved irresistible for
later generations of biographers and were a source of rich material for
historical novelists. Indeed, Cochrane's literary legacy has proved
more significant than his historical legacy. He rarely receives more
than a passing mention in most naval histories but his exploits live on
in the works of Patrick O'Brian, C.S. Forester and others. Captain
Marryat, who had served as a midshipman in the frigate *Imperieuse* and
had taken part in some of the most spectacular of Cochrane's actions,
used his experiences as the basis for *Frank Mildmay, or the Naval
Officer*, the first of his many adventure stories which proved popular
with Victorian readers and were enjoyed by his friend Charles
Dickens. G.A. Henty, a prolific writer whose patriotic tales were
avidly read by schoolboys from Edwardian times until they fell out

of favour in the 1950s, produced a stirring account of the naval hero in his book *With Cochrane the Dauntless; the exploits of Lord Cochrane in South American waters* which was first published in 1909. C.S. Forester drew on events in Cochrane's life for several of his Hornblower novels, notably *The Happy Return*, which is based on Cochrane's exploits with the Chilean navy. Patrick O'Brian freely acknowledged his debt to Cochrane's autobiography. The plots of three of the books in his admired sequence of novels featuring Captain Jack Aubrey and his surgeon Stephen Maturin are taken directly from events in Cochrane's career: *Master and Commander* is inspired by Cochrane's exploits in the *Speedy; The Reverse of the Medal* has Aubrey involved in a scandal on the Stock Exchange; and *Blue at the Mizzen* includes incidents from Cochrane's actions in South America. Although there are similarities between Cochrane's life and some of the adventures of Hornblower and Aubrey, it has to be said that the real-life exploits of Cochrane were often far more daring and more exciting than those of his fictional counterparts.

There is no doubt that Cochrane was his own worst enemy. He had few equals as a man of action but he was lacking in tact and diplomacy. He was constantly upsetting his superior officers, dashing off provocative letters and imagining plots and slights against him. His greatest mistake was to get involved in the politics of his day. It was not unusual for serving naval officers to enter Parliament but Cochrane did not have the necessary qualities for success in that noisy bear garden. His passionate embracing of worthy but unpopular causes, his lack of any political subtlety, his impatience to get results, combined with his personal attacks and his intemperate language, proved a disastrous combination.

What is so striking about Cochrane is the contrast between the combative tone of so many of his letters and speeches and his unusually quiet and reserved manner. The novelist Mary Russell Mitford, who met him in the garden of William Cobbett's home in Hampshire when he was at the height of his fame as a frigate captain, was surprised to find him nothing like the common notion of a warrior: 'A gentle, mild young man was this burner of the French fleets and cutter-out of Spanish vessels . . .'[6] Cyrus Redding, the writer and journalist, found him to be 'a remarkably plain, quiet, fine young man, wholly unassuming'.[7] Maria Graham, the widow of a naval officer and a travel writer of distinction who saw much of Cochrane in Chile, also noted his unassuming manner but was impressed by the man behind the calm front which he presented to the world. 'Though not handsome, Lord Cochrane has an expression of countenance which induces you, when you have once looked, to look again and again. It is variable as the feelings which pass within; but the most general look is that of great benevolence. His conversation, when he breaks his habitual silence, is rich and varied; on subjects connected with his profession or his pursuits, clear and animated; and if ever I met with genius, I should say it was pre-eminent in Lord Cochrane.'[8]

This book began as a study of Cochrane's career in the Royal Navy with the aim of examining his version of the story as it appears in *The Autobiography of a Seaman* and comparing it with relevant contemporary documents. These documents include the logbooks and muster books of his ships; his letters and reports to his commanding officers and the Admiralty in London; the letters and memoirs of his fellow officers; court martial reports; the minutes of the Navy Board and Board of Admiralty; reports in the newspapers and in the *Naval Chronicle*; the observations of people who met him during his years as a frigate captain; charts and contemporary pictures of the ports, harbours and coasts which he visited; and the plans of his ships (curiously neglected by other biographers – we find, for instance, that the brig sloop *Speedy* was steered by a tiller and not by a wheel, and that the hated *Arab* bore little resemblance to a slab-sided collier).

It soon became evident that it was impossible to do justice to Cochrane's achievements as a naval commander without taking into account the truly astonishing feats which he carried out while in command of the navies of Chile and Brazil. It was equally difficult to ignore his activities as a Member of Parliament because these were originally prompted by his desire to draw attention to injustices, corruption and dangerous practices which he came across as a naval officer. His interest in the scientific and engineering advances of his

day also had to be taken into account because he was constantly
experimenting and inventing: he was among the first naval officers to
make use of Congreve's rockets when attacking coastal targets; the
'explosion ships' at Basque Roads were largely of his own devising; he
invented a convoy lamp for the use of merchant convoys; and he was a
leading exponent of steam power for warships and devoted years of his
life to devising and building a rotary steam engine.

In addition to the naval documents there is a great deal of material
available on the other aspects of Cochrane's life. Because he was so
often involved in controversial schemes, in legal battles and in claims
for large sums of money including prize money and back pay, he and
his secretary, and later his family, made sure that copies of his letters
and parliamentary papers, and the records of his dealings with foreign
governments were preserved. These, and much of the correspondence
between him and his wife and their five children, have been deposited
in the National Archives of Scotland and the National Library of
Scotland and are a wonderfully rich resource for students of his life.
The National Maritime Museum at Greenwich has a number of
relevant documents including the correspondence between Cochrane
and his Scottish surgeon, James Guthrie. (It would be interesting to
know whether Patrick O'Brian was aware of the life-long friendship
between Cochrane and Guthrie when he created the ingenious and
fascinating character of Dr Maturin.) And there is also valuable
material in the British Library, notably the Collingwood Papers,
the Auckland Papers and the Minutes of Evidence given before the
House of Lords Committee of Privileges in 1861 – the latter is
particularly revealing about Cochrane's domestic life and the details
of his courtship and runaway marriage to a young and pretty orphan in
defiance of the wishes of his wealthy uncle.

We also know exactly what Cochrane looked like at different stages
of his life. He sat for his portrait on several occasions and these
paintings remain in the family collections. There are also some fine
engraved portraits and a few caricatures by some of the leading
cartoonists of his day. These, together with the descriptions of many
people who met him, indicate that he was impressively tall and

powerfully built, and that his hair was not red, as so many biographers have suggested, but auburn (the descriptions vary between sandy and reddish). He had blue eyes, a prominent nose and a fair complexion which his life at sea caused to be tanned and sun-freckled. Samuel Bamford, the radical activist, said that 'he stooped a little and had somewhat of a sailor's gait in walking'.[9] And since he was born and brought up in Scotland it is not surprising to find that he spoke with a distinctive Scottish accent. His grandson recalled, 'I was a boy when my grandfather died, and I well remember him – his striking personality, his impressive manner of speech, with a lowland Scottish accent, and his kindness to children.'[10] He was always intensely proud of his Scottish roots, and his Scottish friends and connections were a constant source of support during his long and turbulent life.

ONE

A Scottish Upbringing

1775–1793

Culross Abbey House, where Thomas Cochrane and his three younger brothers spent their early years, is situated beside the old abbey ruins on high ground overlooking the Firth of Forth. When the Cochrane family were living there the house had a palatial appearance with rooms on three floors and an imposing façade with square towers at either end. It had been built by Edward, Lord Bruce of Kinross, in 1607 and was based on designs by Inigo Jones. For more than two hundred years the house dominated the skyline of Culross, but in the nineteenth century the house fell into disrepair. It was partly dismantled in 1830 and was rebuilt on a smaller scale with two floors and without the flanking towers. The lower sections of the towers were converted into outbuildings and these, together with the heraldic pediment over the main entrance and the finely proportioned windows, are a reminder today of the house's former grandeur. From the terrace in front of the house there are panoramic views across the tidal waters of the Forth which stretch away into the distance towards the city of Edinburgh, fifteen miles downstream.

Alongside the house is the parish church of Culross. Once part of the old abbey, the church has been much altered over the years and the church tower now has battlements in place of the distinctive stepped roof which appears in old engravings. The churchyard is full of half-buried gravestones and ancient yew trees. It is a peaceful spot and in the summer months the only sounds are those from the sheep in the nearby fields and the cries of the jackdaws among the ruins of Culross Abbey. The abbey, which lies in the shadow of the church tower, was founded by Malcolm, Thane of Fife, in 1217 and for two centuries it was a monastery housing Cistercian monks. According to local legend Lady Macduff and her children were murdered by Macbeth in the vicinity.

Below the dilapidated walls and foundations of the abbey the land falls steeply away and a narrow road leads down to the cobbled streets of Culross which is a remarkably well-preserved example of a small Scottish town of the seventeenth century.[1] The picturesque collection of small houses with roofs of weathered red pantiles and Dutch gable ends extends along the waterfront. At the height of the town's prosperity in the 1600s there were sometimes as many as a hundred merchant ships anchored offshore waiting to transport locally-produced salt and coal from the Culross mines to Scandinavia and the Low Countries. There is little activity on this section of the river today; at low tide the foreshore becomes a vast expanse of mud with gulls and oystercatchers picking their way among the pools left by the receding water.

The Cochranes can be traced back to the eleventh century and beyond but it was William Cochrane, first earl of Dundonald, who founded the fortunes of the family. He was born in 1605 and became the Member of Parliament for Ayrshire in 1641. He was a great landowner with estates at Paisley and others in Renfrewshire and Ayrshire. His staunch support for the Stuart cause was rewarded by King Charles I who created him Baron Cochrane of Dundonald in 1647. He continued to represent Ayrshire in Cromwell's parliament of 1656 but in 1660 he was one of the lords who supported the return of Charles II to England and his restoration to the throne. In 1669 he was created earl of Dundonald and Lord Cochrane of Paisley and Ochiltree. He died in 1685, aged eighty, and was buried at Dundonald, some twenty miles south-west of Glasgow.[2] A fine portrait in the Dundonald family collection shows a man of commanding presence with the prominent nose and cleft chin characteristic of many of his descendants.

The family fortunes suffered a steady decline during the succeeding generations. Taxes, marriage provisions requiring handsome dowries for daughters, and large sums spent on improvements to houses and gardens, were a constant drain. Instead of making money from their lands, or investing in overseas colonies, many of the Cochranes joined the army – a noble enough profession but not a lucrative one. Three members of the family were killed in Marlborough's wars. The seventh earl joined the army of General Wolfe which was despatched to Canada to drive the French from Quebec and the settlements along the banks of the St Lawrence River. He died in 1758 during the assault on the fortress of Louisbourg in Nova Scotia. Following his death the Paisley estates were sold and Major Thomas Cochrane, who became the eighth earl, inherited little more than the Culross Abbey estates

and the surrounding lands. His unwise investments and extravagant bequests further diminished the family fortunes, which did not bode well for the man who would succeed him as the ninth earl of Dundonald. This was Archibald Cochrane, the father of Thomas Cochrane whose adventurous life would lead to him becoming the most famous member of the family.

Archibald Cochrane was a man with a genius for invention but a fatal inability to control his finances.[3] He was born in 1748, the second child and eldest son of the nine children of Major Thomas Cochrane. At the age of sixteen he went into the army as a young officer in the 3rd Dragoons but after a while he left the army and joined the navy. His voyages took him as far as the Guinea coast and he rose to the rank of acting lieutenant but the long and dreary months at sea did not suit his active and enquiring mind. He returned to the family home at Culross to devote himself to civilian pursuits. In October 1774, at the

Culross in the late seventeenth century, viewed across the Firth of Forth. Culross Abbey and the Abbey House can be seen on the hill above the town.

age of twenty-six, he married Anna Gilchrist, the nineteen-year-old daughter of Captain James Gilchrist, a distinguished frigate captain. The Gilchrists lived at Annsfield, Hamilton, in Lanarkshire, a few miles south-east of Glasgow. There is a moving letter from Captain Gilchrist to his friend George Marsh, a commissioner in the Navy Office in London, which describes the feelings of his wife and himself at the thought of losing their daughter. It was written from Annsfield on 10 October 1774, a week before the marriage was due to take place:

> Dear George,
>
> I wrote to you the week before last and intended to have mentioned an event that was likely to happen but Mrs Gilchrist's heart failed her . . . She is set down with tears in her eyes to tell you that we are in one sense to lose one of our dear girls in a few days and I really don't know what I shall do without her as she is truly a fine sweet girl yet can have no objections as I hope its for her good to be joined for life to so good and worthie a young man as Lord Cochrane who I look upon as none such in this deprived age being certainly possessed of every amiable quality and I flatter myself she is possessed of every disposition capable of making a man happy. Its my youngest daughter Annie who [by] way of addition to her goodness everybody reckons handsome . . . They are to be married here Monday next week [at] Culross Abbey which is his house near 40 miles from this.[4]

The marriage would be tragically cut short by Anna's death ten years later but while it lasted it seems to have been an extremely happy one. Archibald Cochrane worshipped his wife and described her as 'the handsomest woman in Scotland'. His brother John said, 'she was an angel of a woman. Her firmness and resolution never left her.'[5]

For the birth of her first child Anna left Culross and went to stay with her parents at Annsfield and it was there that Thomas Cochrane was born on 14 December 1775. He was in good company that year. Jane Austen was born two days later at her father's rectory in Hampshire; with two brothers in the navy she would take a keen interest in naval affairs, and the life of Captain Francis Austen would cross the path of the future Captain Lord Cochrane on more than one occasion. The year 1775 also saw the birth of Charles Lamb, the essayist, and J.M.W. Turner, England's greatest painter of landscapes and seascapes. The war with North America began that same year: a minor skirmish at Lexington in April 1775 lit a fuse which led to the full-scale Battle of Bunker Hill in June. The following year, on 4 July 1776, the United States of America formally declared their independence. The war would drag on for eight years and two of the young Thomas Cochrane's seven uncles took part in the campaign. His naval uncle Alexander was a junior lieutenant in the 74-gun ship *Montague* and was wounded in Rodney's action against the French off Martinique in April 1780. Colonel Charles Cochrane, the second son of the eighth earl, who was serving as an aide-de-camp of General Cornwallis, was killed during the siege of Yorktown, Virginia, in the autumn of 1781. The siege ended with Cornwallis surrendering his army to General Washington, an event which effectively marked the end of Britain's struggle to retain her American colonies.

The Cochrane family at Culross were kept informed of events in North America by occasional letters from Alexander Cochrane to his eldest brother Archibald who was now head of the family.[6] The eighth earl had died on 27 June 1778 and Archibald, at the age of thirty, had inherited the title and the house and estates of Culross Abbey. His eldest son Thomas, who was three years old when his father became Lord Dundonald, now assumed the courtesy title of Lord Cochrane.

Given the mass of material preserved in the Dundonald family archives it is disappointing to find that so little has been recorded of the childhood of Thomas Cochrane and his younger brothers Basil, William and Archibald. However, it is evident from Cochrane's autobiography that they had little or no formal schooling. The parlous state of the family finances discouraged Lord Dundonald from sending the four boys to any of the fine schools in Edinburgh, and he seems to have been too busy with his own projects to have paid much attention to the matter. 'Perceiving our education imperilled,' Cochrane recalled, 'the devotedness of my maternal grandmother, Mrs Gilchrist, prompted her to apply her small income to the exigencies of her grandchildren.'[7] Thanks to her efforts the boys received the rudiments of schooling from a series of tutors, none of whom appears to have been very satisfactory. It was an upbringing that taught them to be self-reliant and practical. They had the run of the rambling great house at Culross, the churchyard and the abbey ruins, and the thick forest of Scots pines which covered the slopes to the east. According to family tradition Cochrane was an adventurous boy and there are tales of him climbing trees, descending a disused coal shaft to look for a nest and sailing a boat on the Forth with bed sheets for sails.

On 15 November 1784, when Cochrane was nearly nine, his mother died in the house of his uncle John with her husband by her side. Lord Dundonald was overcome with grief: 'Life itself is a misery to me since my Dearest, Dear, Dear Annie breathed her last in my arms,' he wrote in a letter to her mother. 'Her last words to me were Take care of the bairns, Farewell, Farewell. Her dying look will never be effaced from my mind, recommending herself to God.'[8] We can only speculate on the effect which her death had on her children because there are scarcely any references to her in their later correspondence. Fortunately for the young family their grandmother, Mrs Gilchrist, stepped

The south front of Culross Abbey House as it looked in the 1780s during the boyhood of Thomas Cochrane. The tower of the Abbey church can be seen on the left.

into the breach and took charge of the household at Culross. She seems to have been a warm and capable woman. Many years later Cochrane's wife would testify that he often referred to the days of his youth in Scotland and 'the happy days with his grandmother'.[9]

It is significant that most of the brief chapter which Cochrane devoted to his boyhood in his autobiography is devoted not to his own upbringing but to his father and his scientific experiments. He admired his father, he learnt much from him and later in life he would prove equally inventive, but he could not forgive him for embarking on one ruinous venture after another: '. . . his discoveries, now of national utility, ruined him, and deprived his posterity of their remaining paternal inheritance.'[10] While Thomas Cochrane was still in his teens the entire Culross Abbey estate was put up for sale and later passed out of the family for ever.[11] The irony of the situation was that if the estates had been well managed they would have brought considerable wealth to Dundonald and his heirs. Beneath the 2,000 acres of land lay rich seams of coal, iron, fire clay and brick clay; above ground the estate included nearly 1,000 acres of Scots pine 'now fit to be cut for waggon-way rails, sleepers and pit-timber'.[12] This was at a time when the Industrial Revolution was gathering momentum and such raw materials were very much in demand.

Lord Dundonald was aware of the riches on his land. He was abreast of the latest developments of the industrial age and was in touch with some of the best scientific minds of the day: Joseph Black, Professor of Chemistry at Edinburgh and a man often regarded as the father of modern chemistry, was a family friend; and so was Matthew Boulton, the partner of James Watt, the Scottish designer of the first commercial steam engine. But Dundonald believed he had made a discovery which would yield riches far greater than any profits to be made from selling timber or extracting iron or fire clay from the Culross estates. He had carried out experiments by heating coal in a kiln and found that this produced a number of useful by-products including coke, ammonia and coal tar. The coke could be sold to the newly established iron works in the region, and the ammonia could be sold to calico printers, but it was the coal tar which he believed to be the most promising. He was aware from his time in the navy of the damage caused to the bottoms of ships by the teredo worm, particularly in tropical waters. He believed that coal tar could be used as an effective anti-fouling and protection against the teredo worm. The navy already used great quantities of Stockholm tar for a variety of purposes: for coating the standing rigging of ships and for sealing the seams of planks after they had been caulked with oakum; and tar diluted with oil was painted on to the topsides of ships as a preservative varnish. But Stockholm tar had to be imported from Scandinavia (it mostly came from the pine forests of Finland and was exported via Stockholm). It was expensive and in times of war there was always a possibility that the supply might be cut off. There were obvious advantages in producing tar from British coal, and if British ships adopted it as a form of underwater anti-fouling, it would be needed in vast quantities.

Dundonald took out a patent for his particular method of extracting coal tar and by 1783 he had established four kilns at Culross which were processing some twenty-eight tons of coal a week. In 1785 he published a paper entitled *Account of the Qualities and Uses of Coal Tar and Coal Varnish* and he decided to expand production by setting up the British Tar Company. Among his partners in this venture was his cousin John Loudon Macadam who, many years later, would become famous as the pioneer of road building – his name for ever associated with 'tarmacadam', or tarmac. Initially the tar-making venture went well and among the admirers of the process were a number of eminent Scots including Professor Black and Adam Smith, the economist. This support prompted Dundonald to set about raising large sums of money to establish kilns at Newcastle and elsewhere. He wrote to his uncle Andrew Cochrane, 'We are encouraged to proceed in establishing the manufacture upon a very large scale in different parts of Great Britain . . . but a capital of thirty to forty thousand pounds will in the course of a few years need to be expended.'[13] He succeeded in raising £22,400 based on the assumption that there would be a clear annual profit of £5,000.[14]

A later generation would recognise the advantages of having a home-grown source of tar but, as is so often the case with inventors, Dundonald was not the one to profit from his new process. He had assumed that the Admiralty would welcome his discovery but the navy had been experimenting with copper sheathing to protect the bottoms of ships. The experiments had proved so successful that between 1779 and 1783 the Admiralty issued orders which resulted in the entire fleet being coppered. It was an expensive and labour-intensive process and had some serious drawbacks, but the Admiralty was committed to coppering and was not interested in Dundonald's cheaper alternative. His efforts to persuade the builders of merchant ships to use tar were similarly rebuffed. Cochrane accompanied his father on some of his visits to London and recalled a visit to a shipbuilder in Limehouse. 'My lord,' said the shipbuilder, 'we live by repairing ships as well as by building them, and the worm is our best friend.'[15] Dundonald received a similar response from ship-builders in the provinces.

Discouraged by his failure to win over the Admiralty, as well as the merchant shipbuilders, Dundonald lost interest in his coal-tar project and began to experiment with the manufacture of salt and sal ammonica. His friend Professor Black paid a visit to him at Culross and warned him against embarking on other projects. 'I endeavoured to dissuade him from the pursuit of these for the present, and advised him to attend to the branches of his manufacture which had already succeeded and were bringing in money.'[16] Dundonald did not heed the warning and continued with his experiments.

His financial situation had been slightly improved by his second marriage. In April 1788, at the age of forty, he married Isabella Raymond, a wealthy widow. Thomas Gainsborough painted her portrait and an engraving based on the picture reveals a good-looking woman with fine features and an abundance of dark hair. Thomas Cochrane was twelve at the time of the marriage and he was now despatched to London with his brother Basil. Their father was determined that they should both join the army and for several months they attended Mr Chauvet's military academy in Kensington

Square. Lord Dundonald's agent provides us with a glimpse of their appearance as they set off for London: 'I have just seen the young gentlemen off by the coach. It is true they have not had very much education, but they are strong and fine to look at and very sensible, and will get on anywhere.'[17] Another source described Thomas around this time as 'a tall thin youth with locks somewhat tending to an auburn tinge'.[18] There is a portrait of him as a boy of around twelve or thirteen in the Dundonald family collection. He looks intelligent and thoughtful and is shown with long, reddish-brown hair, blue eyes and a fresh complexion.

After the years of roaming wild in the vicinity of Culross Abbey it must have been difficult to adjust to the schooling and the surroundings of central London. The military academy provided him, albeit briefly, with the foundations of an education which he would later build on but he was already clear that an army career was not for him. He wanted to follow the examples of his uncle Alexander and his grandfather Captain Gilchrist and join the navy. His father, who had not enjoyed his time at sea, ignored his wishes and procured him a commission in the 104th Regiment of Foot. Thomas never took up the commission. He did not like the military training, he hated the military uniform he was compelled to wear, and he returned to Scotland, telling his father that he wanted to go to sea with his uncle. His father was furious and remained adamant that a military career was the only option. There now occurred a curious hiatus in the young Cochrane's life. 'Four years and a half were now wasted without further attempt to secure for us any regular training.'[19] At an age when boys destined to be naval officers were at sea learning the ropes, Cochrane embarked on a course of self-tuition at home. 'Knowing that my future career depended on my own efforts, and more than ever determined not to take up my military commission, I worked assiduously at the meagre elements of knowledge within my reach.'[20] Exactly what form this self-education took is not known but presumably he studied any books to hand that would help him in his longed-for naval career. It was during this period that the threat of financial ruin looming over the family became a reality.

His father continued with his experiments, turning from one project to another. He set up a factory to produce alum or alumina for silk and calico printers, and discovered a method of producing a form of gum which could replace imported gum senegal. He accidentally discovered that coal gas could be used for illumination but he never followed this up and it was left to others to make their fortunes from gas lighting. He took out several more patents, and published a paper entitled *The Present State of the Manufacture of Salt Explained.* In 1790 he joined the Losh brothers to produce synthetic soda from salt and together they set up a works near Newcastle where Dundonald had already established a tar distillery. Within a few years the partnership was dissolved and the Losh brothers went on to develop a profitable chemical business on their own. Dundonald had borrowed heavily to finance his various projects and the moment came when his creditors lost patience with him. In 1793 he was forced to put the Culross estate up for sale. He wrote and published a detailed description of the assets of the estate which ran to seventy-five pages. He recorded the history of the estate, stressed the value of its mineral deposits and pine forests, and sadly admitted that 'nothing but the Proprietor's pecuniary inability to proceed farther, could make him wish to part with such a property, on which he had expended so much money to render productive, and struggled so hard to retain'.[21]

The year 1793 would prove to be a critical one in the life of his son Thomas. It was the year in which he was faced with the imminent loss of his inheritance and realised that he would have to make his own way in the world. It was the year in which France, having executed its king, declared war on Britain and thus initiated a conflict which would last for twenty-one years and provide the opportunity for several generations of naval officers to make their names and their fortunes. And it was the year in which his father at last consented to him joining the navy. His army commission was cancelled and in the summer of 1793, at the unusually late age of seventeen, he set off from Culross to join the crew of his uncle's ship at Sheerness.

Cochrane's naval uncle, who played such an important role in his life, was a relatively junior frigate captain in 1793 but he would end his days with a knighthood and the rank of Admiral of the White.[22] In many ways his naval career was more distinguished than that of his nephew who did not command a British ship of the line, let alone a squadron or a fleet, until he was an old man and then during a period of peace. The Hon. Alexander Forrester Inglis Cochrane was the sixth son of the eighth Earl of Dundonald and had joined the navy at the age of fifteen. As a midshipman and lieutenant he saw a great deal of action on the coast of North America and in the West Indies where he served under Sir Peter Parker and Sir George Rodney. Promoted to post-captain in 1782, he had a successful spell as a frigate captain before making his reputation in 1801 when he superintended the successful landing of General Abercromby's army on the coast of Egypt. By 1804 he was a rear-admiral and commander-in-chief in the Leeward Islands. In 1806, as second in command to Sir John Duckworth in the West Indies, he played a key role in the Battle of San Domingo ('Duck-worth's Action'), the last fleet action of the wars against Napoleonic France. For his part in this decisive victory he was made a Knight of the Bath and given the freedom of the City of London. Although he was an effective fighting captain, Alexander Cochrane lacked diplomatic skills and managed to annoy a number of influential superiors including Lord Keith and Lord St Vincent. Nevertheless, in a highly competitive profession in which family connections and influence, or what was known as 'interest', was often crucial to promotion and advancement, it did the young Thomas Cochrane no harm to have such an uncle looking out for him.

In 1792 Captain Alexander Cochrane was in command of the 28-gun frigate *Hind* with orders to patrol the east coast of Scotland. He spent that year cruising back and forth from Berwick to Stornaway in the Western Isles. He used Leith Roads in the Firth of Forth opposite Edinburgh as a base and moored there on no fewer than eight occasions, often for several weeks at a time.[23] Since Culross was only a few miles upstream we may reasonably assume that he visited his brother and family on several of these occasions. Knowing that his nephew was keen to join the navy, and seeing him at a loose end, he must have done his best to persuade Dundonald to put aside the army

Shipping off Leith Roads with the city of Edinburgh in the distance.
Lithograph after the painting by J. C. Schetky.

commission for his eldest son and allow him to join the crew of his ship. The threat of imminent bankruptcy no doubt contributed to Dundonald's change of heart. With the nation at war, a naval career offered regular pay and the opportunity for swift promotion and prize money.

By the time Thomas had been equipped with a uniform and was ready to leave home the *Hind* had been ordered south. After several months cruising off Ushant and the Scilly Isles she returned to the Thames estuary for a refit. On 28 July 1793 she anchored at the Nore, the fleet anchorage off the mouth of the River Medway. At dawn the next day, with a pilot on board to guide her past the shoals and mud banks, she sailed up the entrance channel of the Medway and dropped anchor opposite Sheerness dockyard. It was there that Thomas Cochrane's naval career began.

TWO

From Midshipman to Lieutenant

1793–1800

The dockyard at Sheerness, unlike those of Chatham, Portsmouth and Plymouth with their sheltered locations, fine Georgian storehouses and smart terraces of officers' houses, was a bleak, inhospitable place. Built on reclaimed marsh land on the edge of the Isle of Sheppey it was isolated and windswept. There was a low-lying fortress guarding the entrance to the Medway but more prominent in that watery landscape were the warships and old hulks moored to wooden buoys in the main channel.

Cochrane arrived at Sheerness on 29 July 1793 and was rowed out to the *Hind*.[1] It was not a good moment to make his appearance. His uncle had gone ashore in the morning and the first lieutenant was busy preparing the ship for an overhaul by the dockyard carpenters and shipwrights. The guns and barrels of gunpowder were being hoisted out and lowered into barges alongside and preparations were in hand to take down the sails and topsail yards. The first lieutenant was John Larmour, one of those rare men whose seamanship and ability to handle the crew had led to his promotion from an ordinary seaman to commissioned officer. He had been a lieutenant since 1784 but had never lost the habit of getting his hands dirty. When Cochrane first met him he was dressed as a seaman with a marlinspike slung round his neck, and a lump of grease in his hand. 'His reception of me was anything but gracious. Indeed, a tall fellow, over six feet high, the nephew of his captain, and a lord to boot, were not very promising recommendations for a midshipman.'[2] On seeing Cochrane's unusually large sea chest he ordered it to be cut down to size and Cochrane was mortified to find all his belongings turned out on the deck and the chest sawn in half. Larmour accompanied the operation with uncomplimentary observations on midshipmen in general and Cochrane in particular. The newcomer had the good sense to restrain his feelings and within a few days he had impressed Larmour by his obvious desire to learn his trade and to make up for lost time.

For the next three months the *Hind* was in the hands of the dockyard and it was an ideal opportunity for Cochrane to get to know every inch of the ship before they put to sea. When the topmasts had been got down the ship was lashed alongside a hulk so that the sails, much of the rigging and the warrant officers' stores could be unloaded. The ship was then hauled into one of the docks where she spent two weeks while the dockyard men repaired the copper sheathing on her

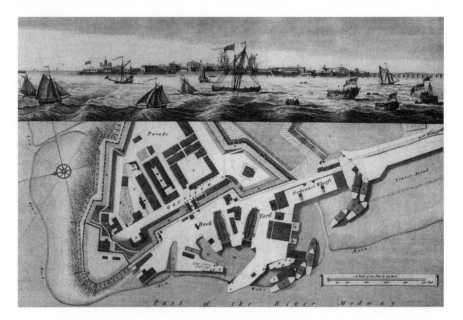

A plan and elevation of His Majesty's dockyard at Sheerness.
Engraving after the pictures by Thomas Milton and John Cleveley, 1755.

bottom and recaulked the topsides. While the ship was being worked on by caulkers and carpenters the crew moved into a hulk which was hauled up on the foreshore nearby and was used as a temporary dormitory.

In the autumn of 1793 Captain Alexander Cochrane learnt that he had been appointed to command the *Thetis*, a larger frigate of 38 guns which had sailed into the Medway on 2 September and was now anchored off the dockyard. From the ships' logs we learn that on 17 October the crew of the *Hind* were 'turned over from his Majesties ship Hind to the Thetis'.[3] After helping to dismantle one ship Cochrane had the chance to help prepare another ship for sea. As one of the young gentlemen and a future officer he could have spent much of this time ashore but he decided to follow Larmour's example and work on board alongside the skilled hands and the dockworkers. He was allowed to do so on condition that he changed out of his midshipman's uniform and wore the clothes of an ordinary seamen. 'Nothing could be more to my taste; so, with knife in belt and marline spike in hand, the captain of the forecastle undertook my improvement in the arts of knotting and splicing; Larmour himself taking charge of gammoning and rigging the bowsprit, which, as the frigate lay in dock, overhung the common highway.'[4]

This determination to master every aspect of the workings of a ship was characteristic of Cochrane. He had inherited from his father a passionate interest in how things worked and how they could be improved. Over the next few years he would make it his business to become accomplished in every specialist trade on board as well as learning the art of handling a ship in all conditions. His practical working knowledge of ships and seamanship would stand him in good stead when he commanded his own vessel and would earn him the respect of the men who served under him. However, he never forgot his debt to Larmour: 'We soon became fast friends, and throughout life few more kindly recollections are impressed on my memory than those of my first naval instructor, honest Jack Larmour.'[5]

Most boys who were destined to become officers joined the navy at a young age, usually between nine and fourteen. Until the system was changed in 1794 it was usual for the boys to be entered on the muster books as captain's servants, sailors, or able seamen as required.[6] When they had served three years at sea they could be rated as midshipmen. After a minimum of six years' service a midshipman could apply to become a lieutenant. He was expected to produce journals and certificates to prove his service; and must then go before a panel of captains and pass an oral examination in which he must demonstrate a sound knowledge of navigation, seamanship and shiphandling.

Cochrane's early life at sea shows how the regulations could be bypassed, and how family connections could hasten a young man's advancement. His father may have been on the verge of bankruptcy but he had a network of powerful friends and relations among the Scottish aristocracy who were prepared to put in a word on his eldest son's behalf.[7] The young Lord Cochrane's rapid rise to lieutenant is a classic example of 'interest' at work. The muster book of the *Hind* shows that Cochrane made his appearance on board the ship on 29 July 1793. His age was noted as seventeen and he was rated 'able seaman'.[8] In fact his uncle had been entering Cochrane's name on his ship's books ever since 1780 when his nephew was only five years old. Cochrane's name was entered as a captain's servant first on the bomb vessel *Vesuvius*, then on the sloop *Caroline* and the frigates *Sophie* and *Hind*, thus securing him a theoretical thirteen years of sea time before he ever set foot on a warship.[9] This practice, known as 'false muster', was not uncommon and could produce some strange results. The most notorious example was Rodney's promotion of his fifteen-year-old son John who had been at sea for no more than a year when he was advanced from midshipman to post-captain in a matter of weeks. Edward Pellew promoted his son at a very early age and Cochrane's uncle Alexander did much the same for his eldest son Thomas John who became a lieutenant at sixteen and a post-captain at eighteen.

The practice of false muster and the effect of interest certainly helped Cochrane to make up for his late start in the navy but he was not given command of his own ship until he had been at sea for seven years and, thanks to his dedicated approach to his profession and his natural ability as a leader, he would prove to be more than capable of

A watercolour by George Tobin depicting the *Thetis* aground on the coast of
North Carolina, December 1794. The sailors in the boats are taking soundings
to find the depth of water before the ship is hauled off.

handling a ship and going into action when the moment came. His first
step up occurred on 18 October 1793, less than three months after
joining the navy. On the day following the transfer of the crew of the
Hind to the *Thetis* his uncle advanced him from able seaman to
midshipman. A few weeks later, on 27 November, the *Thetis* put to
sea and Cochrane's naval training began in earnest.

On an overcast day, with a fresh gale blowing, they sailed out of the
Medway into the Thames estuary and made their way up the east
coast. They reached the Firth of Forth on 11 December and spent a
month over Christmas at anchor in Leith Roads. The ship's log
records that the men were employed 'scraping, cleaning, scrubbing
hammocks, exercising the great guns', but presumably Captain Cochrane and his nephew found the time to visit the family at Culross. On
13 January 1794 the *Thetis* weighed anchor and headed across the
North Sea to Norway. Their orders were to intercept French priva-

teers and to look out for an enemy convoy but neither were sighted. Cochrane was impressed by the rocky coastal scenery and by the hospitality of the inhabitants. The young midshipmen were allowed ashore on several occasions and they spent their time shooting and fishing and racing down the snowy slopes of the fjords on sledges. This pleasant winter holiday was brought to a close towards the end of February when they left the anchorage at Bergen and sailed to Spithead. There they joined a squadron under the command of Admiral George Murray. Their destination was North America and the objective was to protect British commerce and fisheries. Cochrane would spend the next four years cruising the eastern seaboard from Nova Scotia to Florida.

They left Plymouth on 18 May and sighted New York on 24 July. They followed the coast down to Charleston and then sailed back to Sandy Hook Bay and Staten Island. On 18 January 1795 one of the lieutenants of the *Thetis* transferred to another ship and Cochrane's uncle took the opportunity to appoint his nephew acting lieutenant in his place. Admiral Murray confirmed the provisional appointment, and Lord Spencer, the First Lord of the Admiralty, was prepared to let the provisional appointment stand. Writing to his friend Thomas Coutts, the banker, he said that he was aware of Captain Cochrane's application on behalf of his nephew 'and if it should turn out, which I think it very probably may, that the appointment by Admiral Murray was not strictly regular, he shall however be included in my list for promotion when there is a regular appointment'.[10] Coutts was a descendant of the first Earl of Dundonald and had previously assured Captain Cochrane that he would always do what he could on his behalf: 'Your father was kind to me when a boy and I hope I shall never forget a favour done to me.'[11]

On 13 April 1795 Cochrane joined the 64-gun ship *Africa* at Hampton Roads and spent five weeks serving as acting lieutenant.[12] They sailed as far as Bermuda before he was transferred from the *Africa* to the sloop *Lynx*, 16 guns, again as acting lieutenant. When the *Lynx* put into Halifax, Nova Scotia, the *Thetis* was lying at anchor there, and to Cochrane's disappointment he found that he had missed the chance of action. Captain Cochrane, together with Captain Beresford in the *Hussar*, had intercepted five French warships in the seas off the Chesapeake River and captured a frigate and a sloop. Following the action John Larmour had been promoted which created a vacancy on the *Thetis*. Cochrane returned to his uncle's ship as second lieutenant, though still in an acting capacity. Back in London Lord Spencer informed Coutts, 'Captain Cochrane will no doubt be glad to hear that Lieutenant Larmour has been promoted . . . and that Lord Cochrane's commission will be confirmed'.[13] But it was evidently still considered a bit too soon for Cochrane to apply to be examined for lieutenant. Jane, the Dowager Countess of Dundonald, wrote to Captain Cochrane on 12 July 1795 informing him that 'Earl Spencer has said that if he [Lord Cochrane] keeps steady to the sea he will do everything that he can to serve him. He is a man to be trusted when he says so much.'[14]

That summer Cochrane saw some action for the first time. On 16 August the *Thetis* chased and captured a French privateer of 16 guns and four days later they took a sloop of 11 guns. The following August the *Thetis* was part of a squadron which engaged three French frigates off New York and forced one of them to surrender. Such actions were useful in improving the fighting ability of the crew but were insignificant compared with some of the naval actions taking place in Europe. On 28 May 1794 a British fleet of twenty-six ships of the line, seven frigates and five smaller vessels under the command of Lord Howe had engaged a French fleet of similar size in the Atlantic west of Ushant. After a hard-fought action spread over four days one of the French ships had sunk and six had been captured. The Battle of the Glorious First of June was hailed in Britain as a triumph. It would be the first of three major fleet actions which would take place on the European side of the Atlantic while Cochrane remained on the American station.

Meanwhile, in February 1796, he passed his examination for lieutenant; Admiral Murray issued a temporary commission and the promotion was confirmed by the Admiralty on 27 May 1796.[15] Two years and ten months after joining the navy the twenty-year-old

Cochrane became a commissioned officer. Nelson had passed his lieutenant's exam at the age of eighteen and a half but by that time he had accumulated more than six years of service at sea and had completed voyages to the West Indies, the Arctic and the Indian Ocean. Cochrane had been fortunate with his rapid promotion but the next step from lieutenant to master and commander would not be so easy. There were nearly two thousand other lieutenants on the Navy List. Many of them were well connected and the majority of them had far more experience than he had. Nevertheless the family connections continued to operate on his behalf. When Admiral Murray was replaced by Admiral Vandeput as commander of the American station we find Thomas Coutts writing to Captain Cochrane, 'A particular friend of mine is gone to command in your station. Admiral Vandeput, a very Gentleman like man in every respect and I hope you will become intimate with him if you are not so already – pray tell him I have written to you to mention him and that I am sure if it should be in his power to serve you or Lord Cochrane he will be pleased to do it were it only on my account.'[16]

Within a short time of Admiral Vandeput's arrival Cochrane was appointed a lieutenant on his flagship, the *Resolution* of 74 guns. From the small world of a frigate with a crew of 270 men he now joined a ship with more than 500 men. Instead of a single gun deck there were two decks lined with guns from bow to stern, the men eating in the cramped space between the guns and the fortunate sleeping in hammocks slung above them. Unlike the cramped gun room on the frigate, the lieutenants on the *Resolution* had a spacious wardroom: it had a long table running down the centre and there were individual cabins for the officers along the sides. Cochrane took his turn in dining with the admiral. He was dismayed at first by his brusque manner but he soon came to respect him and found him to be one of the kindest of commanders: 'There was not a happier ship afloat, nor one in which officers lived in more perfect harmony.'[17]

Unfortunately for someone as ambitious as Cochrane, life on the American station proved to be tediously uneventful. 'My chance of promotion as a lieutenant of this ship is not worth one farthing,' he complained in January 1798. 'I see Lord Caulfield is made Captain. He was upwards of two hundred under me on the list of lieutenants.'[18] They spent several months moored in the harbour of Halifax, Nova Scotia, its rocky, pine-fringed shores frequently obscured by sea fog. More months were spent lying at anchor in Hampton Roads at the entrance of Chesapeake Bay. There were expeditions ashore and sometimes the young gentlemen of the ship went hunting with hounds in the forests of Virginia, and dined with local families. Cochrane was horrified by the treatment of the black slaves on the plantations and their sufferings during a bitterly cold winter. In a letter to his father he wrote, 'Nine tenths of the Negroes are at this inclement season without blankets or bed and almost without clothes. I have seen enough in this country to cure any advocate of the slave trade of ever wishing to support so horrid an infringement of natural liberty.'[19] Taking pity on an old black man who had worked as a miller for forty-seven years in deplorable conditions, Cochrane and his shipmates gave him some blankets and a few dollars. 'The man was overjoyed in a manner past expressions, shedding tears . . .'[20]

In May 1798 the *Resolution* sailed back to Halifax. Cochrane rejoined his uncle's frigate and they sailed for England. The *Thetis* arrived in Plymouth in November 1798. Much had happened during the four years they had been away. The revolution in France, with its ideals of liberty and equality, had descended into a bloodthirsty purge of the nobility and gentry and thousands of men and women were executed by the guillotine during the Reign of Terror. More ominous for Britain was the emergence of Napoleon Bonaparte from the turmoil of the French Revolution. Trained as an artillery officer at the military academy in Paris, he had come to the fore during the siege of Toulon in December 1793. A brigadier-general by the age of twenty-four, he had been given command of the Army of Italy and had won a spectacular series of victories against Austrian armies in northern Italy during 1796. The next year he was given command of a French army assembled at Boulogne for the invasion of England. An inspection of the troops and the transport ships convinced him that invasion was out of the question until the French navy had command of the English Channel and its approaches. He persuaded the ruling Directory in Paris to mount an expedition to Egypt. In April 1798 he had set sail from Toulon with a vast armada of warships and transports. He captured Malta, landed in Egypt, defeated the local forces at the Battle of the Pyramids and established French rule across the region.

While the Revolutionary armies of France appeared to be invincible, the territorial ambitions of France and her allies were constantly thwarted by Britain's increasingly dominant command of the seas. Spain had declared war on Britain in October 1796 but four months later a Spanish fleet of twenty-seven sail of the line had been defeated by a British fleet of fifteen under the command of Sir John Jervis at the Battle of Cape St Vincent. The victory was largely due to the bold and unorthodox tactics of Commodore Nelson who had left his position in the line of battle, sailed into the main body of the retreating Spanish ships, engaged three ships and captured two Spanish first-rates. Following the battle, Jervis was made an earl and became Lord St Vincent; Nelson was made a Knight of the Bath. The Spanish fleet retreated to Cadiz where it remained blockaded for many years to come.

The French occupation of the Low Countries had put the considerable Dutch fleet at the disposal of the French Republic but this too had been put out of action by the British navy. At the Battle of Camperdown in October 1797 Admiral Duncan defeated the Dutch fleet in a hard-fought action off the coast of Holland, forcing the remnants of the Dutch fleet to retreat to the Texel. The following year Lord St Vincent despatched Nelson into the Mediterranean with a hand-picked squadron to track down the French expedition led by Napoleon. Nelson eventually found the French fleet anchored in a strong defensive position in Aboukir Bay. At dusk on 1 August 1798 the British fleet attacked. During the course of a fierce action thirteen of the seventeen French warships were captured or destroyed. One of the ships to escape was the *Généreux*; she was captured off Malta eighteen months later and Cochrane would be given the task of sailing her to Port Mahon.

News of the Battle of the Nile did not reach Britain until the first week of October so it would still have been a big story when Cochrane and his uncle returned to Plymouth. Celebrations had taken place all over the country: church bells were rung across the land; public buildings were illuminated, and sheep and oxen were roasted in market squares. Having missed out on all the excitement Cochrane was impatient to be sent where there was some action, and at this critical stage in his career he was fortunate to be despatched to the Mediterranean.

Once again we see the influence of the Scottish aristocracy at work behind the scenes. This time Cochrane's patron was Vice-Admiral Lord Keith, a fellow Scot who would play a significant role in his career during the next few years. Created Baron Keith in 1797 as a reward for his successful operations in the Indian Ocean, he was born George Keith Elphinstone and was the fifth son of the Earl of Elphinstone.[21] Like Cochrane's family, the Elphinstones had large estates in Scotland but were heavily in debt. George Elphinstone had left the family seat in Stirlingshire and had joined the navy at the comparatively late age of sixteen. His family was so impoverished that they refused to spend five guineas on a short course of navigation for him. He saw action during the war with America, became the Member of Parliament for Dumbartonshire, and married a young woman from Kinloss. On the outbreak of war with France he played a key role in the capture and defence of Toulon under the command of Lord Hood. Following a series of operations off Cape Town and in the Indian Ocean he returned to England having amassed £64,000 in prize money. Although cautious and methodical by nature Lord Keith would prove a capable commander of fleets. During the course of a long naval career he had under his command at various times four of the navy's boldest and most unorthodox officers: Nelson, Sir Sidney Smith, Sir Home Popham and Lord Cochrane. Though sometimes exasperated by them Keith generally handled them with tact and restraint.

In the autumn of 1798 Lord Keith was preparing to sail to the Mediterranean as second in command to Lord St Vincent. He already had his full quota of officers on his flagship, the *Foudroyant*, but he was prepared to take on Cochrane as a gesture of goodwill to his family. Cochrane joined the ship on 28 November 1798 as a supernumerary and reported to the admiral. He received a remarkably cool reception. 'I fancy he expected I came to talk to him on family matters,' Cochrane wrote to his father, 'as when I entered the room he said he had received papers from you which he did not understand and could not possibly interfere in.'[22] Although acting with the best of intentions Cochrane's father tried the patience of several senior admirals during the course of the next few years by writing long and demanding letters on behalf of his son.

The *Foudroyant* sailed from Plymouth on 5 December and fifteen days later they arrived at Gibraltar, a place which Cochrane would get to know well in the coming years. The British naval base was situated at the foot of the towering slopes of the Rock of Gibraltar. The anchorage was sheltered by the great curve of the Bay of Gibraltar but it was exposed to winds from the south and the dockyard facilities were limited. Its importance lay in its commanding position at the mouth of the Mediterranean and during the long war against France and her allies it would prove a vital base for British operations – along with Port Mahon in Minorca and Valetta harbour in Malta.

Shortly after their arrival at Gibraltar Lord Keith transferred his flag and his crew to the *Barfleur*, a three-decker of 90 guns, and appointed Cochrane as his eighth lieutenant. For the next few months the flagship was part of the British fleet which was keeping watch on the Spanish fleet in Cadiz harbour. Lord St Vincent had imposed a strict regime on the crews of the blockading force but he was now increasingly unwell and was spending most of his time ashore at Gibraltar. Within a few weeks of his joining the crew of the *Barfleur* Cochrane clashed with the flagship's first lieutenant. It was the first of his many brushes with authority and reveals the arrogant side of his nature which would make him enemies in the future. The first lieutenant was Philip Beaver. He was thirty-two years old and came from a family of Oxford academics and clergymen. He was an experienced and capable officer who would soon be promoted to captain and would distinguish himself in actions in the Mediterranean and the Indian Ocean, but he took himself rather too seriously and, according to his biographer, 'his rigidly exact notions did not always quadrate with those of his messmates.'[23]

The cause of the incident was trivial. The *Barfleur* had made a number of trips across the Straits of Gibraltar to Tetouan on the coast of Morocco in order to purchase cattle for the use of the whole squadron. On one of the trips Cochrane went ashore to do some duck shooting with Captain Cuthbert of the marines. When they returned to the ship Cochrane reported his return to the captain but failed to report to Lieutenant Beaver. Since the ship had weighed anchor and the two men had apparently been left on shore Beaver informed the captain of their absence. On finding Cochrane back on board Beaver confronted him and said that he had been made to appear exceedingly ridiculous, having reported the two men missing when they had in fact returned. Lieutenant Jackson, one of the observers of the incident, would later recall what happened next.

Cochrane said 'that he could not help Lieutenant Beaver appearing ridiculous to the Captain' which prompted Beaver to retort 'that unless he was acquainted with the return to the ship, while he was 1st. Lieutenant, Lord Cochrane should not go out of the ship, to which Lord Cochrane in a manner surprised said, "Aye, Lieutenant Beaver!"' According to Cochrane's version he then reminded Beaver that it was a rule of the ship that matters connected with the service were not to be discussed in the wardroom. This enraged Beaver who, according to Jackson, 'made some reply, but what I do not recollect, and before Lieutenant Beaver had finished speaking Lord Cochrane turned his face aft and whistled'. Beaver went straight to the captain and demanded that Cochrane be court-martialled 'for disrespect to me and unofficerlike conduct between the hours of five and six o'clock this evening'.[24]

The court martial was held on board the *Barfleur* on 18 February 1799 and was presided over by Lord Keith. Cochrane was acquitted of insubordination but did not get away scot-free. Keith was exceedingly angry about the whole business:

'Here are all the Flag Officers and Captains called together, at a time when the wind is coming fair, and the ship ought to be under way! I think I am made the most ridiculous person of the whole!' And he concluded the case with some wise advice for his junior officer: 'Lord Cochrane, I am directed by the Court to say that officers should not reply sharply to their superior officers, and a first lieutenant's situation should be supported by everyone; a ship is but a small place where six or seven hundred persons are collected together, and officers should in every part of it avoid any flippancy.'[25]

With so many lieutenants competing for promotion, the court martial could have seriously damaged Cochrane's prospects. However, a letter written by Lord Keith to Captain Alexander Cochrane two and a half years later (at a time when the Cochrane family were lobbying for Cochrane's promotion to post-captain) shows how a powerful patron was more significant than a dispute between lieutenants. Keith told Cochrane's uncle that he had endeavoured to prevent the court martial 'with what influence I had. The trial made nothing against his Lordship. I respect his family and will not lose any opportunity to convince his Lordship if my Lord Spencer alone had the power of confirming commissions.'[26] During the next year Cochrane saw much of the western Mediterranean but very little action.

In April 1799 Vice-Admiral Bruix eluded the British ships keeping watch on the French naval base at Brest and headed south. On 3 May he appeared off Cadiz with a fleet of nineteen ships of the line and ten smaller vessels. His first objective was to join up with the twenty-eight Spanish ships in Cadiz harbour but the British were uncertain whether his ultimate destination was Minorca, Malta, Naples or Egypt. Lord Keith was lying off Cadiz and his fleet of fifteen ships was all that prevented the two enemy fleets from combining into a formidable force. Lord Keith formed a line of battle and prepared to receive the French attack. It was the only occasion in Cochrane's career in the British navy when he might have taken part in a major fleet action, but it was not to be. Whether it was due to a rising onshore gale or the unwillingness of the French admiral to risk damaging his ships and thus imperilling his main objective is not clear. 'To our surprise,' Cochrane recalled, 'they soon afterwards wore and stood away to the south-west; though from our position between them and the Spaniards they had a fair chance of victory had the combined fleets acted in concert.'[27]

On entering the Mediterranean the French fleet headed for Toulon where Bruix received orders to proceed to Genoa with supplies for the French army in Italy which was under threat from the Austrians. Keith followed the French fleet up the Spanish coast. His fleet was within striking distance of the enemy when he received peremptory orders from Lord St Vincent to head immediately for Minorca. St Vincent believed that Port Mahon and its fine harbour was the most likely objective for a French attack. Lord Keith reluctantly abandoned the chase and sailed south. At Port Mahon, on 14 June, he shifted his flag from the *Barfleur* to the *Queen Charlotte*, a first-rate ship of 100 guns and currently the second largest ship in the British navy. Cochrane was among the officers and men who joined the admiral on his new flagship.

Having caused considerable alarm among the limited British forces operating in the Mediterranean, Bruix headed for Cartagena on the south-east coast of Spain and linked up with a Spanish squadron. From there he sailed through the Straits of Gibraltar and headed back to Brest. Keith set off in pursuit. When his fleet passed Gibraltar on 30 July they were only eight days behind the enemy. They raced up the coast of Spain and Portugal and across the Bay of Biscay. Off Cape Finisterre they spoke with a Danish brig which had passed through the combined French and Spanish fleet only two days before. 'We then directed our course for Brest,' Cochrane recalled, 'hoping to be in time to intercept them, but found that on the day before our arrival they had effected their object and were then safely moored within the harbour.'[28]

Bruix had demonstrated that the French navy could elude the British blockade and, in spite of the crushing defeat at the Battle of the Nile, could still pose a serious threat, especially if French ships combined with those of Spain. Lord Keith came in for much criticism in England for failing to find and engage Bruix, but those who understood the situation defended him. With many of his ships in need of repair and short of provisions Keith sailed on from Brest and back to England. He dropped anchor in Torbay towards the end of August 1799. While they lay at anchor in the bay Keith introduced Cochrane to Lord Spencer, who had now been First Lord of the Admiralty for almost five years. Cochrane received a letter from Lord Spencer around this time which makes it clear that the court martial had done him no harm as far as the Admiralty were concerned. 'I shall have great pleasure,' Spencer wrote, 'in paying every attention in my power to forwarding your prospects in the service when opportunities offer themselves for advancing you . . .'[29] Meanwhile, increasing illness had caused St Vincent to resign as commander-in-chief in the Mediterranean and on 15 November 1799 Lord Keith was appointed in his place. He sailed from Spithead in the *Queen Charlotte* and by 6 December he was back in Gibraltar, with Cochrane still on board his flagship as a junior lieutenant.

For the British the situation in the Mediterranean at the beginning of 1800 appeared more hopeful than it had been for some time. The previous year Napoleon had taken his Army of Egypt into Syria and captured Gaza and Jaffa, but his attempt to storm the medieval fortress on the coast at Acre had failed ignominiously. A small force of British seamen led by Sir Sidney Smith had beaten off the attackers, and the arrival of Turkish reinforcements had forced the French to retreat. In August 1799 Napoleon had abandoned his troops and sailed for France. He had taken advantage of unrest in the country and divisions in the Directory in Paris to engineer a coup from which he emerged as First Consul. For several months he was engaged in domestic issues and at this stage the full extent of his ambitions for himself and the French nation was not apparent. Malta was still held by the French but the Grand Harbour at Valletta had been under siege by British ships for months and there was every likelihood that the island would fall to Britain before the year was out. Port Mahon, Minorca, had been available as a British naval base since its capture in November 1798.

In the Kingdom of the Two Sicilies, which occupied the southern half of Italy, some semblance of order had been restored after months of bloodshed. The French had occupied Naples in December 1798 but had since been driven out and, thanks to the controversial intervention of Nelson in the summer of 1799, the corrupt but pro-British regime of King Ferdinand and Queen Maria Caroline had been restored in the capital. It was to Italy that Lord Keith now headed with his squadron. He arrived at Leghorn on 12 January 1800 and a week later Nelson, in the *Foudroyant*, joined him there. It was an uneasy meeting because Nelson had expected to succeed St Vincent as commander-in-chief in the Mediterranean. Both admirals then sailed south to Palermo where Keith was introduced to Sir William and Lady Hamilton and met the king and queen. He did not enjoy his visit and reported, 'the whole was a scene of fulsome vanity and absurdity all the eight long days I was at Palermo'.[30]

Cochrane was less critical. He accompanied Keith ashore and had the opportunity to meet Nelson. Cochrane was a twenty-four-year-old lieutenant and his experience of action was limited to some minor engagements while serving on his uncle's frigate on the east coast of North America. Nelson was forty-one: he had made his name in one fleet action and achieved international celebrity following his victory at the Battle of the Nile; he had fought several lesser actions, and risked his life by leading shore parties against heavy odds – he had lost the sight of one eye at the siege of Calvi in Corsica and had suffered the amputation of his right arm following the disastrous attack on Santa Cruz, Tenerife, in 1797. A head wound at the Battle of the Nile had left him in great pain and to many observers he now appeared old and exhausted. But for Cochrane he was a heroic figure and in a memorable passage in his autobiography he acknowledged his debt to Britain's most famous admiral:

It was never my good fortune to serve under his Lordship, either at that or any subsequent period. During our stay at Palermo, I had, however, opportunities of personal conversation with him, and from one of his frequent injunctions, 'Never mind manoeuvres, always go at them,' I subsequently had reason to consider myself indebted for successful attacks under apparently difficult circumstances. The impression left on my mind during these opportunities of association with Nelson was that of his being an embodiment of dashing courage, which would not take much trouble to circumvent an enemy, but being confronted with one would regard victory so much a matter of course as hardly to deem the chance of defeat worth consideration.[31]

Nelson was indirectly responsible for Cochrane getting the promotion and the independent command that he was impatiently waiting for. On 19 February 1800 a squadron under Nelson's command was sailing off the north-west coast of Malta when enemy ships were sighted on the horizon. They proved to be a storeship loaded with troops and supplies for the relief of the French garrison at Malta, and her escort which consisted of the 74-gun ship *Généreux*, three frigates and a corvette. The storeship and one of the frigates surrendered but the *Généreux* fled north towards Sicily. After a chase of more than six hours Nelson caught up with her and captured her.[32] She was escorted to the Sicilian port of Syracuse by two of the ships in Nelson's squadron.

The capture of the *Généreux* and the need to find a British commander for her enabled Lord Keith to make a series of promotions. The one which directly affected Cochrane was the promotion of Jahleel Brenton to the rank of post-captain and his appointment to a 74-gun ship. Brenton was currently commanding a diminutive warship of 14 guns called the *Speedy* in which he had distinguished himself in a number of actions against Spanish gunboats. On 20 February Lord Keith promoted Cochrane to the command of the *Speedy*, which, when the appointment had been approved by the Admiralty, would lead to his promotion from lieutenant to that of master and commander.[33] However, before Brenton or Cochrane were able to take up their new commands Lord Keith had other tasks for them. Brenton was ordered to take the *Speedy* to Leghorn with despatches, and Cochrane was 'required and directed to take upon yourself the acting command of the French ship Genereux' and to sail her to Minorca for repairs and a refit at Port Mahon.[34]

To be given temporary command of a valuable prize was an opportunity for Cochrane to prove himself but it was also a considerable challenge: he had to make a seven-hundred-mile voyage in a 74-gun ship with a prize crew which was partly made up of sick and invalided men hastily drafted from other ships in the squadron, and partly by local seamen; in addition he had to take with him sixty-three French prisoners with no more than eleven marines to guard them and keep order among the motley crew; and he had to face the unpredictable weather of a Mediterranean winter. He took up his role as acting captain on 20 February and was joined by his eighteen-year-old younger brother Archibald who was signed on as midshipman.[35] They spent a busy week in the harbour at Syracuse carrying out repairs to the rigging, taking on provisions and transporting prisoners to and fro. On 2 March, with a light westerly breeze, they weighed and made sail.[36]

The wind increased steadily during their second day at sea. They took in two reefs but the main topsail split when they were hit by a squall. Two days later they were hit by strong gales and driving rain. By close reefing the topsails and getting down the topgallant yards Cochrane weathered the storm and the wind died to a light breeze. On 9 March they ran into another storm. As the ship rolled and pitched in the rising seas a sudden squall carried away the mizen topmast and the head of the mizen mast. A few hours later another squall split the foresail. This was bad enough but Cochrane was concerned that he might lose the masts: the rigging had been set up so badly that the shrouds were alternately strained almost to breaking point and then loosely drooping as the masts jerked from side to side. They survived another day of rough weather and as soon as it moderated Cochrane got the crew to set up the lower rigging properly and had a new mizen topmast made to replace the missing one. They had a scare on 11 March when a strange warship was sighted. They cleared the ship for action but she proved to be a Portuguese ship of the line and therefore no threat to Cochrane's hard-pressed men.

Fifteen days after leaving the coast of Sicily, they sighted the distant outline of Minorca on the horizon. With light airs and a calm sea they rounded La Mola, the rocky headland at the harbour mouth, and made the signal for a pilot. On the afternoon of 17 March, with the pilot to guide them, they sailed past the battlements of Fort Charles and the round gun towers on the slopes overlooking the narrow entrance and entered the magnificent harbour of Port Mahon. Four miles of deep, sheltered water slowly opened up ahead of them. They passed a few local fishing boats, their lateen sails barely filled by the evening breeze, and sailed past a small island used for quarantine purposes and a larger one with a handsome line of buildings surmounted by a bell tower; this was the naval hospital which had been founded by the British back in 1712. Rounding a bend in the harbour, they saw ahead of them the town of Mahon, a dense cluster of houses with red pantile roofs climbing up the steep hillside and dominated by the grey stone walls of the cathedral. They dropped anchor among the warships and merchant ships which were moored in the great expanse of calm water at the far end of the harbour. The dockyard lay across the water from the town and in the days following their arrival they sent the sails, the spare spars and the gunner's stores to the yard. The French prisoners were taken off and rowed across to the *Courageuse*, a French frigate captured the year before and now used as a prison ship.

The voyage had been a demanding test of Cochrane's seamanship and leadership skills.[37] Two of the wounded men in the crew had died while they were at sea, and he had flogged two seamen with twelve lashes each for drunkenness, but he had brought a ship of the line

A warship entering the harbour of Port Mahon, Minorca. The town and cathedral are just visible beyond the moored vessels in the middle distance.

safely into port. Moreover, the assignment had probably saved his life. During his absence the *Queen Charlotte* had caught fire and blown up while anchored off Leghorn. Early in the morning of 17 March, while Lord Keith was engaged in discussions ashore, a fire had broken out among some hay under the half-deck of the flagship. The flames had rapidly engulfed the boats on the booms and spread to the rigging. All attempts to put out the fire had failed and after raging for four hours it reached the after magazine. The ship had exploded and sunk with the loss of 636 men. Lord Keith had rounded up as many local boats as he could but there was little they could do to help. He wrote to his sister, 'the boats are returned with the sad tidings that not more than 150 will be saved'.[38] On the day after the explosion Captain Brenton and the *Speedy* arrived at Leghorn. A picture, apparently drawn at the time by an artist who was an eyewitness, shows the *Speedy* approaching the wreckage of the *Queen Charlotte* and lowering a boat from her stern davits. In the foreground the crew of another boat are depicted searching for survivors among the shattered remains of masts, sails and spars.

The wreckage of the *Queen Charlotte* at Leghorn in March 1800, with a brig sloop, possibly the *Speedy*, lowering a boat.

In Port Mahon harbour Cochrane and his prize crew continued to
dismantle the *Généreux*. Discipline among the men was evidently a
problem because on 2 April he ordered a seaman to be punished with
thirty-six lashes for drunkenness and disobedience, and the following
day three more seamen were found drunk and given twenty-four
lashes each. Early on the morning of 20 April the *Généreux* was towed
across to the dockyard and moored alongside the wharf so that the
damaged mizen mast could be taken out. Later that morning Captain
Brenton came on board and took over command of the ship. This
released Cochrane from his supervising role on the French prize. On
the afternoon of the same day he was rowed out to the *Speedy* which
was lying at anchor among the other vessels opposite the town. The
ship's log for 20 April notes simply, 'Cloudy weather. Employed
receiving water and stores – at 3 Lord Cochrane read his Commission
and superseded Captain Brenton.'[39] Cochrane had wanted to be given
command of a fine corvette of 18 guns and was not impressed by his
first inspection of the *Speedy* but he would soon become very proud of
the small, two-masted vessel in which he first made his mark as a
coastal raider.

THREE

Commander of the *Speedy*

1800–1801

Cochrane was commander of the *Speedy* for less than fifteen months and yet in that time he carried out a series of raids on Spanish anchorages, he fought and won a single-ship action against overwhelming odds, and, according to his own account, he captured more than fifty vessels, 122 guns and 534 prisoners. How was it possible for an inexperienced commander to achieve so much in such a short time? Cochrane himself described the *Speedy* as 'little more than a burlesque of a vessel of war' and famously claimed to have been able to walk the deck with her entire broadside of 4-pounder shot contained in the pockets of his coat. If she was so small and lightly armed, how was the *Speedy* able to cause such destruction and, in particular, how was she able to overcome a vessel more than three times her size? Did Cochrane, reminiscing as an old man in his eighties, embroider and exaggerate the story of his first independent command?

The documentary evidence is limited but it does confirm the facts set out in Cochrane's autobiography. When we examine the background to the cruise and the tactics he employed we can see exactly why he was so successful. The principal elements were the ship, the crew and the particular talents which Cochrane brought to the art of warfare at sea.

The *Speedy* was what was called a brig sloop. That is to say, she was a two-masted vessel like a coastal brig but she was rated as a sloop on the Navy List because that was the term given to a vessel which was commanded by an officer with the rank of master and commander.[1] She had been built in a private yard at Dover and launched in 1782 so she was nearly twenty years old when Cochrane first stepped on board. Her length on the upper deck was seventy-eight feet three inches and her breadth was twenty-five feet eight inches.[2] If she sailed into a marina today she would appear rather formidable with her broad wooden decks lined with fourteen guns, her long bowsprit, her heavy, sea-stained sails and her sturdy masts supported by taut and heavily tarred shrouds. Her plans, which have been preserved in the National Maritime Museum at Greenwich, show her to have had a profile not unlike a naval cutter with a graceful sheer and a steeply raked stern. She was steered by a long tiller rather than a wheel and had cramped accommodation on the lower deck for a crew of eighty or ninety men. The captain had a tiny cabin at the stern and there were individual cabins for one lieutenant, the master, surgeon, purser, gunner, boatswain and carpenter. An iron stove dominated the forward part of the lower deck and the stores of the carpenter, boatswain and steward were crammed into the forepeak. The crew slung their hammocks in the dark and limited space remaining. The headroom throughout the lower deck was barely more than five foot at its maximum and the numerous deck beams reduced it to four foot in many places so that moving around below deck was not easy.

Cochrane had spent his time as a young officer in ships which would have towered over the *Speedy*. In 74-gun ships like the *Resolution* the captain had an elegant cabin with fine furniture and windows opening on to a stern gallery or balcony. The gun deck was more than twice the length of the *Speedy* and was lined with massive 32-pounder guns capable of reducing a frigate to a dismasted wreck in a matter of minutes. Three-deckers like the *Barfleur* and the *Queen Charlotte* were even larger and had crews of more than seven hundred men. It is little wonder that the *Speedy* must have seemed ridiculously small and lightly armed by comparison.

But although brig sloops were among the smallest of the warships on the Navy List they were well suited for the work for which they were designed: providing protection for convoys of merchantmen from marauding gunboats and privateers; disrupting trade by attacking enemy merchant vessels; carrying out reconnaissance and conveying intelligence. The most authentic picture of one of these brig sloops in action is a watercolour by the marine artist and former sea captain Nicholas Pocock. It depicts the *Childers*, a brig sloop which was almost identical to the *Speedy* in size, rig and armament.[3]

One of the keys to Cochrane's exploits in the *Speedy* was that he inherited a brave and disciplined crew. Under her two previous commanders she had defended herself and her convoys against superior odds and her officers had been singled out for praise. In February 1798, under the command of Hugh Downman, the *Speedy* had beaten off an attack by the *Papillon*, a fast and powerful French brig, and had sent her fleeing over the horizon. The *Speedy* lost five men killed and four wounded in the action and her masts and rigging were so badly damaged that she had to put into Lisbon for a refit.

It was under her next commander, Jahleel Brenton, that the *Speedy* truly proved her worth. Brenton, who was to play a significant role in Cochrane's life during the next two years, had an interesting background. He was born in Rhode Island on the eastern seaboard of North America, the eldest son of an American father and an English mother. His father had been a lieutenant in the Royal Navy and on the outbreak of the war with America he had decided to remain loyal to the British cause. In 1780 he had moved with his family to England and he eventually rose to the rank of rear-admiral. His son Jahleel joined the navy in 1781 at the age of eleven and saw a great deal of action in the ensuing years. He was present at the blockade of Toulon, took part in the Battle of Cape St Vincent as first lieutenant of HMS *Aigle*, and while a lieutenant on board the *Ville de Paris*, the flagship of Lord St Vincent, he so distinguished himself in a boat attack that the admiral promoted him to the command of the *Speedy*, a particularly fortunate move, as he later recalled: 'It was a singular circumstance that I had already served in the *Speedy*, both as second and first

A detail from a watercolour by Nicholas Pocock showing the brig sloop *Childers*, which was very similar to Cochrane's *Speedy*.

lieutenant; and while talking over expected promotion with my messmates, who were naming the favourite sloops to which they should prefer being appointed, I always named the Speedy.'[4]

Brenton joined the *Speedy* in February 1799, and his first task was to escort a convoy from Lisbon to Cadiz. In the Bay of Gibraltar they were attacked by no fewer than twenty-three Spanish gunboats. Brenton ordered the convoy to close up and strictly preserve their order of sailing. The *Speedy* then wore round ahead of the convoy and attacked the gunboats with such determination that they sheered away and enabled the convoy to gain the shelter of the bay where St Vincent's flagship was at anchor. Brenton received the congratulations of St Vincent and the Governor of Gibraltar for his spirited defence of his charges.

In August, while en route from Port Mahon to Gibraltar, the *Speedy*, assisted by a local privateer brig, attacked three armed xebecs – three-masted vessels with triangular lateen sails much used by the Barbary corsairs. The xebecs had anchored in a sandy bay and were captured after a fusilade of fire. In his report of the action Brenton wrote, 'The officers and men under my command behaved in such a manner as would have ensured our success against a more formidable enemy.'[5]

The *Speedy*, under the command of Captain Jahleel Brenton,
attacked by enemy gunboats off Gibraltar in November 1799.

And in November 1799 the *Speedy* and her crew scored a notable victory. They were escorting a transport ship and a merchant brig when they were attacked by a flotilla of enemy vessels as they were approaching Gibraltar. The flotilla consisted of a French privateer of 8 guns, two schooners armed with 24-pounders and ten assorted gun-boats. The attackers tried to cut out the transport ship but the *Speedy* intercepted the attack and enabled the ship to reach her anchorage safely. The enemy vessels then turned their united efforts against the helpless merchant brig. The *Speedy* bore up through the centre of the attacking vessels and after a heated exchange for three-quarters of an hour she forced them to run for shelter. The *Speedy* lost two men killed and one wounded, had most of her rigging cut away and was so damaged by shots below the water line that she headed for the anchorage with water up to her lower deck. In his despatch Brenton again gave full credit to his men: 'I cannot say too much in praise of Lieutenant Parker, Mr Marshal the master, and the remainder of the officers and men under my command; from their spirited exertions, and strict attention to their duties we were enabled to save our convoy and His Majesty's sloop.'[6]

When Brenton's report of the action reached the Admiralty it was accompanied by letters from Admiral Duckworth and the Governor of Gibraltar which paid such fulsome tribute to Brenton's skill and gallantry that Lord St Vincent (who had recently returned to London on sick leave) called on Lord Spencer, the First Lord of the Admiralty, and insisted that Brenton be promoted to post-captain. Spencer was happy to oblige and agreed that he should be put into the first post vacancy which came available in the Mediterranean. The vacancy did not occur until the following year when, as we have seen, the capture of the *Généreux* by Nelson's squadron opened up the field for a series of promotions. Brenton had initially been given command of the *Guerrier* but by the time he had completed the various missions required of him in the *Speedy*, the *Guerrier* had gone to another captain and he was ordered to take command of the *Généreux* at Port Mahon. So it was there that he handed over the *Speedy* to Cochrane, and it was there on the afternoon of 20 April 1800 that Cochrane climbed aboard the battle-scarred vessel, assembled the men on deck and read his commission which was signed by Lord Keith on behalf of the Lords of the Admiralty:

'By virtue of the power and authority to us given, we do hereby constitute and appoint you Commander of His Majesty's sloop the Speedy, willing and requiring you forthwith to go on board and take upon you the charge and command of Commander in her accordingly; strictly charging and commanding all the officers and company of the said sloop to behave themselves jointly and severally in their respective employments with all due respect and obedience. . . .'[7]

As Lieutenant Parker, Mr Marshal, the master, and the rest of the ship's company listened to the familiar phrases they must have regarded Cochrane with some reservations. His character, his leadership and his mode of command would affect all their lives for better or for worse. Brenton had been in the navy for twenty years and had proved himself a courageous and highly competent officer. Cochrane was a twenty-four-year-old Scottish aristocrat with barely seven years seafaring experience. He brought with him his youngest brother, the Hon. Archibald Cochrane, who was signed on the books as master's mate. This was a reminder that family connections were so often the key to advancement. Was Cochrane appointed as their new commander because of his ability or because he had friends in high places? His height and his powerful build were no doubt impressive but how would he perform when they went into action or were struck by a Mediterranean squall off a lee shore?

Cochrane had everything to prove. The *Speedy* gave him the opportunity to make his name and secure promotion to post-captain, the most crucial of all ranks for an ambitious young officer. Once he was on the list of captains his advancement would be by seniority and, provided he survived injury, disease, shipwreck and the other hazards of life at sea, he would rise inexorably to the rank of admiral. This and the opportunities for prize money were to be powerful incentives for his actions in the coming months.

Within two days of Cochrane's arrival the *Speedy* was ready for sea. At 2.00 p.m. on 22 April 1800 they weighed anchor. With a southwesterly wind against them they had to warp the ship the length of the harbour and it was six o'clock before they cleared the entrance and were able to make sail. They headed east for the island of Malta where they had orders to rendezvous with a convoy of merchantmen. The weather was fine with light to moderate breezes which gave Cochrane an ideal opportunity to observe the vessel's performance.[8] On the fourth day out from Port Mahon he decided the brig was under-canvassed and he ordered the sailmaker to enlarge the mainsail and the main topsail, though whether this made any difference to her speed is not recorded. We do know what he thought of his new command. 'Despite her unformidable character, and the personal discomfort to which all on board were subjected, I was very proud of my little vessel, caring nothing for her want of accommodation.'[9]

For a man of his height the cramped conditions below deck must have been a constant annoyance. The living space in the captain's cabin was extremely limited. The floor area was no more than six foot by four and was almost entirely occupied by a table. The remaining space was taken up by lockers which also served as seats. There was no room for a chair and with such limited headroom Cochrane found considerable difficulty in sitting with his feet under the table. Shaving was even more of a problem but he solved this by putting his head through the companion (the skylight, clearly visible on the deck plans of the *Speedy*) and laying out his shaving things on the deck.

It took them no more than a week to reach Malta and on 29 April they dropped anchor in St Paul's Bay on the north coast of the island, a few miles from the strongly fortified harbour of Valletta. From their anchorage along the coast the crew of the *Speedy* could see several British warships cruising off the harbour entrance of Valletta, main-taining the blockade which would soon force the French garrison to surrender.

They spent a day replenishing their supplies of fresh water before setting sail and joining the convoy and her other escort, the brig sloop *Minorca*. The weather continued fine as they headed north-west and once they were safely through the Straits of Messina they parted company with the convoy and sailed north until they sighted the

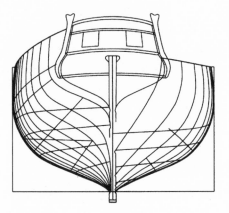

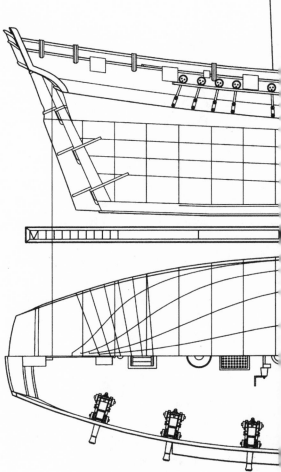

Designed and built by King of Dover
laid down in 1781 and launched in 1782
Dimensions :
Length on the range of the deck   78' 3"
Length of the keel for tunnage   59' 0 1/2"
Breadth extreme   25' 8 1/4"
Depth in hold   10' 10"
Burthen in tons   287 12/94
Armament
14 4 pounder guns and 12 Swivels

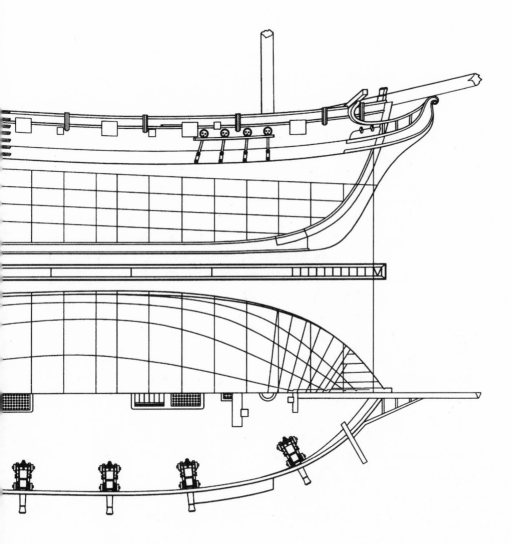

The lines of the brig sloop *Speedy*, drawn by Norman Swales from
the original plans in the National Maritime Museum, London.

mountains of Sardinia. In the early hours of the morning of 7 May they dropped anchor in the great bay of Cagliari on the southern coast of Sardinia. Scattered around the sparkling waters of the bay were fourteen merchant ships waiting to be escorted to the Italian port of Leghorn. At noon on 10 May Cochrane made the signal for the convoy to get under way and with a light breeze filling their sails they crept around the headland at the eastern end of the bay and headed north.

At dawn the next day a strange ship was sighted and, before the *Speedy* could intercept, she had picked off one of the outlying vessels in the convoy and captured her. There was so little wind that Cochrane ordered his crew to get out the sweeps, the long oars used to propel the vessel in calms, and under oar and sail they bore down on the intruder. It only needed a few shots from the *Speedy* to persuade the enemy ship to surrender. She proved to be a French lateen-rigged vessel mounting 6 guns and she became the first of Cochrane's prizes.

On the afternoon of 14 May they sighted Montecristo, the small island off the coast of Corsica which would soon be made famous by Alexandre Dumas. In *The Count of Monte Cristo*, his epic story of wrongful imprisonment and retribution, he described the island as 'a rock of almost conical shape, which appears to have been thrown up by some volcanic cataclysm from the depths to the surface of the sea'.[10] According to Dumas the island was and always had been utterly deserted but, as the *Speedy* sailed past, five rowing boats emerged from one of its rocky inlets and began pulling towards them. The boats converged on the sternmost vessels in the convoy, boarded and took possession of two of them. Cochrane gave orders for the remaining ships in the convoy to make for the shelter of the Bay of Longona while he chased after the gunboats in the gathering dusk. They pursued them during the night and, thanks to clear skies and light winds, they were able to keep them in sight. At one in the morning they recaptured the two merchantmen and took them in tow. On 21 May the *Speedy* and her convoy arrived safely at Leghorn. In his first cruise as a commander Cochrane had successfully defended the ships in his charge and captured one vessel. It was a modestly successful beginning.

After taking in water and provisions the *Speedy* left Leghorn and made for Genoa where Lord Keith, with a squadron of warships, was blockading the port. On 29 May Cochrane went aboard the flagship and received orders from Keith to cruise independently and to harass enemy shipping. For the next four months the *Speedy* sailed to and fro in the seas of the western Mediterranean, intercepting merchantmen and chasing French privateers. By 6 October, when she returned to Port Mahon for repairs, she had engaged in several minor actions and captured three more vessels.

A survey carried out by the dockyard showed that the *Speedy* needed a major refit. She was hauled alongside the sheer hulk (the floating crane used for handling masts) so that her bowsprit could be taken out and repaired. Much of her running rigging was replaced and caulkers came on board to caulk the seams of her internal and external planking. She put to sea again on 21 October but ran into a gale and lost her main boom and one of the boats when a heavy sea broke across her stern. She returned to Port Mahon for further repairs and it was while she lay at anchor near the dockyard that a new surgeon came on board to join the ship's company.

The present surgeon of the *Speedy*, Louis Rimonier, had been appointed surgeon of the 36-gun frigate *Caroline*. His replacement was a Scot by the name of James Guthrie. Many years later Guthrie wrote, 'I joined the Speedy as acting surgeon on the 30th November 1800 and continued in her until she was captured on the 3rd July following.'[11] In fact his warrant, signed by Lord Keith, makes no mention of his being merely acting surgeon and orders him 'to repair on board the Speedy and take upon you the employment of Surgeon. . . . with such allowance for wages and victuals for yourself as is usual for the Surgeon of the said Sloop'.[12] Guthrie had formerly been surgeon's first mate on the 74-gun ship *Foudroyant* and he proved an excellent appointment. He became a lifelong friend of Cochrane and was the surgeon of all the ships he commanded as a captain in the Royal Navy.[13]

The next cruise of the *Speedy* shows Cochrane beginning to get into his stride. They left Port Mahon on 12 December and headed west for

Majorca. Sailing off the mountainous north coast of the island they sighted a number of strange craft, one of which proved to be a French bomb vessel. The *Speedy* was cleared for action and they chased her along the western shores of Majorca and drove her ashore near Dragon Island (Isla Dragonera). They then attacked a French vessel mounting 6 guns, captured her and transferred her crew to the *Speedy*. They replaced the French prisoners with a prize crew which sailed the vessel back to Port Mahon.

A few days later, during the afternoon of 21 December, they were cruising along the coast of Spain near Alicante when they saw a large ship which appeared to be a heavily-laden merchantman. Cochrane decided to investigate but as they approached the vessel she suddenly raised her gunports and they found themselves facing the broadside of a powerful Spanish frigate. Escape was impossible because the frigate could easily outsail them: the only solution was to deceive the Spanish captain into thinking the *Speedy* was a ship of a neutral nation. In his autobiography Cochrane tells how he had been warned at Port Mahon that the Spanish were on the lookout for the *Speedy* and that he had prepared for just such an emergency. He had had the *Speedy* painted in imitation of a Danish brig and had taken on board a Danish quartermaster complete with the uniform of a Danish officer. Confronted with the guns of the Spanish frigate, Cochrane hoisted a Danish flag and instructed his quartermaster to tell the Spanish that the *Speedy* was two days out from Algiers where the plague was raging. Recalling the incident many years later Guthrie the surgeon corrected Cochrane's account:

> The Speedy was from Mahon and had not been at Algiers during the time I belonged to her – I was on deck and heard Lord Cochrane dictate to the quarter master what to say and as no one in the brig for the time being could speak or understand any language except Danish and the Spaniard had only a seaman who had been several voyages to the Baltic who understood a few words of Danish, but the word quarantine being nearly the same in different languages, on its being mentioned the Spanish officer exclaimed, oh! oh! quarantina, quarantina, and desired his boat to keep off – it was dark by this time, so we escaped.[14]

While the frigate disappeared into the night the *Speedy* headed south-west, sailing close inshore along the Spanish coast. In the Bay of Cartagena they had a minor skirmish with two Spanish privateers and succeeded in capturing one of the vessels they were escorting which was laden with wine. Further forays along the coast yielded no more prizes and by 11 January 1801 they were back in Port Mahon to take in fresh supplies of water and provisions.

For the next four months the cruises followed much the same pattern except that the number of prizes taken increased steadily. Cochrane was perfecting the skills which he would later use to such devastating effect as a frigate captain. His cruises in the *Speedy* took him all round the western Mediterranean so that he built up a first-hand knowledge of the bays, anchorages, harbours and fortifications from Malta and Tunis to Gibraltar, Genoa and the islands of Sardinia and Corsica. He became a master of hit-and-run raids; he learnt the value of moving at night and attacking in the early hours of the morning; and he became adept at *ruses de guerre*, in particular the use of false flags and misleading signals – a long-standing seafaring tradition much used by pirates but also by naval warships as an acceptable device for catching the enemy off guard.

A notable example of the successful use of false flags took place on 22 January 1801. Cochrane's description of the incident is brief and again his surgeon provides more detail. According to Guthrie, 'five Danish merchantmen came out of Barcelona, one of whom his Lordship boarded to obtain news and get water from them as they were all in ballast'.[15] At dawn the next morning they were still sailing in company with the Danish vessels when two enemy ships were seen approaching from the west. One was a Spanish brig of 8 guns and the other a French ship of 10 guns. Cochrane hoisted a Danish flag and pretended to act as escort to the Danish convoy.

'The Spanish brig and French ship came right down upon us suspecting nothing and as we were edging towards the latter he hailed wishing to know what we wanted with him to which his Lordship replied it was just him we wanted.'[16] The *Speedy* hauled down the Danish flag, hoisted British colours and opened fire. Within

half an hour it was all over. Both enemy ships were captured and fifty
men were taken prisoner.

But it was an action on 6 May which made Cochrane's name and
was directly responsible for his promotion to the coveted rank of post-
captain. The fight between the *Speedy* and *El Gamo* has acquired a
legendary reputation. It was regarded at the time as a 'very spirited
and brilliant action', and is still generally regarded among naval
historians as one of the most remarkable single-ship actions in the
navy's history. By the beginning of May 1801 the *Speedy* had captured
or destroyed seventeen enemy vessels and had made a number of
audacious raids on vessels sheltering under the guns of Spanish forts.
The Spanish were evidently on the lookout for this menace to their
shipping and had a warship cruising off Barcelona. At dawn on 6 May
the *Speedy* sighted a strange ship and went to investigate. There was a
light breeze and it was some two hours before they were close enough
to identify her. She proved to be a Spanish xebec frigate of 32 guns, a
formidable adversary capable of reducing the *Speedy* to a wreck with
two or three broadsides.

Instead of retreating, Cochrane continued to sail towards the enemy
and gave the order to clear for action. At 9.30 a.m. the *Gamo* fired a
gun and hoisted Spanish colours. Her decks were crowded with
seamen and soldiers who no doubt imagined that the lightly armed
brig with the conspicuously tall officer standing by the tiller would
surrender to them without a fight. If there should be a fight the odds
were overwhelmingly in favour of the Spanish. They had more than
twice the number of guns, and they were able to fire a broadside nearly
seven times the weight of the broadside of the *Speedy*'s 4-pounders.[17]
The *Gamo* had 319 men on board, five times as many as the *Speedy*,
which could only muster fifty-four including officers and boys because
many of her crew had been despatched with prizes to Port Mahon.
Apart from the disparity in size of crew and weight of broadside,
Cochrane also had the problem that his guns had a much more limited
range than those of the Spanish ship. His only hope of overcoming his
adversary was to fight her at close quarters.

As soon as the *Gamo* hoisted the Spanish colours Cochrane

acknowledged by running up an American flag. This produced enough uncertainty in the mind of the Spanish captain to delay the firing of his broadside and enabled the *Speedy* to tack, hoist the British ensign and position herself so that when the Spaniard's first broadside was delivered it caused no damage. Telling his men not to fire until they were close alongside, Cochrane sailed the *Speedy* under the lee of the frigate and locked his yards with her rigging. He had calculated that in this position the guns of the *Gamo* would fire harmlessly over the heads of his men because of the height of her main gun deck above the water. However, by elevating the *Speedy*'s guns and having them treble-shotted he could inflict carnage upon the Spaniards' deck – indeed, the first broadside killed the Spanish captain and his boatswain.

Unable to cause any serious damage with their carriage guns, and finding that the musket fire they directed at the British crew had little effect, the Spanish prepared to board. Given their superior numbers this had to be avoided at all costs. Cochrane managed to extricate the *Speedy*'s yards and sheered away from the frigate, firing a broadside as he went. Twice more the *Speedy* ranged alongside the frigate, fired her guns and then bore away. However, Cochrane was aware that this unequal contest could not last. 'Our rigging being cut up and the Speedy's sails riddled with shot, I told the men that they must either take the frigate or be themselves taken.' In an all-or-nothing bid for victory he decided to lead a boarding party of his entire crew. Only one man would stay behind to take the helm, assisted by two boys. Surgeon Guthrie volunteered for this job and 'placed the Speedy alongside with admirable skill'.

Cochrane had divided his men into two groups, one to board at the head of the frigate and the other to board amidships. The men at the head were ordered to blacken their faces in order to appear more terrifying as they suddenly emerged from the swirling smoke of the bow guns. The Spaniards were taken by surprise, as Cochrane had intended they should be, and, before they could recover, the second group of boarders attacked them from behind. For several minutes there was a mêlée as men and boys engaged in hand-to-hand fighting with cutlasses, pistols and boarding axes. Cochrane, who had that essential gift in a military leader of being able to think clearly in the heat of the action, observed the big Spanish flag billowing above the yelling, screaming figures on the deck and directed one of his men to haul it down. The effect was extraordinary. The hard-pressed Spaniards, who had already lost fifteen men killed and forty-one wounded, assumed that one of their officers had surrendered the ship and laid down their weapons.

The *Speedy* had lost three men killed and eight wounded, including Lieutenant Parker, who was badly injured by a sword thrust in his thigh and a musket ball in his chest. This left only forty-two men available to sail the two ships and to guard 263 unwounded prisoners. Cochrane solved the problem by herding the Spaniards into the hold and pointing the guns down the hatchway. He left a prize crew of thirty men on the *Gamo* under the command of his brother Archibald, now a midshipman, and as soon as they had carried out essential repairs the two ships headed back to Port Mahon. There Cochrane sent his report to Captain Manley Dixon, the senior officer at Port Mahon. Like Jahleel Brenton before him, Cochrane gave full credit to his officers and men for their part in the defeat and capture of the frigate:

'I must be permitted to say that there could not be greater regularity, nor more cool determined conduct shown by men, than by the crew of the Speedy. Lieut. Parker, whom I beg leave to recommend to their Lordships' notice, as well as the Hon. Mr Cochrane, deserve all the approbation that can be bestowed. The exertions and good conduct of the boatswain, carpenter, and petty officers I acknowledge with pleasure, as well as the skill and attention of Mr. Guthrie, the surgeon.'[18] Cochrane's commander-in-chief, Lord Keith, was anchored off Aboukir Bay at the mouth of the Nile when he received the news of the *Speedy's* action. He sent a letter warmly congratulating Cochrane on 'an event so honourable to the naval service' and asked him to pass on to the *Speedy's* officers and men his approbation of their bravery and discipline.

It would be several months before Cochrane's report reached

London, and when it did so it attracted little attention, presumably because the *Speedy* was a small and relatively insignificant vessel.[19] However, the extent of Cochrane's achievement must have impressed some expert observers because Nicholas Pocock, who had now established himself as the leading marine artist of the day, added the fight between the *Speedy* and *El Gamo* to his growing portfolio of naval actions and produced a fine watercolour which was subsequently engraved and published.[20]

The coast near Barcelona was the scene of Cochrane's next exploit in the *Speedy*, a joint operation with the 16-gun brig sloop *Kangaroo*. The principal source of information on this occasion is a detailed despatch from the commander of the *Kangaroo*, Captain Pulling, who had recently arrived on the Mediterranean station and was senior to Cochrane. The two sloops had found a Spanish convoy of twelve sail and five armed vessels anchored in the Bay of Oropeso, protected by the twelve guns of a battery in a large square tower. 'When having so able and gallant an Officer as his Lordship to lead the attack into the Bay,' wrote Pulling, 'I hesitated not a moment to make the attack.'[21] Throughout the afternoon of 9 June 1801 the bay resounded with the booming of guns and the intermittent crack of musket fire as the British sloops and their boats endeavoured to destroy the gunboats and to capture some of the merchant vessels of the convoy. By seven in the evening they had sunk a 20-gun xebec and two gunboats and had silenced the guns in the tower, but 'were annoyed by a heavy fire of musquetry in different directions till midnight, during which time the boats of both brigs were engaged in cutting out the vessels that were found afloat'.[22] By the next morning they had succeeded in capturing three brigs laden with wine, rice and bread, and had sunk or driven ashore all the remaining vessels of the convoy. On receiving Pulling's despatch Lord Keith sent it on to the Admiralty with an accompanying letter in which he drew attention to the zealous and active exertions of Captain Pulling, and 'the continued meritorious conduct, of which Captain Lord Cochrane, and the Officers and crew of the Speedy, have lately furnished so exemplary a proof'.[23]

When he returned to Port Mahon, Cochrane was disappointed to learn that the *Gamo*, potentially the most valuable of all his prizes so far, had been sold for a knockdown price to the Algerines, presumably because her Mediterranean hull form and rig were not considered suitable for the Royal Navy. Apart from the fact that Cochrane would have liked to have been given command of her, he would have earned a handsome sum in prize money if she had been taken into naval service. He was equally disappointed to be told that, instead of returning to the Spanish coast to continue his capture and destruction of enemy vessels, he must escort a packet boat carrying mails to Gibraltar.

Three weeks after his successful action with Captain Pulling he was once again heading for the coast of Spain but instead of remaining safely out of sight of land and the attentions of enemy privateers cruising offshore, he was unable to resist heading inshore. In a bay near Alicante several merchant vessels were observed at anchor. On seeing the *Speedy* sailing towards them they weighed anchor and ran aground on the beach. Cochrane was aware that he would be exceeding his instructions if he sent in boats to haul them off so instead he set fire to them. One of the vessels was laden with oil which burned fiercely through the night and lit up the sky for miles around, attracting the attention of an enemy infinitely superior to the *Gamo*.

On 13 June a squadron of French warships under Rear-Admiral Durand de Linois had left Toulon and was now sailing down the Spanish coast towards Cadiz in order to collect reinforcements for the French army in Egypt. The squadron consisted of the 80-gun ships *Formidable* and *Indomptable*, the 74-gun ship *Desaix* and the frigate *Muiron*. On seeing the flames of the burning vessel they headed inshore to investigate. At daybreak on 3 July the *Speedy* was in sight of the Rock of Gibraltar when her lookout observed the ships on the eastern horizon. At first Cochrane thought that they were Spanish galleons returning from South America but as the light improved it became clear that they were French ships of the line and they were heading their way. The *Speedy* was upwind of the squadron but the wind was so light that they had little chance of outsailing the larger vessels. It was characteristic of Cochrane that he should refuse to surrender his ship without a struggle although the forces ranged against him were overwhelming. He ordered all sail set, got the crew pulling at the sweeps and directed their course towards Gibraltar. With each tack the enemy drew steadily closer. At about 9.00 a.m. Cochrane gave the order to heave all the guns overboard in order to lighten the brig and increase her speed but the French ships continued to close the distance. Soon the 74-gun *Desaix* was close enough to fire her bowchasers and as she turned to go about on the other tack she fired a broadside. Apart from some minor damage to the rigging the *Speedy* and her crew remained unharmed but this could not last much longer. Barrels and casks of stores and provisions followed the guns overboard but made no apparent difference to their speed. Cochrane now waited for the *Desaix* to come level with them and when she was just ahead of their beam he bore up, set the studding sails and attempted to run between the advancing ships. The *Desaix* tacked in pursuit and fired another broadside which again missed the diminutive target.

The *Desaix* now moved in for the kill and when she was within musket shot she let loose a deadly barrage of round shot and grape shot. The *Speedy* was saved from destruction by the fact that the French ship heeled as she turned to bring her guns to bear and most of the round shot fell short. However, the *Speedy* had now lost her main boom, her sails were riddled with holes and much of her rigging was cut and trailing across the deck. Miraculously not a single member of her crew had yet been hurt but Cochrane knew that another broadside at close range would have a murderous effect. At ten o'clock he ordered the colours to be hauled down and surrendered to a ship which had a crew five times the size of his own and was more than forty times more powerful in terms of the weight of her broadside. He had himself rowed across to the *Desaix*, climbed up her massive sides and formally offered his sword to Captain J. A. Christy-Pallière. According to Cochrane's account the French captain politely declined to take it, saying, 'he would not accept the sword of an officer who had for so many hours struggled against impossibility'. The French squadron, with the captured *Speedy* and the packet boat, rounded Europa Point, sailed past the British naval base at Gibraltar and headed across the bay to the Spanish port of Algeciras. There they dropped anchor in a strong defensive position protected by two batteries and a fort.

The nearest British warships were thirty miles away blockading the entrance to the harbour of Cadiz. The blockading squadron was under the command of Rear-Admiral Sir James Saumarez in the *Caesar*. His flag captain was Jahleel Brenton who had moved from the *Généreux* a few months earlier. When news reached Saumarez of the arrival of the French ships he immediately set sail and arrived in the Bay of Gibraltar at 7.00 a.m. on 6 July with a squadron of six ships of the line, a frigate and a brig.

Cochrane was having breakfast in the great cabin of the *Desaix* with Captain Christy-Pallière who saw no reason why an imminent action with a superior force should spoil their meal. However, when a round shot from the British flagship crashed through the stern windows the two men abandoned breakfast and went up on to the quarter deck. A second shot from the *Caesar* hit a file of marines close by and Cochrane decided that further exposure on his part was unnecessary, 'and went below to a position whence I could nevertheless, at times, see what was going on'. The ensuing Battle of Algeciras was a humiliating defeat for the British. They were hampered by a dying breeze and an unfavourable current and were unable to take advantage of their numerical superiority. In the confused and heated action which followed both sides suffered heavy losses in dead and injured. The British 74-gun ship *Hannibal* ran aground and came under a barrage of fire. Her captain fought back but was forced to surrender after losing his foremast and mainmast. The *Pompee* ran into trouble and boats had to be sent to tow her out of danger. At 1.30 p.m. Saumarez gave the order to withdraw and sailed his depleted and battered squadron across to Gibraltar for repairs.

The following day Saumarez sent Captain Brenton across to Algeciras under a flag of truce to arrange an exchange of prisoners. Admiral Linois agreed to the release of the crew of the captured *Hannibal*, as well as the officers and men of the *Speedy*. Cochrane went to stay in the Commissioner's house at Gibraltar. From the garden of the house he witnessed the British squadron set sail on 12 July to retrieve their reputation. The dockyard craftsmen had worked over-time to repair the damaged ships and, together with hundreds of other onlookers, they gathered along the waterfront to cheer the squadron on its way. The band of the Gibraltar garrison thumped out a succession of patriotic tunes, while out in the bay the band on board the *Caesar* could be heard playing 'Hearts of Oak'.

The French squadron had received reinforcements during the course of the past week and Saumarez's squadron of five ships of the line, two frigates and two smaller warships now faced nine French ships of the line, three frigates and a lugger. In the ensuing action, most of which took place in darkness off Cabareta Point, the British were revenged for the earlier reverses. Superior seamanship and gunnery proved decisive in the confusion of a night action. Two Spanish three-deckers fought each other, caught fire and blew up with terrible loss of life and one French ship was captured. The remaining French and Spanish ships retreated to Cadiz.

For Cochrane there was a court martial to face for the loss of his ship before he returned to England and an uncertain future. Mean-while the *Speedy* was taken to the French naval base at Toulon. In the hands of Brenton and Cochrane she had acquired a reputation out of all proportion to her size.[24] She was soon to become a pawn in the diplomatic offensive which Napoleon was waging with Pope Pius VII, whose presence he required at his forthcoming coronation as emperor. On 12 December 1802 the *Speedy* was sailed from Toulon to the port of Rome at Civitavecchia. She was renamed *Saint Pierre* and the words 'Donné par le premier consul Bonaparte au Pape Pie VII' were inscribed in gilt letters on her poop.[25] In 1804 she was entered on the books of the Papal Navy where she remained until 1807 when she was broken up.

FOUR

A Dark Interlude

1801–1804

The court martial for the loss of the *Speedy* was held on board the 80-gun ship *Pompee* on 18 July 1801, less than a week after Sir James Saumarez and his victorious squadron had returned to Gibraltar. The *Pompee* was anchored in Rosier Bay, a sheltered inlet near the dockyard of Gibraltar, and the President of the court was her commander, Captain Charles Stirling. He was assisted in his deliberations by four other officers, all of whom had distinguished themselves in the night action off Cabareta Point. The senior of the four was Captain Richard Keats who had made his reputation as a frigate captain and had played a major role in the recent action as commander of the 74-gun *Superb*. Alongside him was Captain Samuel Hood. He was the cousin of the naval brothers Lord Samuel Hood and Lord Bridport and had achieved fame on his own account as commander of the *Zealous* at the Battle of the Nile. Next in seniority was Captain Aiskew Hollis of the frigate *Thames* who had already taken part in two fleet actions: the Battle of Ushant and the Battle of the Glorious First of June. The junior captain present was Jahleel Brenton. He, of course, knew better than any of them the strengths and weaknesses of the *Speedy* and the fine record of the officers and men that he had helped to train.

Cochrane could expect a sympathetic hearing from men of such experience and the proceedings were conducted in a brisk and seaman-like manner. Cochrane was asked to explain the circumstances relating to the loss of his ship which he did briefly and without heroics. He pointed out that he had endeavoured to keep to windward of the enemy but 'found not withstanding all our endeavours to keep the wind that the French ships gained very fast . . .'.[1] When he had concluded his description he was asked whether he had any reason to find fault with any of his officers or men and he replied that the utmost exertion was used by every person on board. The officers and ship's company of the *Speedy* were then asked whether they could find any fault with the conduct of their captain, to which all replied, 'None'.

Lieutenant Parker, as well as the quartermaster and one of the boatswain's mates, were each questioned about the relative speed of the French ships compared with that of the *Speedy,* and were asked whether every means was taken for the preservation of the king's sloop. Each man confirmed that the French ships sailed much faster even without their studding sails set and that every effort had been made to save the *Speedy.* Surgeon Guthrie was then called to give his version of events. He was asked:

'Are you a sufficient judge of nautical affairs to know whether every effort was used to escape from the force that was pursuing the Speedy?'

He replied, 'I know very little of nautical affairs but it appeared to me that every exertion was used by every person on board. I saw the captain at the helm, and the officers and ship's company at the sweeps.'

'Was you on deck at the time the colours were struck and what distance were the enemy from you at the time of her surrender?'

'I was on deck, and a French two-decker was within musket shot of the Speedy and was firing at us at the time.'

No more witnesses were called and, after checking the views of his colleagues, Captain Stirling announced that the court was of the opinion that Lord Cochrane, his officers and ship's company, had used every possible exertion to prevent the king's sloop falling into the hands of the enemy, 'and do therefore honourably acquit them and they are hereby acquitted accordingly'.[2]

Three weeks later Cochrane was on his way back to England. The order for his passage had been signed by Sir James Saumarez and he was one of twenty-three sailors and soldiers who were travelling as passengers on the schooner *Spider*.[3] The others included two naval captains, a gunner, a boatswain and an army major. After a wait of several days while the schooner took on water and provisions they set sail on 11 August. The *Spider* was a former French privateer and they should have enjoyed a swift passage home but light winds slowed them down and it was not until they were nearing the Lizard that the wind picked up. As they heeled before a freshening breeze off the rocky coast of Cornwall the sky darkened and squally rain showers swept across the surface of the sea. The rain died away as they entered Plymouth Sound and at nine o'clock on the morning of 2 September they moored in Stonehouse Pool. Three weeks later Cochrane was with his family in Scotland.[4]

Cochrane had been away for more than two years and arrived back in Britain at a turning point in the war with France. The conflict had lasted eight and a half years and had almost reached a stalemate with French armies proving invincible on land and the British navy over-coming all opposition at sea. Earlier in the year a British fleet commanded by Sir Hyde Parker had sailed to Copenhagen to chal-lenge the threat posed by the northern League of Armed Neutrality: Denmark, Sweden, Prussia and Russia had agreed on an embargo on British ships which would have cut off the vital supplies of timber, naval stores and grain which Britain imported from the Baltic. Nelson, who was Hyde Parker's second in command, took twelve battleships into Copenhagen harbour on the morning of 2 April 1801. Three ships ran aground on the shoals within range of the shore batteries but Nelson ignored the signal to retreat and, after a hard-fought battle in which British gunnery again proved decisive, the Danes agreed to a cease-fire. Nelson subsequently negotiated an armistice and the Northern League was dissolved.

Set against this much needed victory was the continual threat posed by Napoleon and his territorial ambitions. In June 1800 he had defeated the Austrians at Marengo and in December at Hohenlinden. Austria subsequently made peace with France at Lunéville in February 1801. Spain and most of Italy had already come to terms with the French. In April 1801 Napoleon began assembling an army at Boulogne in preparation for the invasion of England. By August the military encampments could be plainly seen from the highest points of the Kent coast and *The Times* was carrying reports from Dover that 'the greatest activity prevails in the different French ports. The gun boats and flat-bottomed boats are numerous.'[5] The Admiralty provided some reassurance to an anxious British public by appointing Nelson to command the defences in the Channel. The hero of the Nile and Copenhagen led two attacks on Boulogne. On 4 August he bombarded the French harbour with mortar shells fired from bomb vessels but with little effect, and then during the night of 15 August he launched a boat attack on the enemy invasion vessels. The French were surprisingly well prepared for such an attack and the British boats were repulsed with the loss of forty-four men killed and 126 wounded.[6]

Both sides were ready for a pause in the hostilities. Britain in particular needed a breathing space. The country was facing a financial crisis and food shortages and no longer had allies on the Continent. William Pitt, a resolute and courageous war leader, had been replaced back in February by the dull and humdrum Addington, the former Speaker of the House of Commons. Addington represented those interests weary of the war and during the autumn of 1801 he initiated negotiations for a peace with France. The preliminaries were concluded on 1 October 1801 and a formal peace treaty was signed at Amiens on 27 March 1802.

Readers of C.S. Forester's novels will recall the effect of the Peace of Amiens on Lieutenant Hornblower and his friend Lieutenant Bush. In common with hundreds of other naval officers they find themselves out of work and on half-pay. Bush is on a ship in the Caribbean when he hears the news. The crew of his ship cheer wildly because for them it means the end of harsh naval discipline and a return to their homes. But for Bush it means the end of a life he enjoyed. 'He tried to think of a winter's day in England, with nothing to do. No ship to handle . . . No, he simply could not imagine it, and he left off trying.'[7] Back in England he meets Hornblower who is starving and having to spend his days playing whist in the Long Rooms at Portsmouth in order to pay for his lodgings.

For Cochrane the peace also meant unemployment and half-pay. It was one more setback in a series of setbacks he had experienced from the moment of his capture by the French. He had assumed that his taking of the *Gamo* would be rapidly rewarded by promotion to post-captain. Unfortunately the news of the capture of the *Speedy* reached London before the news of the *Gamo* action and he had to wait three months for the promotion to take place. Cochrane's father wrote a long letter to Lord St Vincent complaining about the delay and expressing his surprise and disappointment 'on finding several masters and commanders on the Mediterranean station – his juniors long before, and for several months after, the taking of the Gamo – now placed before him on that list'.[8] St Vincent wrote back to Lord Dundonald explaining the reasons for the delay. He acknowledged that the capture of the *Gamo* reflected the highest degree of credit on Cochrane and his officers and crew, but he went on to say:

'The first account of that brilliant action reached the Admiralty very early in the month of August, previously to which intelligence had been received of the capture of the Speedy, by which Lord Cochrane was made prisoner; and until his exchange could be effected, and the necessary inquiry into the cause and circumstances of the loss of that sloop had taken place, it was impossible for the Board, consistently with its usual forms, to mark the approbation of his Lordship's conduct. Lord Cochrane was promoted to the rank of post-captain on the 8th of August, the day on which the sentence of acquittal for the loss of the Speedy was received, which was all that could under existing circumstances be done.'[9]

This was a perfectly reasonable explanation but for Cochrane, impatient for advancement and currently without a ship to command, the three months' delay was critical because, in the interim period, ten of his rival officers had been advanced to post-captain and would therefore always be senior to him on the captain's list. Cochrane

William Cochrane, founder of the family fortunes. He became the first Earl of Dundonald in 1669.

Thomas Cochrane's father Archibald, the ninth Earl of Dundonald.

Thomas Cochrane as a boy. Following the death of his mother when he was nine years old, Thomas and his brothers were brought up on the family estate at Culross by their grandmother.

The confluence of the Thames and Medway, 1808, by J.M.W. Turner. A breezy depiction
of shipping in the Thames estuary with a sheer hulk removing the masts of a warship
on the left of the picture and Sheerness in the distance.

The harbour and town of Lerwick, capital of the Shetland Islands. Cochrane paid two visits to Lerwick in 1804 while in command of the *Arab*. Lithograph after the painting by J. C. Schetky.

A British squadron under the command of Lord Keith, off Valetta during the blockade of Malta in February 1800, after a watercolour by Rev. Cooper Willyams. Cochrane was a junior lieutenant at this time aboard Keith's flagship, the *Queen Charlotte*, the large warship in the centre of the picture.

Lord St Vincent as First Lord of the Admiralty. It was foolish of Cochrane to make an enemy of such a formidable naval officer. Engraving after the picture by Sir William Beechey.

A portrait of Admiral Lord Keith by William Owen. In 1799 he became commander-in-chief, Mediterranean.

The Rock of Gibraltar viewed from the ruins of Fort St Philip. The town and harbour of Gibraltar can be seen in the distance on the right of the picture. Engraving after the drawing by H. A. West.

The capture of the Spanish frigate *El Gamo* by the British sloop *Speedy*, 6 May 1801, by
Clarkson Stanfield. Cochrane can be seen with raised sword on the poop deck. The artist,
who was a former seaman, was a close friend of Charles Dickens and Captain Marryat.

A detail from a panoramic view of the royal dockyard at Plymouth painted by Nicholas Pocock in 1798. The building slips where Cochrane's frigate *Pallas* was built can be seen on the right of the picture.

A watercolour of Plymouth by J.M.W. Turner. The view looks from Turnchapel, across the shipping in the Cattewater, towards the distant Citadel and the city itself. On the left is the small fort on Mount Batten Point.

subsequently came to believe that the delay was caused by some sinister influence at work and in his autobiography he laid the blame at the door of Lord St Vincent for this and other setbacks.

John Jervis, Earl of St Vincent, had been appointed First Lord of the Admiralty by Addington in February 1801. He had impressive credentials as a fighting captain and admiral. He had played a key role in Wolfe's capture of Quebec in 1759; he had been knighted in 1782 after a single-ship action in which he had captured a French 74-gun ship; he had led a British expedition to the West Indies where he had taken and looted Martinique, St Lucia and Guadeloupe. As commander-in-chief of the Mediterranean Fleet he had led a British fleet to victory off Cape St Vincent and then blockaded the Spanish fleet in the harbour of Cadiz. Appointed to the command of the Channel Fleet in April 1800 he had instituted a close blockade of Brest and imposed a fiercely demanding regime on officers who were having to patrol a notoriously dangerous stretch of coast in all weathers. He was much admired by brilliant and ruthless commanders like Nelson but was feared and resented by those junior admirals and captains that he bullied and treated with contempt. He was a dangerous man to cross and made more dangerous as far as Cochrane was concerned because he had a deep-seated prejudice against Scotsmen.[10]

St Vincent, like all his predecessors as First Lord of the Admiralty, was besieged by letters and personal approaches from naval colleagues, politicians, and members of aristocratic families who wanted him to find ships for their sons, brothers or nephews. But, as he wrote to Lord Keith, 'The list of Post Captains and Commanders so far exceeds that of ships and sloops, I cannot, consistently with what is due to the public and to the incredible number of meritorious persons of those classes upon half pay, promote except upon very extraordinary occasions, such as that of Lord Cochrane and Captain Dundas, who have the rank of Post Captain.'[11] In 1800 only 40 per cent of commanders had ships or active commissions, and more than half the captains listed were out of work and on half-pay.

Unaware of St Vincent's problems, Cochrane embarked on a campaign to promote his first lieutenant, William Parker, a man of conspicuous bravery who had led a number of successful boat attacks and had been severely wounded during the boarding and taking of the *Gamo*. While still in Gibraltar, Cochrane had written to St Vincent on Parker's behalf. He had received no reply to the letter but on his return to England he sent a second letter and then a third which produced a cool response from St Vincent. He was told that his application could not be entertained because 'it was unusual to promote two officers for such a service – besides which, the small number of men killed on board the Speedy did not warrant the application'. This prompted Cochrane to write to St Vincent pointing out that, although only three men were killed on board the *Speedy*, his Lordship's own promotion to an earldom followed a battle in which only one man was killed on his own flagship, 'so that there were more casualties in my sloop than in his line-of-battle ship'. Cochrane may have imagined that his achieve-ments in the *Speedy* and his status as an aristocrat provided him with immunity from the likely repercussions of such a letter. There is no evidence to suggest that it resulted in Cochrane being placed on the black list of the Admiralty, as he imagined, but it did not endear him to St Vincent who later wrote to Admiral Markham, 'Did you ever read such a madly arrogant paragraph as that in Lord Cochrane's public letter, where he lugs in Lieutenant Parker for the avowed purpose of attacking me, his commander-in-chief?'[12]

Having failed to persuade St Vincent to promote Lieutenant Parker, Cochrane turned his attention to the Admiralty Board. Writing from 14 Old Cavendish Street, London, on 17 May 1802 he again put the case for the deserving Parker, only to be informed that it was not proper for naval officers to correspond with their Lordships. Nothing dismayed, he wrote to Evan Nepean, the Secretary of the Admiralty. This produced a final rebuff from Nepean who wrote to say that their Lordships had nothing to communicate to him.

While Cochrane was waging war on the Admiralty, the people of London were going about their usual business in a lighter mood than usual. Fears about Napoleon's threat of invasion were temporarily dispelled by the recently signed Peace of Amiens. When King George III, and the queen and princesses arrived at Somerset House on 1 May to view the pictures in the Royal Academy exhibition a crowd of between two and three thousand people gathered outside and greeted them with loud huzzas and cries of, 'God bless your Majesty! Your Majesty and the Peace for ever!'[13]

Among the pictures on view at the Academy the marine paintings were prominent, reflecting the nation's pride in the exploits of her seamen. Philippe-Jacques de Loutherbourg, who in previous years had exhibited dramatic portrayals of the Battle of the Glorious First of June and the Battle of the Nile, was showing *The Cutting out of the French Corvette La Chevrette by English Sailors,* a vivid depiction of a fierce boarding action which had recently taken place off the Normandy coast. Turner was represented by a vigorously rendered sea piece entitled *Ships Bearing up for Anchorage.* He had exhibited his first picture at the Royal Academy at the age of fifteen, and was now recognised as an artist of exceptional gifts and promise. He was among a number of British artists who took advantage of the peace during the summer of 1802 to travel to Paris to view the amazing collection of paintings and sculptures which Napoleon had looted from Italy.

The stolen art treasures on display in the Louvre were by no means the only attraction. Many English people were intensely curious to see the changes which had taken place in France during the Revolution and the Reign of Terror. Throughout the year there was a constant procession of packet boats and yachts crossing the Channel laden with English tourists. Lord Egremont, who had commissioned Turner's latest sea piece and was to become his greatest patron, sailed from Shoreham in Sussex in the schooner *Lark* with a party of fifty-three ladies and gentlemen and spent three weeks in Paris.

Charles Lamb was thrilled to receive a letter from his friend Thomas Manning who had travelled to Paris earlier in the year. 'It seemed to give me a learned importance which placed me above all who had not Parisian correspondents,' he wrote back. 'Have you seen a man guillotined yet? Is it as good as a hanging? Are the women all painted, and the men all monkeys?'[14] Like everybody else Charles Lamb wanted to know exactly what Napoleon looked like. Manning

told him that the First Consul had a godlike face, but that was not
enough for Lamb. 'What God does he most represent, Mars, Bacchus
or Apollo? . . . Our London prints represent him gloomy and sulky,
like an angry Jupiter.'[15] Fanny Burney, the author of the much
acclaimed novel *Evelina*, saw Napoleon at a military review in the
grounds of the Tuileries and was able to give her father a detailed
description. She was deeply impressed by his pale and melancholy
features, not at all like the warrior she had expected: ' . . . he has by no
means the look to be expected from Bonaparte, but rather that of a
profoundly studious and contemplative man'.[16]

Cochrane was not only out of work and on half-pay. He was also at the
bottom of the captains' list which meant that he had little or no chance of
being given command of a ship. He therefore made an interesting
decision. He had already determined to enter Parliament when the
opportunity arose but he was aware that his 'desultory and imperfect
education' was likely to prove a hindrance to his ambitions. He decided to
return to Scotland and enrol as a student at the University of Edinburgh, first in the Ethics and then in the Chemistry Faculty.

The University of Edinburgh, where Cochrane enrolled as a student following
the Peace of Amiens in 1802. From *Modern Athens! or Edinburgh in the 19th Century*,
a book of engravings based on drawings by Thomas H. Shepherd.

Edinburgh in the early 1800s was enjoying a remarkable upsurge in the arts and sciences. The designs of the Scottish architects James Craig and Robert Adam had transformed the medieval city and created a magnificent series of spacious squares, elegant classical terraces and fine public buildings in the New Town alongside Princes Street. Scottish education in schools and universities was considered by many to be the best in the world – the Scottish novelist Tobias Smollett remarked 'Every peasant was a scholar.' The capital city basked in the recent achievements of Scots who included men as various as the poet Robert Burns, the philosopher David Hume, the economist Adam Smith and the engineer James Watt.

At twenty-seven Cochrane was much older than his fellow students and he made few acquaintances, 'preferring secluded lodgings and study without interruption to the gaiety of my contemporaries'.[17] Among the lectures which he attended were those given by Dugald Stewart, one of the most influential teachers of his day. Stewart was Professor of Moral Philosophy and numbered among his students Walter Scott, Lord Palmerston and Henry Brougham, the future Lord

George Street, Edinburgh, looking west towards St George's Church, which was designed by the Scottish architect Robert Adam. Engraving after the drawing by Thomas H. Shepherd, published in 1820.

Chancellor. He had visited France in the summers of 1788 and 1789 and his subsequent support for the republican aims of the Revolution caused him to be regarded in some quarters as a dangerous radical. His teachings no doubt influenced Cochrane's later decision to stand for Parliament as an independent candidate and a radical.

The Peace of Amiens proved no more than a temporary lull in the hostilities between Britain and France. Napoleon was determined to make France powerful and respected on land and sea, and already had visions of the French Republic becoming an empire, with himself as emperor rather than First Consul. During the year of peace following the Peace of Amiens he annexed Elba and Piedmont, and failed to evacuate French troops from Holland as had been agreed under the terms of the treaty. Early in March 1803 he renewed his preparations for the invasion of Britain by ordering his Minister of Marine to arrange for the building of fifty gunboats and one hundred landing craft to add to those already assembled in the French ports. British politicians of all parties became increasingly resentful of his aggressive policies and on 8 March the king, in his speech from the throne, informed the House of Commons that 'as very considerable military preparations are carrying on in the ports of France and Holland, he has judged it expedient to adopt additional measure of precaution for the security of his dominions'.[18] Attempts to find a compromise that would prevent a renewal of hostilities failed and on 18 May 1803 Britain formally declared war on France.

With the navy back on a war footing Cochrane was more likely to be given a command and once again his family and friends began lobbying on his behalf. Lord St Vincent received letters from Cochrane's father, his naval uncle and the Marquess of Douglas. To the latter St Vincent wrote, 'I have not forgot Lord Cochrane, but I should not be justified in appointing him to the command of an 18-pounder frigate when there are so many senior captains of great merit without ships of that class. I hope soon to be able to place him in one suitable to his standing on the list.'[19] On 5 July he wrote to assure Lord Dundonald that, 'Lord Cochrane will be employed, but the precise moment cannot be ascertained'.[20] No ship materialised so Captain

Alexander Cochrane tried a different tack and wrote to his friend John Markham, who was on the Admiralty Board, asking him to remind St Vincent about Lord Cochrane. 'Many applications have been made in his favour, and promises given, yet he remains on half-pay.'[21]

In the autumn of 1803 Cochrane received the news that he had been impatiently waiting for. He was given command of a ship called the *Arab* and he hurried to Plymouth with high hopes of resuming the glittering career which had been halted so dramatically with the capture of the *Speedy*. On Saturday 15 October he came on board the *Arab*, which was in one of the docks of the royal dockyard, and commissioned the ship. In later years Cochrane maintained that his appointment to the *Arab* was St Vincent's revenge. He recalled how 'a dockyard attendant showed me the bare ribs of a collier, which had been purchased into the service'.[22] A single glance at her naked timbers showed that she would sail like a haystack, and he described how he had to wait patiently while she was patched up with old timber from broken-up vessels.

In fact the *Arab* was not a collier but a former French privateer of 22 guns. Previously called *Le Brave*, she had been captured by the 36-gun frigate *Phoenix* in 1798. She was listed as a sixth-rate and was 110 feet in length (some thirty feet longer than the *Speedy*) and her muster book indicates that she had a complement of 155 men and boys.[23] Plans of the ship show her to have had bluff bows but otherwise to have been closer to the hull form of a small warship of the period than the slab-sided, flat-bottomed shape of a British collier. One can only assume that the disappointment Cochrane felt at not being given a frigate, and the unfortunate experiences which marked his year in command of the *Arab*, left him with such bitter memories that he later blamed the ship, and Lord St Vincent, for what he had to endure.

The *Arab* may not have needed the major repairs to her hull that Cochrane's account suggested but she did need fitting out for sea. In particular she needed new masts, yards and rigging. The day after Cochrane's arrival she was hauled alongside the sheer hulk and her lower masts and bowsprit were swung on board and made secure. She was then moored alongside one of the dockyard hulks and a gang of riggers came on board. They set up the lower rigging, hauled up the topmasts and swayed the lower and topmast yards into place. While the riggers sorted out the endless coils of hemp rope, other men from the dockyard loaded the bilges with iron and shingle ballast. After three weeks of heavy labour the dockyard men had completed their work and the remaining preparations were carried out by the ship's company. There had been a few dozen men on board when Cochrane first arrived and since then a steady stream had joined the ship. They included two lieutenants, the ship's master, the boatswain, two midshipmen; nine seamen who had been rounded up by a press gang; and twenty-nine seamen and five boys sent across from the *Salvador del Mundo.*

On Sunday 6 November Cochrane mustered the ship's company on deck and read the Articles of War, the somewhat haphazard list of rules and regulations which formed the basis for discipline on board. As the men listened to the familiar litany of crimes and punishments a heavy downpour enveloped the harbour. It was the beginning of a spell of blustery weather which culminated in a day of hard gales with thunder, lightning and heavy rain when they moved the ship from alongside the hulk to moorings downstream. There was still much to do. The guns were brought on board, the sails were bent on the yards, 509 pounds of fresh beef were delivered, and a cutter and jolly boat were sent across from the dockyard. At last on Thursday 8 December, nearly two months after Cochrane's arrival, a pilot came on board to take them down the harbour and out into Plymouth Sound.[24]

The first cruise of the *Arab* was uneventful. They escorted a convoy of merchantmen down the Channel, and then headed north to Liverpool. After a fortnight of winter gales, with heavy seas and showers of rain and sleet, they anchored in the River Mersey. A week was spent taking on water and stores and overhauling the rigging; a seaman was punished with twenty-four lashes for drunkenness; and on 31 December a Liverpool pilot guided them out to sea. By 9 January they were back in Plymouth Sound. During the few days that they were moored in the harbour, carrying out repairs and adjustments to the rigging, Surgeon Guthrie came on board and joined the small group of Cochrane's followers who had transferred from the *Speedy* to the *Arab*.

The second cruise of the *Arab* was marred by several unfortunate incidents which Cochrane would no doubt have preferred to forget, and indeed none of them are mentioned in his autobiography. His orders from his commanding officer Lord Keith were to join the other British warships which were keeping watch on the French invasion flotilla being assembled at Boulogne. The *Arab* sailed from Plymouth on 16 January 1804 in company with a convoy, and was sailing past Dungeness when she collided with the gun brig *Bloodhound*, causing her to lose her jib boom, bumkins and associated rigging. There was a stiff southwesterly wind blowing at the time and visibility was cut down by driving rain but, according to Cochrane, the accident was due to the poor sailing qualities of the *Arab* and not the negligence of his officer of the watch. He informed the Admiralty that the *Arab* had gone about on to the larboard tack, the yards were not trimmed 'and the ship, which steers badly at all times, had nearly lost her way. She was therefore unmanageable . . . I was instantly on deck and everything was done that was proper to clear the vessels.'[25] Cochrane played down the damage caused to the gun brig but Lord Keith told Markham at the Admiralty, 'I am obliged to send the Bloodhound to the Nore, all to pieces by the Arab running foul of her. Lord C. gives a sad account of the latter.'[26]

If it had been an isolated incident the collision would soon have been forgotten but three days later, while the *Arab* was at anchor in the Downs, the great anchorage between Deal and the Goodwin Sands, she fell foul of the *Abundance*. This was a large naval storeship and her master promptly put in a claim for damages. Cochrane was mortified and immediately despatched a letter to Lord Keith: 'The Arab having been foul of two vessels in so short a time it is necessary for the justification of my conduct and that of the officers that I apply immediately for Courts Martial . . .'[27] When he received a letter from the Admiralty Board which clearly blamed him for the collision he wrote back with a detailed defence and again demanded a court martial so he could clear his name. 'I am well aware of the value of their

Lordships' good opinion, and that of my brother officers. I do not dread a decision founded on fact; against groundless assertion no man's character is safe.'[28] He was informed that there was no need for a court martial because Rear-Admiral Rowley had already been directed to enquire into the matter.

The troubles of the *Arab* continued unabated. When a boat was sent ashore for water while they were moored off Deal five of the launch's crew deserted. Two days later James White was punished with thirty-six lashes for attempting to desert. On 19 February they crossed the Channel to Boulogne and then sailed along the French coast to Calais. A number of French gunboats were seen cruising inshore. Cochrane anchored and sent a boat with an armed crew in chase, provoking the shore batteries to open fire. Unlike the *Speedy*'s inshore raids, this one achieved nothing, and when they attempted to get under weigh the sailors manning the capstan were knocked down by the capstan bars which were too short, and the *Arab* began drifting ashore. To save her going aground they had to make sail hastily and cut the anchor cable, losing the main anchor and forty fathoms of cable.

A week later, on 27 February, Cochrane caused a diplomatic incident by boarding the *Chatham*, an American ship bound for Amsterdam from New York. He informed her captain that he could not proceed to Amsterdam because the Texel was under blockade, which was not the case, and ordered the ship to make for the nearest British port. This led to a complaint from James Monroe, the American ambassador in London, and a demand from the Admiralty for an explanation from Cochrane. It was around this time that Lord Keith told Markham that Cochrane's uncle, Captain Alexander Cochrane, was a crack-headed, unsafe man who had stirred up dissension in the fleet in the Mediterranean, 'and I am sorry to find that his nephew is falling into the same error – wrong-headed, violent and proud'.[29]

Cochrane now received orders to escort a convoy of Greenland-bound whaling ships as far as the Shetland Islands and then to cruise the east coast and Scottish waters, keeping an eye out for enemy privateers. Few, if any, French privateers ventured north as far as Berwick, let alone the deserted, windswept seas off the Scottish isles.

For a young man thirsting for action and prize money this was a bitter assignment. Routine patrols and convoy protection duties might be the lot of most junior captains but Cochrane believed he was destined for greater things. He blamed official displeasure and malevolence for what he later described as 'naval exile in a tub' and he came to regard the cruise as a blank in his life.

On 24 March the *Arab* joined her convoy at the Nore and sailed from the Thames estuary up the east coast. For a week they endured strong gales and sleet but they made good time and on 31 March the *Arab* and eight whaling ships dropped anchor in the fine harbour of Lerwick, the capital of the Shetland Islands. The gales and sleet continued but they were able to take on water and fresh beef, and carry out repairs to the rigging. After four days it was time to move on and the *Arab* headed out into the North Atlantic with the convoy. When they were within sight of the Faeroe Islands, 250 miles north of the Scottish mainland, they left the whalers to proceed on their way to Greenland and headed back to the Moray Firth. For four days in mid-May they moored in Cromarty Bay and then embarked on an extended cruise which took them around the northern tip of Scotland past Cape Wrath, down through the Hebrides to Barra, and then back through the Pentland Firth and across the Moray Firth towards Peterhead and Aberdeen. They passed Flamborough Head on 12 July and on the 14th they sailed up the Thames estuary and dropped anchor at the Nore.

The fourth and final cruise of the *Arab* under Cochrane's command took them across the Channel to the mouth of the Texel, and then north to Norway. Nearly two months were spent cruising the Norwegian coast, following a similar track to that taken by the *Thetis* when Cochrane was an eighteen-year-old midshipman on his uncle's ship. The cruise of the *Thetis* had taken place during the icy months of the Norwegian winter. This time Cochrane and his crew had the benefit of light breezes and warm summer sunshine. In September they sailed north and returned to the Shetlands where they spent five days in Lerwick harbour before heading south. By 24 October they were back at the Nore.

After four weeks lying at anchor amidst the comings and goings of warships and London-bound merchantmen, they sailed around the

North Foreland and dropped anchor in the Downs. It was there, on 27 November, that Cochrane learnt that his penance on the hated *Arab* was over.[30] Lord St Vincent had been replaced as First Lord of the Admiralty by Henry Dundas, recently created Lord Melville, and a friend of the Cochrane family. Melville was a Scot, he had been Member of Parliament for Edinburgh for many years, he was a former Home Secretary and was a key figure in the political life of Scotland and Westminster.[31] When he was approached on Cochrane's behalf by the Duke of Hamilton, the premier peer of Scotland, and by Cochrane's naval uncle, it did not take him long to find a suitable ship – the new 32-gun frigate *Pallas*. She had been built in the royal dockyard at Plymouth, and launched a few days before the *Arab* returned to the Nore. Cochrane would be her first commander.

To be given command of a frigate was the dream of every young and ambitious captain. Frigates were fast, relatively powerful in terms of their armament, and were equipped for extended cruising. They were used for a variety of tasks: for reconnaissance; for carrying despatches; for escorting convoys of merchant ships; and for raiding enemy coasts and harassing enemy commerce. In the words of an eminent naval historian, 'Their officers and men were recognised (not least by themselves) as a professional elite, honed by independent cruising and frequent action'.[32] Unlike the more heavily armed ships of the line which spent much of their time blockading enemy ports the frigates roamed far and wide and there was ample opportunity for glory and for prize money.

FIVE

The Flying *Pallas*

1804–1806

The royal dockyard at Plymouth is situated on the lower reaches of the River Tamar alongside the broad stretch of water known as the Hamoaze. Unlike the great expanse of Plymouth Sound, which was exposed to the full force of southerly winds until the completion of the breakwater in 1840, the sheltered waters of the Hamoaze provided a secure anchorage for warships guarding the western approaches of the English Channel. It was to Plymouth that ships battered by months of blockade duty off Brest retreated for repairs to hulls and rigging, and Plymouth was often the last port of call for convoys setting off across the Atlantic. Founded in 1690 the dockyard had expanded steadily during the course of the eighteenth century and by 1800 its facilities were comparable with the royal dockyards at Chatham and Portsmouth. A panoramic view of the yard painted by Nicholas Pocock in 1798 shows row upon row of elegantly proportioned brick buildings stretching back in orderly lines from the waterfront. On the extreme right of the painting are three building slips with ships in the course of construction. It was on one of these slips that Cochrane's new ship was built.

In the National Maritime Museum at Greenwich there are plans of the *Pallas* and her sister ship the *Circe* which were issued by the Navy Office on 3 April 1804. One of the drawings is entitled. 'A Draught for building in His Majesty's Yard at Plymouth, Two Frigates of Fir, of 32

Guns, prepared in pursuance of an Order from the Lords Commissioners of the Admiralty of 16th March 1804'. What is interesting
about the plans is that instead of showing the latest development in
frigate design they reveal a modified version of a design which had
been drawn up fifty years earlier. The *Pallas*, the *Circe* and five other
small frigates were based on the lines of the Richmond class which had
been designed back in 1753. The adoption of an earlier design and the
use of fir (a softwood rather than hardy English oak) were largely due
to the disastrous economies forced on the royal dockyards by Lord St
Vincent during his spell as First Lord of the Admiralty. In his
misguided campaign to root out corruption and bad practice in the
yards St Vincent had sacked a fifth of the workforce, destroyed morale
and by series of false economies had drastically reduced the supplies of
hemp, sailcloth and timber, particularly English oak, available for use
in the dockyards. With the renewal of the war against France there
was an urgent need for more frigates. To economise on timber and
have the ships at sea as soon as possible the Admiralty decided to fall
back on the design of the smallest viable class of frigate.[1] The keels of
the *Pallas* and *Circe* were laid down in June 1804 and they were both
built and launched within six months, a notable achievement for the
dockyard. Most of the larger 36-gun and 38-gun frigates took between
one and two years to build.

The day of the launch was a spectacular and colourful occasion.
Joseph Tucker, the Master Shipwright at Plymouth, was determined to
impress the Admiralty with the efficiency of the dockyard and on 17
November 1804 he arranged the simultaneous launch of the *Pallas*, the
Circe and the 120-gun *Hibernia*. On the same day the 98-gun *St George*
was undocked after major repairs. A print commemorating the occasion
shows the waters of the Hamoaze crowded with small boats filled with
cheering spectators. The massive hull of the *Hibernia* is entering the
water; the *Pallas* and the *Circe* are already afloat and are shown in the
centre of the picture with huge launch flags billowing above their decks.

Cochrane's new command may have been based on an old design
and she may have been among the smallest of the navy's frigates but
she was in a different league from the *Speedy*. She measured 127 feet on

her gun deck and so was nearly fifty feet longer than the brig sloop; she had a crew of 215 compared to the *Speedy*'s eighty; and she had more than five times the firepower in terms of the weight of her broadside. Although classed as a 32-gun frigate she had twenty-six 12-pounder guns on her gun deck, and twelve 24-pounder carronades on her quarterdeck and forecastle. Carronades were short, light guns of heavy calibre and low velocity which had been developed by the Carron Iron Company of Falkirk in the 1770s.[2] The navy had been reluctant to use them at first but tests had shown their effectiveness at

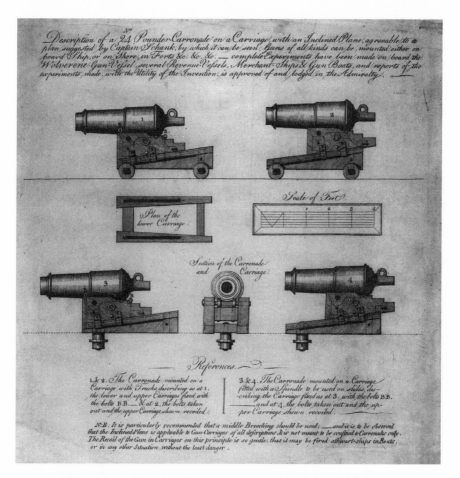

Designs and description of a 24-pounder carronade on a carriage
designed by Captain Schank and 'approved of and lodged in the Admiralty'.

short range. By the 1790s they had become the standard armament on
the upper works of British frigates. Whether loaded with round shot,
grape shot or canister they had a murderous, smashing effect when
fired at close quarters on to a crowded deck. Their shock value had
been confirmed in several successful frigate actions against French
ships. Napoleon, who had trained as an artillery officer, wrote to his
Minister of Marine in 1805, 'In this war, the English have been the
first to use carronades, and everywhere they have done us great harm.
We must hasten to perfect their system . . .'[3]

Cochrane, with his inventive mind and his interest in new technology, would have regarded the rows of Scottish-made carronades on his
quarterdeck with approval. He would also have welcomed the light
and airy space of his quarters which were situated at the stern of the
ship below the quarterdeck. His cabin was illuminated by six well-
proportioned stern windows and there was more than six foot of
headroom. His crew enjoyed better accommodation than the crew of a
ship of the line because in a two-decked 74-gun ship most of the crew
had to eat and sleep in the low, cramped space among the guns. The
principal characteristic of a frigate of this period was that she was
armed with thirty-two to forty guns and her major battery of carriage
guns was mounted on her main deck. The crew's accommodation was
on the unarmed lower deck which gave the men more space per ton
than in any other type of warship. The position of the main battery
well above the water line gave the frigate a distinct advantage in heavy
weather. While a 74-gun ship had to close her lower gunports when
heeled before a strong wind, a frigate could continue to carry a press of
sail and fire her guns while heeled over to a considerable degree.

Within days of hearing the news of his appointment to the *Pallas*,
Cochrane had sent letters to the Admiralty asking for various
members of the crew of the *Arab* to be transferred with him to the
Pallas. He also wrote to Lord Melville and explained that he had raised
the whole ship's company of the *Arab* only twelve months earlier.
'Some of them have been with me since I commanded a ship. I entreat
of your Lordship to recommend to the Board to let them go with me. If
it is necessary I will raise as many for the Arab at my own expense.'[4] It

was not unusual for captains to take able and trusted members of their crews with them when they took up a new command but Cochrane was only allowed to take half a dozen men including James Sutherland the master, Robert Boddy the carpenter, William Wilson the purser, and his friend James Guthrie the surgeon. He now had the difficult task of raising the remainder of the crew.

Captains with a reputation for capturing ships and winning prize money rarely had problems in recruiting good seamen but Cochrane suffered from the disadvantage that his recent cruises in the *Arab* had been singularly lacking in prizes. However, his appointment to the *Pallas* occurred at an opportune moment. Spain, which was currently Napoleon's closest ally, had declared war on Britain in December 1804. This meant that the Spanish treasure ships bringing back gold and silver from the mines in South America were a legitimate target for British cruisers. Indeed, it was the attack on a squadron of Spanish ships bearing treasure which was the major cause of Spain's declaration of war. On 5 October a squadron of four British frigates under the command of Captain Graham Moore had attacked four Spanish frigates in the Gulf of Cadiz. The justification for the attack was that the bullion on board the ships was going to subsidise the French war effort. One of the Spanish ships had blown up during the action killing a large number of seamen and civilian passengers, including the wife and daughters of a returning Spanish governor. The other three ships were captured with cargoes worth around £1 million.[5] Not surprisingly the Spanish authorities were outraged by an attack which was made without warning at a time when Britain was at peace with Spain.

Cochrane's orders were to proceed to the islands of the Azores, which were on the route of homecoming Spanish treasure ships, and to 'cruize in the neighbourhood of them for the purpose of taking or destroying the Enemy's ships of war, and privateers; and for distressing their trade'.[6] On the strength of this he was able to issue a boldly worded recruiting poster which announced that 'The Flying Pallas . . . a new and uncommonly fine frigate' was ready for an expedition. He appealed to seamen and stout hands to join him and hinted at rewards of doubloons from galleons loaded with the treasure of Peru and La

GOD save the KING.

Doublons.

SPANISH
Dollar Bag
Consigned to Boney.

My LADS, The rest of the GALLEONS with the TREASURE from LA PLATA, are waiting half loaded at CARTAGENA, for the arrival of those from PERU at PANAMA, as soon as that takes place, they are to sail for PORTOVELO, to take in the rest of their Cargo, with Provisions and Water for the Voyage to EUROPE. They stay at PORTO-VELO a few days only. Such a Chance perhaps will never occur again,

THE FLYING
PALLAS,
Of 36 GUNS,
At PLYMOUTH,

is a new and uncommonly fine Frigate. Built on purpose. And ready for an EXPEDITION, as soon as some more good Hands are on board;

Captain Lord Cochrane,

(who was not drowned in the ARAB as reported) Commands her. The sooner you are on board the better.

None need apply, but SEAMEN, or Stout Hands, able to rouse about the Field Pieces, and carry an hundred weight of PEWTER, without stopping, at least three Miles.

COCHRANE.

To British Seamen.

BONEY's CORONATION
Is postponed for want of COBBS.

J. BARFIELD, Printer, Wardour-Street.

Rendezvous, at the White Flag,

The recruiting poster issued by Cochrane at Plymouth in January 1805
to enlist men for his cruise to the Azores in the frigate *Pallas*.

Plata. The poster may have encouraged some men to sign on, but he still had to resort to sending out press gangs into the sailors' haunts of Plymouth to round up enough men to be able to take the *Pallas* to sea. This brought him into conflict with the local authorities. The Mayor of Plymouth would not allow press gangs to operate without his permission and Cochrane chose to ignore this. A gang from the *Pallas* led by Lieutenant Crawley was arrested, imprisoned and fined for causing a riot in a public house. The next day violence broke out when local constables attempted to arrest a press gang led by Cochrane himself. This was to result in the Mayor issuing a warrant for Cochrane's arrest on charges of assault. Fortunately the Admiralty stepped in on his side and instructed their solicitor to act on his behalf.[7]

Meanwhile, the *Pallas* was ready to sail. Her masts, yards and rigging had been set up, the iron ballast had been stowed below, and on 1 January 1805 she had been towed from the Hamoaze through the Narrows to moorings in Stonehouse Pool. There the guns and the anchors had been lifted aboard, followed by barrels of gunpowder, and the stores of the gunner, boatswain and carpenter. On 21 January, the same day that the Mayor of Plymouth issued the warrant for Cochrane's arrest, the *Pallas* weighed anchor and made sail. There was a light easterly breeze which died as they headed out into Plymouth Sound and they were forced to moor for the night. At seven o'clock the next morning they hoisted in the boats, sent the pilot ashore and headed out into the Channel.[8] It was a cold, crisp January day with a fresh breeze stretching the new sails and blowing the occasional cloud of salt spray across the newly laid pine decks as the *Pallas* dipped her bows into the waves. For a while the slender column of Smeaton's Eddystone lighthouse was clearly visible on their starboard beam and then the weather closed in and the lighthouse and the distant Cornish coast were hidden by showers of rain.

They intercepted a merchant ship bound for Barbados and a British privateer heading for Madeira before coming across their first prize. She was a Spanish ship from Havana and they sighted her on 6 February. They fired a shot across her bows, forcing her to heave to, and sent the boats across to take possession of her. She was the *Carolina*, bound for Cadiz, and she was laden with logwood and sugar. The crew were taken on board the *Pallas* and replaced by a prize crew who sailed her back to Plymouth. A week later they boarded a second Spanish ship from Havana which, in addition to a valuable cargo, had a consignment of treasure in the form of gold and silver ingots. Again her crew were taken prisoner and the ship was sent to Plymouth. On 15 February they intercepted a Spanish ship, *La Fortuna*, which proved to be the richest prize of all. She was from Vera Cruz and had a cargo of mahogany and logwood as well as gold and silver coin to the value of $432,000. They spent some time ferrying the treasure from the ship to the *Pallas* and had no sooner hoisted in the boats then another sail was sighted on the horizon. They gave chase and within two hours had come up alongside another Spanish ship from Vera Cruz bound for Cadiz. She was the *Sacra Familia*, a fine looking privateer of 14 guns and she too had a rich consignment of dollars on board. For the next week they continued to cruise in the vicinity of the Azores with the two prizes accompanying them. No more Spanish ships passed their way but Cochrane intercepted every other vessel which hove in sight. American schooners and brigs, British merchantmen and privateers, a whaling ship, and even the Falmouth packet boat with mail for the Windward Islands were all stopped and boarded.

Cochrane's orders limited the time he was allowed to cruise in the vicinity of the Azores. 'You are to continue on this service for one month after you shall arrive on your station, and then return to Plymouth, or sooner, if the number of prisoners you take shall make it necessary.'[9] So in mid-March they headed for home. On 24 March they ran into strong gales with heavy rain squalls. They lowered the topsails and foresail and bent on the storm staysails. By dawn the next day the wind had moderated but there was still a heavy sea running. At five in the afternoon the lookout reported strange ships on the horizon. According to Cochrane's autobiography he went aloft and identified them as three French line-of-battle ships in chase of the *Pallas*. The logbook simply records '2 strange sail in the NW supposed to be foreign line of battle ships' and notes that the *Pallas* made sail and got up the topgallant masts. Cochrane provides a dramatic account of what happened next. Realising that the warships were gaining on them, he ordered all the hawsers in the ship to be got up to the mastheads and hove taut in order to take the strain as every possible stitch of sail was set. The French ships continued to draw closer so Cochrane decided on a bold move. He ordered his men to take in every sail, put the helm hard over and wore ship. 'The Pallas, thus suddenly brought up, shook from stem to stern, in crossing the trough of the sea.' The French ships were taken by surprise and shot past at full speed, running on for several miles before they were able to turn and resume the chase. That night, according to Cochrane's account, he lowered a ballasted cask overboard with a lantern in the expectation that the French ships would follow the floating light rather than the *Pallas.* 'The trick was successful . . . we saw nothing of them, and were all much relieved on finding our dollars and his Majesty's ship once more in safety.'[10] The logbook, however, makes no mention of any of this. Was he confusing the sighting of two strange warships out in the Atlantic with the chasing of the *Speedy* by the three French warships off Gibraltar?

What is certain is that the first cruise of the *Pallas* made Cochrane's fortune. There are widely differing accounts of the amount he received in prize money but it was likely to have been at least £40,000 (worth about £1 million today).[11] This was a quarter of the total value of the four Spanish ships he had captured. He would have received three-eighths of the value if he had acquired his orders direct from the Admiralty but William Young, the port admiral at Plymouth, had cut himself in for an eighth share of the prize money by reissuing the Admiralty orders under his own name.[12] Cochrane was deeply aggrieved by this but he could hardly complain at receiving such a windfall for a few weeks' work. His uncle Alexander was well aware of his nephew's lucky break and wrote to Lord Melville, 'this beginning will I hope lay the foundation of his future fortune and I trust he will feel that he owes it freely to your Lordship's kind attention'.[13]

Prize money, which was such a dominating and motivating feature of Cochrane's life, was regulated by a system which had been in force since the passing of the Convoys and Cruisers Act of 1708. This laid down that the entire value of a ship captured from the enemy should be divided among the officers and men who had taken part in her capture. Before the system was revised in 1808, three-eighths of the value went to the captain – unless he was under the orders of an admiral, in which case one of his eighths went to that admiral. One-eighth was divided among the captains of marines, sea lieutenants and masters; another eighth was divided among lieutenants of marines, and the other warrant officers; a further eighth went to midshipmen, surgeons' mates and certain senior petty officers; and two-eighths was divided among the remainder of the crew and the marines.[14] The system was manifestly unfair, particularly for the junior ranks and ordinary seamen who received a tiny proportion of the total sum agreed by the Admiralty Court or the various Vice-Admiralty Courts which were responsible for valuing the captured ship and her cargo. An admiral could accumulate thousands of pounds from ships operating under his command, without leaving his naval base in Antigua, Jamaica or Gibraltar. The captain of a ship of the line involved in blockading Brest or Cadiz had little opportunity for prize money whereas a frigate captain like Cochrane, operating independently of a fleet, could accumulate very large sums of prize money by the capture of merchant shipping.

There are some spectacular examples of riches amassed by individuals during the wars of the eighteenth century. Rear-Admiral Warren accumulated £125,000 in prize money in the 1740s; Admiral Pocock received £122,697 following the fall of Havana in 1762; and Captain Saunders' capture of a single ship in 1746 netted him nearly £40,000 in prize money.[15] The wars against Revolutionary France produced similar examples: Captain Henry Digby, who had captured fifty vessels while in command of the frigate *Aurora* in 1797 and 1798, was one of the four captains present at the capture of the Spanish treasure ships *El Tetys* and *Santa Brigida* in 1799. The total value of the two prizes was £661,206. The admiral commanding the squadron of four frigates got £81,000; Digby and the other three captains £40,730 each and every seaman received just over £182 each – the equivalent of ten years' pay.[16] Such examples were unusual but most sailors had heard of them and the lure of prize money certainly helped recruitment and may have discouraged men from desertion.

The *Pallas* entered Plymouth Sound on 5 April, and anchored in Cawsand Bay to await a pilot. The next day she made her way through the bustling activity of local boats and sailing barges and moored in

Stonehouse Pool. The arrival of the Spanish prizes in Plymouth had already been reported in the local papers and Cochrane underlined the success of his voyage by lashing three very large golden candlesticks to the masts of the *Pallas*. This grandiose gesture was in the tradition of the Elizabethan privateers and was no doubt intended to impress the sailors on the waterfront and ensure that he never again had a problem with recruitment.

Three weeks after her triumphant arrival in Plymouth the *Pallas* set sail for the Solent. The next assignment for Cochrane and his crew was to escort a convoy of merchantmen across the Atlantic to Nova Scotia and Quebec, an unglamorous task with little chance of action or prize money. They spent a week at the fleet anchorage at Spithead, another week anchored in St Helens Roads in the lee of the Isle of Wight and then headed down the Channel in the company of fourteen merchant ships. They were accompanied by the *Harpy*, a brig sloop similar to the *Speedy* and built by the same yard at Dover. They passed the Eddystone lighthouse on 29 April and sailed westwards at the

A watercolour by Nicholas Pocock showing a frigate similar
to the *Pallas* assembling a convoy in St Helens Roads off the Isle of Wight.

speed of the slowest merchantman. While they were trailing across the grey waters of the North Atlantic a British fleet led by Nelson was racing across the warmer waters of the mid-Atlantic to the West Indies in search of Villeneuve and the French fleet which had escaped from the blockading force at Toulon. On learning that Nelson was after him Villeneuve headed back to Cadiz, missing Nelson by a matter of days. In a few months they would meet off Cape Trafalgar.

The *Pallas* and her convoy sailed into the harbour of Halifax, Nova Scotia, on 30 June after a notably uneventful voyage. It had taken them two months compared with the twenty-four days it had taken Nelson and his line-of-battle ships to cover the greater distance from Spain to the Windward Islands. The *Pallas* spent a profitless summer cruising back and forth from Halifax to Cape Breton Island and King Edward Island before taking on a pilot and heading up the St Lawrence River. On 10 October the ship's log noted, 'Came to with the best bower in 27 fathoms, off the City of Quebec. Moor'd ship a cable each way.' Quebec, built on the rocky heights above the river, had been captured from the French fifty years before in an assault led by General Wolfe who had died on the field of battle. His death had been commemorated in heroic paintings and prints which would soon be eclipsed by the outpouring of national grief which greeted the news of the death of Nelson. On 21 October, while the *Pallas* lay at anchor in the shadow of Quebec, the combined fleets of France and Spain joined battle with the British fleet in the seas off Cape Trafalgar. Nelson was hit by a musket ball while pacing the quarterdeck of the *Victory* with Captain Hardy. He was carried below to the orlop deck where he died around 4.30 p.m., having learnt from Hardy that the British had won a great victory.

The return voyage of the *Pallas* was marked by storms. They sailed from Quebec on 29 October with another convoy and as they headed out into the Atlantic they encountered a gale which was accompanied by gusts of driving snow. The crew of one of the merchantmen had to abandon ship and were rescued by a boat from the *Pallas*. Later, as the convoy approached the English coast, they were hit by another gale which split the mainsail of the *Pallas* and then carried away her mizen topsail yard. The weather moderated as they sailed up the Channel and they had an easy run past Beachy Head and Dungeness. They anchored off Sheerness on 10 December. The foreman of the dockyard came on board to examine the state of the ship. It was evident that a major refit was required. The foremast had to be replaced as well as much of the running rigging. The planking needed attention from the caulkers, two of the ship's boats needed repairs and condemned stores had to be removed and replaced. To facilitate the work the ship's company were moved out of the ship for several days and took up residence in one of the hulks moored off the dockyard.

The log of the *Pallas* records that on 24 December, while the men were moving their gear into the hulk, 'passed by HMS Victory with the body of Lord Nelson'. In fact Nelson's body was no longer on board the ship on which he had died. On 22 December Nelson's secretary, John Tyson, had arrived at Sheerness with the coffin made from the mast of *L'Orient*, the French flagship which had blown up at the Battle of the Nile. Tyson had secured permission to fetch the coffin from the undertakers and he arranged for it to be loaded on to the *Chatham*, the dockyard yacht at Sheerness and taken out to the *Victory* which was lying at anchor at the mouth of the Thames estuary waiting for a favourable wind to proceed up the river.[17] Early on the morning of 24 December the *Chatham* set off for Greenwich bearing Nelson's body. As the yacht proceeded up the Thames her progress was marked by the firing of minute guns from the forts at Tilbury and Gravesend and by the tolling of bells from the churches along the river. Later that day the *Victory* passed Sheerness dockyard and headed up the Medway to Chatham.

The repairs and provisioning of the *Pallas* were completed in a little over three weeks and on 14 January 1806 she weighed anchor and sailed for the Downs. They spent a week among the warships and merchantmen lying in the anchorage and while they were there Cochrane spent some of his prize money on the purchase of a galley from the boat builders of Deal. The Deal galleys were long, narrow, clinker-built boats famous for their speed under oar and sail. They were launched off the steep shingle beach at Deal and were used to race pilots out to waiting ships and to rescue ships in distress on the

Goodwin Sands. Cochrane's boat 'rowed double-banked, and required eighteen hands at the oars and this together with her beautiful build rendered her perhaps the fastest boat afloat'.[18] This may not have been an exaggeration. The galley later played a key role in Cochrane's boat actions off enemy coasts and her design so impressed the Admiralty that they ordered drawings to be made of her lines.[19]

Given the restricted space available for storing boats on the smaller types of frigate it seems likely that the galley replaced one of the existing boats of the *Pallas* rather than added to their number. At this period it was usual for frigates to be issued with four or five boats: a launch, a barge or pinnace, one or two cutters and a jolly boat.[20] The largest of the boats were stored in the waist of the ship (the space on deck between the foremast and the mainmast). To lift heavy boats over the side and into the water took some time and involved complicated tackle and a lot of men heaving on ropes. The smaller and lighter boats were hung from quarter davits on either side of the stern and could be launched rapidly in the event of an emergency, such as a man overboard. All the ship's boats could be sailed as well as rowed, and it was usual for the large launch to be fitted with a carronade in her bows. Cochrane later fitted carronades into most of his boats when he carried out his raids on the Mediterranean coasts of France and Spain.

Cochrane now received orders to cruise off the French coast at Boulogne and then to join Vice-Admiral Edward Thornborough's squadron at Plymouth. On 15 February 1806, after two weeks of raiding the Normandy coast, she headed down the Channel to Plymouth Sound. Lying at anchor in Cawsand Bay was Thornborough's squadron: his flagship the *Prince of Wales*, four ships of the line and a cutter. Within a day of the *Pallas* joining the squadron they sailed for France, and for a month Cochrane kept company with the warships. They proceeded south past Ushant and Brest, past Lorient and Belle Ile towards Basque Roads. During the cruise Cochrane made a series of raids on coastal shipping: off the Ile Dieu his boats captured seven fishing boats; he took a lugger loaded with wine and shifted twelve hogsheads on board the *Pallas*; and as they sailed by the coastal town of Les Sables d'Olonne a brig and several other vessels were seen at

anchor in the bay. Cochrane sent the boats inshore and they successfully boarded and captured the brig. Another brig was so alarmed by
the shots fired at her by the *Pallas* that her crew ran her ashore.

On 29 March they rejoined the squadron which was sailing in the
vicinity of Basque Roads. Cochrane went aboard the flagship of
Admiral Thornborough and received orders to cruise independently
and to continue to harass enemy commerce and shipping. He now
embarked on one of the more perilous undertakings of his life as a
frigate captain. He had received information that some French corvettes were lying at anchor in the estuary of the Garonne, the river
which joins the Dordogne near Bordeaux. One of the corvettes was
acting as a guardship and Cochrane decided to make a night attack on
this vessel and cut her out (the naval term for capturing an anchored
ship by sending armed men in boats to overcome her crew and sail her
away). The great estuary of the Garonne, known as Le Gironde, is
nearly nine miles wide at its mouth. The nautical almanac warns the
mariner 'the outer approaches can be dangerous due to Atlantic swell,
very strong tidal streams and currents, extensive shoals and shifting
sand banks', and points out that strong westerly winds and an ebb tide
can produce breaking seas some five metres high.[21] In addition to the
navigational hazards there were gun batteries defending the stretch of
river where the guardship was anchored.

At 8.25 on the evening of 5 April, Cochrane anchored the *Pallas*
near the Cordovan Shoal which lies at the entrance of the Gironde. All
the boats were launched, and under the command of the first lieutenant, John Haswell, nearly 180 men proceeded upstream. The conditions were favourable for a night attack. There was only a moderate
southerly wind, and clouds obscured the moon and stars so that the
boats were able to cover the twenty miles to the target unobserved. At
3.00 a.m. the boats came alongside the corvette which proved to be the
Tapageuse, a French warship armed with fourteen 12-pounder guns.
Her crew of ninety-five were taken unawares and though they put up
some resistance they were easily overcome. However, the firing of
pistols and muskets during the attack alerted the crews of the other
vessels moored upstream. Lieutenant Haswell and his men managed

to weigh anchor and get the *Tapageuse* under way when they were attacked by a vessel which is described in Cochrane's report as a sloop-of-war, and in the logbook as a gun brig. They managed to beat off the attacker, causing as much damage to her hull as the *Tapageuse* suffered in the rigging.

At daybreak Cochrane and the men left behind on the *Pallas* could just see the *Tapageuse* in the distance, way up the river. They also saw three strange ships heading their way. When the ships failed to respond to Cochrane's signal he realised they were the enemy. The *Pallas* was at a considerable disadvantage. Although she was theoretically more powerful than her attackers, three corvettes, she only had forty men left on board to raise the anchor, set the sails and man the guns. To fool the French into thinking he had a full crew Cochrane sent a few men aloft to secure the furled sails with light yarn. As soon as the ship was ready he ordered the yarns to be cut all at once. 'The manoeuvre succeeded to a marvel. No sooner was our cloud of canvas thus suddenly let fall than the approaching vessels hauled the wind, and ran off along shore, with the Pallas in chase, our handful of men straining every nerve to sheet home.'[22]

As they gained on the nearest French corvette, the *Pallas* began firing her bow guns, the only ones that could be manned with their restricted crew. This so alarmed the French captain that he deliberately ran his vessel ashore. They went aground in a sheet of spray, the shock of the impact dismasting the corvette. The crew immediately abandoned ship, took to the boats and rowed ashore. Cochrane paused only to fire several shots into her hull before setting off in pursuit of one of the other corvettes. They came up with her around four in the afternoon, fired the bow guns, and she too was forced to run ashore, losing her masts as she did so. Cochrane anchored for a few hours and during the night he headed back to the Cordovan Shoal in order to rendezvous with the captured *Tapageuse*. The next day, 7 April, they found that the third French corvette had also been run ashore. Cochrane anchored abreast of her and fired two guns at her hull to put her out of action.

At 6.00 a.m. the following day, in light airs and with rain streaming off the sails and drenching the decks, they finally met up with the *Tapageuse*. Leaving a prize crew aboard the French corvette the remainder of Cochrane's men returned to their ship. Two days later they joined the squadron, with their prize in company. Cochrane submitted a report on their exploits, much of which was devoted to praising the conduct of his officers and men. He pointed out that, in addition to capturing the *Tapageuse*, they had driven onshore and wrecked 'one national 24-gun ship, one of 22 guns, and the Malicieuse, a beautiful corvette of 18 guns'. Admiral Thornborough sent Cochrane's despatch to Lord St Vincent with a covering letter which was unstinting in its praise and showed an understanding of the risks of the enterprise:

> It will not be necessary for me, my lord, to comment on the intrepidity and good conduct displayed by Lord Cochrane, his officers and men, in the execution of a very hazardous enterprise in the Garonne, a river the most difficult, perhaps, in its navigation, of any on the coast. The complete success that attended the enterprise, as well as the destruction of the vessels of war mentioned in the said letter on the coast of Arcasson, speaks of their merits more fully than is in my power to do.[23]

St Vincent, who had resumed command of the Channel Squadron and was cruising off Ushant, passed on the despatches to the Admiralty. He accompanied them with a brief note of his own in which he observed that the gallant and successful exertions of the *Pallas* reflected very high honour on her captain, officers and crew, 'and call for my warmest approbation'.

Having sent his report to Thornborough, Cochrane returned to the scene of his recent exploits to make sure that the corvettes which he had driven ashore were totally destroyed. On the afternoon of 14 April one of the corvettes was sighted but the French had erected a gun battery to protect her while repairs were carried out. The guns of the *Pallas* soon silenced the battery, a boat was sent ashore and the stranded vessel was set on fire. The second corvette was found to be breaking up in the surf so they left her to the mercy of a rising gale.

Pounding waves and shallow water prevented them reaching the third. They bore away and headed north past the Ile d'Oléron to Basque Roads where they found Thornborough's squadron lying at anchor. Cochrane anchored in the vicinity of the five British warships, sent boats across to the flagship to replenish his water supplies and received further orders from the admiral. His next job was a typical assignment for a frigate: to reconnoitre the French position in the vicinity of the Ile d'Aix and report on the number and strength of the French warships in the anchorage.

The French had two naval bases on the Atlantic coast of France. The major port and anchorage was at Brest which was strategically well placed; it had a sheltered roadstead large enough for five hundred ships; and, like Portsmouth, was protected by forts on either side of a narrow entrance. During the Napoleonic Wars it was subject to more or less constant blockade by British ships which cruised back and forth among the rocks, shoals and overfalls which guarded the approaches to the port. The other French anchorage was Basque Roads which was sheltered from Atlantic storms by two large islands, Ile de Ré and Ile d'Oléron. The main anchorage was defended by gun batteries on the fortified Ile d'Aix and was served by the port and naval base of Rochefort which was several miles up the River Charente. The disadvantage of Basque Roads for the French was that it was wide open to attack from the sea. The main approach to the anchorage between the islands was more than eight miles across and there were many places where a British fleet could safely anchor out of range of any shore batteries.

In the darkness of the early hours of 25 April the *Pallas* weighed anchor and headed towards the French anchorage. By 10.00 a.m. her crew were close enough to observe the details of the French warships lying at anchor. There was one three-decker, one ship of 80 guns, three 74-gun ships, two heavy frigates of 40 guns, three light frigates and three brigs of 14 to 16 guns. With calculated bravado Cochrane stood in towards the French squadron until they were within gunshot. The logbook records what happened next: 'Perceived a frigate and the brigs get under way – made and shortened sail and tacked occasionally

endeavouring to bring them to action – fired several broadsides . . .'
Cochrane continued to cruise in the vicinity for four hours but the
French ships were not prepared to engage the arrogant British frigate
and retreated to the shelter of the gun batteries on the Ile d'Aix.
However, Cochrane had been able to make a detailed assessment of the
anchorage, and had noted the landmarks, shoals and defences. When
he sent his report to Thornborough with details of the French
warships, he observed that the anchored ships could easily be burnt
and that a military force could take possession of the Ile d'Oléron
'upon which all the enemy's vessels may be driven by sending fire
vessels to the eastward of Ile d'Aix'.[24] Three years later he would have
the opportunity to put this suggestion into action.

While cruising off the French coast Cochrane had observed that the
French had established an effective system of signal posts which were
able to warn local coasting vessels of the presence of British warships
in the vicinity. He therefore resolved to put out of action all those in
the immediate neighbourhood. Two signal posts at Point Delaroche
and one at Caliola were demolished. At Lanse de Repos a party from
the *Pallas* led by Lieutenant Haswell and Robert Hillier, the gunner,
managed to overcome more than a hundred local militia soldiers, burn
the signal house to the ground and come away with a set of signal
flags. And on 9 May, assisted by the crews of the gun brig *Contest* and
the cutter *Frisk*, a landing party from the *Pallas* attacked a gun battery
on the Point d'Equillon. The fifty men manning the battery were
driven off; the three 36-pounder guns were spiked, the gun carriages
burnt, the magazine blown up and all the shells thrown into the sea.
This was a foretaste of the destruction Cochrane would inflict on the
Mediterranean coast of France and Spain in the near future.

Cochrane's final exploit while in command of the *Pallas* was as
spectacular as any of his previous actions although it failed to yield any
prize money. On the morning of 14 May the *Pallas*, with the sloop
Kingfisher, 16 guns, left the anchored British squadron with orders to
make a further reconnaissance of the French ships lying in the vicinity
of the Ile d'Aix. Captain Seymour, in command of the *Kingfisher*, had
orders to keep clear of danger and not to proceed beyond the

Chassiron lighthouse so he waited at the entrance of the Antioch Passage. The *Pallas* sailed on and anchored provocatively within range of the guns of the Ile d'Aix. It was Cochrane's intention to tempt one of the French frigates to come out and fight. Rear-Admiral Allemand, who commanded the French squadron in Basque Roads, responded to the bait and ordered the 40-gun frigate *Minerve* to weigh anchor and attack the *Pallas*. He also ordered the three gun brigs *Lynx*, *Sylphe* and *Palinure*, each of 16 guns, to get under way and support the heavy frigate. Far from being concerned by the sight of this powerful force Cochrane was delighted that 'the long wished-for opportunity was at last arrived'.[25] And yet on paper it appeared to be an unequal contest. The *Minerve*, Captain Joseph Collet, carried a powerful armament of twenty-eight 18-pounders, four 8-pounders and twelve 36-pound carronades and she had a crew of 330 men compared with the 215 men of the *Pallas*.

At around 11.00 a.m. the *Pallas* came under fire from the *Minerve* and one of the brigs, as well as the guns of the forts on the Ile d'Aix. Cochrane waited until the enemy ships were within point-blank range before letting loose a broadside which brought down the main topsail yard of one of the brigs and tore away the aftersails of the frigate. For the next two hours the ships tacked to and fro among the shoals, their guns booming and echoing across the choppy waters of the anchorage, the thick clouds of gun smoke billowing from each broadside before being swept away by the fresh northeasterly breeze.

The guns of the *Pallas* were so effective that the firing of the *Minerve* slackened and Cochrane ordered Mr Sutherland, the master, to run alongside her in preparation for boarding. Such was the headway of the ships that they collided with considerable force so that 'the spars and rigging of both vessels were dismantled. The concussion drove our guns back into the ports, in which position the broadside was again discharged, and the shot tore through her sides with crushing effect, her men taking refuge below . . . The French captain was the only man who gallantly remained on deck.' There was no longer any chance of capturing the French frigate. Admiral Allemand had ordered two of his large frigates to go to the assistance of the *Minerve* and it was now essential for the crew of the *Pallas* to cut themselves free from the wreckage. The foremast and bows of the British frigate had taken the brunt of the collision. The cathead and bow anchor had been torn away, and the foredeck was strewn with the wreckage of the foretopmast, foresail, spritsail yards and most of the fore rigging. However, the crew managed to hack through the tangle of spars, sails and rigging which linked the two ships and they drifted apart. Captain Seymour ignored his orders to keep the *Kingfisher* clear of the action. Seeing the *Pallas* so disabled he hoisted all sail and bore down to give them assistance. A tow line was passed across and before the French frigates arrived on the scene the two British ships were heading for the open sea.

The French ship lost seven men killed and fourteen wounded but the *Pallas* suffered remarkably few casualties: one marine was killed, a midshipman was badly wounded and three seamen were slightly injured. This was a pattern which was typical of Cochrane's career as a naval commander and was a tribute to his leadership, and the training and discipline of his crew. Jahleel Brenton would later recall that 'he admired nothing more in Lord Cochrane than the care he took of the preservation of his people. Bold and adventurous as he was, no unnecessary exposure of life was ever permitted under his command. Every circumstance was anticipated, every provision for success was made.'[26] During the course of his cruises in the *Speedy* and the *Pallas*, Cochrane had perfected his skills as a frigate captain. He had learnt the value of surprise attacks carried out at night or at dawn; he was ingenious in his use of stratagems and simple tricks to throw the enemy off guard; he had thoroughly mastered the essentials of seamanship so that he handled his ship with consummate skill; but above all he never went into action without the most careful preparation. His daring attacks, although sometimes appearing foolhardy, were carried out in the knowledge that his crew were thoroughly briefed and prepared, and that he had worked out the tides, the depth of water and had calculated the strength and weaknesses of the enemy ship or the enemy position. Edward Brenton, the naval historian and brother of Jahleel Brenton, noted that 'Before he fired a shot he reconnoitred in person, took soundings and bearings, passed whole nights in his boats under the enemy's batteries, his lead line and spy glass incessantly at work.'[27] This attention to detail and his natural gifts as a bold and resourceful commander would be dramatically demonstrated when he took his next ship into the Mediterranean.

Meanwhile, there were repairs to be carried out to the rigging of the *Pallas*. When they rejoined the squadron they received two spars from HMS *Kent* to replace those which had been lost. Cochrane now received orders to escort a convoy back to England and on 19 May they set sail in the company of twelve transports carrying naval stores and men. With fresh to strong breezes to help them on their way, they were back in Plymouth Sound within a week.

SIX

Member of Parliament for Honiton

1806–1807

On Saturday 7 June 1806 the local newspaper for Plymouth and the surrounding area published a detailed account of the recent exploits of the *Pallas*. Two of Cochrane's despatches to the Admiralty were printed in full and readers were informed that the *Pallas* had attacked and sunk a 20-gun brig, 'repeatedly annoyed the enemy on his own coast and even in his harbours' and had narrowly escaped capture in the action against the *Minerve*. The newspaper had previously reported the rich prizes captured by the *Pallas* off the Azores and pointed out to its readers that the latest actions of the frigate in Basque Roads provided further evidence of 'the gallant conduct of her noble commander'.[1]

On Sunday, the day after the reports of Cochrane's actions had appeared in the newspaper, the inhabitants of Honiton were treated to the sight of the noble commander and his supporters clattering into the main street in two post chaises each drawn by four sweating horses. The news soon spread that Lord Cochrane had driven from London via Exeter at high speed in order to meet the outspoken political journalist William Cobbett who had arrived at Honiton the day before. Cobbett had embarked on a lifelong campaign to reform the electoral system and to root out bribery and corruption in Parliament. He had selected Honiton as his first target because it was about to have a by-election and was one of the 'potwalloper' boroughs in which the Members of Parliament were elected by a few hundred local householders – men who owned their own house and the pot in the fireplace. These voters were not only open to bribery but, as Cobbett discovered, they relied on it. 'They tell you, flatly and plainly, that the money which they obtain for their votes, is absolutely necessary to enable them to live; that, without it, they could not pay their rents; and that, from election to election, the poor men run up scores at the shops, and are trusted by the shopkeepers, expressly upon the credit of the proceeds of the ensuing election . . .'[2]

Honiton was a small country town lying in a fertile valley a few miles inland from Sidmouth and forty-five miles away from Plymouth. Although it consisted of no more than a scattering of houses gathered around an ancient church it had the right to return two Members of Parliament. One of them was a man called Richard Robson who had been elected in April, and the other was Cavendish Bradshaw whose acceptance of the lucrative post of Teller of the Irish Exchequer meant that he had to seek re-election. Cobbett regarded him with contempt for accepting a worthless sinecure with no responsibilities and for being in the pocket of the government.

In *Cobbett's Weekly Political Register*, the newspaper he founded and edited, Cobbett had appealed for a candidate of honest and independent turn of mind to contest the borough of Honiton; when no one stepped forward he decided to contest the election himself. He had left London on 6 June and driven down to Honiton in company with Cochrane's uncle Andrew Cochrane-Johnstone who apparently wished to do some business with his nephew. Cobbett later described how they were having dinner when:

there came an express from Lord Cochrane, bearing a letter for me, informing me that his Lordship, having read my address to the people of Honiton in the London newspapers, and having perceived that I had resolved to stand myself merely because I could find no other independent man to oppose Mr Bradshaw, he had determined to accept of my general invitation, and that he was actually on his way (dating his letter from

Exeter) to put his purpose into execution. In an hour afterward, having stopped at Exeter to provide lawyers, &c. his Lordship arrived.'[3]

Cobbett welcomed Cochrane's dramatic arrival. He was aware that if he contested the seat himself he was unlikely to have sufficient influence to defeat Cavendish Bradshaw who had been canvassing the electors and had already received promises of support. Cobbett knew of Cochrane's reputation through his friendship with Andrew Cochrane-Johnstone and he realised that Cochrane's glamorous image as a naval hero was far more likely to appeal to the voters of Honiton than his own image as a radical journalist. Although they came from very different backgrounds the two men struck up a friendship which was to last for more than twenty years. They would become neighbours in Hampshire, and Cobbett was to prove Cochrane's most stalwart supporter and champion in his darkest hours.

In some ways the two men were alike. They were both energetic, impetuous and independently minded, some would say bloody-minded. They were both tall and powerfully built and weather-beaten but there the resemblance ended. Cochrane, now thirty, had an aristocratic air with a prominent, aquiline nose and that reddish or sandy coloured hair characteristic of some Scotsmen. He could appear arrogant, and was considered so by many of his superior officers, but to those who knew him well he was quiet and unassuming, with a common touch and a natural sympathy for the ordinary seamen. Cobbett, aged forty-four, had the appearance of an amiable English yokel with bluff, rounded features and a deceptively mild expression. Mary Russell Mitford described him as 'a tall, stout man, fair, and sunburnt, with a bright smile, and an air compounded of the soldier and the farmer, to which his habit of wearing an eternal red waistcoat contributed not a little. He was, I think, the most athletic and vigorous person that I have ever known. Nothing would tire him.'[4] Born at the Jolly Farmer pub in Farnham where his father was the tavern keeper, Cobbett had joined the army and spent seven years serving as a British soldier in New Brunswick on the American–Canadian border. He had become a sergeant-major but left the army under a cloud after an abortive attempt to expose corruption. He had remained in America for another eight years, living in Philadelphia where he had developed his skill as a journalist and pamphleteer. He had returned to England in 1800, established *Cobbett's Weekly Political Register* in 1802 and had rapidly established himself as a formidable commentator on political affairs.

On Monday 9 June an open meeting was held in Honiton to enable the two principal candidates to address the voters. (A third candidate, Mr Courtney, seems to have played no active part in the election and only received two votes when the poll closed.) Political meetings at this period could be rowdy affairs but the weather during June was hot and sunny with prospects of the best harvest for years and this may have helped to put the householders of Honiton in a friendly and receptive mood. They listened in silence to Mr Bradshaw who pointed out the inexperience of his opponent and assured the voters, 'I shall always support every measure that I think conducive to the good of my country and shall always oppose every measure of a contrary description.'

Cochrane was not a natural orator and had a tendency to be rambling and repetitive but he did his best. He began his speech by explaining that he had had no time to meet the individual electors but had been flattered by the reception given him on his arrival. He went on to say, 'The greater part of my life has been spent in the toils of the sea; but those toils have become pleasures when I reflected that they might tend to the security and the honour of this happy land, and to the preservation of those inestimable liberties, to exercise the most important of which, you, gentlemen, are this day assembled. To preserve these liberties unimpaired shall be the business and the pride of my life.' He assured the crowd that he would never accept any sinecure or pension or any grant of public money and that his constant endeavour would be 'to be useful to my country in general, and to this borough in particular'.[5]

The meeting was brought to life by Cobbett who attacked Bradshaw with what the local paper described as 'thundering eloquence'. He called Cochrane's opponent a cynical, place-seeking liar whose sole purpose in Parliament was to retain office, and he denounced him for bribing the corrupt rascals he expected to elect him. The poll opened the next day and the householders were given a week in which to cast their votes. When the poll closed on 18 June and the votes were counted it was found that Cochrane had collected 124 votes but Mr Cavendish Bradshaw had 259 votes and he was duly elected to Parliament. Cobbett was furious but Cochrane, with an eye to the future, made generous use of his prize money and treated the inhabitants of Honiton to a dinner. According to the *Western Flying Post*, 'Lord Cochrane gave an ox roasted whole to the populace, and great hilarity prevailed'.[6]

For the next four months Cochrane divided his time between Plymouth and London where he had lodgings at 67 Harley Street.[7] We know very little about his domestic arrangements during these early years as a frigate captain. Like most naval officers on active service his ship was his main base. The address he gave on his occasional letters to the Admiralty was usually 'Pallas, Plymouth Sound' or 'Pallas, off Hythe' or some other port or harbour. What we do know is that he kept in close touch with his family, particularly his brothers and his uncles, and later he would take rooms in the house of his uncle Basil Cochrane who had an imposing residence in Portman Square.

Towards the end of August 1806 Cochrane was appointed to command a larger frigate, the *Imperieuse*, which was currently undergoing an overhaul in one of the docks at Plymouth.[8] She had no masts and no crew and when Cochrane arrived on 2 September to commission the ship the only people present to witness the brief ceremony were a few shipwrights and caulkers from the dockyard. Even without her masts and rigging the *Imperieuse* was an impressive vessel and was ideal for the sort of actions at which Cochrane excelled. She was listed as an 18-pounder frigate of 38 guns. She was bigger and faster than the *Pallas* and considerably more powerful in terms of her armament: in addition to her long guns she had two nine-pounder and twelve 32-pounder carronades which could be used to devastating effect in close action. Originally named the *Medea* she was a fine example of Spanish ship building. She had been the flagship of the squadron of Spanish treasure ships commanded by Rear-Admiral Bustamente which had been intercepted by the British in the Gulf of Cadiz in October 1804. Her capture, and the capture of two other Spanish ships laden with gold and silver, had precipitated war between Spain and Britain.[9]

Having inspected the ship and spoken to the dockyard workers, Cochrane realised that she would not be out of the dock for another two weeks. He applied for a further leave of absence and returned to London. He was back in Plymouth on 30 September. The ship was still in dry dock and still without a crew. When he had first received the news that he had been nominated to a larger frigate Cochrane had written to the Admiralty requesting that the entire ship's company of the *Pallas* be transferred to his new command and he had evidently been given some assurance that this would be possible. Ignoring the usual protocol, he now went behind the back of the port admiral and wrote once again to William Marsden, the Secretary to the Board of Admiralty: 'Admiral Young informs me that he has not yet received the order for the discharge of the crew of the Pallas into L'Imperieuse which circumstance I beg you will make known to my Lords Commissioners of the Admiralty . . .'[10] On receipt of this letter the Admiralty directed Admiral Young to carry out their earlier orders but reminded Cochrane that he ought to correspond through the admiral in future. Four days later the log of the *Imperieuse* noted that the ship's company of the *Pallas* had arrived on board, so Cochrane evidently got his way. During the course of the next week the ship took on water, wine and large quantities of fresh beef, as well as the stores of the warrant officers.

In October Cochrane learnt that the Cabinet had met in a late-night session and had determined on the immediate dissolution of parliament. A general election gave Cochrane the opportunity to have a second attempt at contesting Honiton before his ship was ordered to sea. The colourful account of the two Honiton elections which appears in his autobiography is not only inaccurate in the chronology of events but gives a misleading version of Cochrane's treatment of the voters.

In his account he maintains that although he rewarded the voters after his defeat in the first election, he did not bribe them before they cast their votes in either election. In view of his later stand as a radical candidate committed to parliamentary reform he obviously wished the record to show that he had been consistent in his opposition to bribery and corruption. In fact he did bribe the voters the second time he contested the seat, and he later admitted as much in a parliamentary debate.

Cochrane arrived in Honiton on 18 October. As on the previous occasion his entrance was dramatic. He had persuaded some of the officers and crew of the *Pallas* to accompany him and they treated the occasion with the jollity and noisy exuberance characteristic of sailors ashore. The sleepy town was woken to the sound of two horse-drawn carriages rumbling down the main street to the accompaniment of much cheering from their occupants. Cochrane emerged from the first carriage accompanied by two of his lieutenants and a midshipman wearing their naval uniforms. The second carriage was filled to overflowing with the boat's crew of the *Pallas* prepared for action: the helmsman was seated on the box and the boatswain 'perched on the roof of the carriage with his whistle in his mouth, kept the whole in order, and enabled all to cheer in due time, every blast being accompanied by a long huzza'.[11] During the course of the day Cochrane and his supporters went from house to house, energetically canvassing the voters. Cochrane also arranged for the town crier to announce that any voter who applied to Mr Townshend would receive the sum of ten guineas. This no doubt convinced any wavering voters that there was only one man to vote for and it was soon reckoned that Cochrane had an unassailable lead over his opponent. Ironically there was no need to bribe the voters on this occasion. Richard Robson had decided to stand for neighbouring Okehampton, leaving two vacant seats at Honiton. As Cochrane and Bradshaw were the only two candidates they were both elected unopposed. The townspeople showed their delight at Cochrane's election by 'conveying him all over the town in an arm chair on their shoulders with his long legs hanging over'.[12]

The JOLLY TARS *of* OLD ENGLAND *on a* LAND CRUISE.

'The Jolly Tars of Old England on a Land Cruise'. A print after J. C. Ibbetson showing exuberant sailors driving a stagecoach which they have commandeered.

Ten years later Cochrane stood up in the House of Commons during the course of a debate on reform and explained his conduct. According to the official record of the debate, 'He remembered very well the time he was first returned as a member to the House, which was for the borough of Honiton, and on which occasion the town bellman was sent through the town to order the voters to come to Mr Townshend's, the headman in that place, and a banker, to receive the sum of £10 10s.' He said that he had kept the bills and vouchers for the money. 'His motive, he was now fully convinced, was wrong, decidedly wrong, but as he came home pretty well flushed with Spanish money, he had found the borough open, and he had bargained for it; and he was sure he should have been returned had he been lord Camelford's black servant or his great dog.'[13]

It is not difficult to see why Cochrane acted as he did at Honiton. His purpose in becoming a Member of Parliament was not to advance his own career; in future years he would frequently attack senior figures in the naval and civilian establishments in the House of Commons and seemed to go out of his way to alienate those who might otherwise have helped his advancement. His primary aim was to expose naval abuses and corruption and to fight the causes of those naval officers and men who lacked influence. His first attempt to win the Honiton seat had failed because his opponent had bribed the voters and he had not. On his second attempt he decided to follow the custom of the day and use his prize money to ensure that he got into Parliament. The end justified the means. His actions did not go unnoticed, however. A year later, when he contested the parliamentary seat of Westminster and stood as a radical candidate opposed to bribery, he was repeatedly accused by a hostile member of the crowd of corrupting the voters of Honiton. Cochrane refused to answer the charge and left the hustings.

Back in Plymouth the *Imperieuse* was slowly being prepared for sea. Iron and shingle ballast had been stowed below and on 20 October the frigate was warped alongside the sheer hulk so that her masts could be lifted aboard. The standing rigging was set up, the topmasts and yards were hoisted aboard and heaved into place, and provisions and stores were brought across from the dockyard. By 13 November she was ready to slip her moorings and run down to Stonehouse Pool where she dropped anchor. The muster book for this period indicates that the official complement of the *Imperieuse* was 284 men. No fewer than 191 were former members of the crew of the *Pallas* and included James Guthrie, the surgeon, and Robert Hillier, the gunner.[14]

The new members of the crew included three of the lieutenants assigned to the ship: the first lieutenant Sam Browne, the second lieutenant David Mapleton, and the third lieutenant Richard Harrison, all of whom would distinguish themselves in coastal raids and cutting-out expeditions during the course of the next three years. A number of boys also joined the ship including William Cobbett's son Henry, and the fourteen-year-old Frederick Marryat whose writings, based on his recollections of his service on board the *Imperieuse*, would play a major part in establishing Cochrane's reputation as a heroic frigate captain. Marryat had been a rebellious and unruly schoolboy and had persuaded his father to send him to sea. His father, Joseph Marryat, was a wealthy London merchant and Lloyd's underwriter who had trading links with the West Indies. It seems likely that Cochrane's naval uncle Alexander, now commander-in-chief of the West Indies station, made the initial introductions.

On 22 September 1806 the young Marryat joined the *Imperieuse* as a 'boy, volunteer of the 1st class'.[15] After serving under Cochrane for three years he went on to become a distinguished naval officer: he received the gold medal of the Royal Humane Society for his bravery in saving lives at sea; he devised and published a code of signals for the merchant service; and he was appointed a Companion of the Bath and a Member of the Légion d'Honneur. But it was as a novelist that he made his name and became a man of wealth and influence. Writing as Captain Marryat, he published a succession of novels between 1829 and 1849, including *Mr Midshipman Easy, Masterman Ready* and *The Children of the New Forest*, which established him as one of the most successful writers of his day. Handsome, charming and jovial, he was a valued and welcome member of the circle of Charles Dickens. The essayist and writer Leigh Hunt said that Marryat's face in a drawing room had the life and soul of fifty human beings and Anthony Trollope recalled his hearty laugh and wrote that 'he warmed the social atmosphere wherever he appeared with that summer glow which seemed to attend him'.[16]

The majority of Marryat's novels were about ships and the sea. He drew on his shipboard experiences in war and peace and he peopled his books with the seafaring characters he had admired, hated, endured and fought alongside. His first novel, *Frank Mildmay, or the Naval Officer*, was a thinly disguised autobiography of his early years in the navy and included detailed descriptions of several of Cochrane's most daring exploits. Marryat was at an impressionable age when he joined the *Imperieuse* and he idolised Cochrane, as did many of his crew. They saw him at his best and in his element. In his memoirs Marryat recalled, 'the coolness and courage of our captain, inoculating the whole of the ship's company; the suddenness of our attacks, the gathering after the combat, the killed lamented, the wounded almost envied; the powder so burnt into our faces that years could not remove it; the proved character of every man and officer on board, the implicit trust and the adoration we felt for our commander'.[17]

Marryat may have hero-worshipped Cochrane but his writings also provide a remarkable insight into daily life on board the *Imperieuse.* His viewpoint from the midshipmen's quarters is a useful corrective to Cochrane's own reminiscences. Here is Marryat's description of the chaotic scene which greeted him on his arrival at Plymouth dockyard:

> The ship was at this time refitting, and was what is usually called in the hands of the dockyard, and a sweet mess she was in. The quarter-deck carronades were run fore and aft; the slides unbolted from the side, the decks were covered with pitch fresh poured into the seams, and the caulkers were sitting on their boxes, ready to renew their noisy labours as soon as the dinner-hour had expired. [Under the half-deck] sat a woman, selling bread and butter and red herrings to the sailors; she had also cherries and clotted cream, and a cask of strong beer, which seemed to be in great demand . . . the 'tween decks was crammed with casks, and cases, and chests, and bags and hammocks; the noise of the caulkers was resumed over my head and all around me; the stench of bilge-water, combining with the smoke of tobacco, the effluvia of gin and beer, the frying of beef-steaks and onions, and red herrings – the pressure of a dark atmosphere and a heavy shower of rain, all conspired to oppress my spirits, and render me the most miserable dog that ever lived.[18]

Within three weeks of Marryat's arrival the *Imperieuse* was abruptly ordered to sea by Admiral Young, the port admiral who Cochrane believed had a grudge against him. Young may have resented Cochrane's going behind his back to secure his crew and was unlikely to have approved of his recent efforts to get into Parliament, but it is more likely that he wanted to impress his superiors by getting all available warships at Plymouth to sea as rapidly as possible. He ignored Cochrane's protests that the ship was far from ready and enforced the order for sailing by the repeated firing of a gun. Cochrane was compelled to weigh anchor with the decks in confusion, guns unmounted and three barges still alongside in the process of loading provisions and gunpowder on board.

As they sailed out into the Channel on Sunday 16 November the crew had to clear the decks, stow the holds and secure the guns while the ship heeled before a rising southwesterly wind. Three days later they were approaching the island of Ushant off the north-west coast of France. Overcast skies had prevented them from taking noonday sights to check their position and the weather was foul with driving rain and squalls. In the early hours of 19 November, as they were scudding before the wind at eight knots, the ship struck a submerged rocky shelf with great violence. Her speed carried her onward, the waves lifted and thumped her massive wooden hull three or four times on the rocks and then carried her forward into deep water. Marryat recalled how a cry of terror ran through the lower decks and men hurried on deck without their clothes. 'Our escape was miraculous: with the exception of her false keel having been torn off the ship had suffered little injury.' According to the ship's log they clewed up the sails, let go two anchors and brought to in thirteen fathoms. As the bleak November dawn lightened the sky they saw that they were anchored between Ushant and the mainland when they should have been outside and to seaward of the island. In the hurry and confusion of leaving Plymouth some iron left too near the compasses in the binnacle had affected the compass needles. The compass error had caused them to steer too far to the east. It was a potentially catastrophic error and the *Imperieuse* could easily have been lost with all hands among the notorious shoals off north Brittany.

Later that morning Cochrane spotted a schooner onshore and, apparently unaffected by their recent brush with death, he ordered the boats to be lowered and sent to chase her down. However, the weather worsened and at 3.00 p.m. the ship's guns were fired as a signal for the boats to return. The next day they headed north, rounded Ushant and set a course for Basque Roads where they were due to rendezvous with a British squadron under the command of Commodore Richard Keats. It was while they were speeding south that an incident occurred which made almost as much of an impression on Marryat as the grounding on the shoal. At one o'clock on the afternoon of 25 November a young marine named John Bennet fell overboard. Several members of the crew promptly jumped into one of the boats hanging from the quarter davits by the ship's stern and asked to be lowered down to save the man. Cochrane 'who was a cool calculator, thought the chance of losing seven men was greater than that of saving one, so the poor fellow was left to his fate'. Marryat was particularly upset because the young man was a strong swimmer and made strenuous efforts to regain the ship. He was still visible when they were a mile to windward. They watched him rising to the top of a large wave and then sinking into the trough beyond. There was a great deal of muttering among the crew about the cruelty of the captain but, with the benefit of his later experience, Marryat had to admit that Cochrane had been forced to make a hard decision and chosen the lesser of two evils.

Four days later, at daybreak on 29 November, a number of strange sails were sighted to leeward. As they drew closer the lookouts on the *Imperieuse* identified the flags and sails of the British squadron they were looking for. There were four ships of the line, three frigates, a sixth-rate ship and a brig sloop. They were cruising off the entrance to Basque Roads, keeping a lookout for any movement from the French warships anchored in the vicinity of the Ile d'Aix. The *Imperieuse* hove to and lowered a boat so that Cochrane could be rowed across to Keats's flagship, HMS *Superb*. The two men had last met in Gibraltar when Keats had been a member of the court martial which was held on the loss of the *Speedy*.

Cochrane's orders were to cruise independently of the squadron and to harass enemy shipping so the next few weeks were spent intercepting and capturing French merchant ships, transports and local trading vessels. With a ship as fast and powerful as the *Imperieuse* there was little opposition and the only action which put serious demands on Cochrane's disciplined crew was an attack on the Bassin d'Arcasson.

The entrance was defended by a fortress called Fort Roquette which was armed with four 36-pound carriage guns, a thirteen-inch mortar and two field guns. Cochrane organised an expedition to storm the fort. The pinnace and the jolly boat, filled with armed men and led by Lieutenant Mapleton, set off before dawn on 6 January 1807. The French soldiers must have fled because Mapleton's force entered the fort without a single casualty, and were able to spike the guns, destroy the gun platforms and gun carriages, burn the military stores and blow up the magazine. Having left the fort itself in ruins Mapleton and his men captured a galliot and a pinnace and returned to the ship. When Cochrane sent his despatch to Keats describing the action he gave full credit to all concerned and he also enclosed details of the vessels captured or destroyed by the crew of the *Imperieuse* since 15 December 1806. In the space of three weeks they had seized eight vessels and destroyed seven. Marryat, who was experiencing life on board a man-of-war for the first time, would later observe, 'The cruises of the Imperieuse were periods of continual excitement, from the hour in which she hove up her anchor till she dropped it again in port; the day that passed without a shot being fired in anger, was with us a blank day; the boats were hardly secured on the booms than they were cast loose and out again; the yards and stay tackles were for ever hoisting up and lowering down.'

For the remainder of January 1807 they continued to cruise in the vicinity of Basque Roads, never far out of sight of the squadron. A final foray took place on 27 January when Cochrane lowered the boats off Les Sables d'Olonne and sent an armed force to attack the French signal posts. The following day the carpenters of three of the squadron's ships of the line came on board the *Imperieuse* to survey her rudder. It was evident that the ship needed dockyard attention and two days later, following a visit by Cochrane to Keats's flagship, the *Imperieuse* was on her way back to Plymouth. They had a rough passage home: on some days the ship was driving into steep seas stirred up by gale-force winds; on others they were hit by sudden squalls accompanied by lightning and flurries of rain and hail. The wind dropped to a fresh breeze as they ran into Plymouth Sound. On

11 February they dropped anchor in seven fathoms as a heavy downpour swept across the anchorage. A week later the *Imperieuse* was towed through the Narrows into the sheltered expanse of the Hamoaze. For the next two months she was out of action and in the hands of the dockyard.

SEVEN

The Westminster Election

1807

The weeks of keeping watch in all weathers off the Atlantic coast of France had taken their toll. Cochrane frequently suffered a relapse when returning home after a demanding spell of active service. On 3 April 1807 he wrote to the Admiralty and explained that he had suffered greatly in his health during the past winter 'from the necessity I was under of being constantly on deck, there being neither Master or Pilot, or any other person on board the Imperieuse to whom I could trust, either by day or night, the pilotage of the ship when close in shore'.[1] He asked their Lordships to appoint a captain to take over command of his ship for two months until he had sufficiently recovered. He followed this with a second letter in which he enclosed a doctor's certificate. Thomas Seagram, surgeon, of 17 Wigmore Street, confirmed that he had examined Lord Cochrane and he 'appears to be in that state of debility of health requiring a respite from duty at present'.[2]

The Admiralty agreed to Cochrane's request and appointed an acting captain in his place. On 17 April the *Imperieuse* put to sea under the command of Captain Alexander Skene and a week later she was cruising the waters between Brest and Ushant. The crew were not impressed by their new captain. According to Marryat, 'our guns were never cast loose, or our boats disturbed from the booms. This was a repose which was, however, rather trying to the officers and ship's company, who had been accustomed to such an active life'.[3]

On 27 April the government led by Lord Grenville, 'The Ministry of all the Talents' as it had been optimistically called, was forced to dissolve parliament and call another general election. Encouraged by William Cobbett, Cochrane decided to forsake the corrupt and demanding voters of Honiton and to stand as a parliamentary candidate for Westminster, the most democratic and high-profile constituency in the country. His impending crusade to reform naval abuses and corruption would, he believed, carry more weight if he represented the City of Westminster rather than a distant borough in which the election process was notably undemocratic. He proposed to stand as an independent member 'disclaiming all attachment to parties or factions', but circumstances led to him being called a radical, a label which suited his naturally rebellious temperament and his habit of questioning authority.

The parliamentary system and election procedures of Britain in the early nineteenth century had changed little since the Glorious Revolution of 1688 and the accession of William and Mary to the throne. The House of Lords and the House of Commons were dominated by the aristocracy and the landed gentry. Elections took place on a limited scale but very few Members of Parliament were democratically elected in the modern sense.[4] In the counties every man with freehold property worth forty shillings a year had the right to vote but in practice it was the local lord or squire who usually determined who should be sent to Parliament. The electoral system in the boroughs was eccentric in the extreme and depended on historic custom and practice. There were seats like Bodmin where only members of the local corporation could vote; in some boroughs the voting was restricted to freemen of the borough; there were the potwalloper boroughs like Honiton and Aylesbury; and there were the rotten boroughs and pocket boroughs where the right to vote was restricted to the owners or occupiers of certain houses or plots of land. Old Sarum, the most notorious of the rotten boroughs, was a mound of earth with no houses on it at all. Only twenty boroughs had more than a thousand electors; Westminster with an electorate of more than 11,000, voters was outstanding and was among the few places where there was open political discussion and actively fought election battles.

Many seats in Parliament could be bought, usually for very large sums of money. At election time newspapers carried advertisements announcing the sale of whole boroughs. Sir Francis Burdett, who was one of Cochrane's political rivals for the seat at Westminster and later became his friend and ally, bought the seat of Boroughbridge in Yorkshire for £4,000 in 1796. He later spent a total of £94,000 in two Middlesex elections. In addition to the buying and selling of seats and the bribery and corruption in the boroughs, there were also a considerable number of safe government seats which were in the patronage of the government of the day.

Within the Houses of Parliament the political process was labyrinthine. The labels of Whig and Tory were applied to the two major groupings of leading politicians and their supporters but the parties bore little resemblance to the political parties of today. Members of Parliament were influenced in their views and their actions, not by party discipline, but by ties of kinship, friendship and patronage, and above all by the interests which they represented. Some members had commercial interests in the West Indies or the East Indies, others had interests in the City, and there were a growing number of wealthy industrialists. A great many had landed interests – when a local squire was returned to Parliament he went as a spokesman for a local community that was self-sufficient and self-governing and he cared little about the political discussions and manoeuvring which took place in Parliament.

It was the task of the king to choose a prime minister who was able to command sufficient support among the various factions to be able to assemble a government. With so many interests at work it is little wonder that governments came and went so frequently. In the thirty years between 1782 and 1812 most administrations lasted no more than two years, some no more than a few months. The first administration of William Pitt the Younger which held power for eighteen years, from 1783 to 1801, was unusual. With the nation at war from

1793 and the growing fear of a French invasion, Pitt was able to rely on the support of the king and persuade a group of his Whig opponents to join his administration.

In spite of its shortcomings the British constitution was regarded with pride by most Englishmen, and was admired by many foreign observers. It seemed to combine the benefits of absolute monarchy, aristocracy and democracy in a subtle system of checks and balances. There were, however, a growing number of critics of the constitution who wanted more equal representation of the people and an end to bribery, patronage and parliamentary corruption. John Wilkes had led the way in the 1760s with attacks on the king and the government which stirred up considerable popular support. Regarded as a danger-ous agitator he was forced to flee England for a time but on his return he was elected MP for Middlesex. His imprisonment in 1768 sparked riots in Southwark with mobs roaming the streets chanting 'Damn the King, damn the government, and damn justice'. The early stages of the French Revolution inspired a wave of republican feeling in England and Scotland, particularly among working people and independent craftsmen. From 1789 onwards there was a rapid growth of clubs and societies dedicated to political reform. These were particularly con-cerned with the unfair and unrepresentative electoral system and the failure of successive governments to tackle serious social problems such as low wages, bad working conditions, overcrowded prisons and the plight of the poor and the elderly.

The advocates of political reform came to be known as radicals and their cause was given added impetus by the publication of Tom Paine's *Rights of Man* in 1791,[5] a hard-hitting rebuttal of Edmund Burke's *Reflections on the French Revolution* published the previous year. Burke had denounced the political theories on which the Revolution was based and warned his countrymen that the popular uprising in Paris would lead to war, tyranny and a military dictatorship. Tom Paine, the son of a Norfolk farmer, had spent twelve years in America where his political writings were much admired and were partly responsible for the Declaration of Independence of 1776. His *Rights of Man* was dedicated to President George Washington and set out his belief that all men have equal rights in nature and therefore the right to equal representation. He questioned the hereditary right of kings and aristocrats to govern, and recommended that a large part of the annual revenue be diverted towards the relief of the poor, the education of children and support for the elderly. Paine had some difficulty in finding a printer prepared to publish his text but when it was published it sold in thousands and became a textbook and inspiration for the radical movement. It sparked off an explosion of popular revolt in Scotland with mob riots in Edinburgh, Glasgow and Dundee.

The setting up of the guillotine in Paris, the execution of King Louis XVI and the French declaration of war on Britain produced a backlash against the radical reformers who were regarded as subversive troublemakers. Tom Paine had to take refuge in France. The working men's clubs were regarded with increasing suspicion and in 1799 the Combination Acts outlawed trade unions and decreed that any worker combining with a group of other workers was liable to be sentenced to three months in jail or two months' hard labour.

For several years the reform movement lay dormant. It revived during the election of May 1807 and the Westminster constituency became the battleground for the radical cause. Cochrane found himself at the centre of a maelstrom of political activity. There were two seats to be contested. At the general election of 1806 the Westminster electors had returned to Parliament an admiral and a playwright. The admiral was Samuel, Viscount Hood, who had made his name at the Battle of the Saints (1782). He had been MP for Westminster since 1784 but did not contest the 1807 election.[6] The playwright was Richard Brinsley Sheridan, the celebrated author of *The Rivals* and *The School for Scandal*. Sheridan had entered Parliament in 1780 and his brilliant oratory and his friendship with Charles James Fox, the leader of the Whigs, had secured him the posts of under-secretary for foreign affairs and then secretary of the Treasury. Now, aged fifty-six, he was heavily in debt and had degenerated into a corpulent and drink-sodden wreck of a man. He had put his name forward for re-election but, in spite of his occasional flashes of oratory, was no longer a serious contender for the seat.

The most serious rival to Cochrane was Sir Francis Burdett. He came from a wealthy family and had greatly increased his wealth by his marriage to the daughter of Thomas Coutts, the banker. He had followed his education at Westminster and Oxford by travelling the Continent on the grand tour and had been in Paris during the early months of the French Revolution. The experience had led to him becoming a supporter of the revolutionary ideals. When he entered Parliament at the age of twenty-six he had embraced the cause of parliamentary reform, and now, at thirty-seven, was regarded as the leader of the radicals. He had the support of Cobbett as well as that of Francis Place, the Charing Cross tailor who was the principal organiser of the local radical organisation. The other candidates were Colonel John Elliott who had replaced Admiral Hood as the Tory candidate, and James Paull, a former merchant who had stood as a radical at the last election and been defeated. Paull had assumed he would be the official radical candidate this time and was so enraged when Sir Francis Burdett entered the field that he challenged him to a duel. *The Times* reported that this took place on Wimbledon Common 'in consequence of a misunderstanding'.[7] At the first firing neither duellist was hit but when they fired their pistols a second time both men fell to the ground. Paull had a minor wound in his leg but Burdett was more severely wounded in the thigh and was prevented from taking an active part in the election campaign.

On 2 May a 'numerous and most respectable meeting of the Independent Electors of Westminster' was held at the St Alban's Tavern in a street off Pall Mall. There it was resolved that 'the known character of Lord Cochrane as a brave and meritorious Naval Officer, and his principles as a Political Man, entitle him to the warmest approbation of this meeting'.[8] It was agreed that Lord Cochrane was a fit and proper person to represent the City of Westminster in Parliament and the meeting resolved to use all possible exertions for promoting and securing his Lordship's election. During the course of the next week Cochrane gave election dinners in Willis's Rooms in St James's and he hired committee rooms in Richardson's Coffee House in Covent Garden as a base for his campaign.[9] A local hack was commissioned to write an election broadside which was headed: 'Victory! Cochrane! Reform!' It combined the patriotic sentiments typical of the naval songs of the period with a reference to reform as a reminder that, although standing as an independent, Cochrane was a supporter of the radical cause:

> All hail to the hero – of England the boast,
> The honour – the glory – the pride of our coast;
> Let the bells peal his name, and the cannon's loud roar
> Sound the plaudits of Cochrane, the friend of her shore.
>
> From boyhood devoted to England and Fame
> Each sea knows his prowess, each climate his name . . .
> While he hurls round the thunder, and rides in the storm
> He is more than all this! – He's the Friend of Reform.

The radicals were sceptical of Cochrane's motives. Henry Hunt, a fiery orator who was to become a leading figure in the movement for parliamentary reform, later wrote, 'So little faith had Sir F. Burdett and his friends in the sincerity of Cochrane's principles that they never drank his health, or even mentioned his name',[10] and the radical organisation led by Francis Place ignored him entirely. This was probably to Cochrane's advantage because it was the other candidates who were subjected to ridicule and slanderous accusations. Sheridan was condemned for his drinking, his sloth and his friendship with the rakish and unpopular Prince of Wales; James Paull was denounced as a beastly drunkard and a base seducer; and Colonel Elliott was dismissed as a feeble-minded imbecile and was dubbed 'Colonel Narcotic'. The character assassination of rival candidates, which was conducted by speeches, hand bills and posters, was a prelude to the high point of the campaign – the appearance of the candidates and their supporters on the hustings.

On Friday 8 May the crowds began to gather early in the morning in Covent Garden. At this date, before the building of Charles Fowler's market building, Covent Garden was one of the largest open spaces in central London. On the south side there were two rows of shops selling fruit, flowers and vegetables, and alongside them an area with trees and shrubs for sale in tubs. The rest of the square was left open for market traders to sell their produce from baskets, hand carts, and horse-drawn farm wagons. The hustings, a raised wooden platform with a roof to shelter the speakers from the elements, was set up in front of the portico of St Paul's church. In the space in front of the church, where street musicians and performers entertain the crowds today, a dense and rowdy assembly of men, women and children gathered to listen to the speeches and to applaud or jeer the candidates.

At ten o'clock the proceedings began and Cochrane was the first to address the crowd. Although he was attended by several naval officers in uniform he began by assuring the electors that he did not come forward on the ground of any merit which he might derive from his military services. He said he was entirely unconnected with any of the great parties in Parliament and, if elected, would vote for every measure which appeared to be right, whoever might originate it. He was a friend to the reform of abuses and, as for parliamentary reform, he did not conceive that it was a business so very difficult as some seemed to apprehend. He made a scathing attack on those who thought that naval officers ought not to be returned to Parliament. What about all those others who were equally unfit? Besides the holders of pensions, places and sinecures there were those whose chief ambition was to display their horses and carriages and their driving skills in Bond Street; those who were principally intent on showing their pretty persons to the ladies; and those who wished to use the House of Commons 'as a mere fashionable evening lounge'. This brought cries of 'Bravo! Bravo!' from the crowd. He concluded by telling his audience that he would not have put himself forward if he had not felt conscious of his own honour and his belief in the independence of the great body of the electors of Westminster. It was reported that 'Lord Cochrane's speech was received with great applause, and without the slightest murmur of disapprobation; his Lordship appeared a great favourite with all ranks.'[11]

Colonel Elliott was not so fortunate. Both he and Colonel Robinson who introduced him were subjected to such a noisy and hostile reception from the crowd that *The Times* correspondent was unable to hear more than a few words of their speeches. James Paull fared better and when he had finished speaking there were loud cries of 'Paull for ever'. Unable to appear because of the wound he had received in the duel, Sir Francis Burdett was represented by a Mr Glossop. The radical supporters in the crowd ensured that he got a good reception. Sheridan, once the toast of the town, decided not to appear in person and was represented by his agent.

With the preliminary speeches concluded, the High Bailiff asked for a vote by a show of hands. *The Times* correspondent reckoned that Burdett and Paull had the most support but the High Bailiff declared that the show of hands was in favour of Lord Cochrane and Colonel Elliott. The supporters of Burdett and Sheridan immediately demanded a poll. At the end of the first day the poll showed Cochrane leading with 112 votes, followed by Elliott with 99 and Burdett with 78. This galvanised the opposition against Cochrane and during the course of the next few days he was subjected to venomous attacks from the Tory supporters of Elliott, and from Francis Place and the radicals who were determined to ensure that Sir Francis Burdett was elected. For several days the crowds continued to gather in Covent Garden. The candidates or their representatives made speeches, and their supporters held meetings and distributed hand bills. When the polls finally closed the efforts of the radicals were rewarded: Sir Francis Burdett topped the poll with 5,134 votes; Cochrane came next with 3,708; Sheridan had somehow managed to accumulate 2,645 votes; Elliott had 2,137, and Paull had 269. Burdett and Cochrane were duly elected as the new members to represent the City of Westminster.

The Westminster election of 1807 came to be regarded as a triumph for middle-class radicalism. Cobbett wrote, 'This election is the beginning of a new era in the history of parliamentary representation.'[12] Elliott and Sheridan, the candidates representing the ruling parties, had been defeated by two candidates pledged to further the cause of reform. Cochrane recalled that when the result of the poll was known Sir Francis Burdett was carried from his town house in Piccadilly to a magnificent dinner at the Crown and Anchor tavern in the Strand. 'A triumphal car was provided, which on its passage through immense crowds of spectators was enthusiastically greeted, the illustrious occupant reclining with his wounded leg on a cushion . . .'[13] For many years afterwards the date continued to be celebrated with a dinner at the Crown and Anchor, and dinners were also held by radical organisations in other parts of the country.

The campaign was summed up in a typically irreverent caricature by James Gillray which showed the scene at the hustings with the five candidates competing to climb to the top of the electoral pole. Sir Francis Burdett is depicted as a republican goose at the top of the pole, with the words 'Conceit' and 'Vanity' on his wings and is being helped on his way by a pitchfork wielded by the radical clergyman Horne Tooke. Cochrane is below Burdett 'flourishing the cudgel of naval reform lent to him by Cobbett'. He is wearing a naval coat and hat but has the striped red and white trousers symbolic of the French revolutionary Jacobins. Cochrane is trampling on Colonel Elliott who is depicted as a beer barrel. Below him is the red-faced, large-bottomed figure of Sheridan, described in the caption as 'an old Drury Lane Harlequin'. James Paull, the unsuccessful radical candidate, is shown falling to the ground at the bottom of the pole 'done over and wounded by the goose . . .'.

The new parliament assembled on Friday 26 June 1807. The King's Speech was read by the Lord Chancellor in the House of Lords. In the House of Commons the new members were sworn in and then a succession of speakers rose to comment on the King's Speech. Cochrane seized the opportunity to make a few brief and mildly critical comments about the two main parties. He saved his ammunition for 7 July when he introduced the first of two motions which would antagonise a great number of his fellow MPs and would put him on a collision course with the naval establishment.

A caricature by James Gillray of the Westminster Election of 1807, with Burdett and Cochrane triumphant at the top of the pole and beneath them the unsuccessful candidates Colonel Elliott, Sheridan the playwright and James Paull.

The House of Commons in which Cochrane first made his mark was burnt down in the fire which destroyed both Houses of Parliament in 1834. The chamber, which had witnessed the oratory of Edmund Burke, William Pitt and Charles James Fox, was smaller, darker and plainer than today's House of Commons. In its general appearance it was not unlike one of Wren's City churches which was not surprising because Wren had been commissioned to carry out major alterations to the gothic chapel of St Stephen's in 1707. He had introduced galleries supported on slender columns on either side of the chamber; he had created three round-headed windows at one end, and lined the walls of the chamber with oak panelling. The Members of Parliament sat on plain wooden benches like pews. The Speaker sat behind a table covered with green cloth and laden with large leather volumes. The floor was plain wooden boards and the only decorative elements were the large brass chandelier hanging from the ceiling and the royal coat of arms above the Speaker's chair.

Pictures of the House of Commons in session show the Members of Parliament gathered together on the benches: a picturesque cross-section of the ruling classes. There were country squires in plain jackets and riding boots, soberly dressed clergymen, wealthy aristocrats with fancy waistcoats and cravats, and a sprinkling of generals and admirals in uniform. The behaviour of the members during debates shocked many observers: 'Some talked aloud; some whinnied in mock laughter, coming like that of the damned from bitter hearts. Some called "order, order", some "question, question"; some beat time with the heel of their boots; some snorted into their napkins; and one old gentleman in the side gallery actually coughed himself from a mock cough into a real one, and could not stop until he was black in the face.'[14] Into this hostile arena Cochrane launched the first of his motions on 7 July: 'That a committee be appointed to enquire into an account of all offices, posts, places, sinecures, pensions, situations, fees, perquisites, and emoluments of every description . . . held or enjoyed by any member of this House, his wife, or any of his descendants.'

He went on to give details of some of the worst cases of parliamentary abuses. There were, for instance, eighteen placemen – paid supporters of the government – who received a total of £178,994 of public money between them. Cochrane's charges produced an angry response from the members present and the Chancellor of the Exchequer dismissed the motion as much too general. However, Cochrane did receive support from Samuel Whitbread, the brewer and philanthropist, and from his former opponent Sheridan who had been elected to another seat. Eventually it was agreed that a list be published of all places and pensions except those in the armed services. It was two years before the list appeared, by which time Cochrane had more pressing matters on his mind.

On 10 July Cochrane rose for a second time and embarked on a long and detailed onslaught on the navy, singling out Lord St Vincent for particular blame for various naval abuses. He said that his aim was to draw the attention of the House to 'circumstances which have embittered the lives of seamen employed in His Majesty's Service'. His first motion was 'That there be laid before this House copies of letters or representations made by the commanders of H.M.s sloop Atalante and schooner Felix, addressed to Captain Keats (commanding off Rochefort) respecting the state and condition of those vessels, and the sick therein.'[15]

Both vessels had recently been lost with all hands and Cochrane had first-hand knowledge of the circumstances which had led to their loss. The commanders of both vessels had repeatedly drawn the attention of their commanding officers to the unseaworthy state of their ships but they had been refused permission to put into port for repairs. Cochrane knew the commander of the *Felix* and considered him one of the best and ablest officers he had ever known; and he had met the commander of the *Atalante* when he had been ordered to revictual the vessel which had been at sea continuously for eight months. He had been told by her officers that the sloop was in a dangerous condition: her foremast and bowsprit were sprung; she was making twenty inches of water per hour; and a gale of wind would cause her inevitable loss. Cochrane had reported the condition of the ship but no action had been taken.

He next drew the attention of the House to the effect of eight- or nine-month cruises on the health and morale of officers and men.

Unable to stock up on fresh provisions men were going down with scurvy, while the refusal to allow shore leave to those who had been months at sea had an extremely bad effect on their morale. 'It is a hard case that in harbour neither officer nor men shall be permitted to go on shore . . . And the injustice appears the more striking, when it is remembered that the Commander-in-Chief resided in London, enjoying not only the salary of his office, but claiming the emolument of prize-money gained by the toil of those in active service.' Here Cochrane was reflecting the widespread resentment within the fleet at the harsh regime imposed on the ships blockading Brest and Basque Roads by Lord St Vincent whose increasing infirmities had caused him to leave his flagship and take up residence ashore.

Finally, Cochrane introduced a motion requesting that there be laid before the House all orders issued by the Commander-in-Chief of HM Ships in the Channel (Lord St Vincent) between 1 March 1805 and 1 March 1807 which restrained or restricted commanding officers from sending men to the naval hospitals. He gave details of men he had sent to hospital with serious illnesses who had been refused admission, and he also condemned the mistaken economies in medical supplies which resulted in a lack on board ships of such basic items as lint for the dressing of wounds.

During the course of his speech Cochrane had been interrupted with cries of 'Order, order' from the three naval officers present who were outraged that a junior officer should be raising matters which ought properly to have been dealt with by the Admiralty and Navy Board and not brought before the House of Commons.[16] Stung by some of their comments he proceeded to make personal insinuations against each of them, which did nothing to further his case. Reminded that he had recently run the *Imperieuse* on to a shoal on the French coast, he then launched into an attack on William Young, the port admiral at Plymouth, for ordering his ship to sea when she was in an unfit condition, with forty tons of ballast still on deck, her guns unfitted and the dockyard men still working on her. At this point the Speaker stepped in to remind the Noble Lord that he must confine himself to the motion before the House.

Cochrane concluded by pointing out to the members that 'All such grievances may seem slight and a matter of indifference to those who are here at their ease; but I view them in another light, and if no one better qualified will represent subjects of great complaint, I will do so, independent of every personal consideration.' It was a passionate, crusading performance on behalf of British sailors, but it was tactically foolish and doomed to failure. All the motions were thrown out without a division. Cochrane had made enemies of key members of the naval establishment and was marked down as a troublemaker. Within two weeks he had been ordered back to sea.

EIGHT

Return to the Mediterranean

1807–1808

The *Imperieuse*, under the temporary command of Captain Skene, had spent four dreary months cruising in the vicinity of Ushant as part of the fleet blockading the French warships in the naval base of Brest. She returned to Plymouth on 11 August 1807 and, 'to the delight of all, we found that the Mediterranean was to be our station and that Lord Cochrane was to resume command'.[1] Cochrane had orders to proceed to Spithead to meet up with a convoy which he was to escort to Malta. He arrived on board the *Imperieuse* on 19 August and found the crew engaged in fitting her out for foreign service: repairs were carried out to the yards and rigging; the stores of the gunner, the carpenter and the boatswain were taken on board, and within a week the ship was ready for sea.

On Friday 28 August they sailed out of Plymouth Sound and ran straight into heavy rain and a squall which split the main topgallant sail. This did nothing to stop their progress and with a brisk wind from the north-west they surged up the Channel and within twenty-four hours were entering the Solent. They moored ship in the anchorage at Spithead opposite Southsea Castle. For several days they lay at anchor among the comings and goings of warships and merchantmen, fishing boats, colliers and innumerable small craft. While they waited for the convoy to gather, the crew were kept busy painting the ship, washing and scrubbing their hammocks and rowing back and forth to fetch provisions and stores from Portsmouth dockyard.

On 11 September the commissioner came on board to pay the ship's company. The people on shore always discovered when a ship was to be paid and from early in the morning the ship was surrounded by wherries and bumboats manned by local traders, many of them women, who clamoured to sell their goods to the crew. There is a vivid description of pay day on a frigate in Marryat's novel *Peter Simple*:

> About eleven o'clock the dockyard boat, with all the pay clerks, and the cashier, with his chest of money, came on board, and was shown into the fore-cabin, where the captain attended the pay-table. The men were called in, one by one, and, as the amount of wages due had been previously calculated, they were paid very fast. The money was always received in their hats after it had been counted out in the presence of the officers and the captain . . . The ship was now in a state of confusion and uproar; there were Jews trying to sell clothes, or to obtain money for clothes which they had sold; bumboat men and bumboat women showing their long bills, and demanding or coaxing for payment; . . . and the sailors' wives, sticking close to them, and disputing every bill as presented . . . There were such bawling and threatening, laughing and crying – for the women were all to quit the ship before sunset.

There was no opportunity for the men to spend their pay in the taverns and whorehouses of Portsmouth and Southsea because the next day Cochrane ordered the signal to be made for the convoy to prepare to sail, and the ship was got ready for sea. At 8.30 a.m. on Sunday 13 September they weighed anchor, fired a gun and flew the signal for the convoy to get under way. Across the anchorage there were shouted commands and the thunderous flapping of heavy canvas as some forty merchant ships and troop transports hoisted their sails and followed the *Imperieuse* across to St Helens and then around the eastern end of the Isle of Wight and out into the Channel.

They enjoyed light breezes and clear blue skies as they crossed the Bay of Biscay and sailed south along the coast of Portugal, past Cape St Vincent and the Rock of Lisbon. They reached Gibraltar on 30 September, spent a few days anchored in the bay, taking in water, fresh beef and barrels of rum and then headed east into the Mediterranean. They sighted the southern end of Majorca and the mountains of Sardinia and still the light airs continued. The convoy was now reduced to twenty-one sail and some of them were proving so recalcitrant that the *Imperieuse* had to fire her guns 'for non compliance with signals'. On 26 October the scattered ships were hit by one of those squalls that come with so little warning in the Mediterranean. Strong winds whipped up the sea and heavy rain drenched the decks. The fore topsail of the *Imperieuse* was split and had to be unbent and replaced. The next day the wind dropped back to light airs and continued so as they approached their destination. They saw the island of Gozo at 6.00 a.m. on 31 October. Two hours later they were sailing along the northern shore of Malta, and at 10.00 a.m. they moored off the custom house in the great harbour of Valletta. On all sides were the towering ramparts and fortifications built by the Knights of St John during the sixteenth and seventeenth centuries as a defence against the Turks. Anchored among the merchant ships and galleys and lateen-rigged local vessels were six British warships, a reminder to other maritime powers that Malta was now a British possession.

Having delivered her convoy, taken on water and carried out repairs to her rigging, the *Imperieuse* headed north to receive further orders from the commanding officer, Vice-Admiral Lord Collingwood who was cruising off Palermo. They sailed along the southern coast of Sicily and then north towards Corsica. On 13 November they passed Montecristo. The winds were so light and variable that Cochrane gave the order to heave to. At daylight the next morning they were still drifting on a flat, calm sea when they spotted two strange sails in the distance. The larger vessel appeared to be an armed polacre (a 3-masted vessel with square sails on the mainmast and mizenmast, and a large lateen sail on the foremast); the smaller vessel was a local trading vessel which had been captured by the polacre. The general

opinion on board the *Imperieuse* was that the armed vessel was a
Genoese privateer. Cochrane, following his usual practice, ordered the
boats to be lowered and sent an armed party led by the Hon. William
Napier to investigate. Aged twenty-one, Napier was a powerfully built
Scotsman who was rapidly gaining a reputation as an outstanding
seaman.[2] As he approached the polacre he was surprised to see a
Union Jack being hung over her gunwale. This checked the oarsmen in
the British boats, but they continued to pull slowly towards the vessel
and, when they were close under her stern, Napier hailed her captain.
He demanded to know the nationality of the polacre and said that if
she was English her captain could have no objection to being boarded
by the boats of an English frigate. According to Marryat (whose
version differs in some respects from Cochrane's account) the captain
of the polacre, Pasquil Giliano, answered that

> he was a Maltese privateer, but that he would not allow them to come on
> board; for, although Napier had hailed him in English, and he could
> perceive the red jackets of the marines in the boats, Giliano had an idea,
> from the boats being fitted out with iron tholes and grummets, like the
> French, that they belonged to a ship of that nation. A short parley ensued,
> at the end of which the captain of the privateer pointed to his boarding
> nettings triced up, and told them that he was prepared, and if they
> attempted to board he should defend himself to the last. Napier replied
> that he must board and Giliano leaped from the poop, telling him he must
> take the consequences. The answer was a cheer, and a simultaneous dash of
> the boats to the vessel's side.[3]

A fierce and bloody action followed. Cochrane later informed
Collingwood that the crew of the polacre fired a volley of grape shot
and musketry 'in the most barbarous and savage manner, their
muskets and blunderbusses being pointed from beneath the netting
close to the people's breasts'.[4] Undeterred by the flying musket balls,
the British seamen scrambled aboard and laid about them with
cutlasses and boarding axes. The polacre had a crew of fifty-two
men who put up a hard fight but they were cut down and forced to

surrender. Within ten minutes Captain Giliano had been killed and the decks were strewn with dying and wounded men. At noon the boats returned to the *Imperieuse* laden with casualties: the British had lost two men killed and thirteen wounded; the polacre had suffered the death of her captain and had fifteen men wounded.

The action proved to be a costly mistake. The polacre was not an enemy vessel but the Maltese privateer *King George*. Both captains had therefore been at fault. Cochrane had failed to display the British flag on his ship before despatching his boats, and his men had then attacked a vessel operating under a letter of marque. Captain Giliano, an experienced and successful Maltese privateer, had been suspicious of the *Imperieuse*, a Spanish-built ship flying no colours, with boats that appeared to be French. He had acted on a hunch and lost his life in the process. Cochrane was furious at the unnecessary loss of life. Marryat later observed, 'I never, at any time, saw Lord Cochrane so much dejected as he was for many days after this affair. He appreciated the value of his men – they had served him in the Pallas, and he could not spare one of them.'[5] Cochrane believed at the time, and always maintained, that the polacre was a pirate ship masquerading as a privateer and in his report to Collingwood he stressed that there were only five British subjects in the crew (three Maltese boys, a Gibraltar man and the captain) and the rest were 'a set of desperate savages', the renegades of a variety of countries most of which were at war with Britain.

The case was tried before the Vice-Admiralty Court at Malta in January 1808. The owner of the polacre, James Briasco, lost his vessel which went to the crown. Cochrane was blamed for failing to display his flag and other irregularities and was ordered to pay legal costs. He was so angry at what he saw as the injustice of the proceedings that he wrote a ten-page memorandum which he sent to the Admiralty Board, but his complaints got him nowhere.[6] The case confirmed his belief that the Vice-Admiralty Court at Malta was a flagrantly corrupt organisation, and he would later embark on a personal crusade to prove the full extent of the corruption.

Five days after the action with the *King George*, privateer, the

Imperieuse joined Collingwood's fleet which was lying off Toulon. Cochrane went aboard the flagship *Ocean* and met the man who had been Nelson's second in command at Trafalgar. Cuthbert Collingwood, now aged fifty-seven, had been the lifelong friend of Nelson and had taken over command of the fleet after Nelson's death. Reserved, modest and deeply conscientious, Collingwood never achieved the public recognition accorded to some of his fellow admirals but he had proved himself brave in action, was unusually humane in his treatment of his men and was a master of strategy and diplomacy.[7] It is evident from Cochrane's writings that he much admired Collingwood and he was determined to impress him and 'to make every exertion to merit his Lordship's approbation'. His orders from the commander-in-chief required him to deliver letters to Captain Patrick Campbell of the *Unité*; to take command of the 22-gun *Porcupine* and the brig sloop *Weazel* and to take up a station to the south of Corfu 'where you will keep a vigilant lookout for any ships or flotilla which may be coming from the Adriatic' and, on discovering any enemy vessels, 'you will use your utmost endeavours to destroy them'.[8] But first he was ordered to return to Malta so that the wounded and the prisoners captured in the recent battle could be sent ashore. The log of the *Imperieuse* shows that she moored in Valletta harbour on 29 November; eight wounded men were sent to the hospital and a week later she set sail for the Adriatic. She spent the next two months cruising off Cephalonia and Corfu before returning to Malta on 27 January 1808.

Cochrane's description of this Adriatic cruise is curious. In his autobiography he maintained that he intercepted a convoy of enemy merchantmen who were carrying passes issued by Captain Campbell and that Campbell subsequently told Admiral Collingwood that he, Cochrane, was unfit to command a squadron. His inference was that Campbell hoped to divert attention from his illegal selling of passes by casting aspersions on the officer who had been appointed to succeed him. Cochrane blamed Campbell for depriving him of the only opportunity he had ever had to take command of a British squadron. The facts do not bear out this interpretation. Serious charges were later made against Campbell in Malta for various illegal practices but

Campbell had nothing to do with the fact that Cochrane did not get command of the squadron. Collingwood had received news that the enemy were planning to transport troops from Italy to Corfu. He therefore ordered Captain Thomas Harvey, who was senior to Cochrane and was in command of a 64-gun ship, to take over command of a strengthened Adriatic squadron which would be better able to obstruct the enemy troop movements.[9]

On 1 February 1808 the *Imperieuse* set sail from Malta. She arrived off the coast of Spain near Barcelona on 10 February and proceeded slowly south. They captured several small vessels and were in the vicinity of Cartagena when they attacked four gunboats. The broadsides of the *Imperieuse* sank two of the gunboats, a third was captured and the fourth escaped. From the prisoners taken in the action they learnt that a large French privateer was at anchor in the Bay of Almeria. Cochrane decided to cut out the privateer but instead of sending in the frigate's boats at night he planned a daylight attack.[10]

At dawn on 21 February the *Imperieuse*, flying an American flag, rounded the headland on the eastern side of the great bay and headed for the town of Almeria which could be seen in the distance, lying at the foot of the Sierra Nevada mountain range. As they drew closer they could see numerous vessels lying at anchor under the protection of the heavy gun batteries which protected the town and the harbour. In theory a daylight attack was foolhardy because one of the batteries was mounted in a tower overlooking the anchorage and the *Imperieuse* offered an easy target for its four guns. However, Cochrane had rightly calculated that his boldness in anchoring under the guns, together with the American flag he was flying, would allay any fears that his frigate was an enemy vessel and would enable him to mount a surprise attack. He anchored between the French privateer, *L'Orient*, and two heavily laden brigs. Springs were made fast to the anchor cables of the *Imperieuse* which would enable the crew to control the position of the ship and swing her round to bring her guns to bear where needed. The boats were hoisted out and lowered and still there was no sound from the batteries around the bay. The boarding parties, armed with pistols and cutlasses, dropped down into the boats where they found several of the younger midshipmen, including

Marryat, who were determined not to miss the action. At a signal from Lieutenant Caulfield, who was leading the cutting-out expedition, the oarsmen dug in their oars and pulled swiftly across the calm water towards the privateer. The crew of the French vessel had evidently been suspicious of the *Imperieuse* because they were not taken unawares. As the boats approached they let loose a hail of musket fire and began running out their carriage guns. Marryat was in the leading boat with Caulfield and recalled what happened next:

'Half of our boat's crew were laid beneath the thwarts; the remainder boarded. Caulfield was the first on the vessel's decks – a volley of musketoons received him and he fell dead with thirteen bullets in his body.'[11] Marryat was immediately behind Caulfield and was knocked down by him as he fell and was then trampled over by his shipmates as they rushed on to the deck. He lay 'fainting with the pressure and nearly suffocated with the blood of my brave leader, on whose breast my face rested, with my hands crossed over the back of my head, to save my skull, if possible, from the heels of my friends and the swords of my enemies'.[12] The British boarders showed no mercy to the crew of the privateer but hacked them down on the deck 'and those who threw themselves into the sea to save their lives were shot as they struggled in the water'.[13] The musket shots, and the yells and screams of the men fighting for their lives, alerted the shore batteries to the enemy in their midst. Soon the whole bay was filled with the booming roar of cannon, and the smooth water was rent and splattered by heavy shot. The log of the *Imperieuse* records that at 8.30 a.m. she opened fire on the town, her crew swinging her round with the springs to bring her guns to bear on one battery after another. The inhabitants of Almeria were so fascinated by the battle taking place in their harbour that large numbers of them lined the shore, at considerable risk of being hit by the guns of the *Imperieuse*.

According to Marryat the fight on the privateer was over in eight minutes. The British seamen who had boarded her cut her anchor cable, set some sail and steered her between the *Imperieuse* and the nearest gun battery. The two merchant brigs were also captured by the men in the boats. Around mid-morning the wind died and for a while the *Imperieuse* and her three prizes were becalmed and at the mercy of the shore batteries. The privateer was hit but not seriously damaged and fortunately a light breeze sprang up. The *Imperieuse*, now flying the British flag, weighed anchor and, accompanied by her three prizes, sailed slowly out of range of the batteries. She had suffered unusually heavy casualties: in addition to the death of Lieutenant Caulfield, one man had been shot in the mouth, his jawbone broken in pieces; one man had been severely shot in the arm and another in the hand 'it is supposed will lose the use of it'; three men had been badly wounded by shot in the back; and four men had received serious head wounds, which would prove fatal for one of them.[14] Two days later they dropped anchor in the Bay of Gibraltar. When he received Cochrane's report of the action Collingwood was generous in his praise: 'Your Lordship's vigilance and zeal in the public service has always been exemplary and the attack of the enemy on the 22nd under circumstances so critical is a brilliant instance of it – highly honourable to all engaged in it, and will be gratifying to the Lords Commissioners of the Admiralty.'[15] They remained at Gibraltar for three weeks. Cochrane arranged for the body of Lieutenant Caulfield to be taken ashore and buried with full military honours. When they returned to the ship the crew were instructed to give the *Imperieuse* an overhaul. They stripped out and replaced the decayed rigging; they restowed and cleaned the hold; and they worked over the ship from stem to stern, closely supervised by Cochrane who had learnt every trade on board from his early days under the instruction of Lieutenant Jack Larmour. When they set sail on 5 March the ship was looking at her most beautiful with freshly painted topsides, blackened yards and tarred rigging, polished brass, scrubbed decks and sails expertly set and trimmed. They passed Europa Point with a fair wind and headed east along the Spanish coast. Marryat was surprised to find that when they were sixty miles from the Rock of Gibraltar they could still see the distinct outline like a blue cloud on the horizon. They sailed close along the shore passing the numerous bays and beaches of the Costa del Sol with the high mountains of the Sierra Nevada rising up behind, their lower slopes covered with vines.[16]

For the next six weeks they prowled around the coasts of Majorca and Minorca. Every strange ship was intercepted and boarded and, if they were French or Spanish, they were captured and despatched to Gibraltar with a prize crew on board. They observed and noted the Spanish warships in the harbour of Port Mahon, and fired on the army barracks at Ciudadella. Crossing over to Majorca they spent several days at anchor in the sheltered waters of Alcudia Bay while the boats went ashore to find fresh water. The water proved to be unfit for use but the boat's crews returned with several sheep, bullocks and pigs. Before leaving the bay they destroyed a tower and dismounted its guns. From Majorca they headed north-west to the Catalonian coast of Spain and on 27 April they sighted the town of Palamos. They headed inshore and sailed south, past the old port of Blanes with its hilltop castle, until they came to the River Tordera. They anchored off the estuary, sent the boats in and were able to fill up the casks with twenty-six tons of clean, fresh water before the local militia arrived. When they opened fire with muskets on the sailors ashore, Cochrane ordered one of the guns of the *Imperieuse* to fire round shot at the soldiers who beat a hasty retreat into the woods. From the River Tordera to Cartagena they carried out a series of coastal raids, capturing a number of vessels in the process. They returned to Gibraltar on 30 May 1808 accompanied by a flotilla of prizes.

On 11 June 1808 Lord Collingwood sent the Admiralty a detailed list of vessels captured by British ships on the Mediterranean station during the period from 1 October 1807 to 4 April 1808. Since no major action involving line-of-battle ships had taken place in the area during that period the British ships on the list were frigates, sixth-rates or brig sloops. Most of them had captured two or three vessels; a few had captured four or five; the brig sloop *Grasshopper* had captured ten vessels, and the *Unité*, under the command of the energetic Captain Campbell, had captured eleven. During the same period Cochrane's *Imperieuse* had captured twenty-nine vessels including four ships, eight brigs, two sloops and a variety of Mediterranean craft such as xebecs, settees and feluccas.[17]

*

During the last few months of 1807 and the early part of 1808 events were taking place in Spain and Portugal which would have a profound effect on the war in Europe. Napoleon's plans to invade Britain had been thwarted by the failure of the French navy to arrive in the English Channel and provide protection for the landing craft and transports he had assembled at Boulogne and several other ports. The Battle of Trafalgar had decimated his fleet and underlined Britain's command of the seas. Napoleon therefore determined to mount an indirect attack on the most stubborn of his enemies and destroy her by economic warfare. In November 1806 he issued the Berlin Decrees which forbade all those countries under French control from trading with Britain. Following his defeat of the Russians at the Battle of Friedland on 14 June 1807, the subsequent Treaty of Tilsit, and the Milan Decrees of November and December 1807, he endeavoured to impose an economic blockade which extended across Europe from the Bay of Biscay to the Urals.

A major gap in the blockade was Portugal, Britain's long-standing ally, which defied the Berlin Decrees. Napoleon's response was to despatch an army under General Junot to enforce his will. Ever since the resumption of the war following the brief Peace of Amiens the French armies had proved invincible and the Portuguese were certainly not capable of halting their progress. Dom João VI, the Regent of Portugal, was persuaded to leave the country and move his government to his South American colony of Brazil. On 30 November 1807, twenty-four hours before General Junot's advance guard arrived in Lisbon, Dom João and his family cleared the mouth of the River Tagus, sailed out into the Atlantic and headed for Rio de Janeiro escorted by a squadron of British frigates. Among the passengers on board the Portuguese flagship was Pedro, the six-year-old son of Dom João. Fifteen years later Dom Pedro would be at the forefront of the rebellion against Portuguese rule in Brazil and Cochrane would play a key part in the battles which would lead to Brazilian independence.

With Lisbon in the hands of French troops Napoleon now determined to increase his hold over Spain. He wanted to ensure that all her ports and harbours were closed to British shipping; he needed Spain to supply him with troops, cash and ships; and he believed that a country which he regarded as primitive, priest-ridden and badly governed would benefit from the reforms he had introduced in France and northern Italy. A French army crossed the Pyrenees into Spain on 16 February 1808, swept aside all opposition and occupied Madrid on 23 March. King Charles IV of Spain was forced to abdicate and three months later Napoleon announced that his eldest brother Joseph was to be King of Spain. With 25,000 troops in Portugal, 95,000 in Spain and his brother on the Spanish throne, Napoleon assumed that the entire peninsula was now under his firm control. He fatally misjudged the terrain and the people.

An occupying army faced major problems in Spain. Much of the country was mountainous with barren uplands and few roads suitable for the moving of horse-drawn artillery and baggage trains. Apart from the people living in the bays and inlets along the rocky coast, the population was scattered in small, impoverished villages or gathered

Grande hàzaña. con muertos.

'What a feat! With dead men!' ('*Grande hazaña. Con muertos.*') Etching by
Francisco Goya, who witnessed and recorded the horrors of the war in Spain.

in isolated cities defended by towering city walls. In addition to the
hostile terrain Napoleon's armies had to contend with a people who
were intensely proud, accustomed to hardship and adept at guerrilla
warfare – a warfare which was frequently accompanied by acts of
barbaric cruelty. The atrocities committed by both sides in the coming
struggle would be depicted with horrific realism in a harrowing series
of engravings by the Spanish artist Francisco Goya who was an
eyewitness to some of the worst excesses of the period. The writings
of Cochrane and Marryat include several mentions of atrocities which
they observed during raids on the Spanish coast.

The first demonstration of Spanish resistance took place on 2 May
1808 when there was a popular uprising in Madrid. It was savagely
put down by French troops but the rebellion spread rapidly to other
cities. There were riots in Toledo and Seville, and in the harbour of
Cadiz the French admiral was forced to surrender his fleet to the local
Spanish forces. The occupying power was further humiliated on

Con razon ó sin ella.

'Rightly or wrongly' ('*Con razon ó sin ella*'). Etching by Goya
depicting Spanish peasants being gunned down by French soldiers, *c.*1810.

20 July when a Spanish army led by General Castaños defeated a French army of nearly 18,000 men under the command of General Pierre-Antoine Dupont at the Battle of Baylen. Napoleon was so angry when he heard the news that he stripped Dupont of his command and imprisoned him.

The Spanish rebellion had immediate and long-term consequences for the British conduct of the war. Spain might be under the nominal control of France but her people were now allies of Britain. Her ports were available to British ships and the navy could now make use of Spain's extensive coastline to land troops unopposed and provide supplies and reinforcements to British forces. News of the Spanish rebellion reached England on 11 May. On 1 August an expeditionary force of 10,000 men landed at Mondego Bay on the coast of Portugal and marched inland. The force was led by Sir Arthur Wellesley, the future Duke of Wellington, who had proved his qualities as a military leader in India. Within a fortnight of his landing he had defeated a French force at Rolica and on 21 August he scored a notable victory at Vimeiro: a French army under General Junot was routed, losing thirteen cannon and 3,000 men. Unlike the Royal Navy the British Army had so far failed to distinguish itself in the war in Europe but Vimeiro marked a change in its fortunes. There would be many reverses during the course of the next six years but Wellington, working closely with Spanish forces and assisted by information supplied by Spanish priests and local people, would slowly but surely drive the French out of Spain and Portugal.

NINE

The Coastal Raids of the *Imperieuse*

1808

Lord Collingwood heard the news of the Spanish rebellion while he and his squadron were keeping watch on the port of Toulon. He was quick to grasp the significance of the developments and sailed at once for Gibraltar which he reached on 8 June. He spent four days in the bay gathering information, and then sailed on to Cadiz where he made contact with the Spanish admirals and waited for orders from Britain. On 20 June he wrote a secret despatch to Rear-Admiral Martin in which he outlined the recent events in Spain and was able to tell him, 'I have the fullest instructions from the Secretary of State to give every possible aid to the operations of the Spaniards.' He said he was sending the *Imperieuse* to the Captain General of Majorca with letters from the British government and he was enclosing a copy of the further orders he had given to the *Imperieuse:* 'You will perceive that the station she is appointed to fill, is one of the first consequences to our present affairs.'[1] From this last remark and the tone of his orders to Cochrane it is clear that he was expecting the *Imperieuse* to play a significant role in the rapidly unfolding events.

The *Imperieuse* had been lying at anchor in the Bay of Gibraltar since 30 May undergoing a thorough overhaul. Her people had cleared the holds and washed and restowed the iron ballast; they had taken on provisions and filled the empty casks with water; and the warrant officers' stores had been drawn from the dockyard. At dawn on 20 June they unmoored the ship, set sail and headed west. Under overcast skies, with a fresh breeze filling the sails, they passed Cape Trafalgar and headed for Cadiz. The next day they sighted the lighthouse of Cadiz and found a fleet of British warships anchored in the bay near the walls of the ancient seaport. Anchoring close by, Cochrane had a boat lowered and was rowed across to Collingwood's flagship to collect his instructions. The orders he received are worth quoting at some length because they help to explain the determination and energy with which he tackled his operations off the Spanish coast during the next six months:

> Whereas it is of the greatest importance that the French troops now at Barcelona which are supposed to be besieged by the Spaniards in the Citadel, should not be reinforced by sea from France or draw supplies from thence. You are hereby required and directed to proceed immediately off that Port and cruise between it and Marseilles for the above mentioned purpose – using every exertion to prevent reinforcements or supplies of any sort getting into the Spanish Dominions from the neighbouring territory of France.
>
> It being His Majesty's intention that during the present struggle of the Spanish Nation to throw off the yoke of France that every assistance and aid should be rendered by the British forces to forward so desirable an object. You will, while employed in the execution of the above service, regulate your conduct towards Spanish vessels which may be carrying despatches or supplies for the use of the Spanish army accordingly; and if circumstances should arise in which you may be able to render assistance to the Spanish patriots, you will do so, as far as your means may render expedient.[2]

That evening the *Imperieuse* parted company with the fleet and headed back through the Straits of Gibraltar.[3] She was now flying British and Spanish flags at her mainmast and when she put into the harbour of Cartagena on 26 June her captain and crew received a warm welcome, in spite of the fact that only five weeks before they had launched a fierce attack on several Spanish gunboats in the vicinity. From Cartagena they headed north-east to Majorca and dropped anchor in the Bay of Palma so that Cochrane could deliver the letter from Collingwood to the Captain General of the Balearic Islands. As at Cartagena they had every reason to expect a frosty reception in view of their recent raids in the area. Cochrane noted that 'the inhabitants were at first shy, apparently fearing some deception' but when he went ashore with the news that Britain and Spain were now allies the mood rapidly changed and they found themselves showered with presents by the people of Palma. Having delivered Collingwood's letter Cochrane wasted no time in heading back to the Catalonian coast of Spain.

The French had some 13,000 troops in the region of Catalonia under the command of General Duhesme. One battalion was based at Figueras, close to the frontier with France, but the bulk of 'The Army of Observation of the Eastern Pyrenees' was stationed in Barcelona. The main road linking Barcelona with France stretched for a hundred miles along the rocky coast, in many places running along the shore and vulnerable to attack from the sea. The *Imperieuse* arrived off Barcelona on 5 July. Cochrane once again hoisted the Spanish and British flags and with typical bravado fired a twenty-one-gun salute to the Spanish authorities, a deliberate affront to the French soldiers in possession of the town. The booming of the guns drew crowds to the waterfront and Cochrane and his crew could see thousands of local people gathering on the rooftops and in the public squares. The French responded by firing at the *Imperieuse* from their gun batteries but their shot fell harmlessly short of the frigate.

From Barcelona they sailed north, the light airs making progress slow. Becalmed in a bay near Blanes they dropped anchor and were told by the inhabitants of a nearby village that the French had recently plundered their church and burnt down forty-five houses, 'a wretched policy truly, and one which did the French great harm by the animosity thus created amongst the people'. On 10 July Cochrane began the first of his many attacks on the coastal road. Anchoring the *Imperieuse* at a point near Mataro where the road ran beneath precipitous rocky cliffs, he sent the boats ashore with a party of seamen who blew down the overhanging rocks, making the road impassable for cavalry and artillery.

On 16 July they sailed to Port Mahon to stock up on water and provisions. Together with the *Hind* and the *Kent* they were ordered to escort a convoy of eight vessels carrying 4,430 Spanish soldiers and artillery from the island to the mainland. Having completed that mission they returned to the task of disrupting the operations of the French army. For five days they carried out demolition work along the coast road between Barcelona and Blanes. While the *Imperieuse* lay offshore, the boats landed parties of seamen who burnt bridges, blew up the roads and systematically destroyed gun batteries. A raft was constructed so that the guns from the batteries could be floated out to the *Imperieuse,* and on one occasion they transferred a number of heavy brass guns from a battery on a cliff top to the ship by making use of the simple mechanical aids that sailors used every day. Marryat recalled how they anchored within pistol shot of the battery and passed long lines from the ship to the cliff: 'We lashed blocks to our lower mastheads, rove hawsers through them, sent the ends on shore, made them fast to the guns, and hove off three of them, one after another, by the capstan.'[4] While they were engaged in these operations they received intelligence from the crew of a Spanish boat that French forces were attacking the castle at Mongat. By the time the *Imperieuse* arrived in the vicinity the advance guard of General Duhesme's forces had captured the castle but Cochrane learnt that the local militia could provide eight hundred men to assist him if he attempted to retake the castle.

Mongat was no more than a small coastal village but its castle was in an important position commanding the road leading from Barcelona to Gerona. At dawn on 31 July the *Imperieuse* anchored two and a half miles from the castle and Cochrane went ashore in the gig to carry out a reconnaissance from the wooded hills overlooking the area. The heat of the Mediterranean sun was tempered by a fresh southwesterly breeze as he climbed to a suitable vantage point. Having decided that an attack was practicable he returned to the ship and ordered his men to clear her for action. As the *Imperieuse* crept closer inshore the Spanish militia, encouraged by the sight of the warship's approach, launched a fierce attack on an outpost the French had established on a neighbouring hill and succeeded in taking it. Anchoring in nine fathoms opposite the castle, the *Imperieuse* fired two broadsides at close range. The gun platform of a warship of even moderate size was a devastating weapon; for the French defenders it was like being attacked by a regiment of foot artillery. The shot of the 18-pounder guns smashed into the masonry, dismounting guns and hurling stone fragments and choking clouds of dust into the air. As the noise of the second broadside died away the French hung out flags of truce.

When Cochrane landed with a party of red-coated marines under the command of Lieutenant Hoare he found that the Spaniards were ignoring the flags of truce and were preparing to storm the castle. The French soldiers were desperately firing back, knowing the consequences if they surrendered to the vengeful Spanish peasants. Cochrane took charge of the situation, persuaded the Spanish to hold their fire and entered the castle where he found the French troops drawn up on each side of the gate. The commandant told Cochrane he would only surrender to him. 'After giving the commandant a lecture on the barbarities that had been committed on the coast . . . I acceded to the request to surrender to us alone and promised an escort of our marines to the frigate.' The French prisoners were marched down to the boats, the marines having some difficulty in protecting them from the Spaniards who subjected them to volleys of abuse. When they were safely on board Cochrane ordered the demolition of the castle. The guns were removed, a fuse was led to the French ammunition store and the entire edifice was blown up. Hundreds of local people now appeared and the Spanish flag was hoisted on the smoking ruins.

That evening Cochrane wrote a despatch to Lord Collingwood informing him that the castle of Mongat 'surrendered this morning to His Majesty's ship under my command'.[5] He praised the Spanish militia, explained that the castle had been levelled to the ground and provided a list of the prisoners captured and the military stores taken. It was an impressive list: 71 French soldiers had been taken, with 2 killed and 7 wounded; and the arms included 5 cannon, 80 muskets, 500 cannonballs and 13 barrels of powder and cartridges. When he received Cochrane's despatch Lord Collingwood sent it on to the Admiralty with an accompanying letter in which he pointed out that the capture of the castle of Mongat was 'one of the many instances in which His Majesty's ships on the Eastern Coasts of Spain have rendered effectual aid to the Patriot Spaniards in resisting, and driving the Enemy out of their country – and of the zeal and indefatigable industry with which Captain Lord Cochrane engages in that service'.[6]

The capture of the castle and the demolition of sections of the road disrupted and delayed the operations of General Duhesme but did not prevent him achieving his objective. Before Cochrane's arrival off the coast at Barcelona, Duhesme had taken a large body of troops northwards to reopen communications with France. On returning to Barcelona he was forced to take his men inland and drag his guns and baggage trains over the hills where they were at the mercy of guerrilla attacks. He was so angry when he eventually reached Barcelona that he turned his guns on the citadel in the town and threatened to destroy it unless his troops were supplied with daily rations of food, wine and brandy.[7] The day after the attack on Mongat the frigate *Cambrian* appeared and Cochrane persuaded her captain to take some of the French prisoners. Four days later the *Imperieuse* sailed into the Bay of Rosas where the *Hind* was at anchor and her captain agreed to take the remainder of the prisoners as he was about to sail to Port Mahon.

From Rosas the *Imperieuse* headed north and east towards the Languedoc coast of France. On 16 August they anchored near the mouth of the Rhône. The nearest town was Aigues-Mortes, once a strongly fortified port but now stranded several miles inland beyond a bleak and windswept expanse of salt flats. The only prominent landmarks in the otherwise featureless stretch of coast were the signal posts and their adjoining cottages. The signal posts were towers with signal arms which could be moved into different positions to convey information about the movement of shipping in the vicinity. The signal arms, which operated on a similar principle to semaphore flags, could pass the information from one tower to the next along the coast and it was evident that the nearest post was signalling a warning that there was a British warship in the area. Cochrane decided that his next objective must be to destroy the enemy communications. On 18 August all the boats of the *Imperieuse* were hoisted out, filled with armed parties of seamen and marines and sent ashore. The offending signal station of Pinide was demolished without opposition. The signal books were captured but to fool the enemy into thinking that they had been destroyed Cochrane ordered that a few half-burnt pages be scattered around with the result that the French authorities did not consider it necessary to alter the codes.

For the next week the *Imperieuse* ranged back and forth along the coast of Languedoc and demolished one signal post after another. Cochrane later reported to Lord Collingwood, 'With varying opposition, but unvaried success, the newly-constructed semaphoric telegraphs – which are of the utmost consequence to the safety of the numerous convoys that pass along the coast of France – at Bordique, La Pinede, St Maguire, Frontignan, Canet, and Fay, have been blown up and completely demolished, together with their telegraph houses, fourteen barracks of *gens d'armes*, one battery, and the strong tower on the Lake of Frontignan.'[8]

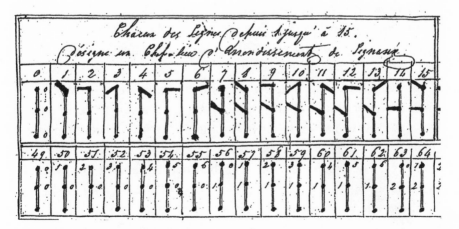

A detail of a page copied from a captured French signal book
which Cochrane sent back to the Admiralty. It shows the semaphore signals
used on the coast between Port Vendres and La Spezia in 1808.

When he had completed his self-appointed mission Cochrane delivered a set of the signal books to Admiral Thornborough who was commanding the British fleet off Toulon; and when he put into Gibraltar in October, he sent a copy of the signal codes to the Admiralty. He explained how the French sent signals four times a day with details of the number, strength, situation, bearing, distance and other details concerning British and other vessels on the stretch of coast between Spezie and Port Vendres. He asked their Lordships to note that the French system 'appears more simple and clearer than the signals now used on our coast made with flags and balls on different staffs'. And to prove his point he enclosed a copy of the signals which he and his crew had noted and deciphered when the *Imperieuse* had been sailing off Vigie de Bandau, near the mouth of the Rhône.[9]

After a week of operations against the signal posts the *Imperieuse* returned to the Bay of Rosas for a few days to take on board fresh supplies of water, wine and cattle. Cochrane now determined to cause further disruption along the enemy coast by subjecting the enemy to rocket attacks. Collingwood had recently expressed an interest in rockets and had told Thornborough that he was 'very desirous that an experiment should be made on Marseilles – Lord Cochrane is expert in these sort of enterprises'.[10] On 2 September the *Imperieuse* met up with the British squadron cruising off Toulon and Thornborough was able to supply Cochrane with six cases of rockets.[11]

The rockets used by the British navy were the invention of Sir William Congreve, the eldest son of Lieutenant-General Sir William Congreve, the Comptroller of the Royal Laboratory at Woolwich. Inspired by accounts of the war rockets used against the British in India, Congreve had carried out experiments with rockets of different calibres and warheads in 1804. Through his father he was able to get a quantity of rockets manufactured at the Royal Arsenal at Woolwich. In the summer of 1805 he met the Prince Regent at the Royal Pavilion in Brighton and persuaded him that a rocket attack should be made on the French invasion flotilla gathered at Boulogne. The Prince Regent was so impressed by the plan that he 'wrote a letter in his own hand to Mr Pitt, recommending his immediate attention to its adoption and sent me round to Walmer Castle (at which place Mr Pitt was) in the cutter which attended His Royal Highness at Brighton that no time be lost'.[12]

That autumn a flotilla of boats armed with rockets, and led by Sir Sidney Smith, sailed to Boulogne but rough weather caused the attack to be abandoned. In October 1806 the navy agreed to try again. This time the boats were led by Captain Owen and some four hundred rockets were fired at the unsuspecting inhabitants of Boulogne. According to *The Times*, 'the enemy were so appalled that it was a considerable time before they manned the shore batteries'.[13] Several buildings were set on fire and the experiment was considered a limited success. Cases of the giant rockets were distributed to a number of British squadrons but they were rarely used. Cochrane, however, was keen to try them out. He had met Congreve in the past and had had some useful advice from him on double-shotting his guns. He could see that rockets, which could be safely fired from the ship's boats because they had no recoil, might prove an effective weapon against coastal towns and ports.

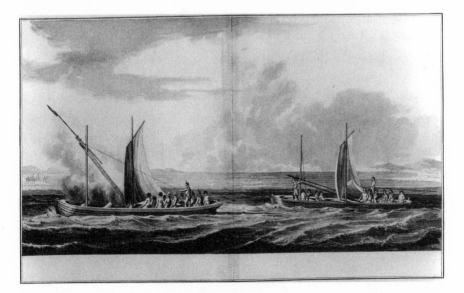

Congreve rockets being launched from boats. An illustration from a treatise on his rocket system published by Major General Sir William Congreve.

The first target of Cochrane's rockets was the fishing port of Ciotat, situated between Toulon and Marseilles. The *Imperieuse* was anchored in the lee of an island and out of range of the guns of the fort defending the harbour. The boats were hoisted out, their masts were stepped and wooden launching frames were set up in the bows. During the course of the afternoon of 4 September they launched several rockets towards the town. Fires were started in two places 'but as the houses were for the most part built of stone, the conflagration was confined to the spot where it had broken out'. Cochrane decided to abandon the rocket attack. He recalled the boats, weighed anchor and, sailing close inshore, he directed the guns of the *Imperieuse* at the fort. The bombardment continued until 8.00 p.m. when the onset of a fierce north-west wind caused them to break off the bombardment and drop anchor in Ciotat Roads.

It was during this period, when Cochrane was at his most active as a coastal raider, that his methods were observed at close hand by another distinguished frigate captain. For several days Captain Jahleel Brenton, in command of the 38-gun ship *Spartan*, sailed in company with the *Imperieuse* and took part in joint attacks on the French coast. He would later testify to the energy, skill and seamanship demonstrated by Cochrane at this time. Brenton had sailed from the Bay of Rosas on 4 September and headed for Marseilles. On 7 September he rounded Cape Couronne and saw the *Imperieuse* firing at three merchant vessels lying at anchor in a small cove. The *Spartan* joined in the attack, directing her guns at the French soldiers who had gathered along the shore while Cochrane sent in his boats to destroy the merchant vessels. The next day the boats from the two frigates were sent ashore and demolished a signal post in the Bay of Saintes Maries. But it was Cochrane's actions on 10 September that made a lasting impression on Brenton. As the two frigates were sailing along the coast near Port Vendres they came under fire from several gun batteries. Cochrane had previously carried out a reconnaissance of the area and was determined to silence the batteries. Before dawn on the 10th the boats from the two ships landed near the southernmost batteries. The enemy soldiers fled at the sight of the armed seamen and marines approaching along the shore. The guns in the battery were spiked, the gun carriages wrecked and the barracks blown up. By the time the boats had returned to the frigates the alarm had been raised up and down the coast and a large body of troops with cavalry and artillery had assembled along the shore.

Cochrane and Brenton now formed their shore parties into two divisions. At around 1.00 p.m. the boats of the first division set off towards the northernmost battery. This was a feint intended to deceive the enemy and caused the troops to set off along the coast to receive them. While they were absent the two frigates moved close inshore and fired their broadsides at the central gun battery which retaliated with a brisk fire, causing some damage to the rigging of the British ships. After an hour of steady bombardment the marines of both ships were sent ashore and had no difficulty in taking the battery and spiking the guns. However, the French troops had now discovered the deception and were heading back along the coast road. In his memoirs Brenton recalled what happened next:

A beautiful instance of ready seamanship was displayed by Lord Cochrane upon this occasion. Having already reconnoitred the coast, he requested he might be permitted to lead upon the occasion. The Spartan was following the Imperieuse, at less than a cable's length distance, the ships going about three knots; when the Imperieuse was observed suddenly to swing round, with much more rapidity than any action of the helm could have produced. The fact was that Lord Cochrane from the masthead saw a squadron of the enemy's cavalry galloping towards a gorge on the coast, which, had they passed, they would have cut off the retreat of our people, who were employed in spiking the guns. His Lordship immediately ordered the ship's anchor to be let go, and then swinging round brought her starboard broadside to enfilade this gorge, by which the cavalry were instantly turned.[14]

The use of the anchor to swing the frigate round at speed so that she could bring her guns to bear on a particular point on shore was a masterly demonstration of ship handling. The cavalry having been driven back with grape shot, the coast was clear for the marines to return to their respective ships. That evening the larger boats, each armed with a carronade in the bows, were sent to destroy the northernmost battery. Having carried out this mission they attacked two anchored vessels with guns and rockets. One was set on fire and the other blown up. The next day they moved up the coast and at 8.00 p.m. they anchored off the French port of Sète. The old harbour was full of fishing boats and merchant vessels and was protected by a mole and gun batteries. The houses were built around the harbour and climbed up the lower slopes of Mont St-Clair, the upper slopes of which were thickly wooded with pines. Oblivious to the picturesque qualities of the town Cochrane decided to launch another rocket attack.

In the early hours of 12 September two boats from the *Imperieuse* and one from the *Spartan* set off in the darkness and fired a succession of rockets at the shipping in the harbour and the buildings on the waterfront. Apart from terrifying the inhabitants the rockets caused minimal damage. Brenton blamed the defective state of many of the rockets, some of which burst because they were decayed, while 'the rockets which were in good order fell either burning a considerable time but meeting with nothing combustible produced no effect'.[15] Later that morning the boats were despatched a second time and burnt two large pontoons and destroyed a signal post in the vicinity of the town.

The next day was grey and overcast with lightning and the distant rumble of thunder giving warning of bad weather to come. As they sailed along the coast they sighted a convoy of nine merchant vessels close inshore. The convoy altered course on seeing the two British warships and took refuge in a deep bay which was protected by shoals off the entrance. By taking careful soundings the *Imperieuse* and the *Spartan* gained access to the bay but once inside they were hit by a fierce northwesterly wind. This drove most of the convoy onshore and the frigates were only saved from grounding by each of them letting go a second anchor. When the wind dropped they hoisted out the boats and took possession of a ship, two brigs, a xebec and a bombard.

These had to be heaved off the shore and they had no sooner anchored them near the frigates than the wind got up again, rose to gale force and continued to blow hard for three days. On 16 September they emerged from the bay with four prizes under sail and the brig under tow. Later that day the *Spartan* parted company, taking the prizes with her. Brenton sent a despatch to Admiral Thornborough in which he described the joint actions carried out with the *Imperieuse* and praised the conduct of Lord Cochrane, describing it as, 'a most animating example of intrepidity, zeal, professional skill and resources.'[16]

The next two months were comparatively uneventful, mainly because autumn gales restricted the opportunities for coastal raids. The logbook for this period is filled with entries such as 'Heavy swell from the SE. Rain and thunder. . . . Squally with lightning . . . Dark and cloudy with thunder, lightning and rain.' After a week lying at anchor in the Bay of Rosas they returned to the mouth of the Rhône. Running low on fresh water for the crew Cochrane devised an ingenious method of collecting it. He got the sailmakers to prepare huge bags from the studding sails and these were taken in the boats up the great river until they reached the point where the water was pure and no longer brackish. The bags were filled, towed back to the ship, and the fresh water pumped into the barrels in the hold by using the ship's fire engine. They were less successful in augmenting their supply of meat. A party was sent ashore to capture some of the cattle seen grazing along the river banks. The area was so marshy that the sailors kept sinking up to their waists and after pursuing the cattle for some way they abandoned the chase. However, it was not an entirely wasted foray because a new telegraph station was spotted nearby. The boats were despatched and the men set the building on fire; when this failed to destroy it they blew it up.

From the Rhône estuary they sailed east past Ciotat and then south to Minorca where they encountered the *Royal Sovereign*, the flagship of Vice-Admiral Thornborough who gave Cochrane despatches to take to Gibraltar. The *Imperieuse* arrived in the Bay of Gibraltar on 12 October and remained anchored there and in the nearby Zaffarine Bay for the next seventeen days. It was an opportunity to clean up the ship and the crew after three and a half months of continuous cruising in which they had made dozens of raids on coastal targets, had frequently been under fire from gun batteries and had ridden out several Mediterranean storms. The ship's company was sent ashore to wash and dry their clothes and bedding; the sails were mended; the rigging was repaired and then tarred; the guns and gun carriages were scraped and painted; and the ship was painted inside and out.

By the time Lord Collingwood received Cochrane's report on his recent raids on the French coast he must already have seen Jahleel Brenton's description of the joint attacks of the *Spartan* and *Imperieuse*. The letter which Collingwood sent to the Admiralty echoes Brenton's praise for Cochrane's energy and skill and it also contains a flattering assessment of the effect of Cochrane's operations:

> I enclose a letter which I have just received from the Right Honourable Lord Cochrane, captain of the Imperieuse, stating the services in which he has been employed on the coast of Languedoc. Nothing can exceed the zeal and activity with which his Lordship pursues the enemy. The success which attends his enterprises clearly indicates with what skill and ability they are conducted, besides keeping the coast in constant alarm – causing a general suspension of the trade and harassing a body of troops employed in opposing him.

On 29 October 1808 the *Imperieuse* left the shelter of Zaffarine Bay, rounded Europa Point and the lines of forts and ramparts beneath the Rock of Gibraltar, and headed back towards Catalonia. The three-week passage along the Spanish coast was similar to their previous one: a warm welcome and much hospitality during a ten-day stop in the harbour of Cartagena; and a rocket attack on a seaport – on this occasion Barcelona, which was still in the hands of the French. The French troops manning the shore batteries proved more accurate than on their previous visit: one shot hit the bows of the *Imperieuse* and another smashed through two of the ship's boats stowed on deck.

On 15 and 16 November, in company with the frigate *Cambrian,* they sailed close inshore and endeavoured to support the Spanish patriot forces in the hills overlooking Barcelona but the heights occupied by the enemy were beyond the range of their guns. On 19 November Cochrane learnt that the French forces had taken possession of the town of Rosas 'and knowing that Lord Collingwood attached considerable importance to this place, I considered it my duty, in accordance with his Lordship's instructions, to proceed in that direction, hoping that the Imperieuse might there render substantial service'.[17]

TEN

The Defence of Fort Trinidad

1808

The old fishing port of Rosas, or Puerto de Roses, lies at the northern end of the great Bay of Rosas. Stretching for eight miles in a sweeping curve, the bay provides shelter for shipping from the fierce north-west wind, the *tramontana*, which can strike from a clear blue sky without warning. The coast along the southern shores of the bay is low and sandy but at the northern end the land rises to a rocky promontory which overlooks the harbour of Rosas. Behind the town are the mountainous slopes of the Pyrenees. Two fortresses used to guard the approaches to the town: Fort Trinidad, which was built out on the promontory, and the larger citadel which commanded the coast road linking Barcelona to the south with the French border twelve miles away to the north.

Collingwood appreciated the strategic importance of Rosas and, following the Spanish rebellion in the summer of 1808, he had ensured that there was a permanent British presence in the bay. When a French division marched on Rosas in July 1808 the British ship *Montague*, Captain Otway, was anchored off the town. Otway sent a party of marines to help the local militia defend the citadel and on 23 July, backed up by the guns of the *Montague*, they succeeded in driving off the enemy. Meanwhile, the French garrison in Barcelona under General Duhesme was under siege from several thousand Spanish troops and by early November was so low on supplies that Duhesme doubted whether he could hold out beyond the end of December. Belatedly Napoleon recognised that more troops were needed in Catalonia and he gathered two divisions from northern Italy and one from Germany. By November there were 25,000 troops on the Spanish frontier under the able command of General St Cyr with orders to relieve Barcelona at all costs. If the Spanish, assisted by the guns and men of the British warships in the vicinity, could delay the advance of St Cyr's army for long enough there was every chance that the French garrison in Barcelona would be forced to surrender to the overwhelming number of Spanish soldiers surrounding the city.[1]

St Cyr despatched 12,000 Italian troops under General Reille to make a major assault on the defences of Rosas. When they reached the outskirts of the town on 7 November there were two British ships in the bay: the 74-gun *Excellent* under the command of Captain West and the bomb vessel *Meteor*, Captain Collins. The citadel was manned by 3000 Spaniards under Colonel Pedro O'Daly but its fortifications were in need of repair and reinforcement. Cochrane later reported to Collingwood that one of its bastions had been destroyed by an explosion in the last war: 'a few thin planks and dry stones had been put up by Spanish engineers, perhaps to hide the defect; all things were in the most deplorable state without and within'.[2] Fort Trinidad was a more impregnable structure but was currently defended by no more than eighty Spanish soldiers and twenty-five marines from the *Excellent*. Although the fort was built on high ground beside the sea there was another hill, Puig-Rom, beyond and higher than the fort. The first action of General Reille's forces was to occupy these heights while the remainder of his army set up camp in front of the citadel and prepared to lay siege to it. On 15 November an attempt was made to storm Fort Trinidad but the attackers were driven off with the loss of sixty men. Captain West sent more of his marines to defend the fort while the enemy set up a battery of three 24-pounder guns on the summit of Puig-Rom. The fire from this elevated position knocked a breach in the walls of Fort Trinidad and threatened the British warships anchored in the bay below.

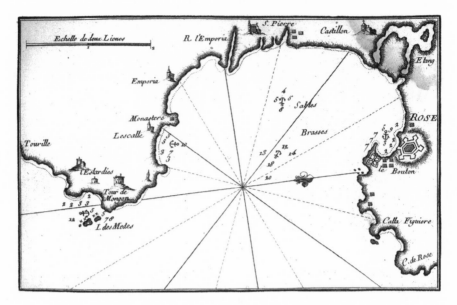

A chart of Rosas Bay by Joseph Roux, 1764, showing the citadel beside
the town of Rosas (Rose) and Fort Trinidad on the nearby headland.

The *Imperieuse* arrived in the Bay of Rosas on Sunday 20 November
1808.[3] The *Meteor* was still lying at anchor but Captain West's *Excellent*
had been replaced by the *Fame*, 74 guns, commanded by Captain
Bennett. Cochrane anchored the *Imperieuse* nearby and went aboard
the *Fame*. He found Bennett much discouraged by the current situation.
He thought that the citadel would soon fall to the invaders, and he had
withdrawn his marines from Fort Trinidad following the breach made
in its walls. Cochrane was the junior officer but believed that his
instructions from Collingwood gave him a free hand. He decided to
investigate the situation for himself and the next morning he headed the
Imperieuse towards the town. The wind was so light and variable that
they made little progress and at 4.30 p.m. the boats had to be hoisted out
and for an hour they towed the ship slowly towards the shore before
coming to anchor in sixteen fathoms. The crack and boom of the enemy
artillery could be heard across the water and from the town and the
citadel grey clouds of gun smoke rose into the still air.

The morning of 22 November was another day of light winds.
Cochrane went ashore and inspected the citadel which was under

sporadic bombardment from enemy shells. He returned to the *Imperieuse* and despatched parties of seamen and marines to help the Spaniards repair the defences of the citadel, work the guns and fire on the enemy who were digging entrenchments and setting up gun batteries. Cochrane's arrival in the bay and his positive attitude encouraged O'Daly and Captain Bennett to launch an attack on the gun battery on Puig-Rom. During the evening of 22 November the *Imperieuse* moved to a position close inshore and anchored opposite the battery. That night the frigate's boats and those of the *Fame* ferried seven hundred of O'Daly's men and thirty marines across to Fort Trinidad. At 2.00 a.m. Cochrane ordered his crew to beat to quarters. The gig, the yawl and the jolly boat were sent westwards towards the town to distract the attention of the enemy from the men advancing on the gun battery, and at 3.00 a.m. the guns of the *Imperieuse* opened fire. The French commander was quick to realise what was happening and promptly sent a force to assist the gun battery. His professional troops had no difficulty in foiling the attack and when the gun battery turned its guns on the *Imperieuse* Cochrane had no option but to get his men to tow the frigate out of range. In the early light of dawn, on a flat calm sea, the boats returned to the shore beneath Fort Trinidad. The Spaniards were taken off the beach and rowed across to the citadel. The marines returned to the ships.

Undaunted by this setback Cochrane went ashore to see whether Fort Trinidad was capable of holding out against a sustained attack from the enemy. He was encouraged by what he found. The thickness of the walls and the construction of the interior of the fort persuaded him that it would be difficult for the enemy to take the place if it was resolutely defended. If they did gain access the defenders would be able to make a rapid retreat down the cliffs to the beach where the boats would be waiting to take them off. The major problem was the breach which had been made by the guns on the heights above but it was typical of Cochrane that he should find a way of turning this to his advantage. The fort was made up of three structures joined together but on different levels: a lower fort some fifty feet high overlooking the sea; a middle fort twenty or thirty feet higher, and a tower 110 feet high which faced the heights of Puig-Rom. The breach which had been made in the tower was some sixty feet from the ground. In his autobiography Cochrane used an interesting analogy to describe the scene:

> A pretty correct idea of our relative positions may be formed if the unnautical reader will imagine our small force to be placed in the nave of Westminster Abbey, with the enemy attacking the great western tower from the summit of a cliff 100 feet higher than the tower, so that the breach in course of formation nearly corresponded to the great west window of the abbey. It will hence be clear that, in the face of a determined opposition, it would be no easy matter to scale the external wall of the tower up to the great west window, and more difficult still to overcome the impediments presently to be mentioned, so as to get down into the body of the church.[4]

The impediments which Cochrane devised were ingenious. The logbook of the *Imperieuse* records that on 24 November the boats were sent to Fort Trinidad and 'two thirds of the ships company employed at the Fort filling up the breach made and on sundry other duties necessary for the defence of the same'.[5] The ship's carpenter, Mr Lodowick, supervised the construction of a wooden ramp or slide which was positioned on the inside of the breach in the walls and was covered with grease from the ship's galley. The enemy would have to use scaling ladders to climb up to the breach and when they got there they would be faced by a man trap: the pressure of men climbing up behind would cause those at the front to slide down the ramp and fall fifty feet to the floor below. Marryat described some of the other hazards: 'We happened to have on board the frigate a large quantity of fish hooks: these we planted not only on the greasy boards, but in every part where the intruders were likely to place their hands or feet. The breach itself was mined, and loaded with shells and hand-grenades; masked guns, charged up to the muzzle with musket balls enfiladed the spot in every direction.'[6]

The crew of the *Imperieuse* worked night and day to make the fort impregnable. They were assisted by the Spaniards who had been dissuaded from abandoning the fort. Captain Bennett reported that Lord Cochrane 'by his example has inspired confidence in the Spaniards, but I fear that it will not last, and that the fort ought to be blown up. I am still of that opinion.'[7] Cochrane was prepared for this eventuality and got the men to lay explosive charges at key points in the fort with short fuses which could be lit if, and when, they had to abandon the place. He also had them filling sandbags and clearing away the rubbish and broken gun carriages which littered the interior of the fort. Marryat was much involved in these labours but did not enjoy the working conditions. They had to sleep on dirty straw infested with fleas, and the food was bad and sometimes non-existent. Worst of all was the threat from the hills above them. The gun battery on Puig-Rom kept up a sporadic fire on the fort from dawn to dusk, the shots thudding against the walls and bringing down piles of stone and rubble inside the fort. In addition to the gun battery a corps of Swiss sharpshooters had taken up a position on another hill nearby and anyone who showed his head above the parapet became the target for a deadly hail of musket shot.

On their second day in the fort Cochrane himself became a victim of this gunfire: 'Being anxious, during an ominous pause, to see what the enemy were about, I incautiously looked round an angle of the tower towards the battery overhead, and was struck by a stone splinter in the face; the splinter flattening my nose and then penetrating my mouth. By the skill of our excellent doctor, Mr Guthrie, my nose was after a time rendered serviceable.'[8] For six days they lay low in the fort. On the evening of 26 November they heard the sound of heavy and sustained gunfire from the direction of Rosas. By the morning the enemy had driven out the defenders and gained possession of the town. Nearly four hundred Spaniards had lost their lives or been captured during the assault. It was inevitable that a major attack would soon be made on Fort Trinidad.

In the early dawn of 30 November the lookouts in the fort became aware that something unusual was happening on the slopes beneath the breach. It was a cold, crisp morning with streaks of mist lying in the valleys and a pale glow in the eastern sky. Cochrane was alerted and, training his telescope on the rough ground below the tower, he could clearly see an advancing body of troops. He quietly roused his men and within three minutes every man was at his post, 'and though all were quick, there was no time to spare, for by this time the black column of the enemy was distinctly visible, curling along the valley like a great centipede; and with the daring enterprise so common among the troops of Napoleon, had begun in silence to mount the breach'.[9] The attacking force was drawn from the 1st and 6th Italian regiments and consisted of more than 1,000 picked men. They came with scaling ladders, and were wearing sombre grey *capots*, or great-coats, over their colourful uniforms which explained why they had been able to get so close without being seen. The early morning calm was now broken by the crackle of musket fire, shouted orders, and then a dull explosion as the defenders set off one of the mines hidden in the rubble below the tower. Earth, stones and bodies were hurled in the air and a gaping hole appeared in the dense mass of the storming party. The British sailors cheered and hurled hand grenades but after a moment's hesitation the enemy continued to advance up the hill, led by a colonel with a drawn sword whose cool composure was admired and noted by Cochrane and Marryat. Within a few minutes some forty of the attackers had climbed up to the breach with their ladders. There was just enough light for them to make out the man trap yawning before them; while they hesitated on the brink they came under ferocious fire from Cochrane's men and were thrown back. The enemy had by now sustained heavy losses and a pile of dead and wounded lay on the rubble at the foot of the tower. The assault was abandoned and, gathering up their wounded, the enemy retreated down the slope accompanied by the derisive cheers and jeers of the defenders. Cochrane reckoned the Italians had lost more than fifty dead. His force had lost three dead, a British marine and two Spaniards.

The next three days were relatively quiet in the fort. The enemy were engaged in setting up new gun batteries. Out in the bay the boats of the *Fame* intercepted and captured a sailing vessel laden with provisions for the enemy troops. The boats from the *Imperieuse* took more sandbags across to Fort Trinidad and returned with two wounded Spaniards and a wounded French prisoner. During the evening of 2 December two warships were seen on the horizon and the next morning the 74-gun *Magnificent* and the bomb vessel *Lucifer* sailed into the bay and joined the three British warships anchored offshore, just out of range of the enemy guns.

On 4 December General Reille's troops began a bombardment of the citadel, directing their fire at the old breach in the walls and enlarging it to such an extent that it was clear that the defending Spaniards would not be able to hold out much longer. On the same day there was a nasty accident in the fort. Some enemy soldiers had begun digging an entrenchment on the slopes below with the obvious intention of cutting off the defenders' retreat and their line of communication with the boats of the *Imperieuse*. Five of Cochrane's men were loading a long brass 24-pounder gun to use against this threat when the gun went off while it was being loaded. The victims were the two men who were ramming the cartridge home: a marine called William Foulkes and William Slaggot, a mizen-top man. In his memoirs Marryat recalled the scene in graphic detail: 'The state of the poor marine was dreadful; his face was blown off to the bones; nose, eyes, lips, every feature, had disappeared, and the remains were left black as charcoal. Both his arms were blown off short at the shoulders; and the flesh of his chest had been carried away, so that you might perceive the motion of the vitals within.'[10] Marryat noted that the man never complained or seemed to feel any pain: 'With his bared and blackened jaws he continued to abuse the French, and to swear that as soon as he was well again he would have his revenge upon them.'[11] The wounded man was laid down in a corner where his voice gradually failed him as he bled to death. He died within two hours. The mizen-top man had one arm taken off in the explosion and was blown over the castle walls. He landed on the rocks below and when his shipmates climbed down to him they expected to find him smashed to death by the fall. They were astonished to find him 'quite sensible and collected'. He was taken across to the frigate, his arm was treated by Dr Guthrie, and he was put into his hammock. He appeared to be uninjured by his fall, made a full recovery and in due course was sent home.

That afternoon, in response to Cochrane's signals, the *Imperieuse*
moved to a position nearer the fort. A stream cable and anchor were
used to warp the ship close under the land. Springs were then made
fast to the anchor cable so the ship could be swung round as necessary
to provide covering fire to the shore party in the event of a retreat. At
daylight on 5 December the enemy renewed the bombardment of the
citadel and Cochrane knew it would not be long before General Reille
threw the full weight of his troops against Fort Trinidad. As always
Cochrane took every precaution to ensure the safety of the men in his
charge. He signalled the *Imperieuse* and ordered the boats to be armed
and ready to make for the shore. The commanders of the *Fame* and the
Magnificent realised what was happening and got under way. There
was an offshore wind but they were able to beat towards the landing
place where they anchored and hoisted out their boats ready to give
assistance.

During the course of the morning the firing around the citadel
ceased. Cochrane assumed that negotiations for surrender were in
progress, and signalled for the boats to make for the shore. At noon
O'Daly surrendered his force of 2,700 men to General Reille. Cochrane, realising that further resistance was futile, began an orderly
retreat from Fort Trinidad. The Spanish defenders were taken off first,
climbing down the rope ladders on the cliffs and embarking on the
boats. While they did so the British seamen spiked the fort's guns and
heaved them over the walls. As they made the final preparations for
blowing up the fort, stones and lumps of masonry began to fall from
the tower as the enemy guns on the heights of Puig-Rom caused
increasing damage to the structure. The British warships now opened
fire on the enemy gun batteries and the enemy troops approaching
along the shore. As the smoke from their broadsides swirled across the
water the sailors and marines of the *Imperieuse* descended to the
landing place and climbed aboard the waiting boats. The last to arrive
were Cochrane and Mr Burney, the gunner, who had stayed behind to
light the fuses of the demolition charges. The log of the *Imperieuse*
records that the embarkation took place 'under a brisk fire from the
enemy forts and small arms on the hills' but notes that at 2.30 p.m. the

Imperieuse 'weighed and made sail having got all the troops off without loss, and having made fire and laid a train to blow up the castle'.[12]

For some reason only one of the explosive charges detonated, blowing up the section of the fort near the breach. This was a disappointment for Cochrane who had hoped to raze the whole structure to the ground. But he could console himself with the fact that his tiny force of sailors and marines had inspired the Spanish defenders of the citadel and the fort to hold out against an army of 12,000 professional soldiers for nearly two weeks. He had lost only five men killed and twelve wounded during the course of the siege and the men under his charge had killed or wounded around 430 enemy soldiers. O'Daly's losses in the citadel before his surrender were around seven hundred. The overall casualties suffered by General Reille during the siege of Rosas were around 1,000 men. The losses suffered by the invading army were serious enough but the resistance at Rosas had also held up the French advance and delayed the relief of the besieged French garrison at Barcelona. The coastal road in Catalonia continued to be dominated by the guns of British warships so that General St Cyr, in overall charge of the French advance, had no option but to take the inland route. Leaving behind his artillery and his reserves of ammunition and provisions he marched his army across the hills. Unfortunately for the British and their Spanish allies, he outmanoeuvred the Spanish forces besieging Barcelona and on 17 December he entered the city and relieved the French garrison. As the historian Piers Mackesy observed in his study of the war in the Mediterranean, 'Once again it had been shown that though ships could harry an invading army, only troops could defeat it.'[13]

The day following the withdrawal from Fort Trinidad, Cochrane sent a despatch to Lord Collingwood in which he was at pains to praise the efforts of his seamen and marines. Among those he picked out for special mention were Mr Burney the gunner, Mr Lodowick the carpenter, and Midshipman Marryat. Collingwood had been much impressed by Cochrane's actions at Rosas, noting, 'His resources for every exigency have no end.' On receiving Cochrane's despatch he sent it on to the Admiralty with an accompanying note in which he pointed out, 'The heroic spirit and ability which have been evinced by Lord Cochrane in defending this castle, although so shattered in its works, against the repeated attacks of the enemy, is an admirable instance of his Lordship's zeal.'[14]

After enduring several days of strong gales and heavy seas the *Imperieuse* headed north along the coast. On 30 December a convoy of merchant vessels accompanied by two small warships was sighted in the sheltered harbour of Cadaques. The *Imperieuse* anchored off the town, bombarded the gun battery on the beach and took possession of eleven vessels laden with wheat, an armed cutter *La Gauloise*, of 7 guns, and what Marryat described as 'a beautiful vessel called the *Julie*, mounting five guns, and a complement of forty-four men'.[15] Cochrane later purchased the *Julie* for use as a private yacht.

At the end of January 1809 the *Imperieuse* joined Admiral Thornborough's squadron at Minorca and Cochrane obtained permission to return to England. He was exhausted by the physical and mental strain of fourteen months of coastal raids and was hoping for some respite when the *Imperieuse* returned to Plymouth. Instead he was to find himself called upon to undertake the most dangerous operation of his naval career.

ELEVEN

Entering the Gates of Hell

1809

When the *Imperieuse* sailed into Plymouth Sound on the afternoon of 19 March 1809, a signal from the port admiral ordered Cochrane to go ashore and await further orders from the Admiralty. A powerful French squadron had recently escaped from the blockade of Brest and sailed south to Basque Roads. There it had joined the French ships lying in the inner anchorage known as Aix Roads near the naval base of Rochefort. The combined force anchored in the lee of the Ile d'Aix consisted of eleven ships of the line and four frigates and was under the able command of Rear-Admiral Allemand.[1] It was known that the intention of this fleet was to sail to the French island of Martinique and from there to launch an attack on the West India trade which was so important to Britain's economy. To prevent this from happening a British fleet under the command of Lord Gambier was currently blockading the entrance of Basque Roads. However, the Admiralty was worried that the French fleet might slip out again and was determined that it should be destroyed. The idea of using fireships to achieve this had been discussed but those naval officers who had been consulted on the matter were discouraging. Lord Gambier, in particular, had reservations. Writing from Basque Roads on 11 March he had reported that 'The enemy's ships lie much exposed to the operation of fire-ships, it is a horrible mode of warfare, and the attempt hazardous if not desperate . . .'[2]

The return of Cochrane to England at this time was providential. He was well acquainted with the waters of Basque Roads, he had an impressive record of daring attacks on coastal targets and it had not been forgotten that he had recommended a fireship attack on the anchorage at Aix Roads in a letter to the Admiralty in 1806.[3] William Johnstone Hope, the Second Lord of the Admiralty, was instructed to write to Cochrane at Plymouth and sound him out on the matter. Johnstone Hope was a fellow Scot and his letter was couched in the most friendly terms. He began by congratulating Cochrane on his safe return after the rigours he had undergone in the defence of Fort Trinidad. He assured him that his exertions were highly applauded by the Board of Admiralty and that Lord Collingwood's despatches had done full justice to them. He went on to say, 'There is an undertaking of great moment in agitation against Rochefort, and the Board thinks that your local knowledge and services on the occasion might be of the utmost consequence, and, I believe, it is intended to send you there with all expedition; I have ventured to say, that if you are in health, you will readily give your aid on this business.'[4]

The letter was followed almost immediately by a telegraphic message from the Admiralty which summoned Cochrane to White-hall. On his arrival in London he was invited to a private meeting with Lord Mulgrave, the First Lord of the Admiralty. Lord Mulgrave was not a naval man. He had been educated at Eton, had spent time in the army and had been a Member of Parliament since 1784. He had been a staunch supporter of Pitt and for a few months had been Foreign Secretary in his last administration. He had resigned after the death of Pitt in January 1806 but had returned to power as First Sea Lord in Portland's administration in 1807. He was undistinguished as a politician but was a notable patron of the arts: his private collection included works by Rembrandt, Titian and Sir Thomas Lawrence.

Cochrane found him affable and persuasive and was flattered to be taken into his confidence. Mulgrave showed him Lord Gambier's letter and pointed out that, although Gambier and other senior officers had doubts about the effectiveness of a fireship attack, the Admiralty Board was determined to strike a decisive blow before the

French fleet had an opportunity to elude the blockade and attack British commerce in the West Indies. He asked Cochrane for his assessment of the situation at Basque Roads. Cochrane agreed with the opinion of other naval officers that sending in fireships on their own against an enemy that was prepared for them was unlikely to be successful. The enemy would have rowing boats standing by to tow the fireships clear of the fleet. However, if the fireships were accompanied by explosion vessels, bomb vessels and rockets, and the attack was made with a fair wind and a flowing tide, there would be no risk of failure. The gun batteries on the Ile d'Aix were in a dilapidated condition and offered no threat to the attacking force and, since the French ships could not escape up the River Charente, their destruction was certain.[5]

Mulgrave was impressed by Cochrane's confidence and expertise and asked him to put his proposals in writing so that he could show them to the Board of Admiralty which was then sitting. The members of the Board were persuaded by the proposals and the minutes of their meeting on 25 March noted 'Orders to Lord Cochrane to proceed with the Imperieuse off Rochefort, and put himself under the command of Lord Gambier – Lord Gambier to take the Imperieuse under his command.'[6] Mulgrave informed Cochrane of their decision and asked him whether he would undertake to put the plans into execution. It must have been a surprise to him when Cochrane, who had a reputation as a bold and ambitious frigate captain, made it plain that he had no wish to take part in the attack himself. Mulgrave's frank talking had alerted him to the political implications of the planned attack and he sensed that he was likely to be the scapegoat if things went wrong. He explained that he was a junior captain and if he was given command it would excite a great deal of jealousy towards him from the senior officers already with the fleet at Basque Roads. He added that his health had been shattered by his recent exertions and he much needed some rest. We have seen before that he sometimes suffered a relapse on returning home after an arduous and dangerous tour of duty so this may well have been a major factor in his reluctance to take on another hazardous enterprise.

The next day Mulgrave sent for Cochrane again and told him that the Board would not entertain any refusal or delay. He must rejoin his frigate and he, Lord Mulgrave, would square things with Lord Gambier and the senior officers of the fleet. A brief letter from Mulgrave followed which made it clear that he expected Cochrane to undertake 'this important service' if his health would allow it, and included a postscript which allowed no further argument: 'I think the sooner you go to Plymouth the better. You will there receive an order to join Lord Gambier, to whom a secret letter will be written, directing him to employ your Lordship on the service which we have settled against the Rochefort fleet.'[7] The letter was dated 25 March and the same day a telegraphic message was sent, via the signal posts on the hilltops, from the Admiralty building in Whitehall to the royal dockyard at Plymouth with instructions to the officers of the *Imperieuse* to hold the ship in readiness for sea. On 29 March, only ten days after their arrival in Plymouth Sound, Cochrane and his crew were on their way. The pilot came on board to see them out of the Hamoaze and through the Narrows and left them when they were in the open water of the Sound. The sails were set and they headed out into the English Channel under a grey sky and a cold grey sea.

Fresh easterly breezes helped them on their way and at six o'clock on the morning of 3 April they sighted the masts of the British fleet in the outer reaches of Basque Roads between the low rocky shores of the Ile de Ré and the Ile d'Oléron. As they drew nearer the full extent of Lord Gambier's fleet became apparent. There were eleven ships of the line, six frigates and half a dozen smaller warships lying at anchor in the morning sunlight: a forest of wooden masts and black rigging, with long pennants streaming from the mastheads and brightly coloured flags and ensigns flying at the bow and stern of every ship. The *Imperieuse* dropped anchor in seven fathoms, a boat was smartly lowered and within minutes of their arrival Cochrane was being rowed across to Lord Gambier's flagship, the *Caledonia*, a massive three-decker of 120 guns.

The Rt Hon. James, Lord Gambier, Admiral of the Blue and commander-in-chief of the Channel Fleet, was a pious man of fifty-three with a high domed forehead and a severe and somewhat humourless expression. He was much derided throughout the fleet for his particular brand of evangelical Christianity which accounted for his nickname 'Dismal Jimmy'. He abhorred alcohol and bad language, subjected his crews to frequent and lengthy church services and annoyed his fellow officers by issuing them with religious tracts which they were expected to read and distribute to their men. Like so many naval officers, including Nelson, and of course Cochrane himself, Gambier's career had been much assisted by family connections. One of his uncles was a naval officer and another was Charles Middleton (later Lord Barham), a formidable comptroller of the Navy for many years and then First Lord of the Admiralty at the time of Trafalgar. Gambier was a post-captain at twenty-two and had made his name at the Battle of the Glorious First of June when he had shown cool leadership as commander of the 74-gun ship *Defence*, which was dismasted in the heat of the action. He subsequently had three spells in Whitehall as a Lord of the Admiralty, at one stage serving under Middleton. In 1807 he led a massive British fleet in an attack on Copenhagen, bombarded the city into submission and returned to Britain with fifteen Danish warships as prizes. He was created Baron Gambier but the unprovoked attack on a neutral country was much criticised in some quarters: it ensured that the Baltic remained open to British ships but lost Britain another ally.

Gambier's correspondence in the days preceding the attack on Basque Roads clearly reveals his own reluctance to undertake the mission. He had already made it clear that he regarded fireships with distaste. He also exaggerated the dangers of an attack on the French position. On 19 March the Admiralty had written to him telling him that it was their Lordships' determination 'to leave no means untried to destroy the enemy's squadron'. They had ordered twelve transport ships to be fitted out as fireships, five bomb vessels were preparing to put to sea and Mr Congreve was under orders to proceed to Basque Roads with a transport containing a large assortment of rockets and a detachment of marine artillery. On receipt of this letter, Gambier had replied with his view of the current situation:

The enemy's ships are anchored in two lines, very near each other, in a direction due south from the Isle d'Aix, and the ships in each line not farther apart than their own length; by which it appears, as I imagined, that the space for their anchorage is so confined by the shoaliness of the water, as not to admit of ships to run in and anchor clear of each other. The most distant ships of their line are within point-blank shot of the works on the Isle d'Aix; such ships, therefore, as might attack the enemy would be exposed to be raked by red-hot shot, etc, from the island, and should the ships be disabled in their masts, they must remain within range of the enemy's fire until they are destroyed – there not being sufficient depth of water to allow them to move to the southward out of distance.[8]

He pointed out that the enemy were not only protected by the guns on the Ile d'Aix but in the event of being attacked by fireships could easily take refuge up the Charente because the same wind and tide that would be favourable for a fireship attack would also carry them up the river. As Cochrane would later prove, Gambier's information was faulty in a number of important respects, mainly because he had failed to carry out a close reconnaissance of the area in question.

Gambier did not pass on his concerns to Cochrane when they met on board the *Caledonia*. According to Cochrane he was received with the greatest courtesy by Gambier himself as well as by his second in command, Rear-Admiral Stopford, and by his flag captain, Sir Harry Neale. However, other officers were to prove less welcoming. Cochrane brought with him a letter from the Admiralty to Gambier which contained their Lordships' latest orders. This began, 'My Lords Commissioners of the Admiralty having thought fit to select Captain Lord Cochrane for the purpose of conducting, under your Lordship's direction, the fireships to be employed in the projected attack on the enemy's squadron off Isle d'Aix, I have their Lordship's commands to signify their direction to you to employ Lord Cochrane in the above-mentioned service accordingly, whenever the attack shall take place . . .'[9] The letter went on to inform Gambier that the twelve fireships were ready, but were currently detained by contrary winds in the anchorage at the Downs, as were Mr Congreve and his rockets.

When news of these orders reached the other officers of the fleet they provoked fury in some quarters. Rear-Admiral Eliab Harvey, who had commanded the *Temeraire* with distinction at the Battle of Trafalgar, came storming on board the *Caledonia* and told Gambier that if he were passed over and Lord Cochrane, or any other junior officer, were appointed to command the fireship attack, he would immediately strike his flag and resign his commission. When Gambier explained that he had direct orders from the Admiralty to employ Lord Cochrane and could not deviate from them, Harvey let loose a tirade of personal abuse. Speaking 'in a high tone and disrespectful manner' he accused Gambier, while a member of the Admiralty Board, of having failed to recognise or reward the eminent services he had performed at Trafalgar; and he was sure that Gambier had written to the Admiralty to recommend a junior officer to supersede him in the execution of the proposed attack on the French fleet.[10] Having vented his anger on Gambier in the great cabin he went below to the flag captain's cabin where he found Sir Harry Neale in conversation with Cochrane. Captain Neale recalled what happened next: 'When he came into my cabin he went up and shook hands with Lord Cochrane saying he should have been very happy to have seen him upon any other occasion than the present, that his being ordered to execute the service in question was an insult to the service and he would strike his flag so soon as the service was executed.'[11]

Cochrane explained the circumstances which had led to his appointment and made it clear that he had never sought any part in the forthcoming operation. Harvey declared that Lord Gambier was unfit to command a fleet. That instead of sending boats to sound the channel and find out whether the enemy had placed a boom in front of their line of ships, he had amused himself mustering the ships' companies. Gambier's piety seems to have particularly irritated Harvey. Cochrane recalled him saying, 'I am no hypocrite, no canting Methodist. I am no psalm singer, I do not cheat old women out of their estates by hypocrisy and ranting.'[12] Unable to contain his anger Harvey then stumped up to the quarterdeck and within earshot of every officer present he continued his rant about Gambier's vindictiveness towards him and his unfitness to be in command of the fleet. It was one thing to express his anger in private to Gambier but by his public denunciation of his commander-in-chief he sealed his fate. Gambier had no option but to send him home to face a court martial for 'treating him in a manner so contemptuous and insulting as to amount even to mutiny'.[13]

Cochrane did not allow the attitude of Harvey or other officers of the fleet to deflect him from the matter in hand. At first light the next day the *Imperieuse* weighed anchor and made sail. With the wind from the east-north-east they worked their way towards the anchored enemy fleet, tacking occasionally. They got close enough to the Ile d'Aix to note that the gun batteries, which Gambier so feared, appeared to be in ruins. The next morning, 5 April, Cochrane made a second reconnaissance trip to the island and at 7.30 he deliberately fired a shot at the enemy batteries in order to gauge the response. When nothing happened he tacked the *Imperieuse* and fired an exploratory shot at the enemy fleet. This provoked some of the anchored ships to fire their broadsides but their shot fell harmlessly short. Belatedly, at 8.10 a.m., one of the batteries on the Ile d'Aix opened fire with round shot and shells but failed to reach its target. On returning to the British fleet Cochrane reported what he had seen to Lord Gambier.

'I reported to the commander in chief the ruinous state of the Isle d'Aix, it having the inner fortifications completely blown up and destroyed, which I not only ascertained from the deck with perfect precision as to the side towards us, but also as to the opposite side from one of the tops of the ship.'[14] From his aerial position in the fighting tops of his frigate Cochrane had counted thirteen mounted guns and some mortars. This was later confirmed by Captain Rodd of the *Indefatigable*. John Spurling, the master of the *Imperieuse*, reckoned there were at the most twenty to twenty-four cannon on the entire island. Gambier replied that his pilots had observed three tiers of mounted guns directed at the shipping and he insisted that the batteries were exceedingly strong. However, he was happy to go along with Cochrane's suggestion that, instead of waiting for the

arrival of the fireships from England, they should convert into fireships seven of the transports currently with the fleet.

During the next few days the first constructive preparations for the
fireship attack were put in hand. Men from the *Imperieuse* were
despatched in boats to help convert two of the transports into fireships
and there was much rowing back and forth as they loaded barrels of
gunpowder and shells on to the selected vessels to create a 'fire room'
amidships. William Richardson, the gunner of the *Caesar*, supervised
the fitting out of the *Thomas*, a 350-ton victualling brig from North
Shields. He recalled how they created a series of wooden troughs on
the lower deck and 'in the square openings of these troughs we put
barrels full of combustible matter, tarred canvas hung over them
fastened to the beams, and tarred shavings made out of brooms, and
we cut four port-holes on each side for fire to blaze out and a rope of
twisted oakum well tarred led up from each of these ports to the
standing rigging and up to the mastheads; nothing could be more
complete for the purpose'.[15] Later, when Congreve arrived with his
rockets, many of the fireships were fitted with rocket-carrying frames
on their yardarms. Richardson was rightly sceptical about these. He
suspected that the rockets would be as likely to fly into the boats used
by the fireship crews for their escape as they were to hit any of the
enemy ships.

While this work was in progress Cochrane concentrated on his
particular project, which was the fitting out of four explosion vessels.
These would lead the fireship attack and so terrify the enemy when
they exploded that they would abandon any attempt to tow the
fireships out of harm's way. Working under Cochrane's supervision
the vessels were packed with large casks filled with gunpowder. 'These
casks were set on end, and the whole bound round with hempen cables,
so as to resemble a gigantic mortar, thus causing the explosion to take
an upward course.'[16] The floor of each vessel was reinforced with logs
packed together, and around the casks were packed several hundred
shells and some 3,000 hand grenades. Richardson was given the job of
fitting up a captured *chasse-marée* as an explosion vessel. Having
stowed thirty-six barrels of gunpowder in the hold, he constructed

a fuse consisting of a canvas hose filled with prime powder which led from the barrels through a small hole cut in the vessel's quarter. It was calculated that this would burn for twelve to fifteen minutes 'so as to give the people alongside in the boat who set it on fire sufficient time to escape before she exploded'.[17]

Meanwhile, the additional ships promised by the Admiralty but delayed by contrary winds arrived from England. On 6 April the bomb vessel *Aetna*, commanded by Captain Godfrey, and with William Congreve on board, joined the fleet. And during the afternoon of 10 April a convoy hove in sight which proved to be the fireships escorted by the brig sloops *Beagle* and *Redpole*.[18] In addition to the explosion vessels Cochrane now had at his disposal a total of twenty fireships. Nineteen had been converted from transports and other relatively small vessels; one of them was larger, a 44-gun two-decker called the *Mediator*.[19] Cochrane had asked for two heavy vessels to be fitted as fireships to break through any boom the French might have rigged up to protect their anchored ships. In the event he only got the *Mediator* but this ship would play a crucial role in the coming action. Two brig sloops, the *Redpole* and the *Lyra*, were designated as light ships and they were to proceed in advance of the night attack and to anchor on either side of the channel between the Boyart Shoal and the Ile d'Aix. They would show lights which would guide the invading flotilla towards Aix Roads and the anchored French fleet. All now depended on a wind from the north-west quarter coinciding with the incoming flood tide and, preferably, a moonless dark night.

The French suspected that the British might attempt a fireship attack and had taken a number of precautions. When Admiral Allemand had taken over command of the French fleet from Admiral Willaumez on 17 March he had found it moored in three lines in an exposed position near the entrance of the passage into Aix Roads. He ordered the ships to move south-east and anchor much closer to the guns of the Ile d'Aix. The eleven ships of the line were placed in two lines, their broadsides facing the approach channel, and the ships so positioned that those in the rear line had a clear field of fire between those in the front. Ahead of the ships of the line were four frigates which were positioned to guard the floating boom. The boom was formidable and was theoretically capable of preventing the passage of any fireship and all but the largest of warships. A massive cable, thicker than the main anchor cable of a first-rate ship, was suspended by wooden buoys and secured by chains to anchors weighing five and a quarter tons. Apart from the floating boom, and the guns of the anchored ships, the best defence of the anchorage should have been the guns on the Ile d'Aix – as Lord Gambier constantly stressed. A ship was at a disadvantage when facing a land-based battery partly because the guns of a stationary gun battery handled by an experienced gun crew were inevitably more accurate than the guns fired from a moving and pitching ship, and partly because a land battery could fire red-hot shot and set a ship alight. Moreover, the Ile d'Aix was no ordinary island. It was a military base – a heavily fortified island with ramparts, walls and gun emplacements and a garrison town, much of which remains today. It was to be made famous by Napoleon who fled to Rochefort after his defeat at Waterloo and would spend his last nights on the island before surrendering to Captain Maitland on board HMS *Bellerophon*. When Napoleon arrived in 1815 the military garrison and its defences were in good order, but the gun batteries were in a poor state in 1809 and the 2,000 troops on the island were mostly raw conscripts.

When Admiral Allemand observed the arrival of the twelve transports on 10 April his suspicions about an impending fireship attack were confirmed. He ordered more than seventy armed launches and boats from his fleet to take up positions near the boom so that they could tow away any fireships. He also issued orders for all the ships of the line to strike their topmasts and topgallant masts and get them down on deck, and to send below all unnecessary sails to reduce the chance of the ships being set alight. On 11 April the wind was blowing from the north-west which, as Allemand well knew, was the quarter most favourable for a fireship attack. 'About sunset it still blew hard, and I gave each captain the liberty to act according to circumstances.'[20]

By midday on 11 April the British preparations for the attack were complete. Crews had been selected for the fireships and explosion vessels, all of them volunteers because, according to the understanding of the day, fireships were outside the rules of warfare and their crews would be executed if they were captured. Most of the crews consisted of four or five men led by a lieutenant. Cochrane himself would lead the attack in an explosion vessel and he would be accompanied by five members of the crew of the *Imperieuse*, including his brother Basil and Lieutenant Bissel. The second explosion vessel was likewise manned by men of the *Imperieuse* and was led by Lieutenant Johnson together with Midshipman Marryat and three seamen. The crew of the third explosion vessel was led by Lieutenant Baumgardt of the *Gibraltar*, and the fourth by Lieutenant Davies of the *Caesar*. The crew of the largest of the fireships, the *Mediator*, was commanded by Captain Wooldridge and he had with him two lieutenants, a gunner and one seaman. Small, narrow, four-oared gigs were selected as escape vessels and these would be towed behind the fireships until the moment came to light the fuses.

The wind was rising and stirring up increasingly angry waves but it was blowing in the right direction. Low tide that evening would be at about eight o'clock and for the next six hours it would be flooding in along the channel towards the anchored French fleet. With wind and tide favourable for the night attack Lord Gambier gave Cochrane the order to proceed.

At 4.00 p.m. the *Imperieuse*, accompanied by the frigates *Aigle*, *Pallas* and *Unicorn*, weighed anchor and headed south-east towards Aix Roads. When they were about three miles from the enemy they anchored in nine fathoms alongside the Boyart Shoal. Here they were in a good position to receive the returning boats of the fireships' crews. As dusk fell the *Lyra* and the *Redpole* took up their designated positions on either side of the approach channel and hoisted their distinctive lights as markers for the attacking fleet. The wind was now so strong that the bomb vessel *Aetna*, which had orders to anchor near the Ile d'Aix with a spring on her cable to bring her broadside to bear on the gun batteries, was unable to maintain her position. With 150 fathoms of cable out she was still being driven towards the rocky shore of the island and Captain Godfrey was forced to release the spring and allow her to come head to tide.[21]

By the time the explosion vessels and fireships cut their cables and began to sweep down the channel there was a heavy sea running and the night was as dark as any invading force could have wished. Cochrane, who seems to have been fearless on such occasions, gives a clear but curiously emotionless account of his headlong advance in command of what was nothing less than a floating bomb. He had to estimate the position of the French ships because it was too dark to make them out. 'Judging our distance, therefore, as well as we could, with regard to the time the fuse was calculated to burn, the crew of the four men entered the gig, under the direction of Lieut. Bissel, whilst I kindled the portfires; and then, descending into the boat, urged the men to pull for their lives, which they did with a will, though, as wind and tide were strong against us, without making the progress calculated'.[22] The wind caused the fuses to burn much faster than the expected fifteen minutes and within a few minutes the vessel blew up, lighting up the sky and hurling into the air a mass of burning timbers and exploding shells and grenades. The explosion caused the sea to rise in a tidal wave that lifted the escaping boat on its crest and then dropped it into the trough behind. The skill of Cochrane's seamen enabled them to ride the wave and emerge safely from the trough. As darkness descended again they pulled towards the *Imperieuse* whose lights could be seen faintly in the distance.

Marryat, who was on board the explosion vessel following in Cochrane's wake, recalled the terror he felt as they set off: 'Being quite prepared, we started. It was a fearful moment; the wind freshened, and whistled through our rigging. And the night was so dark that we could not see our bowsprit. We had only our foresail set; but with a strong flood-tide and a fair wind, with plenty of it, we passed between the advanced frigates like an arrow. It seemed to me like entering the gates of hell.'[23] Marryat and Lieutenant Johnson steered the ship, while the other three men were in the boat being towed astern: one of them held the rope ready to let her go, another steered and the third bailed out the water which threatened to swamp the boat. The explosion vessel hit the floating boom with a crash and swung broadside to it. The force of the tide and the wind on her foresail caused her to heel over, while the boat astern was almost lifted over the boom. However, they lit the fuse, scrambled down into the boat and rowed with all their might. They were 200 yards away when the vessel exploded:

> A more terrific and beautiful sight cannot be conceived . . . The shells flew up in the air to a prodigious height, some bursting as they rose, and others as they descended. The shower fell about us, but we escaped injury. We made but little progress against the wind and tide; and we had the pleasure to run the gauntlet among the other fire-ships, which had been ignited, and bore down on us in flames fore and aft. Their rigging was hung with Congreve rockets; and as they took fire they darted through the air in every direction, with an astounding noise, looking like large fiery serpents.[24]

Some of the fireships were set on fire and abandoned by their crews too early. The master of the anchored *Imperieuse* noted in his log that the fireships came down in a very irregular manner: three of them were ignited half a mile to windward of the *Imperieuse*; one of them grounded on the point of the Ile d'Oléron and several others were three-quarters of a mile from the enemy fleet as they passed harmlessly by. But some of the fireships were handled with bravery and

British fireships, with Congreve rockets, bearing down on
the anchored French fleet at Basque Roads on the night of 11 April 1809.

competence, none more so than the former warship *Mediator* which was steered directly at the enemy. Her weight, combined with the strength of the wind and the tide, broke the boom. As the crew were preparing to abandon ship, the flames caused an explosion which blew them overboard, killing the gunner James Seggess. The others managed to reach the gig and row back to the waiting frigates but Captain James Wooldridge was severely burnt and his two lieutenants and a seaman received minor burns.

The awesome sight of the burning fireships illuminating the dark and windy night made a deep impression on all who witnessed it. William Richardson, who was with the anchored British fleet, recalled that all hands were gathered on deck to witness the spectacle 'and the blazing light all round gave us a good view of the enemy'.[25] An officer on board the *Valiant* thought the fireships 'appeared to form a chain of ignited pyramids, stretching from the Isle d'Aix to the Boyart Shoal; while Congreve's rockets, flying through the air in various directions, and like comets dragging a fiery train behind, formed a scene at once the most grand and terrific that can well be imagined'.[26]

The French were aware that a fireship attack was imminent. Admiral Allemand had observed the approach of the four British frigates and watched them anchor on the western side of the channel. In his later report he noted, 'they had fire signals and appeared to be intended for beacons to the fireships'.[27] But the rising gale seems to have led Allemand and his fellow officers to assume that the fireship attack would not take place on such a stormy night. The armed launches and open boats stationed by the floating boom were withdrawn and the first warning the French had of the impending attack was when Cochrane's leading explosion vessel blew up a few hundred yards from their anchored ships. As men scrambled up on deck to see what was happening the second explosion vessel blasted the night and threw up a deadly shower of grenades and shells and flaming wreckage which was scattered across the anchorage. In the darkness which followed the explosion the French sailors could see a distant but ever-increasing number of floating fires as the crews of the twenty fireships set them alight. 'A brig on fire was sent against part of the fleet,' wrote Allemand, 'and afterwards a number of other brigs and three-masted ships advanced in full sail in flames.'[28] Only four of the fireships reached the French fleet but the sight of these, following the blowing up of the explosion vessels, caused alarm and panic among the French crews and their commanders. The three frigates which were anchored ahead of the main fleet cut their anchor cables, made sail and attempted to retreat behind the anchored battleships, but then found that every one of the French line-of-battle ships, except the *Foudroyant*, had also cut or slipped their cables and were adrift. The *Cassard* managed to bring up again with an anchor and ended up near the *Foudroyant* but these were the only French ships to remain afloat that night.

An officer of the flagship *Océan* provided a vivid account of the chaotic scene in the anchorage as the crews made desperate efforts to keep clear of the advancing fireships. The *Regulus*, which was lying in the front line beside the *Océan*, became entangled with a fireship. Her crew managed to cut themselves free but in doing so forced the *Océan* to cut one of her cables to keep clear. As the *Océan* was brought up on her second cable her crew saw three fireships bearing down on them. They cut loose, hoisted the foresail and a staysail and tried to steer clear of the rocks of the Palles Shoal.

> At 10 we grounded; and immediately afterwards a fireship, in the height of her combustion, grappled us athwart our stern. For the ten minutes that she remained in this situation, we employed every means in our power to prevent the fire from catching our ship. Our engines played upon and completely wetted the poop: with spars we hove off the fireship, and with axes we cut the lashing of her grapnels fastened to the ends of her yards . . . Two of our line-of-battle ships, the *Tonnerre* and *Patriote*, at this time fell on board of us. The first broke her bowsprit in our starboard main rigging, and destroyed our main channels.'[29]

In their desperate efforts to fend off the fireship and disentangle themselves from the other two ships they lost at least fifty men, most of them falling into the sea and drowning. They escaped the clutches of another fireship by firing a broadside at her which brought down her mainmast and caused her to change direction and drift harmlessly by them.

The explosion vessels and the fireships failed to set light to a single enemy vessel but they caused mayhem in the anchorage. The wind and the tide did the rest. Within a few hours of the first explosion taking place, thirteen of the fifteen French warships in Aix Roads had been swept on to mud banks and rocky shoals and gone firmly aground.

TWELVE

The French Fleet Aground

1809

The crews of the fireships had a long and exhausting row back to the safety of the anchored frigates. Pulling into a headwind and driving rain they had to bail constantly to prevent the boats being swamped by the rough seas. Cochrane and his crew had nearly three miles to cover and it was after midnight when they bumped alongside the wooden sides of the *Imperieuse* and were helped aboard by their shipmates. They learnt that a fireship in flames had come so close to the *Imperieuse* that it had been necessary to veer out the anchor cable to keep clear, and there had been no option but to cut free the third explosion vessel which had been made fast to the frigate's stern. Cochrane had intended to use this vessel at a later stage once the way had been cleared by the initial wave of explosion vessels and fireships. The fourth explosion vessel never left her moorings. Any disappointment which Cochrane felt at the incompetent handling of so many of the fireships was dispelled by the sight which greeted him at dawn on 12 April.

It was a grey and misty morning with a fresh breeze. Where the previous day an entire fleet had been lying at anchor in orderly lines beside the Ile d'Aix, now there were only two warships still afloat. To the south of them, lying at strange angles on the Palles Shoal, were a great number of ships aground. Among them could be seen the massive hull of Allemand's flagship, the *Océan* of 120 guns. Faintly visible beyond this group were more ships aground, lying in the shallows at the entrance of the River Charente. High water had been at 2.00 a.m. and the outgoing tide was causing the grounded ships to tilt further and further over on their bilges, leaving their bottoms exposed to shot. Only the two 74-gun ships floating in the anchorage were capable of offering any resistance. The remainder were helpless until the tide came in again, or their crews were able to haul them off, an operation which would take some time because they would have to lay out anchors and then lighten the ships by throwing guns and other heavy gear overboard. Cochrane saw at once that here was a golden opportunity to finish the work that the fireships had begun, and destroy the French fleet. He ordered the boats to be hoisted aboard, and at 4.00 a.m. the *Imperieuse* weighed anchor and made sail. They worked their way out of range of the guns on the Ile d'Aix and headed towards the distant British fleet which was three miles from where the *Imperieuse* had anchored and some six from the nearest French ships. At exactly 5.48, according to the signal book on the flagship *Caledonia*, Cochrane sent a signal to Lord Gambier: 'Half the fleet can destroy the enemy: seven on shore.'[1] The signal was acknowledged with an answering pennant, but no further message followed.

As the skies brightened the men in the tops of the *Imperieuse* could see the remaining French ships aground on the far side of the Charente. At 6.40 a.m. Cochrane sent a second message to Gambier, 'Eleven on shore', and this too was acknowledged. Impatiently Cochrane waited for Gambier to order some of his warships to proceed to Aix Roads. When nothing happened he sent a third message, 'Only two afloat', to make sure that his commander-in-chief understood the current situation. At 9.00 a.m., with the tide on the turn, Cochrane wore ship and headed back towards the Ile d'Aix to check on the state of the grounded French ships. Now was the ideal time for the British force to attack because they could sail in with the flood tide, destroy the enemy and sail out with the ebb – but there was no time to lose because the rising tide would enable some of the French ships to float off and he could see the crews of several of them heaving their guns and stores overboard. At 9.25 he sent a fourth signal to Gambier: 'Enemy preparing to haul off.'[2] At 10.00 a.m. Cochrane anchored close to the spot where the *Imperieuse* had spent the night. While waiting for the fleet to respond to his messages, he sent a boat to take soundings and test the depth of the channel leading to the inner Aix Roads.

From the distant position of the anchored British fleet it was possible to see most of the grounded French ships and Gambier had certainly taken note of Cochrane's signals. However, he was reluctant to commit his ships to a general attack. Low water was around 8.20 a.m. and he was worried about the narrowness of the channel and whether there was sufficient depth of water for his ships of the line. He was particularly concerned about his ships going aground and being at the mercy of the guns on the Ile d'Aix as well as the guns of the French ships which were still afloat. His worries were confirmed by Edmund Fairfax, the master of the fleet and the man responsible for the navigation of the flagship. As they were working from inaccurate charts and had not carried out a reconnaissance of the area or taken soundings, they had some reason to be cautious – unlike Cochrane who had a copy of a French chart and had checked the depth of water in several key places. He also knew the true state of the gun batteries.

Gambier may have wished to play safe but he was aware that Cochrane's messages required some action to be taken. Soon after receiving the fourth signal from the *Imperieuse* he ordered the fleet to get under way. The impressive gathering of ships of the line, frigates, brig sloops and attendant vessels heaved up their anchors, set sail and slowly made their way up the channel. At 11.00 a.m., when they were still out of range of the guns of the Ile d'Aix, the *Caledonia* shortened sail and came to anchor in thirteen fathoms, and the rest of the fleet followed suit. Gambier later explained in his despatch to the Admiralty that he had intended to proceed with the fleet in order to effect the destruction of the enemy ships. 'The wind, however, being fresh from the northward, and the flood-tide running, rendered it too hazardous to run into Aix Roads (from its shallow water), I therefore anchored again at a distance of about three miles from the forts on the island.'[3]

Instead of risking his ships of the line, Gambier ordered the bomb vessel *Aetna* to proceed to a position from which she could bombard the grounded French ships. Three gun brigs, *Conflict*, *Growler* and *Innocent*, were despatched to support her, and the *Bellona*, *Revenge* and *Valiant* were ordered to take up an advanced position ahead of the main fleet. As far as Gambier was concerned the fireships had done their work and the damage caused by a single bomb vessel with a thirteen-inch mortar would be sufficient to complete the action.

Cochrane had been anxiously watching the British ships and was greatly relieved when he saw them getting under way. He was surprised that they had not done so after the receipt of his first signal four hours before but there was still time to inflict lasting damage on the enemy. When he saw Gambier drop anchor out of range of the guns of the Ile d'Aix he realised that the commander-in-chief had no intention of committing his fleet to a general attack. His exasperation at the wasted opportunity was shared by several other officers and seamen present. Lieutenant Gordon of the *Illustrious* later recalled, 'I cannot describe the indignation expressed by all hands when the signal was made to anchor again.'[4] Cochrane decided to take matters into his own hands and force Gambier into action by attacking the enemy with the *Imperieuse*. By acting without orders he was risking his commission and he knew perfectly well that a lone frigate was no match for the guns of the French 74-gun ships, but he was prepared to take the consequences. 'It was better to risk the frigate, or even my commission, than to suffer a disgraceful termination to the expectations of the Admiralty, after having driven ashore the enemy's fleet.'[5]

Cochrane was as ingenious as ever in his method of approach. At 1.00 p.m. he ordered the anchor cable of the *Imperieuse* to be hauled in until the anchor began to drag along the bottom. This allowed the incoming tide to drift them stern first towards the enemy. 'I did not venture to make sail, lest the movement might be seen from the flag-ship, and a signal of recall should defeat my purpose of making an attack with the *Imperieuse*; the object of this being to *compel* the commander-in-chief to send vessels to our assistance, in which case

I knew their captains would at once attack the ships which had not been allowed to heave off and escape.'[6] As they slowly drifted south-east along the edge of the channel they observed frantic movements taking place among the enemy ships. The advance of Gambier's fleet had led the French to assume that they were about to be attacked. The two ships afloat in the anchorage, the *Foudroyant* and the *Cassard*, cut their cables and made sail for the Charente. They proceeded a mile up the river but then went aground on the bar at the river entrance near the castle of Fouras. Several other ships had laid out anchors and were now hoisting sails to help drive them off the shoals. Seeing that the opportunity for a successful attack was slipping away, Cochrane sent a signal to Gambier, 'The enemy ships are getting under sail.' This was received by the flagship at 1.30 p.m. Cochrane then set the topsails of the *Imperieuse* and headed for the group of French ships which were still aground on the north-western end of the Palles Shoal. One of the ships was the *Jean Bart*, which was an abandoned wreck. She had run aground two weeks before and her battered hull served as a useful marker to the edge of the shoal. Three grounded ships lay on the outer edges of the shoal near the wreck: they were the *Calcutta*, the *Ville de Varsovie* and the *Aquilon*. Behind them lay the *Tonnerre* which was so firmly aground on the rocks that it would prove impossible for her crew to float her.

As the *Imperieuse* gathered way and heeled before the wind Cochrane sent a challenging signal to Gambier, 'The enemy is superior to the chasing ship, but inferior to the fleet', and five minutes later he followed this with a signal which he knew could not be ignored: 'The ship is in distress and requires to be assisted immediately.'[7] Within minutes of this the *Imperieuse* shortened sail and fired a shot at the *Calcutta*. Cochrane now dropped anchor in five fathoms with a spring on the anchor cable so that he could bring the frigate's broadside to bear on the *Calcutta* as well as the *Aquilon* and the *Ville de Varsovie*. At 2.00 p.m., according to the log of the *Imperieuse*, they commenced close action with the three French vessels, all of them ships of the line. It was near high water so the ships were floating upright and in theory their heavier armament should have enabled them to inflict crippling damage on the British frigate, but the French had thrown many of their guns overboard in order to lighten the ships, and crews were demoralised following the fireship attack and the sixteen hours they had spent on the Palles Shoal.

For half an hour the *Imperieuse* fought alone but then a succession of British ships joined the action in response to Cochrane's last signal. The bomb vessel *Aetna* was the first to arrive and began throwing shells among the French ships. She was followed by the brig sloop *Beagle* whose crew gave Cochrane three cheers as they passed by. The three gun brigs *Conflict, Growler* and *Innocent* were next on the scene. They were followed at intervals by seven warships which had been ordered to get under way by Lord Gambier. These were the 74-gun ships *Revenge* and *Valiant* and the frigates *Aigle, Indefatigable, Pallas, Unicorn* and *Emerald*, the latter commanded by Captain Frederick Maitland.[8] This was not the general attack that Cochrane had originally hoped for but it was more than enough fire power to overcome the French ships still aground on the Palles Shoal. The sight of the approaching British ships caused the crew of the *Calcutta* to abandon her. Cochrane sent a midshipman and a boat's crew to take possession of her, and they were joined by a boat from the *Beagle* under the command of a lieutenant. Acting apparently on his own initiative the lieutenant set fire to the French ship but the fire burnt so slowly that it was dusk before the flames reached the magazine.

Now that reinforcements had arrived Cochrane was able to give his gun crews a rest. At around 3.30 p.m. he gave the order to cease fire, 'the crew being thoroughly exhausted by fatigue; whilst I was so much so, as to be almost unable to stand'.[9] The *Imperieuse* had taken heavier casualties than was usual under Cochrane's command. Three men had been killed and eleven wounded. Henry Crookman, the captain of the forecastle, had had his head taken clean off by a cannonball, according to Marryat, who also recorded 'a very curious instance of muscular action'. An eighteen-year-old seaman was on the forecastle when he was hit by a shot which cut away the whole of his bowels, scattering them over Marryat and another midshipman and nearly blinding them. 'He fell – and, after lying a few seconds, sprang suddenly on his feet, stared us horridly in the face, and fell down dead.'[10] Among the wounded were George Gilbert, assistant to Dr Guthrie, and Mark Marsden, the ship's purser. The French guns had also caused considerable damage to the ship herself: the foremast was shot through, one of the boats was smashed, there were shot holes in the ship's sides and deck and the sails and rigging required urgent attention. The carpenter, the boatswain and the sailmaker and their assistants took advantage of the interlude to carry out essential repairs including 'knotting and splicing the running and standing rigging it being much cut by the enemy's shots'.[11]

The crews of the *Aquilon* and the *Ville de Varsovie* were now facing a steady bombardment from a miscellaneous group of British warships ranged in a crescent formation in the deeper water at the northern end of the shoal. By the time the *Revenge* and *Valiant* joined the fray the thunderous boom of broadsides could be heard for miles around and dense clouds of grey gun smoke were swirling among the embattled ships and drifting across the estuary. It was an unequal contest. The French had difficulty in bringing their broadside guns to bear and had to rely on firing their stern chasers. For two hours they kept up a gallant resistance but they were taking heavy losses and at 5.30 p.m. both ships surrendered. The *Tonnerre* was so far on the reef that she was out of range of the British guns. Unable to haul her into deeper water her crew decided to set her on fire and take to the boats. They rowed across to the safety of the Ile Madame, a mile and a half away to the south-east. At around 7.30 the *Tonnerre* blew up, and at 8.30 the *Calcutta*, which had been slowly burning for several hours, also exploded. The *Calcutta* had been the storeship for the French fleet and was carrying large quantities of ammunition in addition to her own magazine. An eyewitness on board the *Valiant* described the resulting explosion as 'the most terrific and sublime spectacle the human mind could contemplate or the eye survey without emotions of terror!'.[12]

The heavy bombardment of the grounded French ships had encouraged Lord Gambier to send in more reinforcements under the command of Rear-Admiral Stopford. At 5.30 p.m. a flotilla consisting

The boarding and taking of the Spanish xebec frigate *El Gamo* by His Majesty's sloop *Speedy*, commanded by Captain Lord Cochrane, after a close action off Barcelona on 6 May 1801. Engraving after the picture by Nicholas Pocock.

Boats being launched from the *Thames* during the action off Gibraltar on 12 July 1801 between British squadron under Saumarez and the French squadron which had captured the *Speedy* a few days before. Pen and wash drawing by Pierre Ozanne.

A portrait of Cochrane's uncle, Admiral the Hon. Sir Alexander Cochrane. Engraving after the portrait by Sir William Beechey.

A portrait of the gallant Captain Jahleel Brenton, who preceded Cochrane as commander of the *Speedy*.

A multiple launching of warships at Plymouth on 17 November 1804. Cochrane's frigate *Pallas* and the frigate *Circe* are shown with their launching flags in the middle distance. The ship entering the water on the right is the *Hibernia*, 120 guns.

The Right Hon. Lord Collingwood, Vice-Admiral of the Red, from an engraving of 1806 after the picture by Bowyer.

Admiral Sir Edward Thornborough, who was Cochrane's commanding officer during his coastal raids. Portrait by Samuel Lane.

n aquatint after Nicholas Pocock showing the closing stages of the action on 14 May 1806,
hen Cochrane's *Pallas* attacked the French 40-gun frigate *Minerve* (on the left of the picture)
ithin sight of the anchored French fleet.

Aquatint after the picture by Robert Dodd described as 'The attack on the Enemy's Fleet by Fire Ships on the Night of the 11th April 1809'. The fire ship *Mediator* is shown breaking the boom and heading for the anchored French ships.

Cochrane's *Imperieuse*, followed by other British frigates, advances to attack the grounded French ships on the morning of 12 April 1809. Aquatint after the picture by Robert Dodd.

A portrait of Admiral Lord Gambier by Joseph Slater. Gambier was in command of the British fleet at Basque Roads in April 1809.

A cartoon which expresses the popular view of the Basque Roads action and Lord Gambier's court martial. Cochrane and a British sailor burst into Gambier's cabin and demand action against the French fleet.

Lord Ellenborough, Lord Chief Justice of the Court of King's Bench, who presided over the Stock Exchange trial. Engraving after the portrait by Sir Thomas Lawrence.

The principal entrance of the King's Bench Prison in Southwark, where Cochrane was imprisoned. Behind the high wall topped with spikes was a large courtyard. Engraving after the drawing by Thomas H. Shepherd.

General José de San Martin, who led the armies that liberated Chile and Peru from the colonial rule of Spain. He became Protector of Peru in 1821.

A portrait of the young Pedro I, Emperor of Brazil, who was a friend and supporter of Cochrane. Engraving after the picture by Jean Baptiste Reville.

The two principal ships of the Greek Navy under Cochrane's command: the American-built frigate *Hellas* on the left of the picture, and the steam warship *Karteria* (formerly the *Perseverance*). Engraving by Steingrubel after the picture by Krazeisen.

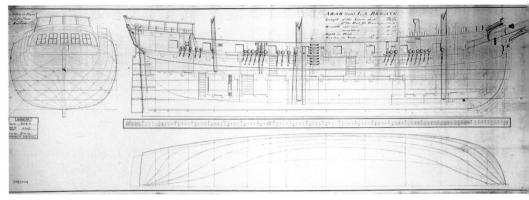

The lines of the *Arab*, 22 guns, formerly the French privateer *La Brave*, which had been captured by the British in 1798. Cochrane took command of her in 1803 and described his cruises in her as 'naval exile in a tub'.

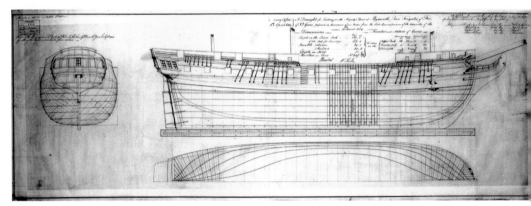

The lines of the two 32-gun frigates *Pallas* and the *Circe*, which were built at Plymouth and launched on 17 November 1804. Cochrane's cruises in the *Pallas* off the Azores in 1805 earned him a fortune in prize money.

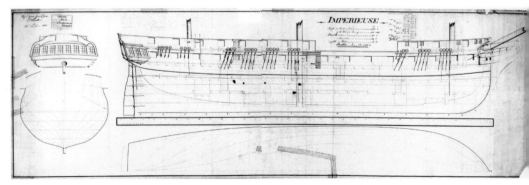

The lines of the frigate *Imperieuse*, of 38 guns, which under Cochrane's command became one of the greatest of all coastal raiders. Built in Spain, she was formerly the *Medea*, flagship of Admiral Bustamente, and had been captured in a controversial action off Cadiz in October 1804

of three fireships, the 74-gun ship *Theseus* and Stopford's 80-gun flagship *Caesar* set sail and headed for Aix Roads. The *Caesar*'s gunner, William Richardson, found the gun batteries on the Ile d'Aix to be as ineffective as Cochrane had reckoned they would be: 'In passing the Aix batteries,' Richardson wrote later, 'where our French pilots had said there were as many guns as days in the year, we could not find above thirteen guns that could be directed against us in passing; and these we thought so little of that we did not return their fire, although they fired pretty smartly at us too with shot and shells, which made the water splash against the ship's side . . .'[13] But at 7.40 p.m., just as they were drawing clear of the Aix batteries, the *Caesar* ran firmly aground on the Boyart Shoal on the south side of the approach channel to the Aix anchorage. They were now a sitting target for the gun batteries on the Ile d'Oléron as well as long shots from the Ile d'Aix. The ship began to heel as the tide fell but the gathering darkness saved them from the French guns. Richardson described how they jettisoned thirty tons of water to lighten the ship and ran the after guns forward to bring her more on an even keel. They had a grandstand view of the blowing up of the *Calcutta* which was only half a mile away. 'Fortunately none of her fiery timbers fell on board our ship: everything went upwards, with such a field of red fire as illuminated the whole elements.'[14] The *Caesar* floated off with the rising tide at 10.30 p.m. and they anchored her in deeper water. The fireship attack had to be abandoned because by midnight the wind was no longer favourable as it was blowing from the south-west.

The extremely low water caused by the spring tides was causing difficulties for other British ships as well as for the French. The *Imperieuse* and the frigate *Indefatigable* went aground for a while but both were afloat again by 9.30 p.m. Cochrane then sent the boats of the *Imperieuse* to take off the crews of the *Aquilon* and the *Ville de Varsovie*. It took several hours and was not helped by the weather which was blustery with squally rain showers. During this operation an incident occurred which was noted by several people because it demonstrated that Cochrane, in spite of the extreme hazards and dangers he had been exposed to, had luck on his side. The captain of the *Aquilon* had told Cochrane that he had left his personal possessions and charts behind on his ship. Cochrane volunteered to go back on board with him and collect them. As they left the *Aquilon* and were being rowed back towards the *Imperieuse*, a stray shot from a heated gun on the burning *Tonnerre* hit their boat. According to Cochrane the shot 'struck the stern sheets of the boat on which he and I were sitting, and lacerated the lower part of the gallant officer's body so severely that he shortly afterwards expired'.[15] Cochrane, who was sitting beside the French captain, was untouched.

At 3.00 a.m. Captain John Bligh, the commander of the *Valiant*, gave the order for the *Aquilon* and the *Ville de Varsovie* to be set on fire, a controversial decision which was later questioned by Cochrane and others who felt that the ships could have been floated off and retained as prizes; the *Ville de Varsovie* in particular was considered to be one of the finest two-deckers in the world. As the flames of the two burning ships illuminated the darkness of the estuary, some of the other grounded French ships opened fire on them, believing them to be more fireships sent in by the British.

By seven on the morning of 13 July the only British ships remaining in the vicinity of the Aix Road anchorage were the *Imperieuse*, the frigate *Pallas*, the bomb vessel *Aetna*, the brig sloop *Beagle* and eight smaller vessels. The ships of the line and the other frigates had headed back to join the fleet in Basque Roads in response to a signal of recall made by Rear-Admiral Stopford. Cochrane decided to ignore the signal on the grounds that it only applied to the ships that Gambier had sent to the assistance of the *Imperieuse*. There were still a number of French ships aground at the entrance of the River Charente, notably Allemand's flagship *Océan*. All these ships were at the mercy of an attacking force. Cochrane believed it was his duty, in accordance with the orders he had received from the First Lord of the Admiralty, to destroy what remained of the French fleet. The water was too shallow for the frigates to sail into the Charente (low tide was around 9.00 a.m.) so he ordered the *Aetna* and the other shallow-draft vessels to attack the *Océan*, the *Régulus* and the *Indienne*. At 11.00 a.m. the flotilla of small warships dropped anchor and opened fire. The demoralised crews of the grounded French warships found themselves bombarded by the shells of the *Aetna*, the guns of the *Beagle, Conflict, Contest, Encounter, Fervent* and *Growler,* and the rockets of the schooner *Whiting* and the cutters *Nimrod* and *King George.* According to some accounts Cochrane transferred to the *Aetna* and directed the action from the deck of the bomb vessel, but there is no mention of this in the logbooks of the *Aetna* or the *Imperieuse,* nor does he make any reference to it in his autobiography.[16]

For five hours the anchored British ships and the grounded French ships pounded away at each other. Casualties were surprisingly light during this phase of the action, probably because the shallowness of the water prevented the British gun brigs getting too close, while the rocket vessels and bomb vessel usually operated from a distance. However, the damage caused to the ships was considerable. An officer of the *Océan* later provided a detailed description of the state of the flagship:

> Our principal damages were: a shot cut our mizen mast through to the spindle, our boom cut half in two, 6 main shrouds cut through and 2 mizen shrouds, two chain plates cut away, our main top-sail yard cut through near the slings, two top-gallant yards cut to pieces. Many shot, fragments of shells, and fire-arrows (rockets) struck us, two poop carronades dismounted, all the stanchions and lockers of the cabin cut away, and the deck pierced by shot.[17]

Around midday the brig sloops *Dotterel, Foxhound* and *Redpole* anchored near the *Imperieuse* and one of them had a letter for Cochrane from Lord Gambier. The first part of the letter urged Cochrane to return to the fleet as soon as possible: 'You have done your part so admirably that I will not suffer you to tarnish it by attempting impossibilities.' Gambier explained that he needed information from Cochrane so that he could complete his despatches. The second part of the letter appeared to give Cochrane authority to continue his actions against the French ships: 'I have ordered three brigs and two rocket-vessels to join you, with which, and the bomb, you may make an attempt on the ship that is aground on the Palles, or towards the Ile Madame, but I do not think you will succeed.'[18]

Cochrane decided to overlook the first part of the letter and respond to the second. 'I have just had the honour to receive your Lordship's letter,' he wrote. 'We can destroy the ships that are on shore, which I hope your Lordship will approve of.'[19] He sent one of the brig sloops back to Gambier with his reply and at the same time sent a telegraph signal to the flagship, 'Can destroy the enemy.' By 4.00 p.m. the tide was running out fast and the *Aetna*, *Beagle* and other vessels had to abandon their bombardment of the French ships and make their way out of the Charente towards deeper water. Rain was now sweeping across the great estuary and a blustery wind was whipping up steep waves as the flotilla of small warships rounded the northern end of the Palles Shoal and headed for the *Imperieuse* which was anchored in the Maumusson Passage, an area of deep water to the south of the Boyart Shoal.

The morning of 14 April brought more rain and fresh gales from the west. At least four of the French warships had managed to heave themselves off the mud during the night and had proceeded up the Charente towards Rochefort. Those French ships which were still aground could be seen unloading guns and stores into local vessels lying alongside them. Cochrane was convinced that these ships, which included the flagship *Océan*, could still be destroyed but before he could organise another attack a boat came alongside with a second letter from Lord Gambier: 'It is necessary I should have some communica-tion with you before I close my despatches to the Admiralty. I have, therefore, ordered Captain Wolfe to relieve you in the services you are engaged in. I wish you to join me as soon as possible, that you may convey Sir Harry Neale to England, who will be charged with my despatches, or you may return to carry on the service where you are.'[20] While the last phrase was somewhat ambiguous, Cochrane had no option but to hand over operations to Captain Wolfe of the frigate *Aigle* and report to the flagship. That afternoon the *Imperieuse* weighed anchor, sailed out of Aix Roads with the ebb tide and joined the fleet.

In his autobiography Cochrane gives a colourful description of his encounter with Gambier in the great cabin of the *Caledonia*. He wrote that he 'told Lord Gambier that the extraordinary hesitation which had been displayed in attacking ships helplessly on shore, could only have arisen from my being employed in the attack, in preference to senior officers.'[21] He maintained that he urged Gambier to send in Admiral Stopford with frigates and other vessels to rectify the situation, because it would be impossible, as matters stood, to prevent a noise being made in England. 'His Lordship appeared much displeased; and making no remark, I repeated, "My Lord, you have before desired me to speak candidly to you, and I have now used that freedom." '[22] But according to the evidence of William James, who was Gambier's secretary, Cochrane said nothing of Gambier's conduct or misconduct and told the admiral that if the British ships had been despatched in response to his signal he calculated that three or four of them would have been lost.[23] Whatever was said, Gambier was impatient for his despatches to be sent on their way. He gave Cochrane written orders to proceed to England with Sir Harry Neale. The following morning, the *Imperieuse* made sail and stood out to sea. There was a heavy swell in the Bay of Biscay but with strong westerly winds they made rapid progress. In less than a week they sighted the Isle of Wight and on the morning of 21 April they ran through the Needles Passage and dropped anchor among the shipping at Spithead.

Lord Gambier remained at Basque Roads for two more weeks. The weather for the first week was atrocious with gales and driving rain which hampered further operations against the enemy and gave the French crews time to get three of their ships afloat and safely up the river to Rochefort. The captain of the *Indienne*, having failed to float his ship, set her alight on 16 April. By the beginning of the second week only the *Régulus* was still aground in the river near Fouras. The French officer of the *Océan*, who provided such a useful running commentary on events, noted on 19 April, 'The enemy continue in the Isle d'Aix road, to the number of 20 sail. They have not made any movement whatever for these three days: which is a thing not at all to be understood, for they might with ease attack the Régulus, and oblige her crew to abandon her.'[24]

On 20 and 24 April, Gambier ordered a flotilla of shallow-draft vessels, led by the bomb vessels *Aetna* and *Thunder*, to attack the *Régulus* but they failed to drive off her crew or cause serious damage to the ship. On 29 April the French finally got her afloat and sailed her upriver. The same day Gambier received orders to return to England and he sailed in the *Caledonia*, leaving Rear-Admiral Stopford, and a much reduced fleet, to keep watch on the enemy's movements.

Considering the size of the two fleets involved, and the quantity of shot, shells, rockets and fireships expended during a series of actions spread over two weeks, the net result of the Battle of Basque Roads was disappointing. Five French warships had been burnt and destroyed – two of them set on fire by their French crews to prevent them falling into British hands. An American deserter from the *Cassard* reported that three other warships were so damaged that they were to be cut down and converted into mortar vessels, and the master of a galliot reported that the frigate *Elbe* was condemned as a wreck.[25] The French had lost 200 men killed and 650 taken prisoner. The British casualties were ten men killed and thirty-seven wounded. If the battle had taken place at the beginning of the French wars it would have been regarded as a triumph on a level with the Battle of the Glorious First of June, but after Nelson's crushing victories at the Nile and Trafalgar, a mere victory by numbers would not do; nothing less than annihilation could be counted as a victory.

The bare figures of French losses fail to do justice to the audacity of the Basque Roads action and its effect on French morale. A French officer told his captors that 'they had now no security from the English in their harbours, and they expected we should next go into Brest and take out their fleet whenever it suited our convenience'.[26] Four of the French captains were put on trial. The court martial was held on board the flagship *Océan* at Rochefort, and exposed the full extent of the panic and confusion caused by the fireship attack and its aftermath. Captain Jean-Baptiste Lafon was found guilty of shamelessly abandoning the *Calcutta* in the presence of the enemy and was condemned to death. He was shot on the deck of the *Océan* at 4.00 p.m. on 9 September. Captain Lacaille was sentenced to two years in prison and Captain Proteau to three months. Captain Clément de la Roncière was found not guilty of the loss of the *Tonnerre* and was acquitted. Many years later, when he was in exile on St Helena, Napoleon was asked his views about Cochrane and the fireship attack. He was scathing about the panic-stricken reactions of the French crews but he also condemned Gambier for failing to support Cochrane as he ought to have done. 'The terror of the *brûlots* (fireships) was so great that they actually threw their powder overboard, so that they could have offered very little resistance. The French admiral was an *imbécile*, but yours was just as bad. I assure you that if Cochrane had been supported he would have taken every one of the ships.'[27]

Of all the ups and downs of Cochrane's life, the fireship attack at Basque Roads must rank as the high point. It was his greatest single exploit as a naval commander and it brought him honours and international fame. The boldness of the attack on a powerful enemy in an apparently impregnable position was comparable with the exploits of Drake, de Ruyter and Nelson. And yet the action at Basque Roads has come to be regarded as a wasted opportunity, a bungled and confused affair, and has been relegated to little more than a footnote in naval history. There is even confusion about the name of the action which is variously called the Battle of Aix Roads, or the Battle of Basque Roads, or simply Basque Roads, 1809 – the latter is probably the most accurate as it was not a battle in the usual sense of the word. Whatever the name, it became for Cochrane a lasting source of bitterness, largely due to his own handling of the outcome of the action and the resulting court martial of his commander-in-chief, Lord Gambier. Instead of enjoying his triumph he became embroiled in a controversy which made him more enemies among the naval high command. It was to prove one more step on the path to his downfall.

THIRTEEN

The Court Martial of Lord Gambier

1809

Within five hours of the arrival of the *Imperieuse* at Spithead the Admiralty had received Lord Gambier's despatches and the following day, 22 April, *The Times* published a report which began:
'GLORIOUS NAVAL EXPLOIT: Yesterday, about two o'clock, Sir Harry Neale, first captain of the Fleet under Lord Gambier, arrived at the Admiralty with an account of the partial destruction of the French fleet in Basque Roads.' This was followed by a letter from the First Lord of the Admiralty, Lord Mulgrave, announcing that 'a successful attack was made by frigates, fire-ships, and bomb-vessels on the enemy's fleet in Basque Roads, under the immediate command of Captain Lord Cochrane, on the night of the 11th inst.' The text of Gambier's despatch was printed in its entirety and the newspaper's editorial comment probably reflected the thoughts of many British people at a low point in the long war with Napoleonic France: 'We have neither time nor space to comment on the above glorious action; suffice it to say, therefore, it is not only worthy of a place in the annals of the British Navy, but has likewise occurred, like some of our other victories, at a most peculiarly fortunate crisis, namely at the commencement of a fresh Austrian war. It will give spirit to our Allies, and we sincerely hope is a happy indication of a change in the fortunes of our adversaries.'[1]

The past six months had brought bad news from the Continent. The Spanish rebellion had prompted Napoleon to take personal charge of the French army in Spain. He had defeated a Spanish force at Trudela, entered Madrid in triumph on 4 December 1808 and then headed north-west with an army of 250,000 men. Sir John Moore, in command of the British Army in Spain, had only 30,000 men at his disposal and had no option but to retreat over the mountains to the coast. He lost 6,000 men during the forced march across the mountains of Galicia in the bitter cold of winter but fought a heroic rearguard action at Corunna on 16 January 1809. This gained sufficient time for his exhausted troops to embark on the waiting transport ships and sail for England. Sir John Moore was killed during the action, his death later commemorated in Charles Wolfe's evocative poem 'The Burial of Sir John Moore after Corunna' which begins, 'Not a drum was heard, not a funeral note, / As his corse to the rampart we hurried.' Within days Napoleon was back in Paris and by April he was assembling another army to attack Austria.

The last major battle by the British navy had been back in February 1806 when Sir John Duckworth had defeated a French squadron off the West Indian island of San Domingo. Cochrane's uncle Alexander, who was commander-in-chief on the Leeward Islands station, had played a key role in the victory. Gambier's bombardment of Copenhagen in 1807, which led to the surrender of the Danish fleet, was a fleet action but not a sea battle in the usual sense of the term. Since then most of Britain's warships had been occupied with the essential but unrewarding tasks of escorting convoys of merchant ships, safeguarding Britain's overseas possessions and keeping watch on the French naval bases. The escape of the French squadron from Brest in February 1809 had been an alarming development but Gambier's despatch from Basque Roads meant that there was no longer an immediate threat to Britain's West Indian colonies.

As the news of the fireship attack circulated, a war-weary nation indulged in the sort of celebrations which had not been seen for four years. Bonfires were lit, public buildings illuminated and patriotic ballads hastily compiled, printed and circulated. One such ballad ran:

We poured in our shot and our rockets like hail
Till at length that their courage began for to fail,
Some were taken and destroyed, and some got on shore,
The rest ran up harbour and would fight no more.
With the chorus:
So success to our sailors that sail on the sea,
Who with COCHRANE undaunted, whenever they're wanted,
They'll fight till they die, or gain victory.[2]

The Amphitheatre at Westminster Bridge staged a dramatic performance every night in which the *Imperieuse*, 'and her undaunted commander, the brave Lord Cochrane', was depicted discharging her guns at the panic-stricken enemy while the house shook to repeated applause. It was reported that 'the attack and burning of the Gallic fleet surpasses anything of the kind ever witnessed'.[3] The naval officers who had distinguished themselves at Basque Roads were rewarded with promotions: the commanders of the brig sloops *Beagle* and *Redpole*, and the bomb vessels *Aetna* and *Thunder*, became post-captains; twelve of the lieutenants who had been in charge of fireships or explosion vessels were promoted to the rank of commander and their crews received £10 each.[4] James Wooldridge, who had so courageously guided the leading fireship *Mediator* on to the boom, and been badly burnt when he and his crew were blown overboard, was singled out for special reward: in addition to promotion to post-captain, he received a gold medal from the king and was given a presentation sword from the Patriotic Fund. Cochrane, who was everywhere recognised as the hero of the action, was made a Knight of the Bath. This was an honour usually reserved for admirals and generals and it had seldom been awarded to naval captains in the past. There were only thirty-six Knights of the Bath at any one time and these included Cochrane's old enemy Lord St Vincent who had been made a KB when, as captain of the *Foudroyant*, 80, he had captured a French 74-gun ship in a single-ship action off Brest in 1782.

Within days of the news of the Basque Roads action reaching

London, however, doubts were being expressed about the extent of the damage inflicted on the French fleet. A letter published in *The Times* on 25 April noted that Lord Cochrane's signal to the admiral of the fleet indicated that seven of the enemy's ships were on shore and might be destroyed. 'The question which hereupon naturally suggests itself to the mind is, "Why then, if seven might be destroyed, were there only four?"' It was not long before rumours were going round that Cochrane was critical of the conduct of his commander-in-chief and would be voicing his opinions in the House of Commons. William Wordsworth told his friend Thomas de Quincey that he had not seen the private accounts about Lord Cochrane but his own feeling was that 'that noble Hero would be greatly disappointed in the result; and I strongly suspected that, if the matter were investigated, heavy blame would be attached to Gambier for not having his ships where they could be brought up in time. Nothing effectual can be done in cases of this sort without considerable risk: excessive caution in such cases is cowardice.'[5]

The doubts about Gambier's conduct were given a more public airing during the court martial of Rear-Admiral Eliab Harvey which was held at Portsmouth on 22 May and was later reported in the newspapers. Most of the proceedings were devoted to Harvey's outburst on board the *Caledonia*. The assembled court heard how Harvey had threatened to impeach Gambier for misconduct and bad management and had told Sir Harry Neale and Lord Cochrane that Gambier was unfit to command the fleet; that instead of carrying out a reconnaissance of the enemy's position he had amused himself mustering the ships' companies; and that 'if Lord Nelson had been there he would not have anchored the Fleet in Basque Roads but have dashed at the Enemy at once'.[6] The court listened to the evidence and concluded that the charges against Harvey for treating his commanding officer in an insulting manner were proved. He was ordered to be dismissed from His Majesty's service. He was later to be reinstated on the strength of his past record but he was never again employed at sea.

Harvey's court martial fuelled the gossip concerning Gambier's failure to follow up the fireship attack but it was Cochrane who brought matters to a head. On learning from Lord Mulgrave that there was to be a formal vote of thanks given to Gambier in the House of Commons, he warned that in his capacity as a Member of Parliament he would oppose any such proposal. Mulgrave did his best to dissuade him but in vain. The Admiralty wrote to Cochrane demanding to be informed of the grounds of his complaint. Cochrane simply referred the Admiralty Board to the logs and signal books of the fleet but the damage had been done. Gambier had no alternative but to demand a court martial in order to clear his name.

The court martial was held on board the *Gladiator*, once a 44-gun ship but now a hulk moored in Portsmouth harbour and the setting for a number of courts martial, including that of Admiral Harvey in May. The proceedings began on 26 July. The charge against Gambier was that on the twelfth day of April, 'the enemy's ships being then on shore, and the signal having been made that they could be destroyed, did for a considerable time neglect or delay taking effectual measures for destroying them'.[7] All the relevant letters and despatches were produced as evidence, together with the logs and charts of Basque Roads. Cochrane was cross-examined at length but the regulations governing the conduct of courts martial prevented him from questioning any of the other witnesses and excluded him from the court when Gambier's defence was presented. In addition to Cochrane and Gambier, the court cross-examined sixteen of the captains who had been with the fleet, five of the ships' masters, the signal lieutenant and signal mate of the *Caledonia*, and Gambier's secretary, James Wilkinson. A notable absentee was Captain Frederick Maitland, the Scottish captain of the frigate *Emerald* which had played a significant part in the action on 12 April. According to several commentators Maitland and his ship were despatched to the Irish station because he was known to be critical of Gambier's conduct.[8]

The President of the court at Gambier's trial was Admiral Sir Roger Curtis. As commander-in-chief at Portsmouth he was the obvious choice for the role but this was unfortunate for Cochrane because he was a friend of Gambier. Equally unfortunate was the fact that the second most senior officer present was Admiral William Young, another of Gambier's friends, who had served with him as a Lord of the Admiralty from 1795 to 1801. While port admiral at Plymouth he had ordered the *Imperieuse* to sea before she was ready and Cochrane had later denounced him in Parliament for endangering his ship and his crew. Young gained his revenge during the court martial by subjecting Cochrane to hostile questioning and by frequently interrupting him when he was giving his evidence. The third officer present was Vice-Admiral Sir John Duckworth, a tough and experienced fighting seaman who was not popular among the men he commanded. Three other vice-admirals, a rear-admiral and four senior captains completed the heavyweight panel of naval officers seated in the great cabin of the *Gladiator*.

What the court martial had to establish was whether, given the state of the wind and tide and depth of water during the morning of 12 April, Gambier should have sent in his line-of-battle ships sooner, or whether such an action would have resulted in the wanton destruction of the ships. When Cochrane was called in to the great cabin he began by consulting notes he had prepared earlier but these were ruled out of order. Without his notes Cochrane's answers to many of the questions were confused and long-winded and put him at the mercy of Admiral Young. Asked whether the frigates alone were sufficient to destroy the enemy's ships between eleven and one o'clock, he replied that when he saw the British fleet weigh and stand towards the enemy and then anchor again he presumed that Gambier had delayed his attack to give the seamen time to have something to eat and drink. Sir Roger Curtis told him this was not an answer to his question.

'If, when it is written,' Cochrane said, 'it shall appear not an answer to the question, then I humbly submit it may be struck out.'

'Yes,' Admiral Young pointed out, 'but if the court is of the opinion their time is taken up with any thing which is not relevant, they may I apprehend stop it, when they see that which you are saying has no sort of connection; they may I conceive determine whether it shall be taken.'

'I apprehend that cannot be seen till the court see what it is I am about to say,' Cochrane said and he explained that although he regretted the fleet's delay in attacking, 'yet I consoled myself by the supposition that his Lordship intended a grand blow on the island and the ships at once, although I thought this neither necessary in order to effect their destruction or prudent with the whole fleet; I could not in any other way account for a proceeding that thus enabled the helpless French ships to endeavour their escape undisturbed to the River Charente: twelve o'clock arrived, no signal was made to weigh anchor; half past twelve, still no signal . . .' He was interrupted by Admiral Young.

'This is really very improper; this has no sort of connection whatever with the question which is asked, and is only a series of observations to the disadvantage of the prisoner.'

'I wish to speak the truth, the whole truth and nothing but the truth.'

'This really has nothing at all to do with the question which is asked of you, which arises merely out of the statement which you have made.'[9]

The cross-examination continued in this manner and concluded with questions about the charts consulted during the action. These were to prove a crucial element in Gambier's defence. Cochrane and Captain Broughton of the *Illustrious* had both used copies of the *Neptune François*, the French chart of the anchorage. This showed the width of the approach channel between the Ile d'Aix and the Boyart Shoal to be more than two miles across, with a depth of water of thirty-five feet at low water off the Boyart. It also showed an area to the south of the approach channel (the Maumusson Passage) where at least six ships of the line could anchor out of range of the guns on the Ile d'Aix. Cochrane was told, 'This chart is not evidence before the court because his Lordship cannot prove it is accurate', and it was therefore ruled to be inadmissible. In its place the court relied on charts drawn up by Mr Stokes, the master of the *Caledonia*, and by Edmund Fairfax, the master of the fleet. These showed the approach channel to be barely a mile wide and the depth to be considerably less than that shown on the *Neptune François*. Cochrane would later come to the conclusion that Stokes and Fairfax had fabricated the details on their charts to support Gambier's defence. This may have been the case but the naval historian John Sugden has suggested another explanation. Fairfax based the outlines of his chart on a French chart taken from the *Armide* and he may have used the wrong scale to convert the French measurements into British nautical miles.[10] But based on the evidence of the Stokes and Fairfax charts Gambier had every reason to be reluctant to send in his line-of-battle ships along a narrow channel with the almost certain risk that they would run aground and be at the mercy of the guns of the Ile d'Aix.

The majority of the captains supported Gambier. Since advancement in the navy depended to a large extent on the recommendation of senior officers it would have been foolhardy to criticise a commander-in-chief in front of his fellow admirals. Only four captains – Broughton, Seymour, Malcolm and Newcombe – were prepared to question the actions of Gambier. Captain Broughton had been within gunshot of the fortifications on the Ile d'Aix and reckoned there were only between fourteen and twenty guns commanding the roadstead and no furnaces for heating shot. 'I think it would have been more advantageous if the line-of-battle ships, frigates and small vessels had gone in at half flood, which I take to be about 11 o'clock.' He added that his French chart showed a safe anchorage with thirty to forty feet of water out of range of shot and shells in any direction. And he thought that two sail of the line would be quite sufficient to silence the batteries of the Ile d'Aix.[11]

Captain Seymour likewise thought that ships of the line should have been sent in sooner and confirmed that there was ample anchorage out of range of the enemy guns. For four days the court closely questioned the naval officers present about the depth of water in the anchorage, the direction of the tide at critical moments in the action and the range of the guns on the Ile d'Aix. After a break on Sunday 30 July, the court reassembled and Gambier's defence was read for him by the Judge Advocate. His carefully argued case takes up thirty-four pages of the printed minutes of the court martial. He concluded his evidence by stating that, if he had acted on Cochrane's signals, 'I am firmly persuaded that the success attending this achievement would have proved more dearly bought than any yet recorded in our naval annals; and far from accomplishing the hopes of my country, or the expectations of the Admiralty, must have disappointed both.'[12]

After sitting for nine days the court retired to consider its verdict and on 4 August came to the conclusion that the conduct of Lord Gambier 'was marked by zeal, judgment, and ability, and an anxious attention to the welfare of His Majesty's service'.[13] He was honourably acquitted and Sir Roger Curtis handed him back his sword which had lain on the table throughout the trial. There is a brief and embittered account of the proceedings in Cochrane's autobiography. In his view the object of the court martial was 'the suppression and invalidation of my evidence by any means that could be brought to bear, rather than an inquiry into the conduct of the commander-in-chief on the merits of the case'.[14] A careful reading of the minutes of the court martial confirms that this was indeed the case. In the circumstances this was not surprising. Cochrane was regarded as a loose cannon by many senior admirals. He had upset several of them by his attacks in Parliament on naval corruption, and he had alienated others by his support of the radicals who were regarded as unpatriotic and a danger to the established order. He had a glittering record as a frigate captain but that did not give him the right to question the actions of his commander-in-chief. Inevitably the naval establishment closed ranks and sided with the admiral against the junior captain.

Every detail of Lord Gambier's court martial had been reported in the newspapers and *The Times* had even included a map of Basque Roads showing the position of the ships. The news of Gambier's acquittal was received with considerable satisfaction by his fellow admirals. 'It will be a lesson to restless and inexperienced young officers not to hazard a mischievous opinion tending to weaken the respect and confidence due to able and tried officers – particularly to commanders-in-chief,' wrote Admiral Bowen,[15] and even Collingwood, who had been unstinting in his praise of Cochrane's exploits in the Mediterranean, prayed for release from such 'wrongheaded people'. Gambier's friends were equally delighted. William Wilber-force, founder of the Church Missionary Society and a leading campaigner against the slave trade, heard the news as he was returning from church in Eastbourne and sent his congratulations, 'animated with a grateful sense of the Goodness of Him who has established your righteous cause'.[16] The most damning comment on Cochrane and his radical friends came from Hannah More, a promi-nent member of the Blue Stocking Society, and a prolific author of religious tracts. In a letter to Gambier's uncle, Lord Barham, she wrote, 'What a tempestuous world do we live in! Yet terrible as Buonaparte is in every point of view, I do not fear him so much as those domestic mischiefs – Burdett, Cochrane, Wardle, and Cobbett. I hope, however, that the mortification Cochrane, &c., have lately experienced in their base and impotent endeavours to pull down reputations which they found unassailable, will keep them down a little.'[17]

It was around this time that Cochrane acquired a property in Hampshire – a small house called Holly Hill which he had bought from his uncle Basil Cochrane.[18] It was situated in the village of Titchfield near Fareham and was conveniently close to Portsmouth and the fleet anchorage at Spithead. It was also close to the home of his friend William Cobbett. In July 1805 Cobbett had bought a tall, red-brick house at Botley with three acres of land and lawns which swept down to the River Hamble. Cobbett and his wife Nancy were sociable and welcoming, and the house was always full of children, guests and visiting friends. There is a vivid and much-quoted passage in the recollections of the novelist Mary Russell Mitford which describes a visit she made to Botley with her father Dr George Mitford, a man about town who shared Cobbett's love of country pursuits.

'I never saw hospitality more genuine, more simple or more thoroughly successful in the great end of hospitality, the putting of everybody at ease,' she wrote. 'There was not the slightest attempt at finery or display or gentility. They called it a farm-house and every-thing was in accordance with the largest idea of the great English yeomen of the old time. Everything was excellent, everything abundant, all served with the greatest nicety by trim waiting damsels.' Guests came and went and included an earl and his countess, a clergyman with his wife and daughter, and two literary gentlemen from London.

'Lord Cochrane was there, then in the very height of his warlike fame, and as unlike the common notion of a warrior as could be. A gentle, mild young man was this burner of the French fleets and cutter-out of Spanish vessels, as one should see in a summer-day. He lay about under the trees reading Selden on the Dominion of the Seas, and letting the children (and children always know with whom they may take liberties) play all sorts of tricks with him at their pleasure.' We then learn that James Guthrie was present. 'His ship's surgeon was also a visitor, and a young midshipman, and sometimes an elderly lieutenant, and a Newfoundland dog; fine sailor-like creatures all.'[19]

For Cobbett this idyllic, pastoral existence came to an abrupt halt during the summer of 1810. For several months he had known that his enemies were determined to prosecute him for his outspoken attacks on the royal family, the church and the government, and for revealing numerous cases of injustice and corruption. When he learnt that five soldiers in Ely had been flogged with five hundred lashes each for mutiny he took up their cause and wrote a damning piece about the floggings in his *Weekly Political Register*.[20] This proved the last straw for the government and he was brought to trial before Lord Ellenborough, the Lord Chief Justice. He was accused of inciting the troops to further mutiny and holding the government and constitution up to contempt. On 9 July he was sentenced to imprisonment and a fine of £1,000 and spent the next two years in Newgate Prison.

While Cochrane was being put in his place by the admirals at Portsmouth, his ship was taking part in a venture which would prove to be one of the most humiliating fiascos of the war. On 30 July the *Imperieuse*, with Thomas Garth as her acting captain, set sail from the anchorage at the Downs with a vast fleet of warships and transports. The aim was to occupy the island of Walcheren at the mouth of the River Scheldt and destroy the dockyards at Flushing and Antwerp which were building warships for the French navy. The Walcheren expedition was a joint services operation, the army providing 29,715 infantry soldiers and 8,219 cavalry, and the navy supplying 37 ships of the line, 24 frigates, 70 smaller warships and 400 transports.[21] Such a force should have been overwhelming and indeed Flushing surrendered on 15 August after being subjected to more than two days of heavy bombardment by the fleet. According to Marryat, 'a tremendous roar was kept up with shell, shot, rockets and musketry, enough to tear the place to pieces'.[22] But then other forces came into play. The strong tides and numerous mud banks of the Scheldt caused frequent groundings and delays, and while the army commander Lord Chatham dithered, hundreds of soldiers and sailors succumbed to mosquito-borne malaria, or 'Walcheren fever', which was endemic in some of the canals and waterways. The *Imperieuse* had a brief moment of glory when she attacked a gun battery at Terneuze. She used the carronades on her foredeck to fire shrapnel shells. These were a recent invention by Lieutenant-General Shrapnel and consisted of cases filled with bullets and an explosive charge fired by a time fuse. By a lucky chance one of the shells exploded in the enemy's magazine causing 3,000 barrels of gunpowder to blow up. But Antwerp proved to be too strongly defended and by the end of August a decision was made to abandon the expedition. Troops and ships were belatedly evacuated during October and November and the remnants of the fleet finally put to sea on 23 December, by which time around 4,000 men had died and more than 10,000 were ill with fever.

Cochrane had offered the Admiralty the benefit of his advice on the Walcheren expedition (he had, among other things, suggested sending in ten explosion vessels) but his advice was not taken. He devoted much of the autumn of 1809 to preparing a detailed examination of the evidence which had led to Gambier's acquittal. His bitterness and determination to revenge himself is revealed in a letter he wrote to James Guthrie. Writing from London on 15 December he promised to come and see Guthrie and the crew of the *Imperieuse* when they

returned from Walcheren. His opening remarks about a boat he was
having built at Deal make it clear that he still intended to resume
command of the *Imperieuse* in due course and continue his raids on the
French coast:

> You will see at Harrisons the Builder who made my former Gig a noble
> boat on the Stocks 50 feet keel and 6½ broad – she will pull like the Devil
> and if I get to the Rochefort station in the spring the wine vessels will
> suffer severely – she will answer excellently to go up the Garonne to
> Verdun Roads at night.
>
> I have got the review of Gambiers Court Martial quite finished but <u>ruin,
> inevitable damnation</u> hangs over both the Court and the Witnesses – all of
> whom fall under the penalty attendant on perjury, except Broughton,
> Malcolm, Newcombe, and Seymour. I have a great mind to prosecute them
> all as soon as my pamphlet is out. It will kick up a noble row. What a base
> pack of rascals they are! I have got their bollocks in a cloven stick and I will
> squeeze them.
>
> I send this letter to Deal where I suppose the Conquerors of Walcheren
> will first anchor. I long to hear the story from you.'[23]

His efforts to reverse the decision of the court martial only stirred
up more opposition against him. When Parliament assembled in
January 1810 a motion to propose the long-delayed vote of thanks
to Lord Gambier was introduced in the House of Lords. Cochrane
attempted to block the vote by introducing a motion of his own in the
House of Commons. On 29 January he asked for the minutes of
Gambier's court martial to be presented to Parliament. He wanted to
initiate a debate on the conduct of the proceedings and hoped to put his
point of view more forcibly than he had been able to do at Portsmouth.
His motion was supported by Joseph Marryat, the father of Cochrane's
midshipman, and by his political allies, including Sir Francis Burdett
and Samuel Whitbread.

'Lord Gambier's plan,' Burdett was reported as saying, 'seemed a
desire to preserve the fleet – Cochrane's plan, to destroy the enemy's
fleet. He had never heard that the Articles of War held out an

instruction to preserve the fleet. What if Nelson, at the Nile or Trafalgar, had acted on this principle?'

As a judgement on the Basque Roads action this reflects the views of most naval historians[24] but in the Parliament of 1810 Cochrane and his friends were in a minority. William Wilberforce spoke for many when he pointed out that to ask for the minutes would be to throw a stigma on all the members of the court martial. Cochrane's motion was amended so that only the sentence of the court was laid before the House. This was agreed and passed. Since the sentence honourably acquitted Gambier and praised his zeal and judgement, this was a total vindication of the commander-in-chief at the expense of his accuser. During the debate on the vote of thanks Cochrane was subjected to considerable personal abuse and the result was a foregone conclusion. The vote of thanks to Gambier was passed by 161 votes to 39 in January 1810.

Cochrane had been soundly defeated by the naval high command and by the political establishment but he had considerable support outside Parliament. Jane Austen's naval brother, Captain Francis Austen, writing to Cochrane many years later, expressed the view of many seamen: 'I must in conscience declare that I do not think you were properly supported, and that had you been the result would have been very different. Much of what occurred I attribute to Lord Gambier's being influenced by persons about him who would have been ready to sacrifice the honour of their country to the gratification of personal dislike of yourself, and the annoyance they felt at a junior officer being employed in their service.'[25]

The popular view of the Basque Roads affair was summarised in a satirical cartoon typical of the age of Cruikshank and Gillray. Published in August 1809 it showed Gambier sitting in his cabin reading a passage from Sternhold and Hopkins' edition of the psalms. A sailor warns Gambier that they had better throw some shells at the French fleet and Cochrane, with his sword drawn, says, 'Why Admiral, Damn their eyes they'll escape if we don't make haste.' Gambier's chaplain raises his hands in horror: 'Oh the wicked dog he has put us quite out, he is insensible of the beauties of Divine Poetry.'

Cochrane now turned his energies to a variety of other causes: to supporting his radical friends in and out of Parliament; to attacking naval abuses and revealing corruption in the Vice-Admiralty Courts; and to courting and marrying a woman young enough to be his daughter.

FOURTEEN

Riots and Romance

1809–1814

The dismal failure of the Walcheren expedition had a number of dramatic consequences. The first was that George Canning, the Foreign Secretary, fought a duel with Lord Castlereagh, Secretary for War and the Colonies. There had been fierce disagreements between the two men over foreign policy, and the recriminations over Walcheren led Castlereagh to throw down a challenge to his bitter rival. The duel was fought with pistols at ten paces on Putney Heath early on the morning of 21 September 1809. Their first shots missed but when they fired a second time Canning was hit in the thigh. His nankeen trousers were soaked with blood and he was hurried away in a coach. Castlereagh suffered no more than the loss of a button which was shot off the right lapel of his coat. Canning soon recovered but both men resigned from the government. With his administration in disarray and deeply unpopular, the strain proved too much for the Prime Minister, the elderly Duke of Portland, who suffered a seizure while travelling to his country residence in Buckinghamshire. He resigned his office and died on 30 October. His place was taken by Spencer Perceval, who had been Chancellor of the Exchequer in the Portland administration.

In February 1810 a House of Commons committee was set up to enquire into the conduct of the Walcheren expedition but the new ministry decided to exclude the public from the meetings to prevent the full extent of military incompetence from coming out into the open. This angered the radicals of Westminster, particularly John Gale Jones, an earnest apothecary who was secretary of a debating society in Covent Garden called the British Forum. He posted hand-bills on the walls around Westminister protesting against this in-fringement of democracy. He was arrested and thrown into Newgate Prison without trial. On 12 March, Sir Francis Burdett stood up in Parliament and denounced his imprisonment as an infringement of Magna Carta. When his motion was defeated Burdett published his speech in *Cobbett's Weekly Political Register*, together with a passionate address to the electors of Westminister. The House of Commons judged this to be a breach of privilege and ordered Burdett to be arrested and sent to the Tower of London.

There followed several days of disorderly scenes in which Cochrane played an active part. As news of Burdett's impending arrest spread, a mob of radical sympathisers gathered outside Burdett's house and pelted any passers-by with mud and garbage if they refused to shout 'Burdett for ever'. Crowds blocked the approaches to the Tower and violence broke out in Piccadilly, Albemarle Street and St James's Square. The windows in the houses of Lord Castlereagh, Spencer Perceval and other prominent figures were smashed, and some houses were broken into and vandalised. Bearing in mind the Gordon Riots of 1780 and the more recent horrors of the French Revolution, the government took drastic action. The guns of the Tower of London were mounted and made ready, and the moat was flooded; a battery of artillery was drawn up in Berkeley Square; and the Horse Guards, the Foot Guards and the 15th Light Dragoons were ordered to stand by. Piccadilly was the scene of several cavalry charges by the Horse Guards until some enterprising members of the crowd blocked the road with ladders from a nearby building site.[1]

Barricaded in his house, Sir Francis Burdett held several meetings with Francis Place and other radical leaders. Cochrane was present at some of these meetings but on Sunday 8 April he decided it was time for action. He arrived in a coach with a cask of gunpowder and was let into Burdett's house by the porter. Some writers have asserted that he started to hack away at the front wall of the house with the intention of preparing a man trap along the lines of the one he had devised for the defence of Fort Trinidad. According to Henry Hunt, he did not get that far but simply told Burdett and his friends that he proposed to undermine the foundations of the front wall and deposit the gunpowder there 'so that he might blow the invaders to the devil'. Burdett was horrified at the proposal and said he had no intention of violently resisting arrest. Hunt tells us, 'The gallant tar then retired, apparently very much disconcerted, and he was particularly requested to take away with him the cask of gunpowder which he did immediately.'[2] Early the next morning the serjeant at arms and his attendants broke into the house through a servant's window, arrested Burdett and drove him off to the Tower where he remained in custody until parliament was dissolved on 21 June. For the rest of the session Cochrane represented Burdett in Parliament and presented a petition protesting against his imprisonment which was signed by his constituents.

Not content with identifying himself with the radicals who were now, more than ever, regarded as enemies of the state, Cochrane embarked on a crusade to expose abuses and injustices in the system of naval pensions. In doing so he targeted and angered some of the most influential families in the land. His cause was admirable but his approach was too blunt to have any hope of reforming the system. On 11 May he stood up before a noisy House of Commons and let loose a barage of statistics. His purpose was to compare the pensions of officers (and the widows of officers) who had spent years at sea and risked their lives for their country with men and women who had lived comfortable lives ashore.

'An admiral, worn out in the service, is superannuated at £410 a year, a captain at £210,' he began, 'but a clerk of the ticket office retires on £700 a year! The widow of Admiral Sir Andrew Mitchell has one third of the allowance given to the widow of a commissioner of the navy!' He went on to point out that the thirteen daughters of admirals and captains who had died while on active service received a sum less than Dame Mary Saxton, the widow of a commissioner.

Expanding on this theme he listed the case of 'the brave Sir Samuel Hood, who lost his arm, has only £500, whilst the late Secretary of the Admiralty retires, in full health, on a pension of £1,500 per annum!' He calculated that the pensions of all the wounded officers of the whole British navy and the wives and children of those killed in action amounted to less that the sinecure of £20,358 paid to Lord Arden.

'Is this justice? Is this the treatment which the officers of the navy deserve at the hands of those who call themselves His Majesty's Government? Does the country know of this injustice? Will this too be defended? If I express myself with warmth I trust in the indulgence of the House. I cannot suppress my feelings.' He then launched an attack on the Wellesleys, the powerful family of the Duke of Wellington:

'I find upon examination that the Wellesleys receive from the public £34,729, a sum equal to 426 pairs of lieutenant's legs, calculated at the rate of allowance of Lieutenant Chambers' legs. Lord Arden's sinecure is equal to the value of 1022 captain's legs. The Marquis of Buckingham's sinecure alone will maintain the whole ordinary establishment of the victualling department at Chatham, Dover, Gibraltar, Sheerness, Downs, Heligoland, Cork, Malta, Mediterranean, Cape of Good Hope, Rio de Janeiro, and leave £5,460 in the Treasury.'[3]

He continued to reel off similar statistics to the amusement of many of those present and the annoyance of others.

When he had finished William Wellesley-Pole got to his feet. 'Lord Cochrane has thought proper to make an attack on the Wellesley family of which I am a member,' he said, and he proceeded to justify the sinecure which was paid to the head of the family. Wellesley-Pole had until recently been Secretary to the Admiralty Board and he was well aware of Cochrane's distinguished record as a naval officer. What he had to say next no doubt reflected the views of most of those present in the House: 'Let me advise him that adherence to the pursuits of his profession, of which he is so great an ornament, will tend more to his honour and to the advantage of his country than a perseverance in the conduct which he has of late adopted, conduct which can only lead him into error, and make him the dupe of those who use the authority of his name to advance their own mischievous purposes.'[4]

Further pressure for him to return to sea was applied a few weeks later by Charles Yorke who had recently replaced Lord Mulgrave as First Lord of the Admiralty. Yorke told Cochrane that the *Imperieuse* was ready for sea and as the current session of parliament was coming to a close, 'I presume that it is your intention to join her without loss of time'. Cochrane replied that he had not yet completed his parliamentary duties but Yorke insisted that he must know whether or not Cochrane had any intention of joining his ship. 'I shall be pleased to receive an answer in the affirmative because I should then entertain hopes that your activity and gallantry might be available for public service.'[5]

Cochrane had no intention of resuming his naval career at this stage. His plans for the use of explosive ships against Walcheren had been turned down but he wanted to experiment further with incendiary devices. He also had some unfinished business which needed to be resolved in Malta. This arose out of his determination to expose the corrupt dealings of the Prize Courts in the Mediterranean which he believed were charging exorbitant fees at the expense of the captains and crews who had captured enemy vessels.

Cochrane had a long-standing grudge against the Vice-Admiralty Court at Malta which, in his view, had cheated him out of the prize money due on the *King George*, the ship he had captured after a hard fight in which two of his men had been killed and a number seriously wounded. Although the ship had been registered as a Maltese privateer, Cochrane had always maintained that it was a pirate and was infuriated that he lost the case and had been charged £600 in legal expenses by the Vice-Admiralty Court at Malta. He had brought up the matter of Admiralty Courts in Parliament on 3 June but had got nowhere and he was determined to obtain first-hand evidence to back up his case. During the winter of 1810–11 he sailed to the Mediterranean in the *Julie,* the French gunboat he had captured at Cadaques

and subsequently bought at Gibraltar for use as a private yacht.[6] He
sailed her as far as Gibraltar but, fearing she might be mistaken as a
warship in the Mediterranean, he took passage on a British brig of war
to Sicily where he held meetings with the army commander, General
Sir John Stuart, and with Captain Richardson of the *Diadem*.[7] At
Messina he carried out a number of experiments with a new form of
mortar which he had devised. He also discovered the lethal effects of
sulphur dioxide. Sicily was a source of sulphur and when visiting the
sulphur mines he noticed that when burnt it produced clouds of
sulphur dioxide which killed everything in the immediate vicinity. He
could see the potential of this and would later draw up elaborate plans
for the use of poison gas as a military weapon.

From Sicily Cochrane sailed on to Malta and he arrived in the
Grand Harbour at Valletta on 20 February 1811.[8] Vice-Admiralty
Courts had been set up during the course of the seventeenth century in
Antigua, Bermuda, Jamaica, Gibraltar, Halifax and elsewhere to deal
with piracy, the condemnation (valuation) of prizes, and with other
maritime matters which were better handled at a local level than by
the High Court of Admiralty in London.[9] Their proceedings were
governed by various acts of Parliament which determined the composition of the courts and the fees to be charged.[10] Many sailors were
sceptical about the decisions of some of the courts. Lord Collingwood
observed in 1808 that, 'The Admiralty Court in Gibraltar appears to
me to be very oddly constituted, and wants regulation.'[11] The court at
Malta was certainly irregular. The scale of fees had been drawn up by
John Sewell, the judge, and one man, Mr Jackson, acted as both
proctor and marshal which was illegal and meant that he employed
himself and paid fees to himself. Cochrane's first action on arriving at
Malta was to look for the table of fees which by law should have been
on public display in the courtroom. He found it on the back of a door in
a room behind the court which the officers used as a robing room.[12] He
removed it but he was observed folding it up and putting it in his
pocket. He was issued with a summons ordering him to return the
paper to the court within two days. He ignored the summons and
when an attempt was made to arrest him he refused to submit on the

basis that the man sent to arrest him had no authority because he was appointed by Jackson who could not act as marshal if he was also the proctor. For several days Cochrane defied the authorities and enjoyed the acclaim and approval of his fellow seamen.

On 28 February he was apprehended by Mr Stevens, the deputy registrar, outside the Naval Arsenal which he had been visiting with the Navy Commissioner and with Captain Maxwell of the *Alceste*. Mr Stevens showed him a new warrant and told Cochrane that he was his prisoner. When Cochrane refused to accompany him to the jail, Mr Stevens summoned four Maltese guards who bundled him into an open carriage and took him to the Castellanea Prison where he was accommodated in some comfort and allowed to entertain his naval friends at public expense. On 2 March he was escorted to the court and charged with the theft of the table of fees and with having resisted arrest. Cochrane refused to acknowledge the legality of the proceedings and protested that he had no counsel, that no evidence had been called and that he had not been allowed to cross-examine any witnesses. Judge Sewell sent him back to prison for contempt of court.

Cochrane's defiance proved increasingly embarrassing for the authorities while his popularity among the British sailors in the port seemed likely to lead to them storming the jail. On the night of 4 March he escaped from the prison by sawing through the bars of his cell and using a rope to lower himself into the street. According to Cochrane the rope and a file were supplied by his servant, Richard Carter, the jailer was made drunk by his naval friends, and a naval gig was standing by in the harbour ready to take him out to the English packet boat which was lying offshore. No doubt his friends did assist his escape but it also seems likely that the authorities colluded in it to avoid further confrontations.

Cochrane was back in London on 11 April but once again found that his direct but unconventional methods had failed to produce the desired results. Sir William Scott, the Judge of the High Court of Admiralty, received reports of his conduct in Malta and after due consideration the judge and the law officers came to the conclusion that the actions of the Malta court had been justified in the circum-

stances 'and that the conduct of the noble Lord was marked throughout by a spirit of contempt which it was the duty of the judge to
repress for the vindication of the jurisdiction over which he presides'.[13]
On 6 June Cochrane initiated a debate in Parliament on the conduct of
Vice-Admiralty Courts. To demonstrate the exorbitant fees charged
by the Malta court he produced the Proctor's Bill for the case of the
King George privateer. He had pasted the various charges on to a single
sheet which he said was six and a quarter fathoms in length. When he
unrolled the bill it stretched from one end of the debating chamber to
the other and caused considerable hilarity among the members
present. It was agreed that the matter should be gone into further
but when Cochrane later proposed that a committee should be set up
to enquire into the court's behaviour his motion was defeated.
Although Cochrane abandoned this particular crusade his complaints
about the corrupt nature of the Malta court were justified by subsequent events. Jackson tried to get his own brother appointed
marshal and when this failed a man called Northcott was appointed.
He promptly made off with the proceeds of a number of prize sales and
was said to be living in Sicily under the name of Smyth.[14] A few
months later Mr Stevens, the deputy registrar, also absconded with
the cash from the sale of a condemned ship.

In the remaining weeks of the parliamentary session Cochrane
turned his attention to the pay and conditions of ordinary seamen and
the plight of prisoners of war. A long-standing grievance of seamen,
and one of the causes of the fleet mutinies at Spithead and the Nore in
1797, were the long delays they frequently experienced before receiving their pay. This was particularly the case with the crews of ships on
foreign service. Cochrane produced examples in Parliament to show
that many seamen went for years without payment which was hard
enough for the men but even harder for their wives and families. He
gave a number of examples to prove his case. Charles Yorke, the First
Lord, replied that it was too late in the parliamentary session to go
into the points raised, and 'as to ships being detained so long upon
foreign and distant stations, it is much to be regretted but it is often
unavoidable'.[15]

It was probably Samuel Whitbread who drew Cochrane's attention to the miserable conditions suffered by prisoners of war. Cochrane paid a visit to Dartmoor where 6,000 prisoners were incarcerated in shocking conditions. On his return to London he stood up in the House of Commons and drew the attention of the members to the state of the prison where he had observed men queuing for hours in the pouring rain to receive inedible food. 'Consequently one thousand are soaked through in the morning, attending to their breakfast, and one thousand more at dinner. Thus a third are consequently wet, many without a change of clothes.'[16] The overcrowding of prisoners at Dartmoor was largely caused by Napoleon's refused to exchange prisoners of war. Cochrane received support from the small body of committed reformers in the house but with the nation at war against a formidable enemy most of the members were indifferent to the sufferings of the thousands of French prisoners confined in rotten hulks in Portsmouth harbour or in bleak prison buildings on distant moors.

The year 1811 had proved to be a surprisingly eventful one for Cochrane, even without the excitements that were an essential part of his life as a naval commander. The following year was to prove equally eventful. He devised ambitious plans for attacking enemy harbours by the use of a combination of explosion ships and poison gas.[17] He submitted detailed plans to the Prince Regent in March 1812 and these were considered by a high-level committee chaired by the Duke of York, commander-in-chief of the army, later in the year.

This was also the year in which Cochrane, at the age of thirty-six, fell in love, apparently for the first time. Although he maintained that he was without a particle of romance in his composition, his courtship and marriage had a romance and a drama that were curiously in keeping with the mood of the times – the Romantic age of Byron, Keats and Sir Walter Scott. In appearance and character the girl he called Kate, Katie or Mouse bore a striking resemblance to the heroines of the poets and writers of his day. She was very young and very pretty with sparkling eyes and an infectious laugh. She seemed to be meek and delicate and feminine but she could also be mischievous and flirtatious and had a resilient and spirited nature. Cochrane adored her from the moment he first set eyes on her to the end of his days. They were often separated for months at a time but their letters are as touching as any love letters can be. 'My lovely Kate', he wrote in 1814, 'Oh my dear soul, you do not know how much I love you . . .'[18] And she later implored him to 'keep your mind at rest my dearest and most beloved Cochrane and for my sake take care of yourself'.

Restless, energetic, constantly engrossed in new projects or old vendettas, Cochrane must have been exceedingly difficult to live with. Kate patiently suffered his obsessions and his extended absences for many years. Her correspondence suggests that she had a love affair with Lord Auckland around 1825 but she remained loyal to Cochrane, bore him two more children and went out of her way to help him clear his name in the years following his return from Greece.[19] It was not until Cochrane was in his sixties that they drifted apart. He remained faithful to her and, apart from her feelings for Lord Auckland, Cochrane was always the most important man in her life. Shortly after his death Lady Dundonald, as she was then called, was cross-examined by a House of Lords Committee of Privileges. This had been set up to establish their eldest son's legitimacy and his right to inherit the earldom (their third son, Arthur, had challenged the legality of their Scottish marriage in the hope of gaining the title). Interrogated under oath by the Lord Chancellor and other lawyers, Kate revealed the details of Cochrane's courtship of her, their elopement and marriage, and their subsequent life together. During the course of the extended interviews she was suddenly overcome by the memory of him and launched into a passionate defence of the man she had loved and worshipped.[20]

Kate was an orphan. Her full name was Katherine Corbett Barnes (although she sometimes signed herself Catherine Corbet Barnes, and when this was questioned by the Committee of Privileges she said she was a careless girl when it came to spelling). Her father was Thomas Barnes of Romford in Essex and her mother was believed to be a Spanish dancer.[21] When Cochrane first met her she was living with her widowed aunt, Mrs Jackson, at 9 Bryanston Street, close to Portman Square. Mrs Jackson's husband had kept a stationer's shop in nearby Oxford Street, but the house in Bryanston Street had been given to Mrs Jackson by her brother, James Corbett. Mrs Jackson was responsible for bringing up Kate and had sent her for two or three years to a school at Great Marlow in Buckinghamshire.

The exact date of Kate's birth is not known but she told the Committee of Privileges that when she first met Cochrane she was sixteen or seventeen years old.[22] They were introduced by Captain Nathaniel Cochrane who had been a friend of Mr Jackson and was a cousin of Cochrane. He had been flag lieutenant to Rear-Admiral Alexander Cochrane in the West Indies and, according to Kate, was 'a very fine fellow'.[23] In 1812 Cochrane was still living with his rich uncle Basil Cochrane in his grand house in Portman Square. He had called to see Kate on several occasions during January and February and after a while had proposed to her but she had refused him. 'I refused all sorts of things of the kind,' she recalled. Around this time Cochrane fell seriously ill, 'and they sent his servant, Richard Carter, to me to tell me he was dying, and also Captain Nathaniel Cochrane came to say how very ill he was, and to ask me if I would walk in front of the house in the square, that I might let him see me, which I did; and he was lifted up to the window of his bedroom, looking like a corpse. My heart was softened to see that great man, the hero of a hundred fights.'[24]

When he recovered from his illness Cochrane had an interview with Kate's aunt. He told her that he wished to marry Kate but would have to marry her secretly in Scotland because his uncle had someone else in mind for him to marry – a rich heiress and the daughter of an Admiralty official. Basil Cochrane wanted to restore the fortunes of the Dundonalds and he was prepared to leave his nephew, the heir to the earldom, a very large portion of his estate if he married the heiress. Cochrane did not wish to upset his uncle but had no intention of marrying for money. His solution was to sweep Kate off to the village of Annan on the Scottish border a few miles beyond Gretna Green. Kate's aunt eventually agreed to the arrangement on the understanding that Cochrane gave his written promise that he would marry Kate as soon as they reached Annan and he must agree that her servant, Ann Moxham, accompany them and witness the ceremony. Ann was 'a bettermost woman of that class', according to Kate. 'She was older than I was considerably, but we, being girls together used to talk and laugh, and she sang remarkably well.'[25]

On 6 August 1812 Cochrane and his bride-to-be set off for Scotland. They took a post chaise which was sometimes drawn by two horses and sometimes by four. Kate, Ann Moxham and Cochrane travelled inside the carriage, and Richard Carter, Cochrane's servant, travelled outside with the driver. It was more than three hundred miles from London to the Scottish border and they journeyed at speed through the day and the night, changing horses as they went. Kate remembered little of the journey or any of the sights en route. 'I was very tired, I was very worn. I was young. I did not think of castles or towns, or anything else. We went rolling on and on, and I slept, and so did he.' They clattered through Carlisle, caught a glimpse of the glistening waters of the Solway Firth and as they passed through Gretna Green, Cochrane breathed a sigh of relief.

'It's all right Mouse, we are all right now,' he said. 'Here we are over the border now, and nothing but God can separate us.' Kate recalled that he snapped his fingers in the way Scotsmen did when they were pleased. They arrived at the village of Annan on the evening of 8 August. The steaming horses came to a halt outside the Queensbury Arms which was run by an elderly and bad-tempered landlady who spoke with such a broad Scottish accent that Kate had difficulty in understanding her. Cochrane was in a jovial mood but he was also in a hurry. He seated himself at the table in the main room, and wrote away on a piece of paper:

'I, Sir Thomas Cochrane commonly called Lord Cochrane of the Kingdom of Scotland being desirous for particular reasons to avoid a public marriage do hereby acknowledge and receive Catherine Corbett Barnes as my lawful wife.' He signed his name and then got Kate to copy out the following words which he had written out for her: 'I Catherine Corbet Barnes of the Parish of Marylebone in the county of

Middlesex do accept and declare Sir Thomas Cochrane commonly called Lord Cochrane to be my lawful husband promising faithfully to keep secret this deed of marriage until I shall be permitted in writing under the hand of my said accepted husband to disclose the same.'[26]

When she had signed her name Cochrane called Richard Carter and Ann Moxham.

'Dick,' he said, 'I want you to put your name to that. You must read it and sign it.' Carter did so, and then Ann Moxham added her signature. When the servants had gone to their rooms Cochrane astonished Kate by raising his hands in the air and dancing a sailor's hornpipe. He told her that now she was his for ever. Kate was not so sure.

'I do not know,' she said, 'I have had no parson and no church. Is this the way you marry in Scotland?' Cochrane assured her that all was well, and then sprang another surprise. He told her he must hurry back to London immediately. His uncle was going to be married on the 11th or 12th and he was expected to be at the wedding. He said that he had given full instructions to Dick and he would bring her back as soon as arrangements could be made. He kissed her, said he had no time to lose and went off in the post chaise.

Kate was tired and thought she would retire to her room. The old lady lit the way upstairs to the bedroom. When Kate said she would like to have a bath, she was told:

'No, you cannot have a bath. There are no baths at the Queensbury Arms.'

'Can you give me some soft water?'

'No, you cannot have any soft water,' said the landlady and told her that she had been doing a lot of washing and had already used up all the soft water.

'What kind of place do you call this,' said Kate, 'where you have no soft water for people and no bath.'

'It is the Queensbury Arms at Annan,' she was told.

Kate, Dick Carter and Ann Moxham stayed two nights at the inn and then headed south in the Glasgow to London stagecoach. They reached London on the evening of 13 August and Kate went back to

stay with her aunt in Bryanston Street. She recalled finding a packet of
wedding cake in the house and when Cochrane came round to see her
he explained that he had attended his uncle's wedding and that his
uncle had now left town.

Unable to acknowledge publicly that Kate was his wife, but frustrated by the restrictions imposed by seeing her at the house of her
aunt, Cochrane decided that they would spend a delayed honeymoon
on the Isle of Wight. On 18 August, accompanied once again by Dick
Carter and Ann Moxham, they travelled to the south coast and took a
boat across the Solent to Ryde. They spent a month in a cottage close
to that of Lord and Lady Spencer who were family friends. Lord
Spencer, when First Lord of the Admiralty, had smoothed the way for
Cochrane's advancement from midshipman to master and commander.
From Ryde they travelled to Cochrane's house at Holly Hill and they
remained there until the next session of parliament opened and
Cochrane had to return to London to take up his parliamentary duties.

The year 1813 was comparatively uneventful. Cochrane continued
to work on various inventions, in particular on the design of an
effective lamp for the use of ships in convoys, and on the design of gas
lamps for street lighting. He continued to speak his mind in parliamentary debates but his views on naval abuses and his criticism of the
way in which the Admiralty were conducting the war at sea were not
helpful to the war effort. He made little or no effort to lobby his fellow
MPs and his speeches were inevitably regarded by most of them as
subversive and unpatriotic. In 1814 the naval and political establishment were at last given the opportunity to put down the troublemaker
in their midst.

FIFTEEN

The Stock Exchange Scandal

1814

While Cochrane was preoccupied with his marriage, his inventions and his parliamentary battles, momentous events were taking place on the Continent. In June 1812 Napoleon marched into Russia with an army of more than 650,000 men gathered from twenty nations. At Borodino the Russian army made a stand and for twelve hours Napoleon's troops fought the most bloody and costly battle of the war. The Russians lost nearly half their army, and the French lost 30,000 men including fifty generals. Napoleon pressed on and entered Moscow on 14 September. The city was empty and abandoned and was soon on fire. The Russians refused to parley and in mid-October, with dwindling food supplies and winter approaching, Napoleon ordered the retreat from Moscow. It was five hundred miles to the Russian border, the countryside had been laid waste and by the second week of November the temperature was thirty degrees below zero. Men and horses died from cold, starvation and the attacks of marauding Cossacks. By 18 December, Napoleon was back in Paris having lost between 500,000 and 570,000 of his Grand Army. He blamed everyone but himself for the disaster. Chaptal, who was one of his ministers, observed, 'after his return from Moscow those who saw most of him noticed a great change in his physical and moral constitution . . . I did not find the same consistency in his ideas or

the same strength in his character; one noticed only inconsequent
leaps of imagination. There was not the old taste and faculty for hard
work.'[1] The Russian campaign had shown the world that Napoleon
was no longer invincible, and there were other signs that his domination of Europe might be drawing to an end.

In Spain the British Army, with the support of Spanish guerrillas,
was relentlessly driving the French troops out of the country. In July
1809 Wellington had advanced to within seventy miles of Madrid and
at Talevera he had defeated an army led by Marshal Soult and
Napoleon's brother, Joseph. There were setbacks and retreats during
the next three years but on 22 July 1812 Wellington fought and won a
crucial battle at Salamanca and three weeks later he entered Madrid.
During the course of the next fourteen months he would fight his way
northwards and lead his army across the frontier into France.

The British government's concern with defeating Napoleon had
diverted attention from an increasingly hostile United States. America's trade and shipping were constantly disrupted by the actions of
British warships; the impressment of American sailors by the British
navy was deeply resented; these and other grievances, together with
the ambitions of a number of American congressmen who were
looking for an opportunity to conquer Canada, led to the United
States declaring war on Britain in June 1812. The resulting 'War of
1812' began badly for Britain, particularly at sea. In August the
American frigate USS *Constitution* defeated the British frigate *Guerriere*
in the first of a number of single-ship actions in which American
warships were victorious. American privateers proved remarkably
successful at intercepting and capturing British merchantmen, while
on Lake Erie a squadron of British ships was soundly beaten by an
American squadron under Commodore Perry. 'We have met the
enemy and they are ours,' Perry reported. 'Two ships, two brigs,
one schooner and one sloop.'[2] The only break in this humiliating
sequence of events for the Royal Navy was a single-ship action which
took place off Boston: on 1 June 1813 the British frigate *Shannon*
commanded by Captain Philip Broke engaged the American frigate
Chesapeake, Captain Lawrence. Like Cochrane, Broke had trained his

men to a remarkable pitch, and the speed and accuracy of the *Shannon*'s gunnery proved decisive in a ferocious action which lasted barely fifteen minutes and left the decks of both ships strewn with dead and dying seamen.

There had been rumours in some English newspapers that Cochrane might be sent to America with a squadron of frigates. The *Morning Chronicle* had claimed on 6 July 1813 that 'Lord Cochrane is appointed to command the *Saturn* for North America'. Such speculation suggests that, in spite of his very public quarrels with the Admiralty, he was still regarded in some quarters as a second Nelson. But it was his uncle Alexander who gave him a chance to resume his naval career. Vice-Admiral Sir Alexander Cochrane had recently been appointed commander-in-chief of the North American station. He was known to be tough and capable and it was hoped that he would breathe fresh life into the navy's efforts across the Atlantic. He invited Cochrane to become his flag captain and when he sailed for America in a frigate to take up his new appointment, he left Cochrane to oversee the fitting out of his flagship, the 80-gun *Tonnant*, which was lying at Chatham. When the ship was ready for sea she had orders to escort a convoy of merchantmen to America.[3] Cochrane now divided his time between Chatham dockyard, and the factory in the City which was producing the prototype for his convoy lamp, and his new home in Green Street, where Kate was pregnant with their first child.

For five years Cochrane had been on half-pay but as flag captain of a ship of the line he would earn a respectable salary, while his particular skills as a coastal raider were well suited to action on the American seaboard. Unfortunately this bright future was to be blighted by the machinations of the youngest of his seven uncles. The Hon. Andrew Cochrane had changed his surname to Cochrane-Johnstone when he married Lady Georgiana Johnstone, daughter of the Earl of Hopetoun. He and Cochrane had always got on well, but he was a completely untrustworthy character, his life a catalogue of dishonest dealings. Lord Dundonald, his eldest brother, described him as 'an unprincipled villain, swindler and coward'.[4] He had joined the army at the age of sixteen and had reached the rank of colonel by 1797 when he was appointed Governor of Dominica. His rule in the West Indian island became notorious for corruption, extortion and brutality and according to one authority, 'he drove a brisk trade in negros and kept a harem'.[5] He was recalled in 1803 to face a court martial but was acquitted. His wife had died in Dominica and he had married a rich Creole heiress but they soon divorced. On his return to Britain he became a friend of William Cobbett (it was he who had first introduced Cochrane to Cobbett at the time of the Honiton election) and he was elected Member of Parliament for the rotten borough of Grampound. He returned to the West Indies and his naval brother Alexander, then commander-in-chief of the Leeward Islands, appointed him navy agent for the Prize Court at Tortola where he was accused of bribery and corruption. Alexander told his brother Basil, 'I shall ever sincerely regret that my attachment to him as a brother induced me to repose in him the trust that I did.'[6]

In May 1813, Andrew Cochrane-Johnstone met and became friends with a Prussian aristocrat in his early forties who called himself Captain De Berenger, a man of many talents with contacts in the highest quarters – he had given advice on military matters to the Duke of Cumberland, and made drawings for the Prince Regent.[7] Cochrane-Johnstone persuaded his brother Alexander that De Berenger had useful skills to offer Cochrane in preparing the flagship for America. As a talented marksman he would be able to train members of the crew in sharp shooting (there were reports that American ships had been employing sharpshooters to good effect). De Berenger also had ideas for new methods of boarding and had developed a flame-throwing device. 'It was thus,' Cochrane wrote in his autobiography, 'that I was subsequently brought into contact with a man who eventually proved my ruin.'[8] Exactly when Cochrane first met De Berenger is not clear. Cochrane says he was first introduced to him at a dinner given by his brother Andrew in January 1814 but it seems they actually met in the previous December when Cochrane asked De Berenger to make drawings for his convoy lamp patent. Whatever the circumstances of their meeting, Cochrane's involvement with Andrew Cochrane-Johnstone and De Berenger was to prove disastrous. Between them the disreputable uncle and the Prussian adventurer had devised an ingenious plot to make large sums of money on the Stock Exchange by spreading a rumour that Napoleon was dead.[9]

Early on the morning of 21 February, De Berenger knocked on the door of the Ship Inn at Dover and demanded to see the landlord. He said that he was the bearer of important news and must have a horse and rider to send a message to Vice-Admiral Foley, the port admiral at Deal. De Berenger was wearing a grey military coat over a red uniform jacket with a large star on the chest (the colour of the coat and jacket would be of vital importance in the subsequent court case). Sitting down in the inn he wrote a letter to Admiral Foley explaining that he had just arrived on a ship from Calais and must proceed to London at once with despatches. The Allies had obtained a final victory and 'Bonaparte was overtaken by a party of Sachen's Cossacks, who immediately slayed him and divided his body between them. General Platoff saved Paris from being reduced to ashes. The Allied Sovereigns are there and the white cockade is universal; an immediate peace is certain.'[10] He signed himself Lieutenant-Colonel R. Du Bourg, Aide-de-Camp to Lord Cathcart, who was the British ambassador to Russia.

A postboy was despatched with the letter to Deal, and De Berenger summoned a post chaise and horses to take him to London. Fog shrouding the southern counties prevented Admiral Foley from using the visual telegraph system to communicate with the Admiralty but De Berenger made sure that he spread the news wherever he changed horses and he lavishly tipped grooms and coachmen with gold napoleons. On reaching the outskirts of London he transferred to a hackney carriage and drove to Lord Cochrane's house in Green Street. Cochrane was not there. He had breakfasted with Andrew Cochrane-Johnstone and Richard Butt, his stockbroker, and then gone on to Mr King's factory in Cock Lane, near the old Smithfield Market, to check on the progress of his convoy lamp. He had been there a short while when his footman, Thomas Dewman, arrived and told him that an army officer was at his house and wanted to see him urgently. Cochrane presumed the officer must have news of his brother, Major

William Cochrane, who was serving with Wellington's army in Spain and so hurried back to Green Street where he was surprised to find De Berenger waiting for him. De Berenger told him that he was in serious financial difficulties and was currently a debtor in the King's Bench Prison. He begged for a passage to America on the *Tonnant* so that he could escape from his creditors. Cochrane said that he could not take him as a passenger on the warship without the Admiralty's permission. De Berenger then announced that he must change out of his military uniform and asked for the loan of a civilian hat and overcoat. He explained that if he returned to the King's Bench Prison in uniform the warden or his servants would suspect that he was planning to abscond and the privilege which allowed debtors some liberty of movement would be withdrawn. Cochrane lent him a black coat and an old hat, and De Berenger left the house with his uniform rolled up in a towel.

The rumours of Napoleon's death were already circulating in London and were causing considerable excitement on the Stock Exchange. The price of shares, particularly the government stock known as Omnium, began to rise sharply from 27½ to 30.[11] By midday the Lord Mayor had still received no official news to confirm the rumours but any doubts which people might have had were dispelled when a coach and horses was driven across London Bridge and down Cheapside. The coach was decorated with laurel leaves and was carrying three French officers wearing white cockades in their hats and scattering papers inscribed with the words '*Vive le Roi! Vivent les Bourbons!*'. By the afternoon the price of Omnium had risen from 30 to 32½. By the morning of the next day, 22 February, there was still no official confirmation of Napoleon's death and the Omnium share price dropped down to 27½ again.

As soon as it became clear that the news of Napoleon's death was a hoax, the Stock Exchange appointed a committee to carry out an investigation. They soon discovered that six people had made large sums of money by selling Omnium shares at the height of the boom on the 21st. Andrew Cochrane-Johnstone had sold Consols and Omnium shares to the value of £510,000; Richard Butt had sold Consols and

Omnium to the value of £392,000; Cochrane had sold his entire holding of Omnium shares valued at £139,000; the other speculators were Stock Exchange gamblers named Holloway, Sandom and McRae and they were identified as the three men dressed as French officers who had driven the coach through the City. On 4 March the Stock Exchange committee offered a reward of £250 for the arrest of the man called Colonel Du Bourg. A few days later an anonymous informant told the committee that the foreign colonel was really De Berenger and that he had been seen entering Lord Cochrane's house in Green Street on the day of the hoax. On learning of this Cochrane immediately drew up a sworn affidavit setting out his movements on 21 February. He described De Berenger's visit to his house and the story which De Berenger had told him about needing to change his uniform, and he explained why he had been prepared to lend him a hat and coat. A warrant was issued for De Berenger's arrest on 17 March and on 8 April he was arrested at the port of Leith near Edinburgh.

In addition to De Berenger's presence in his house on the day of the hoax, Cochrane's sale of his Omnium shares inevitably invited suspicion that he was closely involved with the plot. The argument usually made in his defence is that he had been investing his prize money in stocks and shares for several weeks before the hoax and in the case of his Omnium shares he had given standing instructions to his stockbroker, Richard Butt, to sell if the price rose by 1 per cent. His Omnium shares had been bought at 28¼ and were sold when the price rose to 29½. He would have made double the profit if he had waited and sold when the price reached its peak of 32½. Cochrane had known Butt for several years and always maintained that he was an innocent party in the fraud. Butt had been a pay clerk in Portsmouth dockyard before becoming a speculator on the Stock Exchange. Unlike Andrew Cochrane-Johnstone, he was not in debt at the time of the hoax but was fairly prosperous. However, the very large sum which he had made by his sale of Omnium shares on 21 February was deeply suspicious and, as with Cochrane, his involvement in the scandal ruined him.

The evidence against Cochrane continued to accumulate. When he was arrested in Scotland, De Berenger was found to have in his possession some bank notes drawn in Cochrane's name. At around the same time a waterman called George Odell, who had been dredging for coals in the Thames near Old Swan Stairs, fished up a weighted bundle tied up with window line. The bundle contained a red uniform coat, which had been cut to pieces, together with some embroidery, a star and a silver coat of arms. This was identified by Mr Solomon, a tailor, who confirmed that it had been sold to De Berenger three days before he had masqueraded as Colonel Du Bourg. The Admiralty were watching developments closely and when the Stock Exchange committee expressed its suspicions about Cochrane's involvement in the fraud, John Wilson Croker, the Secretary to the Admiralty, wrote to him demanding an explanation. On 22 March Cochrane replied with a letter defending his position and enclosing affidavits from his servants. The Admiralty had already appointed an acting captain to replace him as commander of the *Tonnant*, and on 7 April the ship set sail for Bermuda under the command of Captain Alexander Skene.[12]

To add to Cochrane's worries, his wife Kate became seriously ill during the final weeks of her pregnancy. She later recalled, 'I was all but dead; I had a most awful confinement; I had the puerperal fever and the measles, and my child was extremely delicate.'[13] She gave birth to a boy on 18 April. He was baptised Thomas Barnes Cochrane in the nearby church, St George's, Hanover Square. Kate was too ill to attend the christening but was well looked after by their nurse, Mrs Tait, whom she described as 'an excellent good old Scotch body'.[14] Two days after the birth the newspapers announced that De Berenger, Lord Cochrane, Richard Butt, Andrew Cochrane-Johnstone, Ralph Sandom, Alexander McRae, Peter Holloway and Henry Lyte were charged with unlawfully conspiring by false news to induce the subjects of the King to believe that Napoleon Bonaparte was dead, 'and thereby to occasion a rise in the prices of the public Government Funds'.[15] They were to be tried in the Guildhall on 8 June before Lord Ellenborough, Lord Chief Justice of the Court of the King's Bench.

As with the court martial of Lord Gambier, the odds seemed to be weighted against Cochrane from the moment the trial began. The legal team for the defence was impressive and included William Best (later Chief Justice of the Common Pleas), James Park (later Baron Park, Chief Justice of the Court of the Exchequer) and Henry Brougham (later Lord Chancellor). There is evidence that they considered anxiously whether or not Cochrane should be separately represented so that he could in his own defence, if necessary, dis-associate himself from his co-defendants. In the event this was not done, with the inevitable result that the mounting evidence pointing to the guilt of De Berenger and his uncle reflected adversely on Cochrane also. The fact that Lord Ellenborough was to judge the case was also unfortunate. He was a formidable lawyer with an impressive background. The son of a bishop, he had been educated at Charter-house and Cambridge. He had read for the Bar at Lincoln's Inn and as a young King's Counsel had defended Warren Hastings. He been an MP, Attorney General and Speaker of the House of Lords. But he was also a High Tory and a notable enemy of the radicals – he had sent Cobbett and Henry Hunt to jail following trials that were politically motivated. Equally ominous for Cochrane was the fact that the Admiralty Solicitor at the trial was Germain Lavie who had acted for Lord Gambier at his court martial. Cochrane later maintained that his appointment was the result of 'collusion between a high official at the Admiralty and the Committee of the Stock Exchange'[16] although there is no evidence to prove that this was the case.

The trial began at 9.00 a.m. at the Court of the King's Bench at the Guildhall and such was the public interest in the case that the courtroom was crowded with spectators. Lord Ellenborough's ap-pearance as he made his way to his appointed place was disconcerting and somewhat alarming. He had an awkward and ungainly walk. 'When he entered the court he was in the habit of swelling out his cheeks by blowing and compressing his lips, and you would have supposed that he was going to snort like a warhorse preparing for battle.'[17] Richard Gurney opened the case for the prosecution. He began by outlining the events of 21 February: the share dealings of the defendants; the part played by the bogus French officers; and the movements of De Berenger from his arrival at Dover until his appearance at Cochrane's house. He called as witnesses the innkeeper at Dover, the postboys, the Thames waterman who had found the uniform and the tailor who had sold it. He then turned to the case against Cochrane. He pointed out that Cochrane had borrowed money from Richard Butt and that he had gained from the sale of Omnium shares. But he concentrated on the matter of the colour of the military uniform worn by De Berenger. In his affidavit Cochrane had sworn that when De Berenger arrived at his house he was wearing a green sharpshooter's uniform under his military greatcoat, and his servants had confirmed that this was the case. But a key prosecution witness, the hackney carriage driver William Crane, swore that De Berenger was wearing a scarlet uniform when he delivered him to the door of Cochrane's house. If his evidence was correct then not only had Cochrane perjured himself in his sworn statement but he must be complicit in the plot because otherwise he would have been suspicious of the man masquerading in the scarlet uniform of a staff officer.

The evidence for the prosecution was finally concluded at 10.00 p.m. After a session lasting for thirteen hours it seemed reasonable to expect that the judge would defer the hearing of the case for the defence till the next day. However, Lord Ellenborough insisted that Serjeant Best proceed because, he said, 'there are several gentlemen attending as witnesses who, I find, cannot, without the greatest inconvenience, attend tomorrow'.[18] The men in question were Lord Yarmouth, Colonel Torrens and the First Lord of the Admiralty, Lord Melville.[19]

Mr James Park, for the defence, mildly objected to this. 'The difficulty we feel, I am sure your Lordship will feel as strong as we do, is the fatigue owing to the length of our attendance here.'[20] When Ellenborough repeated his objection to a postponement, Mr Park, was more forceful: 'I have undergone very great fatigue, which I am able to bear; but I would submit to your Lordship the hardships upon parties who are charged with so very serious an offence as this if their case is heard at this late hour.'[21] However, Lord Ellenborough insisted that they must proceed with the defence. Serjeant Best got to his feet and addressed the court. He pointed out that the charge was a grave one: 'Upon the issue of this question depends whether the accused are to hold that situation in society which they have hitherto held, or whether they are to be completely degraded and ruined.'[22] He reminded them of Lord Cochrane's illustrious past and his services to his country and asked the jury whether such a man was likely to commit so sordid a crime. He made the point that if Cochrane was really complicit in the plot he would not have been so foolish as to meet the chief conspirator so openly at his own house; he convincingly explained away the matter of the bank notes found on De Berenger; and he showed that Cochrane had been selling stock as far back as November, and that his instructions to Butt to sell when the Omnium shares rose by 1 per cent had been given a long time before. He was less convincing on the matter of the uniform and suggested that Cochrane might have been mistaken about the colour. Cochrane was used to seeing De Berenger in his green sharpshooter's uniform and when he wrote his affidavit three weeks later he assumed he was wearing green, 'there being nothing to fix on his Lordship's mind the colour of the uniform'.[23]

Best was still speaking at midnight and it was 1.00 a.m. before Serjeant Park addressed the court on behalf of De Berenger. He was followed by Serjeant Pell, the defence counsel for the other defendants. The first session of the trial eventually finished at 3.00 a.m. How many of the jurors were still awake in the candle-lit gloom of the medieval hall is not recorded.

The trial resumed at 10.00 a.m. Lord Melville and others were called to prove that it was Cochrane's uncle Alexander who was De Berenger's patron and that Cochrane's only connection was in offering to ferry De Berenger across the Atlantic in the *Tonnant*. But the main point at issue was still whether De Berenger had arrived at Cochrane's house in the red uniform of a staff officer or in his own green uniform of the sharpshooters. The cross-examination of a score of witnesses was followed by another long speech by Gurney pressing home his attack on the point of colour.

Lord Ellenborough began his summing up on the afternoon of the second day. He summarised all the evidence, commenting as he proceeded, and then drew attention to the matter of De Berenger's uniform which he clearly regarded as damning evidence:

> De Berenger stripped himself at Lord Cochrane's. He pulled off his scarlet uniform there, and if the circumstances of its not being green did not excite Lord Cochrane's suspicion, what did he think of the star and the medal? It became him, on discovering these, as an officer and a gentleman, to communicate his suspicions of these circumstances. Did he not ask De Berenger where he had been in this masquerade dress? It was for the jury to say whether Lord Cochrane did not know where he had been. This was not the dress of a sharpshooter, but of a mountebank. He came before Lord Cochrane fully blazoned in the costume of his crime.'[24]

At 6.10 p.m. the jury retired and at 8.40 they returned with a verdict of guilty on all the defendants. At this period it was usual for there to be an interval of several days between the verdict of the jury and the delivery of the sentence which gave the defendants an opportunity to lodge an appeal. Cochrane had not been present at the trial but had spent most of his time at Mr King's tin factory working on his convoy lamp. Considerably shaken by the verdict, he wrote to his uncle Basil, 'All my fortitude is required to bear up against this unexpected and unmerited stroke.'[25] Belatedly aware of the seriousness of the situation and realising the crucial importance of De Berenger's uniform in the prosecution's case, he and his defence team found a number of new witnesses in Lambeth including a butcher and a fishmonger who were able to supply sworn affidavits that De Berenger had arrived at his door wearing his green sharpshooter's uniform. (It later emerged that Crane, the hackney coach driver, was an unreliable witness who was prepared to perjure himself for money.) However, when Cochrane presented his new evidence to Lord Ellenborough on 14 June he was informed that it was inadmissible because two of the conspirators, Andrew Cochrane-Johnstone and McRae, were not present at the hearing – they had both fled the country on hearing the verdict.

On 20 June, Cochrane, De Berenger and the remaining defendants appeared before a panel of four judges consisting of Lord Ellenborough and Justices Le Blanc, Bailey and Dampier. Before the sentence was passed Cochrane was allowed to put his case. This he did eloquently and with considerably more restraint than his subsequent speech in the House of Commons:

> It has been my very great misfortune to be apparently implicated in the guilt of others with whom I never had any connexion, except in transactions, so far as I was apprised of them, entirely blameless. I had met Mr De Berenger in public company, but was on no terms of intimacy with him. With Mr Cochrane Johnstone I had the intercourse natural between such near relatives. Mr Butt had voluntarily offered, without any reward, to carry on stock transactions in which thousands, as well as myself, were engaged in the face of day, without the smallest imputation of anything incorrect. The other four defendants were wholly unknown to me.'[26]

He blamed De Berenger for having involved him by coming to his house but he made no comment on the part played by his uncle. He concluded, 'I cannot feel disgraced while I know that I am guiltless. Under the influence of this sentiment I persist in the defence of my character. I have often been in situations where I had an opportunity of showing it. This is the first time, thank God, that I was ever called upon to defend it.'[27]

The next day Mr Justice Le Blanc sentenced all the defendants to twelve months' imprisonment. Cochrane and Butt were also fined £1,000, and in addition to this Cochrane and De Berenger were to stand in the pillory opposite the Royal Exchange for an hour. Cochrane was devastated. According to one eyewitness, 'His appearance today was certainly pitiable. When the sentence was passed he stood without colour in his face, his eyes staring and without expression and it was with difficulty he left the court like a man stupefied.'[28]

He was taken across London Bridge to Southwark and confined in the King's Bench Prison which was situated on the corner of Borough Road and Borough High Street, near the more famous Marshalsea

Prison. Surrounded by a very high wall topped with a line of spikes, the King's Bench Prison was for debtors and those convicted of libel. John Wilkes, Tobias Smollett and the artist George Moreland had been inmates there, and Charles Dickens has the recklessly improvident Mr Micawber confined there for some weeks in *David Copperfield.* The prisoners' rooms were on four floors of a large Georgian building which overlooked a central courtyard. Cochrane had two rooms on the top floor. He was allowed visitors but he was expected to pay for his food and his lodging. The conditions were comparatively easy for a man who had spent years enduring the rigours of life at sea and initially he seems to have been buoyed up by his belief that he was innocent and the victim of injustice. A few days after he had been committed to prison he wrote to Elizabeth Cochrane-Johnstone, the eighteen-year-old daughter of his uncle who was now a fugitive on the Continent;

> 'My dear Eliza – The feelings which you must have experienced, unused as you have been to the lamentable changes of this uncertain life, must have even exceeded that which I suffered in mind from the unexpected and unmerited ruin in which I am unhappily involved. Shocked as I am, and distressed as I am, yet I feel confidence. God is my judge that the crime imputed to me I did not commit . . . I am distressed on your account more than on my own; for knowing my innocence, and unable to speak of the private acts of any other, I cannot bring myself to believe that I shall be disgraced and punished without cause.'[29]

Cochrane's outspoken attacks in Parliament, and the part he had played in the court martial of Lord Gambier, had made him many enemies. They now took the necessary steps to complete his disgrace. At a dinner of senior naval officers at Portsmouth the Prince Regent expressed his determination to order his degradation and his removal from the Navy List. 'I will never permit a service, hitherto of unblemished honour, to be disgraced by the continuance of Lord Cochrane,' he declared. 'I shall also strip him of the Order of the Bath.'[30]

A cartoon depicting 'Things as they have been. Things as they now are.'
Cochrane the naval hero is contrasted with Cochrane the disgraced civilian.
On the right are the walls of the King's Bench Prison.

Within a week of the trial the Admiralty issued an order which ended Cochrane's career as an officer of the Royal Navy. This was followed by a further blow on 5 July when the government introduced a motion in the House of Commons to order his expulsion from Parliament. Sir Francis Burdett and Samuel Whitbread were among those who spoke on his behalf but Cochrane, who had been released from prison in order that he might address the House, launched into such a violent attack on Lord Ellenborough and the jury that Castlereagh warned the reporters present that they could be prosecuted for libel if they published the speech as given. Numerous asterisks replaced Cochrane's swear words in the Hansard report.[31] Most of the members present felt that he had damaged his cause by his intemperate language but his outburst evidently convinced a number of MPs of his innocence. When the vote was taken 144 members voted for his expulsion but 44 members were prepared to vote against the motion.

Cochrane's speech revealed the extent of his bitterness. He had previously enjoyed considerable fame as a naval hero and a parliamentary crusader but these worlds were now closed to him. It is little wonder that he had moments of despair. Mary Russell Mitford, who had seen Cochrane in his heyday playing with the children on the lawns of William Cobbett's house, wrote to a friend, 'Did papa tell you that he had seen poor, poor Lord Cochrane, that victim to his uncle's villainy, almost every day? He wept like a child to papa. And they say that the last dreadful degradation, the hacking off the spurs of knighthood, is actually to be put in force upon him.'[32]

The Prince Regent's threat to strip Cochrane of his knighthood was duly carried out. On 11 August a strange midnight ritual took place at Westminster Abbey. Cochrane's coat of arms and banner were taken down from King Henry VII's Chapel by Mr Townshend, the Bath King of Arms. The banner was then kicked out of the chapel and down the steps 'according to the ancient form, by the King of Arms'.[33] To strip him of the honour he had been awarded for his heroic role in the fireship attack at Basque Roads was the ultimate revenge of the establishment. Many years later, under a more forgiving regime, he would fight to have this honour restored.

The Prince Regent, the Admiralty and the politicians had done their best to bring him low, but Cochrane still had many friends and supporters. His radical friends and associates in and out of Parliament were his most forthright defenders. William Cobbett wrote a thundering series of articles in the *Weekly Political Register* which resulted in a record circulation of 7,000 copies. And most heartening of all was the reaction of Cochrane's Westminster constituents. Following his expulsion from Parliament a writ was issued for a by-election at Westminster. On 11 July, Sir Francis Burdett addressed a mass meeting of 5,000 electors. He urged them 'to vindicate the character of an illustrious person who had rendered great services to the country' and he condemned the malice of his enemies. To prolonged applause from the assembled crowd he said that if Lord Cochrane was to stand in the pillory he should feel it his duty to stand beside him. Richard Brinsley Sheridan, who had been Cochrane's opponent in previous elections, announced that he would not stand against him as a candidate, and Henry Brougham and Major Cartwright followed his lead. On 16 July, Cochrane was returned unopposed by the electors of Westminster as their Member of Parliament.

This encouraging news was followed three days later by further good news. The young Lord Ebrington, supported by Lord Nugent, had put forward a motion in Parliament asking for the pillory sentence to be rescinded on the grounds of Cochrane's outstanding services to his country. On 19 July, Lord Castlereagh announced that a royal pardon had been extended to all persons currently under sentence of the pillory. There is little doubt that there would have been a riot and much smashing of windows by sailors and Westminster electors if Cochrane had been subjected to this medieval punishment.

The trial, the verdict and the sentence imposed on Cochrane aroused considerable controversy at the time and continued to do so for many years, fanned by Cochrane's subsequent attempt to impeach Lord Ellenborough, and by the accusations which he made in his autobiography that the trial was politically motivated and 'that a higher authority than the Stock Exchange was at the bottom of my prosecution'.[34] His vendetta against Lord Ellenborough prompted

Ellenborough's family to respond and resulted in several publications challenging his accusations. The most comprehensive analysis of the circumstances surrounding the trial, J. B. Atlay's *The Trial of Lord Cochrane before Lord Ellenborough*, was commissioned by one of Ellenborough's grandsons. All except two of Cochrane's many biographers have argued more or less passionately that he was innocent of involvement in the fraud, but the tendency of most of them to accept Cochrane's autobiographies uncritically somewhat weakens their arguments. The most detailed and scholarly account of Cochrane's early life has concluded that 'the question of his guilt cannot be satisfactorily resolved' but nevertheless provides compelling evidence to show that he was an innocent victim of his uncle's plotting.[35]

Legal opinion over the years has been critical of the manner in which Lord Ellenborough conducted the trial, and several high-ranking lawyers (including three Lord Chancellors) who reviewed the case during the course of the nineteenth century concluded that Cochrane should have been found not guilty. While his conviction would certainly be regarded as 'unsafe' in the present state of the law, it is almost impossible to apply today's standards to a trial that took place in 1814.[36] However, it is worth noting that there are a number of points on which lawyers then and now agree. The first was expressed by Sir Fitzroy Kelly, who became Attorney General in 1858 and later Lord Chief Baron. He wrote of Cochrane's trial, 'I have thought of it much and long during more than forty years, and I am profoundly convinced that, had he been defended singly and separately from the other accused, or had he at the last moment, before judgement was pronounced, applied with competent legal advice and assistance for a new trial, he would have been unhesitatingly and honourably acquitted.'[37] Because Cochrane was not separately represented it could not be said on his behalf that, although he was closely associated with Cochrane-Johnstone, Butt and De Berenger, he was not personally aware of what they were up to – the line he took at the sentencing procedure after the verdict.

The second point concerns Lord Ellenborough's insistence that the defence must begin presenting their case at 10.00 p.m., after the jury had already spent thirteen hours listening to the case for the prosecution. Today this would have been grounds for setting aside the verdict, probably leading to a fresh trial. James Scarlet, one of the defence counsel at the time and subsequently Lord Abinger, remarked many years later that he was satisfied of Cochrane's innocence, 'and I believe it might have been established to the satisfaction of the jury, if the judge had not arbitrarily hurried on the defence at a late hour'.[38]

Finally there was no evidence produced to show that Cochrane was personally involved in, or had any knowledge of, a plot before De Berenger arrived at his house. It is possible that he realised or suspected then that something was wrong and it is conceivable that he joined the conspiracy but only at that late stage. But if that was the case why was he not separately represented and why was his defence not run on those lines? It has been suggested that a combination of aristocratic disdain and his belief in his own innocence convinced him that he was invulnerable, and that he should do his best to help the others to be acquitted. Henry Brougham was certain that family loyalty contributed to Cochrane's downfall: 'I take upon me to assert that Lord Cochrane's conviction was mainly owing to the extreme repugnance which he felt to giving up his uncle, or taking those precautions for his own safety which would have operated against that near relation.'[39]

Cochrane's sense of family loyalty is underlined by a letter he received from Cochrane-Johnstone's daughter Elizabeth more than forty years after the trial when he was busy preparing his autobiography. She had been living in her father's house at the time of the hoax and so presumably had some inkling of what he was up to. 'Many years I cannot wish for you,' she wrote,

> but may you live to finish your book and if it pleases God may you and I have a peaceful deathbed. We have both suffered much mental anguish tho' in various degrees for yours was indeed the hardest lot that an honourable man can be called on to bear. Oh, my dear cousin, let me say once more, while we are still here, how ever since that miserable time, I have felt that you suffered for my poor father's fault – how agonising that conviction was

– how thankful that tardy justice was done you – may God restore you fourfold for your generous tho misplaced confidence in him and for all your subsequent forbearance.'[40]

While Cochrane tried to settle down to the restrictions of life behind the walls of the King's Bench Prison, Napoleon was having to get used to exile on the Italian island of Elba. During the course of February 1814 he had fought a series of rearguard actions as the Allied forces advanced on Paris. He still had the support of his soldiers and his generals but the people of France were weary of war and the Parisians in particular were not prepared to die to defend their homes. When Tsar Alexander of Russia, King Frederick William of Prussia and Prince Schwarzenberg of Austria entered Paris at the end of March they encountered no opposition. The French Senate deposed Napoleon and on 6 April he was asked to abdicate. He accepted the inevitable. 'Very good, gentlemen,' he said, 'since it must be so, I will abdicate. I have tried to bring happiness to France and have not succeeded. I do not wish to increase our sufferings.'[41] It was agreed that he must leave the shores of France and take up residence as Emperor and Sovereign of the Isle of Elba. On 26 April 1814 he arrived at the little port of St Raphael, near Cannes, and two days later he embarked on the British frigate *Undaunted*. He was wearing the uniform of the Old Guard with the star of the Légion d'Honneur on his chest. He greeted Captain Ussher of the *Undaunted* 'with great condescension and politeness' and plied him with questions about his ship and the passage to Elba. In fifteen months' time, following his escape from Elba and his defeat at Waterloo, he would surrender to Captain Maitland of the *Bellerophon* and ply him with similar questions.

SIXTEEN

The Wilderness Years

1814–1818

The damaging effect of the Stock Exchange trial on Cochrane's life cannot be exaggerated. In the words of one historian, 'At a stroke all his prospects were destroyed, and Lord Cochrane confronted a future devoid of any means of income, without resources, and possibly without honour.'[1] It was not the sentence itself which was so painful: imprisonment could be endured and overcome, as it was by Sir Francis Burdett, William Cobbett, Henry Hunt and other outspoken writers, journalists and politicians of this period. It was the consequences of the guilty verdict which were so damaging: Cochrane lost his livelihood as a naval officer, the profession he had so thoroughly mastered and which had brought him fame and prize money; and he lost his political credibility – it is true that his crusade for naval reform and his support for the radicals had made him enemies but his distinguished naval record and his position as the heir to an earldom had given him a certain authority. He now became an outsider, seen by many as an embittered man fighting for lost causes. But most wounding of all was the stain on his honour and on his family name. The rest of his life would be a long-running campaign to restore his damaged reputation and to clear his name. There would be numerous diversions and adventures but he could never forget the 'period of my life in which occurred circumstances beyond all others painful to the feelings of an honourable man'. When he came to compile his autobiography at the age of eighty-four he was still bitter and would recall how, at the news of his conviction and sentence 'my heart for the first time sank within me, as conscious of a blow, the effect of which it has required all my energies to sustain.'[2]

After his initial depression Cochrane settled down to life in the King's Bench Prison. Throughout the autumn and winter he continued to work on his designs for the convoy lamp and his plans for the gas lighting of street lamps. He prepared a long and rambling letter to Lord Ellenborough, and he had visits from his family and friends. He could walk with them in the courtyard and watch his fellow prisoners playing draughts and skittles. Kate visited him regularly but he discouraged her from coming to live with him in the prison: 'My lovely Kate. You know the inconvenience of this place, and how impossible it is for me to make a single room in a prison comfortable to you. I would not willingly put you to inconvenience, and induce you to sacrifice anything to my satisfaction. No, not for the whole world. This is not a place favourable to morality. I wish you to remain, as you are, uncorrupted by the wickedness of this world.'[3]

He had completed eight months of his sentence when he decided to escape. He would later explain that his decision was prompted by his determination to assume his seat in Parliament and to remind the members 'that their sentence of expulsion had been reversed by the People' and to demand a 'strict investigation into the cause of my suffering, and into the conduct of my Judge'.[4] No doubt he also became increasingly restless at being confined behind the prison walls and the idea of a daring escape appealed to his sense of adventure. It was a foolish idea and gained him nothing but further notoriety and harsher conditions. A servant had smuggled in some lengths of rope and on the night of 6 March 1815 he made his attempt. The windows of his room were level with the top of the outer prison wall and only a few feet from it. For a sailor accustomed to working with ropes at a considerable height above a moving deck, it was a simple operation. He made a loop in the end of the rope and when the night watchman had made his rounds he threw the rope across so that the loop caught in the spikes on top of the wall. He swung himself across, climbed over the spikes and let himself down on the far side of the wall. All would have been well had the rope not snapped when he was still more than twenty feet from the ground. He fell heavily on his back and was knocked unconscious. He recovered, found there were no bones broken and made his way to the nearby house of a former servant of the family. By the time the prison authorities had discovered that he had escaped, he was on his way to Holly Hill, his house in Hampshire.

There was an immediate hue and cry, and a poster was issued advertising a three hundred guinea reward for his capture. The poster included a description which scarcely did justice to his impressive height and powerful physique: 'Escaped from the King's Bench Prison, on Monday the 6th day of March, instant, Lord Cochrane. He is about five feet eleven inches in height, thin and narrow chested, with sandy hair and full eyes, red whiskers and eyebrows.'[5]

There were rumoured sightings of him in the City of London, in Hastings, in France and in the Channel Islands. That he might be at his Hampshire home does not seem to have occurred to anyone. He remained there for two weeks enjoying the company of Kate and their baby son Tom and then headed back to London. On the afternoon of 21 March he walked into the Clerks' Room in the Houses of Parliament dressed in his usual grey trousers and greatcoat and told them he intended to speak in the Commons. He was informed that he could not take the necessary oath to speak until the writ for his election at Westminster had been fetched from the Crown Office in Chancery Lane. While he waited for the writ to arrive, Cochrane entered the debating chamber and, according to the official account of the incident, 'he sat down on the Privy Councillors Bench on the right hand of the chair, at which time there was no member present, prayers not having been read'.[6] An urgent message must have been sent to Southwark because after a while the Marshal of the King's Bench Prison arrived with two or three of his officers and some assistants and told Cochrane that he was arresting him. Cochrane refused to acknowledge his authority and said that he had no right to arrest a Member of

Parliament. There was a struggle, Cochrane was overpowered and taken back to the King's Bench Prison.

Instead of returning to his comfortable rooms on the top floor of the prison, he was locked in a damp, subterranean room. A visiting Member of Parliament who was inspecting prison conditions wrote, 'I found Lord Cochrane confined in a strong room fourteen feet square, without windows, fireplace, table or bed. I do not think it can be necessary for the purpose of security to confine him in this manner. According to my own feelings it is a place unfit for the noble Lord, or for any other person whatsoever.'[7] William Cobbett called on his friend on several occasions and later recorded his memories of the cell in his *Weekly Political Register*. He described the smell as worse than a soap boilers' premises, or those places where butchers deposited the garbage of the slaughter houses or barracks emptied the contents of their privies. 'I dined there by candle light at two o'clock in the day,' he wrote; 'the walls were so damp that, in putting my hand against them, I felt a chill run through my whole body.'[8]

Cochrane still had two months of his sentence to serve but after three weeks in the cell his health had deteriorated to such an extent that his brother called in a doctor to examine him. Dr Buchan reported that Cochrane had severe chest pains, a low pulse, cold hands and many of the symptoms of a person about to succumb to typhus or putrid fever. He blamed the stagnant air in the cell for his condition. Cochrane was moved to another room. Before he could be released from the prison on 20 June he had to pay the £1,000 fine which had been imposed on him when he was sentenced. As a matter of principle he refused to pay, but eventually his family and friends persuaded him that he must do so. Reluctantly, he wrote a bank note for the required amount, adding a defiant endorsement: 'My health having suffered by long and close confinement, and my oppressors being resolved to deprive me of property or life, I submit to robbery to protect myself from murder, in the hope that I shall live to bring the delinquents to justice.'[9]

Cochrane emerged from prison on 3 July 1815. The long war with France was over. Napoleon had escaped from Elba and resumed command of the French army but on 18 June he had been defeated at the Battle of Waterloo by a combination of forces led by the Duke of Wellington and Field Marshal Blücher. He was now at Rochefort and was planning to escape to America in one of the French frigates anchored in Aix Roads. In Vienna the representatives of the major powers of Europe, led by Lord Castlereagh and Count Metternich, had gathered to draw up a peace settlement and redraw the map of Europe.

Cochrane returned to Holly Hill and for a while he took a rest from politics. When he learnt that James Guthrie's ship had returned to port he invited him to 'take up your quarters here, where you will find plenty of good milk, fresh eggs, and all other country fare; besides you shall see a system of farming which Cobbett and I are pursuing to the astonishment and horror of all the surrounding farms'.[10] He continued to work on his designs for gas street lights and in his next letter to Guthrie he asked him whether there had been any attempt to introduce gas lamps in Edinburgh. He also revealed that he was about to launch an attack on his enemies: 'The campaign will soon open now, and I hope to expose the real actors in the mischief . . . All this is ruinous work but it must be gone through, let the consequences be what they may. . . By God I would rather eat dry bread than submit to injustice.'[11]

On 5 March 1815 he introduced a motion in the House of Commons for the impeachment of Lord Ellenborough on thirteen charges of 'partiality, misrepresentation, injustice, and oppression'. Sir Francis Burdett loyally supported him but when the motion was put to the vote not a single Member of Parliament was prepared to back them. Cochrane was undismayed and promised that as long as he had a seat in the House he would continue to bring forward the charges year after year until the truth had been established. In July he caused a major disruption at a public meeting of the Association for the Relief of the Manufacturing and Labouring Poor which was held at the London Tavern. The meeting was an august gathering of members of the royal family and leading churchmen and politicians. It was chaired by the Duke of York and joining him on the platform were the Duke of

Kent, the Duke of Cambridge, the Duke of Rutland, the Archbishop of
Canterbury, the Bishop of London, the Chancellor of the Exchequer
and William Wilberforce. The aims of the meeting were admirable
and a motion proposed by the Duke of Kent neatly summarised some
of the problems facing the country: 'That the transition from a state of
extensive warfare to a system of peace has occasioned a stagnation of
employment and a revulsion of trade, deeply affecting the situation of
many parts of the community, and producing many instances of great
local hardship.'[12]

The coming of peace after more than twenty years of war had led to
a recession, widespread unemployment and an increasing tide of
unrest among the labouring poor in town and country. The imposition
of the controversial Corn Laws in March 1815 had raised the price of
bread and provoked widespread protests – notably in Westminster
where soldiers fired into a crowd of rioters and killed several people.
In the north of England newly installed machinery was smashed by
Luddites who feared the loss of their jobs, and in the southern counties
starving farm workers set fire to haystacks as a form of protest. The
meeting at the London Tavern was intended to raise money for the
benefit of those in need. Cochrane was the first to speak from the floor
but when he rose to his feet he was unable to make himself heard, 'his
voice being lost in the huzzas and hisses which his presence called
forth'. When the noise died down he said that most of the money
raised by the government was taken up by interest on the national
debt or went into the pockets of placemen. He challenged the Duke of
Rutland to surrender his sinecure of £9,000 a year and said that, if he
and others who enjoyed similar incomes did not sacrifice them, 'their
pretended charity is little better than a fraud'. This caused an uproar
but the distinguished members of the committee persevered and
proposed raising a subscription for the benefit of their fellow subjects.
Cochrane denounced the subscription as wholly inadequate and
blamed the Chancellor of Exchequer and His Majesty's ministers
for the state of the country. This provoked an even more violent
uproar. Further motions were proposed and were shouted down. The
Duke of York withdrew and the meeting broke up in confusion.

In August 1816 Cochrane was summoned to the Surrey Assizes at Guildford on the belated charge of having escaped from the King's Bench Prison. Burdett and other friends accompanied him and on arrival they found the court crowded with spectators. Cochrane conducted his own defence and made use of the opportunity to launch a spirited attack on the Marshal of the King's Bench for brutality and taking bribes from prisoners. The jury decided that Cochrane was guilty of escaping from prison, but recommended mercy on the grounds that he had been adequately punished already. The judge was not prepared to let him off entirely and imposed a fine of £100 which Cochrane refused to pay. Judgement was delayed until November when he was sent back to the King's Bench Prison. 'You will see by the papers that I am again in my old quarters in defiance of the verdict of the jury at Guildford,' he told Guthrie on 28 November. 'I am glad of this – most sincerely glad for I will now be able to get my Westminster friends to look into the cruel injustice that has been done to me. I have now no doubt of beating all my enemies most completely, and of exposing such a scene of villainy as scarcely ever before was carried on.'[13] He told Guthrie that Kate and Tom were pretty well and living at Holly Hill where he hoped to join them soon. In fact the Westminster electors organised a subscription and raised the money to pay his fine, enabling him to leave the confines of the prison and return home.

In spite of setbacks in and out of Parliament, and encouraged by the support of his friends and constituents, Cochrane continued to play a prominent role in the movement for parliamentary reform which was seen by the leading radicals as the key to ridding the country of an oppressive government and addressing some of the nation's most deep-seated problems. As neighbours in Hampshire, Cochrane and Cobbett met frequently to discuss how they could best advance the cause of reform. During the course of their conversations in the summer of 1816 Cochrane persuaded Cobbett that he must write an essay with popular appeal which would set out the case for reform while discouraging violence and machine-breaking. They decided that the high price of the *Weekly Political Register* (it sold for just over one shilling) was preventing it from reaching a wider readership. 'Hence came the observation from one of us,' wrote Cobbett, 'that if, for this one time, for this particular purpose, the price could be by some means or other, reduced to twopence, then the desired effect could be produced.'[14] The result was what came to be called the 'Tuppeny Trash'. The first issue contained a stirring piece by Cobbett called 'Address to the Journeymen and Labourers'. It was published as a single sheet alongside the *Weekly Political Register* on 3 November. By the end of the month the twopenny sheet had sold 40,000 copies, and by the end of 1817 more than 200,000 copies were in circulation. Samuel Bamford, the Lancashire weaver and political activist, reckoned that Cobbett's writings were read in nearly every cottage hearth in the manufacturing counties in the Midlands and in the Scottish manufacturing towns. 'Their influence was speedily visible; he directed his readers to the true cause of their sufferings – misgovernment; and to its proper corrective – Parliamentary Reform.'[15]

The next step was to gather petitions from across the country and present them to Parliament when the next session opened on 28 January 1817. By this time Cochrane had moved his London residence from the rented house in Green Street to 7 Palace Yard, Westminster.[16] Samuel Bamford, who was among the delegates who came to London to present the petitions, later wrote an account of the day's proceedings which includes a vivid picture of the part played by Cochrane and his wife. He described how the delegates met Hunt at Charing Cross and moved in a noisy procession to Cochrane's residence:

> On arriving at his house in Palace Yard, we were shown into a room below stairs, whilst Lord Cochrane and Hunt conversed above; a slight and elegant young lady, dressed in white, and very interesting, served us with wine. She is, if I am not misinformed, now Lady Dundonald. At length his Lordship came to see us. He was a tall young man, cordial and unaffected in his manner. He stooped a little, and had somewhat of a sailor's gait in walking; his face was rather oval; fair naturally, but now tanned and sunfreckled. His hair was sandy, his

whiskers rather small, and of a deeper colour, and the expression of his countenance was calm and self-possessed.[17]

Bamford described how Cochrane took charge of the petition, which included signatures from Bristol and the north of England, and was hoisted in a chair and carried on the shoulders of the crowd to the doors of Westminster, accompanied by enthusiastic cheering. Later in the day Bamford and some of the other delegates visited Sir Francis Burdett's house where they were disappointed by their cool reception. Burdett was one of the idols of the radical movement.

Still I could not help my thoughts from reverting to the simple and homely welcome we received at Lord Cochrane's, and contrasting it with the kind of dreary stateliness of this great mansion and its rich owner. At the former place we had a brief reflection, bestowed with a grace which captivated our respect; and no health was ever drunk with more sincere good will than Lord Cochrane's: the little, dark haired and bright eyed lady seemed to know it, and to be delighted that it was so. But here, scarcely a servant appeared, and nothing in the shape of refreshment was seen.[18]

One of the demonstrators had thrown a stone at the Prince Regent as he was driven in a carriage to the opening of Parliament. The Prince was unhurt but the Cabinet immediately went into emergency session and several Members of Parliament demanded that draconian measures be taken against further public uprisings. The general mood of unrest now prompted the government to rush a bill through Parliament which suspended the Habeas Corpus Act, prevented the holding of seditious meetings, and forbade the publication of literature 'of an irreligious, immoral or seditious tendency'. Cobbett, who had already endured two years in Newgate Prison, was aware that his latest writings would provide an excuse for his enemies to throw him back into prison. He called his family up to London from Hampshire and told them that he must go to America. On 24 March 1817 he arrived at Liverpool with his two eldest sons and they embarked on a ship for New York. They did not return until November 1818.

Cobbett had been a good friend and a staunch supporter of Cochrane over the past ten years and his departure must have saddened and discouraged him. It was followed by another setback when a few weeks later he was informed that a court order had been issued for the seizure of Holly Hill on the grounds that he owed creditors £1,200 for unpaid expenses incurred during the Honiton election in 1806. Cochrane surrounded the house with bags of charcoal and let it be known that they contained explosives. For several weeks these discouraged the Sheriff of Hampshire and his constables from entering the house but in the end they did so and Cochrane paid the bill. He subsequently made arrangements to sell the property. He had no regular income and he had incurred heavy legal bills during the course of the Stock Exchange trial and its aftermath.[19]

In April 1817 an envoy from Chile arrived in Britain. His name was Antonio Alvarez and he was seeking support for the liberation movement in his country which was fighting for independence from the colonial rule of Spain. Alvarez had come with $100,000 and orders to recruit naval officers and seamen for the Chilean navy. The end of the wars in Europe and America had made thousands of British seamen redundant and put hundreds of officers on half-pay so that Alvarez had no difficulty in signing up experienced sailors and purchasing a brig-of-war and two armed East Indiamen. It is not known exactly when he first approached Cochrane but his visit came at an opportune time in Cochrane's life. He was forty-one years old. He needed an income to support himself and his family, and his parliamentary career was going nowhere. He might be popular with the Westminster electors and the delegates of working men from the provinces but he and his radical friends were regarded with increasing hostility by the majority of Members of Parliament and large sections of the community outside. This was clearly demonstrated by the behaviour of the audience at a meeting in Winchester. Shortly before leaving for America, Cobbett had accompanied Cochrane and Hunt to a meeting in the Hampshire town. A loyal address to the Prince Regent was proposed by a gathering of local grandees and clergymen. When Cochrane suggested that reference should be made to the fact that the constitution was established by Magna Carta, the Bill of Rights and Habeas Corpus 'for which our forefathers fought and bled', one of the parsons present stood up on his chair and spat on Cochrane's head. Cochrane turned round and said:

'By God, sir, if you do that again I'll knock you down.'

Parson Baines replied, 'You be damned. I'll spit where I like.'

When Cochrane struck at him, the parson jumped down and, putting his hands to his mouth, began hallooing like a huntsman. Another parson kicked Cobbett's heel while he was speaking and when Cobbett urged him to stop, he shouted:

'You be damned, you be damned, Jacobin.'

Cobbett dug his elbow into the man's ribs which temporarily silenced him but the meeting dissolved into uproar with the audience shouting, whistling, stamping and thumping the floor with their canes and umbrellas. Cobbett later wrote, 'As Lord Cochrane and I were going back to London, he said that, so many years as he had been in the navy, he never had seen a band of such complete blackguards.'[20]

Burdett and Cochrane had a less hostile but equally depressing experience when Burdett introduced a bill for parliamentary reform on 20 May. They were the only two members present to speak in favour of the bill and they were the only two to vote for it when the house divided. It is little wonder that when Alvarez offered Cochrane the role of commander-in-chief of the naval forces of Chile, he decided to take up the offer. On 12 January 1818 Alvarez wrote to José Zenteno, the Minister of Marine in Chile, and announced the news:

I have extreme satisfaction in informing you that Lord Cochrane, one of the most famous and perhaps the most valiant seaman in Great Britain, has determined to travel to Chile in order to direct our navy and co-operate decisively in the consolidation of liberty and independence. He is a person highly commendable, not only for the liberal principles with which he has upheld the cause of the English people in Parliament, but because he possesses a character superior to any ambition . . .[21]

Kate was now pregnant with their second child and, having sold Holly Hill, Cochrane agreed that she should go and stay with Mr and Mrs Simpson in Tunbridge Wells. Mrs Simpson was Kate's first cousin. Cochrane kept on the rooms in Palace Yard which were convenient for his parliamentary duties and commuted back and forth. On learning about the proposed move to Chile, the Simpsons strongly urged Kate to have a 'proper legal English marriage' before she went abroad. She later recalled that 'they were old-fashioned excellent people, and they did not understand Scotch marriages, and they wished to have this marriage made in England'. When this was put to Cochrane he assured her that the Scotch marriage was binding but he was very happy to go through with another ceremony. Indeed, he said, he would marry her in a hundred churches. So they were married by the Rev. Thomas Knox at Speldhurst, a small village close to Tunbridge Wells. On 8 March 1818 Kate gave birth to a baby son who was christened William Horatio Bernardo Cochrane. The name Horatio was obviously a tribute to Nelson; the name Bernardo was an act of faith in the new life which they were about to embark on – the leading figure in Chile's most recent struggle for independence and now Supreme Director of Chile was General Bernardo O'Higgins.

Like his father, Cochrane was often a step ahead of advances in technology and he was convinced that steam power was going to revolutionise naval warfare. He therefore determined that he must bring to Chile an armed steamship and he persuaded Alvarez that such a vessel would play a decisive role in any conflict with the Spanish fleet. He had located a ship in Brent's Yard at Rotherhithe which was being built to a revolutionary design. Named the *Rising Star* she had the outward appearance of a traditional 3-masted sailing ship of 22 guns with the addition of two tall, slim funnels amidships. She had an internal, retractable paddle wheel driven by two steam engines, so that she 'combined the endurance of a full sailing rig with the tactical power of steam and an effective, unencumbered battery.'[22] Cochrane was not, it seems, entirely out of funds because he invested £3,000 of his own money in the venture. It was evident that the vessel would not be ready for sea for many months and so he put his brother William in charge of fitting her out and, in due course, sailing her out to South America.

On 2 June Sir Francis Burdett made a second attempt to introduce a motion in the House of Commons proposing parliamentary reform and Cochrane used the occasion to make his farewell speech to Parliament. He was as outspoken as ever:

> As it is probably the last time I shall ever have the honour of addressing the House on any subject, I am anxious to tell its Members what I think of their conduct. It is now nearly eleven years since I have had the honour of a seat in this House, and since then there have been very few measures in which I could agree with the opinions of the majority . . . I will say, as has been said before by the great Chatham, the father of Mr Pitt, that if the House does not reform itself from within, it will be reformed with a vengeance from without. The people will take up the subject and a reform will take place which will make many Members regret their apathy in now refusing that reform which might be rendered efficient and permanent.

He warned them that commotions would arise which would shake the whole framework of government and society to its foundations. He thanked his constituents for their support and for rescuing him from the wicked conspiracy which had nearly ruined him, and he concluded, 'I shall not trespass on your time longer now – perhaps never again on any subject. I hope His Majesty's ministers will take into their serious consideration what I now say. I do not utter it with any feelings of hostility – such feelings have now left me – but I trust that they will take my warning, and save the country by abandoning the present system before it is too late.'[23]

Thirteen years would pass before a Whig government led by Lord Grey would attempt to drive the first great Reform Bill through a reluctant Parliament. When it was rejected there were riots and demonstrations across the country as Cochrane had warned. Public buildings were set on fire in Bristol; in Birmingham the church bells were muffled and tolled as if for a funeral; and in London the papers came out in mourning and the windows of the Duke of Wellington's house were smashed. Lord Grey threatened to create fifty new peers to force the bill through the House of Lords but the opposition caved in and on 7 June 1832 the Reform Act became law, removing the old rotten and pocket boroughs, allocating seats to the new industrial towns and greatly increasing the size of the electorate.

At the beginning of August the Cochrane family and their servants travelled to the Sussex port of Rye where they boarded a fishing smack and sailed across the Channel to Boulogne. There they boarded the *Rose*, a merchant ship of 300 tons, and on 15 August they set sail for South America. It would be seven years before Cochrane returned to Britain.

SEVENTEEN

The Liberation of Chile and Peru

1818–1822

The voyage across the Atlantic and around Cape Horn to Valparaiso took more than three months. They reached the bleak coastline of Tierra del Fuego without incident. The only signs of life in those cold, southern seas were colonies of penguins gathered on the rocky shores and the occasional albatross soaring overhead on outstretched wings. A fierce westerly wind hit them as they approached Cape Horn. For three days the ship laboured in heavy seas, her decks swept by rain and flurries of snow. They headed south where they picked up a favourable wind and were able to round the Horn and turn north into the calmer seas of the Pacific. A rugged, mountainous region of fiords and glaciers and islands slowly gave way to a densely forested landscape with the distant blue slopes and snow-covered peaks of the Andes in the background. At last, on 29 November 1818, the *Rose* reached Valparaiso and dropped anchor among the shipping moored in the bay. Built on the steep hills which curved around the harbour was a dense cluster of houses rising one above the other, many with small gardens overflowing with beautiful shrubs and fruit trees. Narrow, steeply sloping streets led down to the waterfront and the centre of the town with its markets and shops, a large church and a square overlooked by the grand façade of the governor's residence.

Cochrane arrived in the New World at a critical moment in its history. For more than three hundred years the vast continent of South America had been under the rule of Spain and Portugal. The pioneering voyages of Christopher Columbus in the 1490s had been followed by the expeditions of the conquistadors and within less than fifty years Spain effectively controlled much of South and Central America. Only Brazil lay outside Spain's control and that country was ruled by Portugal, the other great seafaring power of the age of exploration. During the course of the sixteenth and seventeenth centuries the two colonial powers had extended their rule over the continent. They had established estates and plantations, and built towns and cities with churches, cathedrals and plazas along the lines of those to be found in Seville, Cadiz and Lisbon.

As the South American countries grew in economic strength the local people came increasingly to resent the restrictions placed on their trading activities and wanted more control over their own affairs. The American Revolution of 1776 leading to the declaration of independence by the United States had shown the way, but it was the invasion of Spain and Portugal by Napoleon's armies in 1808 which encouraged armed resistance to the colonial powers. Within a few years of the overthrow of the monarchy in Spain there were uprisings against the Spanish royalists in the New World. A military junta declared the State of Paraguay independent and in Buenos Aires there was an armed rebellion which ejected the Spanish viceroy and established a republic in what is now Argentina. The independence movement in the north was led by Simon Bolivar and his campaigns eventually led to the establishment of the independent republics of Colombia and Bolivia.

In the south the key figures were General José de San Martin and General Bernardo O'Higgins, both of whom would play a crucial role in Cochrane's life. San Martin had been born in Argentina, trained as an army officer in Spain and fought against Napoleon's invading army with distinction. He had returned to South America in 1812 to join the patriot forces under General Belgrano and had fought a number of actions against royalist forces in the region of the Rio de la Plata. In January 1817 he led an army over the high mountain passes of the

Andes into Chile. On 12 February this army fought and won a crucial battle with Spanish forces at Chacabuco, and a few days later San Martin entered Santiago. He declined the offer to head the independent republic of Chile, leaving it to his friend General Bernardo O'Higgins to become Supreme Director.

O'Higgins, whose Irish father had been Spanish viceroy of Peru, had been sent to England for his education, returned to the family estate in Chile and joined the patriot army. He had displayed conspicuous bravery and leadership in numerous skirmishes and hard-fought actions, and eventually joined forces with San Martin. He took part in the epic march over the Andes and led the infantry at the Battle of Chacabuco. It was O'Higgins who said, 'This battle and one hundred more will be meaningless unless we control the seas.'[1]

Both men were in their early forties when Cochrane arrived in Chile and were very different in character and appearance. San Martin was tall and imposing with the air of a man of the world. 'He has a dark attractive countenance, with black, expressive and penetrating eyes,' noted one observer. 'His manners are dignified, easy, friendly.'[2]

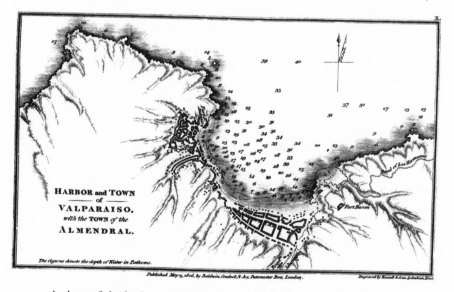

A chart of the harbour of Valparaiso in 1826. The town of Valparaiso is in the top left corner of the bay and the town of Almendral (now called Vino del Mar) is at the bottom of the illustration.

O'Higgins was round-faced and stocky and lacked the worldly manners of San Martin. However, the writer and traveller Maria Graham admired 'the plain simple good sense, honesty and right feeling of O'Higgins' and it was O'Higgins that Cochrane warmed to and most respected.[3] The two men remained on good terms through all the difficulties of the next four years.

When the news reached O'Higgins that the merchant ship *Rose* had dropped anchor in the bay at Valparaiso, he left the presidential palace in Santiago, boarded his carriage and hurried to greet the new commander of the Chilean navy. Cochrane and his party were invited to join the Supreme Director in Santiago. They arrived at the country's capital on 4 December and were entertained for several days with a series of lavish banquets and balls at which the young and beautiful Lady Cochrane made a great impression. Cochrane made less of an impression, according to George Worthington, the American agent in the city. 'His first appearance is not prepossessing. He is about forty years old, very tall and not corpulent, rather of a stripling appearance; not courtly in his address, but very plain and bold in his remarks and opinions; yet not authoritative nor pompous.'[4] When Worthington met Cochrane at a dinner given by General San Martin a few days later he was more enthusiastic and noted that he was 'very much pleased with him as a man of no ordinary talents, of great frankness and an advocate of civil liberty'.[5]

Cochrane appreciated the hospitality of the Chileans but he thought that the festivities and feasts were 'prolonged for so many days as to amount to a waste of time'.[6] He reminded O'Higgins that his purpose in coming to his country was to fight rather than to feast. On 11 December he became a Chilean citizen and was formally appointed vice-admiral and commander-in-chief of the Chilean navy. His pay and allowances were to be $6,000 a year (£1,200). On 9 January 1819 he received his orders from Zenteno, the Minister of Marine. He was to lead an expedition which was to 'blockade the port of Callao, to cut off the maritime forces of the Viceroy of Lima . . . and by so-doing enable them to be defeated in detail'.[7] The expedition was intended as a preliminary foray to encourage patriot resistance, gather intelligence and to seize all ships and property belonging to Spain. Cochrane was ordered to keep clear of shore batteries, to avoid action with superior forces and to ensure that nothing should put at risk the invasion of Peru which was planned for the following year.

Callao was chosen as the first objective for Cochrane's naval campaign because it was Spain's principal naval base on the Pacific coast and it was the port for Lima, the capital of Peru and the administrative centre for the Spanish colonial empire in South America. As long as the Spanish navy controlled the seas in the region there would be a constant threat to the independence of Chile and it would be difficult for San Martin to achieve his long-term aim – the liberation of Peru. There were differing accounts of the strength of the Spanish navy. Commodore William Bowles of the British squadron operating off South America reported that in 1817 'the whole naval force of His Catholic Majesty in these seas consists of the *Venganza* and *Esmeralda* of 36 guns each, and three corvettes of 16 or 8 guns'.[8] Other accounts reported that the Spanish had fourteen warships including three frigates and four brigs, as well as six armed merchantmen and twenty-seven gunboats.[9] The Spanish may have had a notional force as large as this scattered up and down the coast but few of the ships were ready for sea, and the gunboats were only suitable for port defence.

The Chilean squadron under Cochrane's command consisted of seven vessels in all, three frigates, three brigs and a sloop.[10] Two of the frigates were former East Indiamen but the *O'Higgins* was a powerful Spanish warship of 50 guns. Formerly the *Maria Isabel* she had recently been captured in Talcahuano Bay while escorting a convoy of transports. For Cochrane, who had spent three years in the Spanish-built frigate *Imperieuse*, the rig and fittings of the *O'Higgins* must have been reassuringly familiar and he had no hesitation in making her his flagship. While inferior to a British squadron of similar size, the Chilean vessels were perfectly adequate for Cochrane's purposes. He described the squadron as 'a force which, though deficient in organisation and equipment, was very creditable to the energy of a newly emancipated people'.[11]

Chile had no naval tradition and was therefore reliant on foreign sailors to man the ships. A recruiting campaign in Britain and North America had proved remarkably successful and by 1819 had attracted 1400 officers and seamen. Two-thirds of the seamen and almost all the officers were British or American. In addition to the sailors a force of some four hundred marines was recruited, all of whom were Chilean.[12] The senior officers of the squadron varied considerably in background and experience. The Chilean-born Manuel Blanco Encalada was the youngest and least experienced but he had proved his bravery as an artillery officer in the liberation struggle and before Cochrane's arrival he had been made commodore and commander-in-chief of the new Chilean navy. His only previous naval experience was as a midshipman in the Spanish navy but he had justified his promotion by capturing the *Maria Isabel.* He was now twenty-eight and became Cochrane's second in command with the rank of rear-admiral. The third in command was Robert Forster from Bamburgh, Northumberland. He had spent twenty years in the British navy in frigates and ships of the line and seen action in the Bay of Biscay and the Baltic and also in America where he had impressed Alexander Cochrane when serving as first lieutenant of the *Asia.* Cochrane had recruited him in London and now appointed him flag captain of the *O'Higgins.* This created some ill will because Captain Martin Guise was three months senior to Forster on the Navy List. Guise, who was also a Royal Navy veteran with considerable fighting experience, had arrived in Valparaiso several months before Cochrane's arrival and had brought with him the former British brig *Hecate* (now called the *Galvarino*). He was given command of the 44-gun frigate *Lautaro* but he and his friend Captain John Spry, who commanded the *Galvarino*, would cause problems for Cochrane in the future. The best officer by far, who would prove his gallantry on numerous occasions, was Major William Miller, formerly a British artillery officer and now the Commandant of Marines.[13] He had fought with Wellington's armies in the Peninsula, and in due course would rise to the rank of general. His memoirs provide a valuable corrective to the version of events which Cochrane published in his last years to justify his actions in South America.

As always Cochrane was impatient to get going and on 16 January

1819 he set sail with four ships, leaving the remainder to follow as soon as they were ready. The departure was accompanied by a minor drama. Lady Cochrane had said goodbye to her husband and returned to their house when she looked out of the window and was horrified to see their five-year-old son Tom being carried on the shoulders of a cheering crowd to the waterfront. He had slipped out of the house and told a lieutenant that he wanted to see his father. As the last gun was fired to summon all hands on board, the lieutenant and Tom clambered aboard the ship's launch and were rowed out to the *O'Higgins.* The ship was already under way as they came alongside so it was too late to send Tom ashore. He joined the crew of his father's ship and was soon fitted out with a miniature midshipman's uniform.

It took them more than a month to cover the 1,500 miles from Valparaiso to Callao. They sailed past a constantly changing coastline of great natural beauty: bleak, rocky headlands alternated with sheltered bays and deep, wooded valleys; at first the windblown trees, undulating hills and pastures resembled those of Devon or Cornwall but as they headed north the climate and vegetation became more Mediterranean with olive groves and palms, and barren plains covered by coarse grass and scrub; and always, rising up in the background, were the snow-covered mountain peaks of the Andes. The port of Callao was situated in a semicircular bay on low-lying land and was heavily defended by more than 160 guns. Charles Darwin, who visited the place a few years later during his voyage in the *Beagle,* noted in his diary, 'Callao is a most miserable, filthy, ill-built, small seaport; the inhabitants both here and at Lima present every imaginable shade of mixture between European, Negro and Indian blood. They appear a depraved, drunken set.' However, he thought that, 'The fortress, which withstood Lord Cochrane's long siege, appears very imposing.'[14]

When the squadron arrived off the town a carnival was taking place and Cochrane determined to attack the anchored Spanish frigates while everyone was distracted by the noisy festivities. His plan was foiled by a dense sea fog which shrouded the coast for a week. When the fog lifted on 29 February, Cochrane sailed in with his flagship and the frigate *Lautaro,* both ships flying American colours, but light winds and more fog hampered their movements. At one stage they were becalmed for two hours and subjected to heavy gunfire from the gun batteries and the anchored Spanish warships. When Captain Guise was severely wounded and the *Lautaro* withdrew from the action, Cochrane had to accept the inevitable: 'I was reluctantly compelled to relinquish the attack and withdraw to the island of San Lorenzo, about three miles distant from the forts.'[15]

Young Tom had a narrow escape during the action. He had refused to remain in the after cabin and had climbed through the quarter gallery window and joined his father on deck. Cochrane allowed him to remain and gave him the job of handing gunpowder to the gunners, but while he was doing this a round shot took off the head of a marine standing by him. Major Miller later recalled, 'The shot scattered the brains of the marine in the child's face. He ran up to his father, and, with an air of hereditary self-possession and unconcern, called out, "Indeed, papa, the shot did not touch me; indeed I am not hurt." '[16]

The Spanish authorities were using San Lorenzo as a prison island. Thirty-seven Chilean soldiers taken prisoner eight years before were being forced to work in chain gangs and when Cochrane learnt that there were prisoners being kept in even worse conditions in Lima he wrote to Don Joaquim de la Pezuela, the Spanish viceroy, proposing a general exchange of prisoners. The viceroy politely parried the request and expressed his surprise at finding a nobleman of Great Britain, 'a country in alliance with the Spanish people', commanding the naval forces of a rebel government. This prompted Cochrane to engage in a lengthy correspondence with the viceroy during the course of which he came up with a statement which could be said to encapsulate his political beliefs: 'A British nobleman is a free man, capable of judging between right and wrong, and at liberty to adopt a country and a cause which aim at restoring the rights of oppressed human nature.'[17]

On 22 March, Cochrane attempted a second raid on Callao using an explosion vessel to lead the attack but the vessel was harmlessly sunk by Spanish gunfire and again he was forced to retreat. He decided on a change of tactics. Leaving Admiral Encalada to set up a blockade of Callao, Cochrane embarked on a series of coastal raids in his flagship.

For several weeks the *O'Higgins* roved up and down the coast of Peru, intercepting ships and sending landing parties ashore to plunder towns and distribute propaganda leaflets encouraging the local people to embrace the cause of liberty. A raid on Patavilca yielded $67,000 belonging to the Spanish treasury; the capture of the French brig *Gazelle* at Guambucho (Guanbacho) yielded cargo and bullion valued at $60,000; the Spanish fortress at Paita was captured; and at Supe a mule train carrying gold and silver bullion worth an estimated $120,000 was ambushed. Cochrane justified these raids by the need to raise money for the Chilean cause and to pay his men, but he was also after prize money and some of his raids, like those of Sir Francis Drake before him, amounted to outright piracy.

Shortage of supplies had compelled Admiral Encalada to abandon the blockade of Callao and return to Valparaiso and in June 1819 Cochrane also returned and was reunited with his family. Compared with his coastal raids in the Mediterranean his first campaign as commander-in-chief of the Chilean navy had been disappointing to say the least, but the Chilean government was delighted. He had fulfilled the orders given him and entirely justified his appointment. The National Institute of Santiago issued an extravagant eulogy describing his operations at Callao, and the Supreme Director, Bernardo O'Higgins, travelled from Santiago to offer his personal congratulations. Cochrane spent the next three months of the Chilean winter making preparations for a second campaign against Callao. An assistant of William Congreve had arrived to supervise the manufacture of Congreve rockets which, together with fireships, were to play a key role in the attack. Cochrane also persuaded O'Higgins to raise his salary to $10,000 (£2,000) per annum by following the British navy's practice of increasing an admiral's income by the provision of an entertainment allowance, or what was called 'table money'.[18]

On 12 September 1819 the squadron headed north and once again anchored in Callao Roads. On the night of 2 October, Cochrane ordered a preliminary attack to test the harbour defences. Rafts for launching the rockets were towed into position by the three brigs and the sleeping seaport was rudely awakened by gunfire and the hissing flare of the few rockets which were successfully ignited. The Spanish were prepared for the attack and retaliated with such a barrage of fire from the shore batteries that the Chilean ships were forced to withdraw. On 6 October the main attack took place, led by a fireship which, as in the action at Basque Roads, was intended to break the protecting boom and cause panic among the anchored Spanish ships. This time the attack was thwarted by a sudden calm which halted the progress of the fireship. Riddled with shot by the Spanish guns she began to sink, and had to be set ablaze prematurely, causing her to explode before she reached the boom. The Congreve rockets were as unpredictable as ever, most of them veering off course and plunging harmlessly into the sea.

Realising that the forces at his disposal were unable to take the heavily defended seaport, Cochrane turned his attention to easier targets. Captain Guise, with a force of marines led by Colonel Charles, was despatched south to attack Pisco and procure provisions. The attack was successful but Colonel Charles was killed during the action and Major Miller was wounded. Cochrane then led his squadron north to the mouth of the River Guayaquil where, on 28 November, he captured two armed Spanish vessels and took possession of the village of Puna.[19] It was around this time that he came up with a bold plan which lay outside the orders given him by Zenteno but would more than compensate for his failures at Callao. With his flagship alone he determined to attack and take the southern stronghold of Valdivia. He sent three of his ships back to Valparaiso with the large number of men who had fallen sick, ordered the remaining ships to keep watch on Callao, and headed south in the *O'Higgins*.

Valdivia, situated five hundred miles south of Valparaiso, was the first port of call for ships rounding Cape Horn from Europe. It was the last stronghold on the coast of Chile which was still in Spanish hands and its capture would be a major coup. It would, however, be a difficult place to mount a surprise attack because, in common with European naval bases like Brest and Portsmouth, it had a large, sheltered anchorage with a narrow entrance which was strongly protected by forts and gun emplacements. The town itself was sixteen miles up the river estuary.

HARBOR
of
VALDIVIA,
with its
Fortifications.

Ancla Point

Molino Point

Churin Rivulet

Valdivia River

Carbonero Point

Carbonero Battery

REY
ISLAND

Niebla Castle

Piojo

Mount Gonzalo

Aguada del Ingles

Ingles Battery

San Carlos

Amargos

Chorocomoyo Alto

Aguada del Coral

Coral Castle

Sa Rosa Point

Manzanera Island

Cabron I.

Toro I.

Trinidad Point

Frenton Point

Piena del Lobo

S.t Julian Point

Corbone Island

Legisia Island

Mount of San Juan

Ensenada of San Juan

Castile Rivulet

Lienot Giru

Russell & Sons sculpsit.   Published May 15, 1826, by Baldwin, Cradock, & Joy, Paternoster Row, London.

A chart of the harbour of Valdivia in 1826 showing the numerous forts.
Cochrane attacked the Spanish naval base in February 1820.

Cochrane arrived at Valdivia on the evening of 17 January 1820 with Spanish flags flying from the masts of the *O'Higgins* to allay the suspicions of the defending garrison. As it happened the Spanish were expecting the arrival of one of their frigates, and so they naturally assumed that Cochrane's Spanish-built frigate lying off the harbour entrance was the long-awaited ship. Very early the next morning Cochrane had himself rowed around the anchorage in his gig so that he could take soundings of the depth of water and note the position of all the forts and gun emplacements. Soon after his return to the ship a boat came alongside with a pilot accompanied by a Spanish officer and four soldiers. They were promptly made prisoner and from them Cochrane learnt that the Spanish brig *Potrillo* was due shortly with money for the payment of the Valdivia garrison. On the third day the *Potrillo* hove in sight and she too was deceived by their Spanish colours. She was captured without a shot being fired and proved to have on board $20,000 in silver and military stores worth some $40,000. Almost as valuable for Cochrane's purposes were her navigational charts which included an excellent chart of the harbour of Valdivia.[20]

Having made his reconnaissance, acquired a local pilot and captured a valuable prize, Cochrane now headed up the coast to obtain reinforcements for his intended raid. On 20 January he anchored at Talcahuano and travelled a few miles inland to the town of Concepción where he met General Freire, the Chilean governor of the province. Freire gave him a hospitable welcome, 'and after explanation of my plans, placed two hundred and fifty men at my disposal, under the command of a gallant Frenchman, Major Beauchef'.[21] Lying in Talcahuano Bay were a Chilean schooner, the *Montezuma*, and a Brazilian brig, the *Intrepido*, and these were persuaded to join the expedition.

On 25 January 1820 the diminutive squadron set sail for Valdivia and under Cochrane's confident leadership embarked on the most desperate enterprise of his career. In theory an attack on Valdivia with such a small force was suicidal. The place was defended by nearly 2,000 men and, according to the engineer John Miers, was 'unques-

tionably the strongest in the whole continent of South America'.[22]
The fire from the guns of the four principal forts crossed each other
and commanded the entrance, the anchorage and the channel leading
to the town. Once inside the entrance an attacking force would be a
sitting target for more than one hundred of these guns. However,
Cochrane had noted that the guns were intended to resist an attack
from the sea. He proposed to land a force at night and use the element
of surprise to attack the forts and gun batteries from the landward
side. It was a tactic which Sir Henry Morgan had employed with
spectacular success in 1668 when, with no more than five hundred
buccaneers, he had captured Portobello, the strongly defended Spanish
treasure port on the northern coast of Panama. As Cochrane explained to Major Miller, 'Cool calculation would make it appear that
the attempt to take Valdivia is madness. This is one reason why the
Spaniards will hardly believe us in earnest, even when we commence;
and you will see that a bold onset, and a little perseverance afterwards,
will give a complete triumph; for operations unexpected by the enemy
are, when well executed, almost certain to succeed, whatever may be
the odds; and success will preserve the enterprise from the imputation
of rashness.'[23]

The enterprise nearly came to grief before they even sighted their
objective. They were lying off the island of Quiriquina on the night of
29 January in a dead calm. Cochrane had gone to his cabin for a rest,
leaving the ship's only lieutenant in charge with strict orders to wake
him if a breeze sprang up. The lieutenant decided that he too would
retire and left a midshipman to take his place. A sudden wind caught
the ship unawares and the midshipman was unable to prevent her
being swept on to a rocky shoal. Cochrane came on deck to find the
ship aground with the jib boom entangled among the branches of a
tree and fragments of the ship's false keel floating on the surface of the
water. If the swell increased the ship would inevitably break up. A
sounding revealed five feet of water in the hold and an attempt to work
the pumps showed they were out of order.

The first reaction of the crew was to abandon the ship but the
mainland was forty miles away and Cochrane reminded them that it

was inhabited by Indians who were likely to torture and kill them. There was no sign of the schooner and the brig. Their lives depended on getting the pumps working. The practical training which Cochrane had received from his first naval instructor, Jack Larmour, saved the day. 'Our carpenter, who was only one by name, was incompetent to repair them; but having myself some skill in carpentry I took off my coat, and by midnight got them into working order, the water meanwhile gaining on us, though the whole crew were engaged in bailing it out with buckets.'[24] With the pumps at last operating they managed to stem the increase of water in the hold and by laying out an anchor they eventually managed to heave the ship off the reef.

They headed south and when they caught up with the schooner and the brig, Cochrane shifted his flag to the *Montezuma*, and transferred all the soldiers and marines from the leaking *O'Higgins* to the two smaller vessels. The powder magazine and most of the ammunition on the flagship had been soaked and rendered useless by the incoming water. This would have been enough to cause most commanders to call off the attack but Cochrane assured his men that they would succeed by the use of bayonets alone. On the afternoon of 3 February the schooner and the brig anchored off Valdivia near the Aguada del Ingles, the only possible landing place outside the harbour. To prevent the defenders from suspecting anything was amiss both vessels were flying Spanish colours, the troops were ordered to remain below deck and the launches which would take the men ashore were lowered on the seaward side of the ships out of sight of the shore. Cochrane sent a Spanish-speaking officer ashore in a boat to ask for a pilot. He was met by a detachment of Spanish soldiers who were not convinced by his story that the two vessels had come from Cape Horn and been separated from their squadron in a storm. At around 4.00 p.m. the guns of Fort Ingles opened fire on the anchored vessels, the shot smashing into the hull of the *Intrepido* and killing two soldiers. Cochrane ordered the attack to commence at once.

Major Miller with forty-four marines embarked in the launches and headed for the landing place. There was a heavy swell and they had to contend with thick seaweed clogging the oars as well as a hail of musket balls fired at them from the shore. Miller counted seventy-five enemy soldiers and was nearly killed by one shot which passed through his hat and grazed his head. On landing they attacked the Spaniards with such ferocity that they drove them off and within an hour they had landed three hundred men. By now it was dark and a picked force, led by one of the Spanish soldiers they had captured on their previous visit, climbed a precipitous path from the beach to Fort Ingles on the rocky heights above. On reaching the fort one group caused a noisy diversion by yelling and firing those guns which still had dry powder, while another group crept silently round the back of the fort, uprooted a palisade and used this as a bridge to cross a defensive ditch. Attacked from two sides the Spanish defenders fled towards Fort Carlos whose gates were opened to receive the fugitives. The Chileans poured in after them and, using their bayonets to bloodthirsty effect, they soon captured the fort. The next fort was taken in a similar manner and the attackers moved on to Castle Coral, a formidable structure overlooking the anchorage which should have been able to hold out against such a small force. Shaken by the noise and confusion of the night attack in which a hundred men had been killed and many more taken prisoner, many of the Spanish defenders abandoned their posts and escaped across the harbour in boats, leaving Colonel Hoyos, the commander of the castle, with little option but to surrender to Major Miller. By dawn all the forts on the western side of the harbour were in the hands of the Chileans.

The schooner *Montezuma* and the brig *Intrepido* now entered the harbour. They were fired on by the guns of Fort Niebla on the eastern side of the entrance, but without effect, and they dropped anchor in the deep water near Castle Coral. Cochrane ordered two hundred men to embark on the vessels in preparation for an attack on the eastern forts but while they were doing so the *O'Higgins* sailed into the harbour. At the sight of a 50-gun ship, which they assumed was bringing re-inforcements, the Spanish abandoned the remaining forts and fled towards the town of Valdivia. In fact the *O'Higgins* was still leaking so badly that Cochrane ordered her to be beached on a mud bank to prevent her sinking.

On 6 February the *Montezuma* and the *Intrepido*, with Major Miller's marines and Major Beauchef and the Chilean troops on board, sailed up the river towards Valdivia. The *Intrepido* ran aground in the channel and was so badly damaged that she had to be abandoned but this was of little consequence. Before they reached the town a party of local people appeared with a flag of truce and the news that the Governor of Valdivia, Colonel Monoya, had fled. The town was in a state of confusion. The fleeing Spanish soldiers had looted many of the private houses and Cochrane's first task was to restore order.

Valdivia was an important military depot so that in addition to capturing the town, the harbour and the fortifications, Cochrane found himself in possession of 10,000 cannon shot, 128 guns, 1,000 hundredweight of gunpowder, 170,000 musket cartridges, a large quantity of small arms, and the ship *Dolores* which was later sold for $20,000. That evening he wrote a despatch to Zenteno, the Minister of Marine in Santiago. He described their successful action, assured him that he had restored order in the town, and concluded, 'At first it was my intention to have destroyed the fortifications, and to have taken the artillery and stores on board; but I could not resolve to leave without defence the safest and most beautiful harbour I have seen in the Pacific, and whose fortifications must have cost more than a million dollars.'[25]

The authorities in Santiago had received no word of Cochrane's movements since mid-January, when he had left Callao, so the news of his astounding victory came as a complete surprise. The universal reaction was one of jubilation. The Supreme Director announced that all the officers and soldiers who had braved the dangers of 'that noble conquest' would be awarded distinctive medals in recognition of their gallantry; the National Institute of Santiago and the City Council issued proclamations which praised the achievements of Cochrane and his men; and Zenteno wrote a public letter to Cochrane which stressed the magnitude of the capture of such an impregnable fortress: 'The memory of that glorious day will occupy the first pages of Chilean history and the name of Your Excellency will be transmitted from generation to generation by the gratitude of our descendants.'[26] O'Higgins also ensured that the government rewarded Cochrane in financial terms. His pay was doubled, he received the full amount of prize money owed him and he was given an estate of 20,000 acres along the banks of the River Clara.

Although he received a hero's welcome when he returned to Valparaiso on 6 March, Cochrane became convinced that some of the people in power were jealous of his achievements and were plotting against him. He had learnt that Zenteno had remarked in private that the attack on Valdivia was against the orders he had been given and had risked the lives of the patriot forces. This criticism so angered Cochrane that he decided that Zenteno was his bitter opponent, 'obstructing all my plans for the interests of Chile'. He also came to believe that Zenteno and various ministers wished to dispense with his services altogether. Writing some time later to San Martin he observed that 'plans and intrigues were set afoot for my dismissal from the Chilean service'. The written evidence does not support Cochrane's suspicions. Zenteno, a former lawyer, was not a very likeable character. In the words of Maria Graham, 'His manner is cold; but as he is always grave and sententious, and possesses much of the cunning and quickness commonly attributed to his former profession, he passes for clever.'[27] He was, however, a dedicated and able administrator. With few staff, and little help from an almost empty treasury and an impoverished people, he had managed to assemble, maintain and supply the Chilean navy. His correspondence with Cochrane was invariably courteous and friendly, and he dealt patiently with his numerous complaints. And there was no question of anyone in the government wishing to dispense with Cochrane's services. On the contrary, his name, his reputation and his recent exploits were a source of pride, and O'Higgins and his ministers had given him ample proof of their appreciation.

Given the circumstances of a revolutionary government which was struggling to establish a new and independent state, there were inevitable problems. The most serious as far as Cochrane was concerned was that on his return to Valparaiso he found that the officers and men of the Chilean squadron had not been paid. Many of the foreign seamen had lost patience and were deserting their ships. In

April the commissioned officers and warrant officers joined together to present a formal petition for their pay. Cochrane supported their protest and wrote a letter to Zenteno threatening to resign unless the men were paid. By 30 May the government had managed to raise enough money to pay the squadron.

Cochrane also experienced problems with Captain Guise and Captain Spry, although the problems seem to have been largely of his own making. Both men had played a leading role in the attacks on Callao and the subsequent coastal raids, but Cochrane believed they had been plotting against him since his arrival in Chile. On his return from Valdivia he became convinced that they were involved in a plot with Zenteno to have him court-martialled. But although there were plenty of disagreements and disciplinary problems among the officers and seaman in the squadron there is no evidence of any plot against the commander-in-chief. However, Cochrane's followers seem to have been providing him with damaging allegations against Captain Guise. On 11 July, Cochrane had him arrested for disobedience and for endeavouring to 'bring into contempt the authority of his superior officer, the commander in chief'.[28] The charges scarcely warranted such drastic action and when Cochrane asked for a court martial the Chilean government refused his request. This prompted Cochrane to tender his resignation again. O'Higgins and Zenteno strenuously urged him to change his mind and in the end he did so. The priority for the government at this time was assembling ships and men for the invasion of Peru. Preparations for a combined army and navy operation were almost complete and Cochrane's active participation was regarded as essential.

Meanwhile, Cochrane's wife had been experiencing adventures of her own. Kate had seen very little of her husband during their first year and a half in Chile. If he was not away on extended cruises he was engaged with the administration of the squadron or visiting Santiago for meetings with O'Higgins or Zenteno. Like any sailor's wife, Kate was having to get used to these prolonged absences but in Valparaiso she was never lonely. She was the belle of every ball and beguiled many a visiting naval officer, but she also had her share of alarms and adventures. The first of these was nearly fatal. When Cochrane departed for the second raid on Callao, Kate took the children and servants to a country house at Quillota. She was tracked down by an agent of the Spanish regime who threatened to kill her if she did not reveal her husband's secret orders. There was a struggle and before her screams brought the servants to her aid, she had been wounded by the intruder's stiletto. The man was taken away and condemned to death. Kate persuaded the authorities to spare him and his sentence was commuted to banishment for life.

In March 1820, shortly after Cochrane's return from Valdivia, Kate gave birth to their third child, a girl who was christened Elizabeth Katherine. Cochrane's letters home around this time are full of optimism, in spite of his local difficulties. 'You will be glad to hear that I am doing famously here, and have prospects for the future better than the past, as we are now in earnest preparing for the future invasion of Peru,' he wrote to his brother William on 10 April. 'What a noble country this will be in a few years . . . They have presented me with a farm of twenty thousand acres almost as big as the New Forest, and I am in treaty to purchase eighty thousand more of which you shall have a good slice when you can do nothing better.'[29] Before he sailed for Peru he had acquired the estate of Herradura, in the beautiful valley of Quintero, some eight miles north along the coast from Valparaiso.

The Liberating Expedition to deliver Peru from the colonial rule of Spain sailed from Valparaiso on 20 August 1820, cheered on by an enthusiastic crowd of onlookers gathered on the waterfront. There were seventeen transport ships carrying artillery and supplies, 800 horses and an army of 4,200 men, mostly Chileans but with a reinforcement of veteran freedom fighters from Argentina. The transports were escorted by eight warships under the command of Cochrane who was again accompanied by the gallant William Miller, now raised to the rank of colonel. General San Martin was in overall charge of the expedition. They sailed north for two weeks until they reached the town of Pisco, 130 miles south of Callao and Lima. Here San Martin decided to disembark his troops and here they remained for the next six weeks, to the surprise and annoyance of Cochrane who believed that a pre-emptive strike on Lima 'was by no means difficult of execution, and certain of success'. This marked the beginning of a rift between the two leaders which would become increasingly bitter during the coming months.

The two men had a very different approach to warfare. Cochrane believed in taking the enemy by surprise and launching a bold and overwhelming attack. San Martin was an experienced leader of irregular forces who had achieved impressive results in the past, but he had depended on superior numbers and the patriotic fervour of his troops to overcome an enemy usually better armed and better trained. He was aware that his liberating army was greatly outnumbered by the Spanish troops in Peru. It was therefore San Martin's aim to avoid pitched battles and to encourage the people to rise up against their colonial rulers. At Pisco he issued a proclamation to the people of Peru which began, 'You shall be free and independent. You shall choose your own government and laws by the spontaneous will of your representatives.'[30] It was a strategy which took time but would eventually prove successful. The first breakthrough came towards the end of September when Pezuela, the viceroy of Lima, sent an envoy to San Martin under a flag of truce. An armistice was signed but negotiations broke down. Then came news that the province of Guayaquil in the north had declared its independence. A few weeks later one of the Spanish regiments deserted and joined the patriots.

On 28 October San Martin re-embarked his troops and the expedition sailed to Ancón, a fishing village a few miles north of Lima. The troops were sent ashore but it soon became clear that San Martin was in no hurry to advance on the capital. Exasperated by this cautious approach, Cochrane decided it was time for drastic action. Without informing San Martin of his intentions, he took three of his ships – the frigates *O'Higgins*, *Lautaro* and *Independencia* – and sailed into the bay of Callao. His plan was simple, audacious and almost as hazardous as the attack on Valdivia. He intended 'to cut out the Esmeralda frigate from under the fortifications, and also to get possession of another ship, on board of which we had learned that a million of dollars was embarked . . .'.[31] The *Esmeralda* was the flagship of the Spanish fleet, a fine 44-gun frigate with a well-trained crew, and her capture would be a major coup. The problem was that she was protected by a strong boom of spars chained together and was anchored beneath the guns of the fortress which had recently been reinforced and now mounted some three hundred guns. In addition she was surrounded by twenty-seven gunboats.

For this venture Cochrane made the most careful preparations. Alexander Caldecleugh, who watched him at work in the bay of Callao, recalled that he 'frequently rowed about the bay in his gig with the lead in his hand, sounding with the greatest nonchalance, while shot of all shapes and sizes were directed at him from the shore batteries and gunboats'.[32] He spent three days in planning, reconnaissance and preparing his men for the attack. On 5 November he issued a rousing proclamation in English and Spanish, and promised them a share in the prize money of all the vessels captured. When he asked for volunteers all the marines and seamen on board the three ships offered their services. His officers selected 160 seamen and 80 marines. They were informed that the attack would take place that night. Fourteen of the ships' boats would set off at nightfall with their oars muffled to prevent them banging on the thole pins (a type of rowlock projecting upwards from the boat's gunwale) and would head for the gap in the floating boom. To ensure that every man knew what was required of him Cochrane issued a detailed set of orders which covered every eventuality.

To prevent the Spanish from expecting an attack that night Cochrane sent the *Lautaro* and the *Independencia* out of the bay as if in pursuit of some vessels off the coast. At 10.00 p.m. the ships' boats, loaded with armed sailors and marines, set off into the darkness towards the distant lights of the harbour. The oarsmen heaved on the muffled oars and the only sound was the splash of the blades in the water. They arrived at the gap in the boom around midnight where Cochrane's boat was intercepted by one of the guardboats. 'The challenge was given, upon which, in an undertone, I threatened the occupants with instant death, if they made the least alarm.'[33] The threat was effective and a few minutes later the boats drew silently alongside the *Esmeralda* and the men clambered up her sides. As Cochrane boarded the ship he was hit by the butt end of a Spanish sentry's musket, causing him to fall back on to a thole pin of the boat. The pin entered his back near the spine inflicting a severe injury which was to cause him years of suffering. 'Immediately regaining my footing, I reascended the side, and when on deck was shot through the thigh, but binding a handkerchief tightly round the wound, managed, though with great difficulty, to direct the contest to a close.'[34] Apart from the sentries, the Spanish crew had been asleep at their quarters and were taken completely by surprise. British and American seamen and Chilean marines laid into them with cutlasses and boarding axes. One group of Spanish sailors retreated to the forecastle where they put up a gallant fight but they were cut down and the rest leapt overboard or fled below to the hold to escape the slaughter. The fighting tops of the ship had been secured by sailors shinning up the shrouds and within fifteen minutes the ship had been taken.

The uproar on the ship alerted the soldiers of the garrison who opened fire on the *Esmeralda*, killing several Spanish sailors and wounding Captain Coig, the commander of the ship. There were two foreign warships at anchor in the harbour, the British frigate *Hyperion* and the American frigate *Macedonian*. Cochrane had noted that they hoisted distinctive signals at night to prevent them being fired upon in the event of a night attack. Similar lights were now hoisted on the *Esmeralda* and this so confused the gunners in the fortress that the ship ceased to be a target. There are conflicting accounts of what happened next but it seems that some of the British seamen broke into the spirit room and got drunk while the Chileans began plundering the ship. Cochrane's injuries compelled him to hand over command to Captain Guise who decided the best course was to ignore his orders, cut the anchor cables, loose the topsails and sail the ship out of the bay. This put paid to Cochrane's ambitious plans to capture all the other shipping but ensured that the *Esmeralda* was secured without further damage. The operation had been achieved at the cost of eleven men killed and thirty wounded. The Spanish had suffered 160 men dead or wounded.

The capture of the *Esmeralda* from under the guns of Callao was recognised by many observers as an extraordinary achievement. Captain Thomas Searle, commander of the *Hyperion*, considered it 'a most brilliant affair' and was astonished by the speed of the operation. 'This was done so quick and in so masterly a style that I had scarcely time to get out of the line of fire.'[35] Captain Basil Hall, commanding HMS *Conway* which was anchored in Callao Roads, praised Cochrane's 'matchless intrepidity and inexhaustible resources in war' but also pointed to the wider significance of the Spanish flagship's capture: 'The loss was a death-blow to the Spanish naval force in that quarter of the world; for although there were still two Spanish frigates and some smaller vessels in the Pacific, they never afterwards showed themselves, but left Lord Cochrane undisputed master of the coast.'[36] When General San Martin received the news he wrote to Cochrane congratulating him on 'the importance of the service you have rendered to the country by the capture of the frigate Esmeralda, and the brilliant manner in which you conducted the gallant officers and seamen under your orders',[37] and he sent Cochrane's despatches to O'Higgins with an accompanying letter which was full of praise for 'the daring enterprise of 5th November'.[38]

It was now the turn of Lady Cochrane to experience more adventures. In late October 1820 she had set off on a family expedition across the Andes to Mendoza. She was apparently unperturbed by the precipitous mountain tracks or the discomforts of the journey. They had to leave much of their baggage behind and had to sleep in mountain shelters without beds, but she was able to assure her husband, 'I can safely say that I never slept better except when in the arms of my beloved Cochrane.' They encountered a piercing wind on the top of the Cordillera and 'there I experienced much inconvenience from faintness caused by the rarefied air ... I never remember so unpleasant a sensation but I was very soon recovered'.[39] Soon after her return to Valparaiso she embarked on HMS *Andromache* with her children and headed north to join her husband in Peru. She arrived at Callao early in January 1821. Shortly after her arrival she accepted an invitation to visit the estate of a member of the local Spanish aristocracy. The estate was at Quilca in the mountains behind Lima, and Kate took her eleven-month-old daughter Elizabeth with her and several attendants. They travelled on horseback through dramatic mountain scenery but on arrival at Quilca they were warned that a party of Spanish royalists were planning to take Kate and her child hostage. There was no alternative but to leave at once. On the return journey they had to cross a deep ravine by means of a cane and rope bridge. Kate was halfway across with the child in her arms when the swaying of the bridge proved too much for her and she had to lie down and wait to be rescued by one of her servants. They eluded their pursuers, reached the coast safely and were reunited with Cochrane on board his ship. However, Kate's adventures were not yet over. On learning that a Spanish warship in the harbour was planning to escape with a cargo of bullion, Cochrane decided to get under way at once and intercept the ship. As they went into action Kate found herself on deck next to a gunner who seemed reluctant to fire while she was standing beside him. Kate seized the man's arm 'and directing the match, fired the gun. The effort was, however, too much for her and she immediately fainted and was carried below.' There was a sad ending to all these excitements. The young Elizabeth had contracted a fever during the journey inland and died a few weeks later. By mutual agreement Kate and Cochrane decided that she and the other two children must return to England, at least for the time being. In March 1821 they set sail in HMS *Andromache*, accompanied by the wife of the recently deposed viceroy of Peru who had also decided that the time had come to leave the perils and uncertainties of Peru and head for the comparative safety of Europe.

Cochrane would continue as Admiral of the Chilean navy for another two years but a quarrel with San Martin, and problems over prize money and pay led to him becoming increasingly bitter and disillusioned. As so often in the past some of his troubles were of his own making. His long-running vendetta with Captain Guise and

Captain Spry came to a head some weeks after the capture of the *Esmeralda*. San Martin proposed that the captured ship should be renamed *Valdivia* to commemorate the taking of the Spanish stronghold. This posed difficulties among the sailors, partly because half of those who took part in capturing the *Esmeralda* had not been at Valdivia and partly because the Chileans did not want to serve on a ship named after Pedro de Valdivia, a Spanish conquistador. When Guise sent a letter to Cochrane signed by most of the officers, Cochrane chose to interpret this as a rebellious plot and ordered them to be court-martialled. Guise protested and resigned in protest but the court martial went ahead and five officers were dismissed from the navy. When Captain Spry refused to put to sea as a gesture of solidarity with his friend Guise, he too was court-martialled and dismissed from his command.

Meanwhile, in spite of Cochrane's belief that only positive military action would produce results, San Martin's waiting game was having the desired effect. The blockade of the port of Callao and the threatening presence of the patriot army was causing the break-up of Spanish rule. Not long after Viceroy Pezuela had been deposed by an army coup, the Spanish forces in Lima evacuated the city. San Martin entered the capital as a liberator on 22 July 1821 and proclaimed the independence of Peru. When the news reached England it was Cochrane who was given much of the credit for the liberation of the country. A few months earlier *The Times* had been reporting numerous complaints from Valparaiso that Cochrane had been blockading the Peruvian coast and detaining British merchant ships.[40] However, on 1 December, under the headline 'Lord Cochrane's entry into Lima' *The Times* reported his triumphal arrival into the city in a magnificent chariot drawn by four cream-coloured horses. He was conducted to the Palace 'amidst the most enthusiastic shouts from the people of "*Viva la Patria*" and "*Viva l'Almirante*".' On reading the newspaper accounts Lord Byron, a leading light in the movement to liberate Greece, wrote, 'there is no man I envy so much as Lord Cochrane', and noted that Cochrane's entry into Lima was one of the great events of the day.[41]

On 3 August San Martin became Protector of the new republic. With a population suffering from food shortages, and troops roaming the countryside, he imposed an authoritarian regime to prevent the rash of looting and civil unrest from degenerating into anarchy. Cochrane put the worst possible interpretation on this. In his view San Martin had betrayed the cause they were fighting for and instead of establishing a liberal democracy he had set himself up as a dictator. Events would show that he entirely misjudged San Martin.[42] A demand on behalf of the sailors for the payment of prize money and arrears of pay brought the simmering differences between the Admiral of the Chilean navy and the Protector of Peru to a head. Cochrane put in a claim for the immediate payment of $420,000.[43] San Martin accepted responsibility for the payment of prize money but pointed out that the pay of the squadron was the responsibility of the Chilean government and not the new Peruvian republic. An acrimonious meeting on 5 August settled nothing, and disgruntled seamen began leaving Cochrane's fleet and joining the fledgling Peruvian navy. When Cochrane learnt that San Martin had arranged for the contents of the state treasury to be shipped to Ancona in the schooner *Sacramento*, he intercepted the schooner and seized the money which amounted to $283,000 (£56,600). This caused an outcry but, apart from returning $117,000 which belonged to private individuals and the army, he kept the rest and used most of it to pay the squadron the prize money and pay which was owing to them.[44] His high-handed action, his indiscreet language and his complaints about San Martin led to him being ordered to return to Chile. On 6 October he set sail from Callao with the ships of the Chilean navy.

Instead of heading for Valparaiso, Cochrane sailed north in search of the last two Spanish frigates known to be still at large. He took the squadron as far as Acapulco but when they eventually tracked down the frigate *Venganza* in the roadstead at Guayaquil they found she had already surrendered to San Martin's men and was flying the Peruvian flag. The crew of the other frigate had given themselves up at Callao. When Cochrane returned to Callao on 25 April 1822 he was given a cool reception. His former second-in-command, Blanco Encalada, was now on secondment as commander of the Peruvian navy and his seamen were on their guard to prevent Cochrane from attempting to seize another prize. San Martin tried to heal the rift between them by offering Cochrane an estate, and the newly constituted Order of the Sun, and the post of First Admiral of Peru. Cochrane was unrelenting in his response: 'I will not accept either honours or rewards from a Government constituted in defiance of solemn pledges; nor will I set foot in a country governed not only without law, but contrary to law.'[45] And with that he bade farewell to Peru and set sail for Valparaiso.

EIGHTEEN

Brazil and Beyond

1822–1825

On the morning of 2 June 1822 Maria Graham was having breakfast in her cottage in Valparaiso when the child of one of her neighbours came running in and screamed:

'Señora, he is come! He is come!'

'Who is come, child?'

'Our admiral, our great and good admiral; and if you come to the veranda, you will see the flags in the Almendral.'

It was cold and raining but when Maria looked out she saw the cheerful red, blue and white colours of the Chilean flag flying from doors and windows across the town. Lying out in the bay were two ships which had not been there the day before. They were the *O'Higgins* and the *Valdivia*, 'and all the inhabitants of the port and suburbs had made haste to display their flags and their joy on Lord Cochrane's safe return.'[1] The sailors had been away for nearly two years and they were welcomed back as heroes. Zenteno, the Minister of Marine, announced that the Supreme Director had ordered that a medal be struck for the officers and men of the squadron, 'for their gallantry and in proof that Chile rewards the heroes who advocate her cause'.[2]

Maria Graham had arrived in Valparaiso five weeks before in the saddest of circumstances. Her husband Thomas Graham, a naval captain who had served as a midshipman with Cochrane in the *Thetis*, had died during the voyage out. Governor Zenteno arranged for him to be buried in the grounds of the fortress and many people in the town attended the funeral service in the church. Maria had already published books about her travels in India and Italy and would later produce a vivid account of her time in Chile and Brazil.[3] She was an accomplished artist as well as a writer and in years to come she would marry the artist Sir Augustus Wall Callcott and, as Lady Callcott, would publish the best-selling children's book *Little Arthur's History of England*. She was now thirty-seven, a woman of striking good looks but subject to frequent illness. She was greatly cheered by Cochrane's arrival, 'not only because I want to see him whom I look up to as my natural friend here but because I think he ought to have influence to mend some things, and to prevent others'.[4]

Cochrane had gone ashore to see William Hoseason, who was acting as his prize agent and was meant to be handling his financial affairs. Maria Graham walked across the town to Hoseason's house, 'and there I found Lord Cochrane. I should say he looks better than when I last saw him in England, although his life of exertion and anxiety has not been such as is in general favourable to the looks.'[5] In due course they would see much of each other and became good friends but first Cochrane had to sort out the finances of the squadron. He travelled to Santiago and presented the squadron's accounts to the authorities; these included his own demands for the prize money he reckoned he was owed for the capture of the *Esmeralda*. Unfortunately the cost of raising and paying the troops and supplying ships and men for the liberating expedition to Peru had put severe demands on the finances of Chile. There was barely enough money to pay the seamen and no money to carry out much-needed repairs to the warships. However, when the government auditors examined the squadron's accounts they found so many irregularities that they rejected them, to the annoyance of Cochrane who felt that the accounts should be passed without question in view of his heroic contribution to the cause of independence. The resulting arguments put a strain on Cochrane's relations with O'Higgins and the government, which were not helped by suspicions in some quarters that he was shipping back to England a

fortune in gold and silver. We know from his letters to his brother
William that he had come out to America with the hope that he would
make his fortune, and there is evidence to show that around this period
he was sending home considerable sums of money on British warships.[6]

There were lighter moments during his last months in Chile.
Following his triumphal return to Valparaiso he had been granted
four months leave. Early in July he decided to pay a visit to his estate at
Quintero and determined to make the journey on board the steamship
Rising Sun which had recently arrived from England. He invited along
a party which included Don Zenteno and his daughter, three naval
captains and other officers from the squadron, and Maria Graham who
later noted in her journal 'It was with no small delight that I set foot
on the deck of the first steam-vessel that ever navigated the Pacific.'[7]
They travelled under steam power for twenty miles and were nearly
abreast of Quintero when the engines stopped and a headwind forced
them to sail back to Valparaiso.

Maria Graham later made the journey to Quintero on horseback
and was charmed by the beauty of the scenery. The house which
Cochrane was having built looked across a green valley with woods
and low hills, a freshwater lake swarming with waterfowl, and
extensive pastures with grazing cattle. 'After dinner we walked to
the garden, which lies in a beautiful sheltered spot, nearly a league
from the house. At the entrance lay several agricultural implements,
brought by his Lordship for the purpose of introducing modern
improvements into Chile, the country of his adoption.'[8] Cochrane
had ambitious plans to set up a business in partnership with John
Miers, an English engineer. They would raise beef to supply visiting
warships, set up die-making machines for producing coins for the
government and farm the land using some of the methods he had once
discussed with William Cobbett.

His future plans were thrown off course in November when he
received a letter from Antonio Correa da Camera, the Brazilian
agent in Buenos Aires, offering him command of the Brazilian navy.
Brazil was embarking on a war of independence and the patriot

leaders in Rio de Janeiro were aware that seapower would be a key element in the future conflict with the Portuguese forces which still dominated most of the coastal towns and cities. Cochrane was not inclined to take up the Brazilian offer at first but a number of factors led to him changing his mind. The Chilean government had decided that it could not afford and did not need a navy any more. The officers and men were being paid off which meant that Cochrane no longer had an active role to play. On 19 November central Chile was hit by the first of a series of earthquakes of devastating force. Most of the houses and public buildings in Valparaiso were reduced to rubble and the tidal waves which followed the earthquakes caused further damage and loss of life. Cochrane's house at Quintero was among those destroyed. And following on the heels of the natural disasters came the spectre of civil war. Much of the population was disillusioned by the effects of independence and General Freire, the Governor of Concepción, decided to capitalise on the general mood of discontent. He gathered an army and began a slow march towards Santiago where he intended to supplant O'Higgins and his government. He invited Cochrane to join him but Cochrane's first loyalty was to O'Higgins and he had no wish to become enmeshed in the internal politics of Chile.

On 29 November Cochrane wrote and accepted the Brazilian offer and tendered his resignation to the government of Chile. He issued farewell addresses to the Chilean people, to the trading community and to the officers of the Chilean navy and made his preparations for leaving. On 18 January 1823 he went aboard the brig *Colonel Allen* accompanied by his secretary William Jackson, four British naval officers and Maria Graham – her house had been destroyed by the earthquake and he was concerned about her safety. 'He could not bear, he said, to leave the unprotected widow of a British officer thus on the beach, a castaway as it were in a ruined town, a country full of civil war.'[9] A low-key but moving ceremony took place as Captain Crosbie lowered Cochrane's flag from the masthead of the schooner *Montezuma* and presented it to him on the poop deck of the *Colonel Allen*.

They sailed around Cape Horn and on 13 March, nearly two
months after leaving Valparaiso, they reached Rio de Janeiro. Low
clouds and driving rain hid the surrounding backdrop of high-peaked
mountains but the lower slopes of the Sugar Loaf Mountain were
clearly visible as they entered the great Bay of Guanabara. They
passed a number of forts guarding the harbour entrance and dropped
anchor among the ships lying off the waterfront of Rio. A port officer
came on board and, learning that they had come from Chile, he asked
Maria Graham whether she knew Lord Cochrane. 'When he found his
Lordship was actually on board, he flew to his cabin door, and
entreated him to kiss his hand; then snatched his hat, and calling
to the Captain to do as he would and anchor wherever he pleased
without ceremony, jumped over the side to be the first, if possible, to
convey to the Emperor the joyful intelligence.'[10]

Prince Pedro, who had recently become the constitutional emperor
of Brazil, was the son of the King of Portugal. When Napoleon's
armies had invaded Portugal in 1807 and the Portuguese royal family
had fled to Brazil, he had been nine years old. He was now twenty-
three and had the intelligence and courage which his father conspicuously lacked. He was a gifted musician and a fine horseman, and
he would prove a capable leader during the conflicts of the next few
years. At the end of the Napoleonic Wars in 1815 his father had
returned to Portugal: after eight prosperous years as the capital of the
Portuguese empire with the same rights and freedoms as the mother
country, Brazil reverted to its former, downtrodden status as a colony.
Prince Pedro had remained in Rio and had been persuaded to lead a
rebellion which led to him making his historic declaration on 7
September 1822, 'Independence or Death!' The next stage was to
confront and overcome the Portuguese forces which were dominant in
the northern regions of Brazil. The guiding spirit behind the independence movement was José Bonifácio de Andrada, a distinguished
scholar and former scientist who was now Chief Minister. It was he
and his Minister of Marine who had created a Brazilian navy by
commandeering all the Portuguese warships stationed at Rio de
Janeiro. They partially solved the problem of manning the navy by

recruiting sailors from North America and Britain but they still had to rely on a considerable number of Portuguese seamen of questionable loyalty.

Within hours of his arrival in Rio, Cochrane was introduced to Prince Pedro and his Chief Minister, and the following day he was rowed out in the company of the young emperor to see the ships which would be under his command. There was one ship of the line, three frigates, two corvettes, three brigs and a number of schooners. The ship of the line was a two-decker of 64 guns named the *Pedro Primiero*. She had recently undergone a refit in the dockyard and after some initial disappointments would prove a powerful weapon in Cochrane's hands. Having inspected the fleet, Cochrane entered into negotiations on his pay and conditions with the Minister of Marine. He was in a strong position and exploited it ruthlessly. There were already two admirals in the Brazilian navy and, because he was determined that he should have clear authority over them, the rank of First Admiral was specially created for him. He rejected the pay he was offered and insisted on being paid the same as he had received in Chile. Recent research has shown that he named a considerably higher figure than he was actually paid in Chile.[11] The sum of $17,960 per annum which was finally agreed upon was three times more than any other Brazilian flag officer and considerably more than he would have received as a British admiral. The worst interpretation that can be put on his behaviour is that he was dishonest and avaricious. In his defence it could be argued that he was aware of his formidable talents and outstanding record and, as a mercenary for hire, he demanded what he considered he was worth.

On the morning of 1 April 1823, barely two weeks after his arrival in Rio, Cochrane put to sea with the only four ships which were ready to sail. A fifth would follow later. He would be away for the next seven months and the actions of his squadron during that time would play a crucial part in securing the independence of Brazil. Maria Graham was with the crowd gathered on the waterfront to cheer the men on their way. She observed that as the guns of the fort began thundering out a salute, the sun broke through from behind the clouds and a brilliant yellow light illuminated the ships so that 'they seemed to swim in a sea of glory'.[12] Unfortunately their first encounter with the Portuguese fleet was anything but glorious. They headed north and sighted the coast of Bahia on 3 May. The following morning they were confronted by the distant sails of the enemy. On learning of Cochrane's approach, no fewer than eleven warships, including five frigates and one 74-gun ship, had set sail from Salvador and were bearing down on the five ships of the Brazilian squadron.[13] Following Nelson's advice, 'Never mind manoeuvres, always go at them', Cochrane headed straight for the centre of the advancing line. His flagship cut through the Portuguese line firing sporadically as she did so. His powerful ship failed to inflict any damage on the enemy and when he signalled to his other ships to attack the four Portuguese vessels he had detached from the main fleet, they ignored his signal. Heavily outnumbered as he was, Cochrane had no option but to call off the action and retreat to the harbour of Morro de São Paulo. It transpired that on his own ship some of the Portuguese seamen were preventing the powder from the magazine reaching the guns. In his despatch to the Chief Minister, Cochrane explained his problems with the crews and pointed out the numerous defects in his ships (rotten sails, defective cartridges and mortars) but he remained positive. 'I am aware of the difficulties under which a new government labours and am ready to do all in my power under the circumstances.'[14]

He decided to cut his losses and to put the best officers and men into three of his ships and rely on these to carry out a plan which was as audacious as anything he had devised in the past. He intended to blockade Salvador and then attack the harbour and the assembled fleet with the assistance of fireships. The city had been under siege from the land by patriot forces for nearly a year and was therefore dependent on supplies coming in by sea. When Cochrane began intercepting vessels bound for the harbour the inhabitants of San Salvador faced an increasingly desperate situation. After blockading the coast for three weeks Cochrane decided to make a reconnaissance raid to test the defences. On the night of 12 June, while the Portuguese commanders were distracted by a ball which was being held in the town, he sailed the *Pedro Primiero*, accompanied by two other ships of his squadron, into the Bay of Bahia towards the anchored fleet.[15] Unfortunately the wind dropped and they found themselves becalmed under the guns of the forts and in the presence of the Portuguese warships. Cochrane had taken account of the tides when planning the raid so he used the ebb tide, and skilful seamanship, to drift back to the open sea. The news that the Brazilian flagship had sailed into their midst and that a fireship attack was being planned caused consternation among the Portuguese leaders. Under pressure from the inhabitants who were now suffering severe hardship from the shortage of food, General Madeira de Melo, the Governor of Salvador, ordered the evacuation of the city. On 2 July an armada of seventeen warships and seventy-five transports and merchantmen loaded with Portuguese citizens, troops and the contents of the arsenal, headed out to sea. Within hours of their departure an advanced detachment of Brazilian soldiers entered Salvador and hoisted the flag of independent Brazil over the city.

What happened next was a rout on a scale not unlike that of the Spanish Armada in 1588. Spread out across the ocean the Portuguese warships seemed incapable of defending themselves and their convoy from the persistent attacks of the tiny Brazilian squadron. While Cochrane used his flagship to mount hit-and-run attacks on the warships, his other four vessels concentrated on the helpless transports. Within a week sixteen ships and more than 2,000 troops had been captured. 'I have the honour to inform you,' he wrote in a despatch to the Minister of Marine in Rio, 'that half the enemy's army, their colours, ammunition, stores and baggage have been taken. We are still in pursuit, and shall endeavour to intercept the remainder of the troops, and shall then look after the ships of war . . .'[16] Cochrane made most of his attacks on the warships at night. At three in the morning of 16 July he crowded on sail, swept alongside one of the frigates and fired a broadside at close range. While tacking to give them the other broadside the mainsail split in two and he decided to abandon the chase. He ordered Captain Taylor in the 38-gun frigate *Niteroi* to continue the pursuit of the remains of the convoy. Taylor followed the ships across the Atlantic to Portugal and in the sea lanes off the mouth of the Tagus he captured or destroyed more than a dozen merchantmen.

After carrying out running repairs Cochrane headed for São Luis, the capital of the province of Maranhão. The town was situated in the steamy atmosphere of the equator a few hundred miles from the mouth of the River Amazon. He now proceeded to put in effect one of the boldest acts of deception that he had ever attempted. On 26 July he sighted the town and headed for the anchorage, flying British colours to fool the inhabitants into thinking that the *Pedro Primiero* was a British ship coming to help the Portuguese cause.[17] This convinced the authorities who sent out a brig with despatches to welcome them. When the brig's captain stepped on board the *Pedro Primiero* he was astonished to find himself surrounded by British and American sailors in the service of the rebel emperor. With the town now in range of his guns Cochrane replaced the British colours with the Brazilian flag and sent the captain ashore with a message to the commandant informing him that the province of Bahia had been liberated and that the *Pedro Primiero* was the forerunner of a mighty fleet of warships and transports full of troops which had come 'to liberate Maranhão from foreign oppression and to allow the people to choose their system of government'.[18] Of course there was no Brazilian fleet in the vicinity but the commandant was not to know that.

The next day the local junta, accompanied by the bishop, came aboard Cochrane's flagship and swore allegiance to the Emperor Pedro. Captain John Pascoe Grenfell went ashore with a detachment of marines to take charge of the fortifications. On 28 July church bells rang out across the town as independence was formally declared and the Brazilian flag was raised on the public buildings and the warships in the harbour. A new provincial junta was sworn in, and to make sure that his hoax was not discovered until it was too late, Cochrane encouraged the commandant and his Portuguese troops to board merchant ships and sail home to Portugal. With the town at his mercy Cochrane proceeded to strip the place of its assets in a manner reminiscent of the actions of Sir Henry Morgan and his buccaneers at Panama and Portobello. He announced that the money in the provincial treasury, the arms and gunpowder in the forts and all the goods in the government storehouses were enemy property and now belonged to the captors. All the ships in the harbour were seized, including a handsome brig, a schooner, eight gunboats and sixteen merchant vessels. He also confiscated the goods and private property owned by Portuguese citizens and began shipping tons of merchandise back to Rio. His actions caused uproar. The new junta naturally regarded the town and its treasury and other assets as Brazilian and could see no justification for the seizures. Cochrane was unrelenting although he did agree to release funds to pay the Brazilian irregular troops occupying the interior when they sent representatives to the town demanding payment.

The deception at São Luis had been so successful that Cochrane decided to use the same method to liberate the province of Para which encompassed the basin of the Amazon. Captain Grenfell was des-patched in a captured brig to the town of Belem, the capital of Para. He arrived on 11 August flying the Brazilian flag and sent ashore letters from Cochrane which demanded the surrender of the Portuguese authorities in the town and warned that the First Admiral and a large fleet was at the mouth of the Amazon. Disturbed by the news that the provinces of Maranhão and Bahia had already fallen to the patriot forces, the Portuguese handed over power to a Brazilian junta and another region gained its independence. In less than four months the capital cities of three provinces and a vast territory extending along the coast for nearly 2,000 miles had been liberated from Portuguese rule.

Unaware that Cochrane had left Valparaiso and was now First Admiral of Brazil, his wife had been planning to join him in Chile. Kate had hired spacious accommodation on the merchant ship *Sesostris* and set off from England with furniture for the house in Quintero. She was accompanied by a dozen servants and attendants – and the latest addition to the family, a daughter, Katherine Elizabeth, usually called Lizzie. (It will be recalled that their first daughter, Elizabeth Kather-ine, had died of a fever. Kate must have been pregnant with Lizzie when she left Peru and set sail for England in March 1821.) The ship called in at Rio de Janeiro on 13 June and there Lady Cochrane learnt that her husband was now commanding the Brazilian navy and was engaged in operations off the coast of Bahia. The merchant who had arranged her passage and accompanied her on the voyage wrote at once to Cochrane: 'I hasten to announce the safe arrival here this day of your amiable Lady and Child in the *Sesostris*, after a passage of 50 days from England, in excellent health and spirits, so much so that I never saw her Ladyship look better during her residence in Chile. She is at present overcome with the joy of being so near to your Lordship and the fortunate escape of a prolonged absence round Cape Horn.'[19] As the wife of their celebrated First Admiral, Kate was welcomed into the society of Rio and enjoyed the hospitality of the court and the aristocracy. Maria Graham's comments about her are brief and guarded. It is evident that Maria, with her enquiring mind and keen intelligence preferred the company of Rio's politicians and intellectuals to the unsophisticated Lady Cochrane to whom she referred in her journal as 'my pretty countrywoman'. Three weeks before Cochrane's return Maria embarked on a ship for England. She had been invited to become governess to the daughter of the empress but had decided to return home for a while before she took up her post. 'I saw the Empress, who is pleased to allow me to sail for England in the packet the day after tomorrow,' she wrote in her journal on 19 October. 'I confess I am sorry to go before Lord Cochrane's return. I had set my heart on seeing my best friend in this country after his exertions and triumph. But I have now put my hand to the plough, and I must not turn back.'[20]

The *Pedro Primiero* sailed into the great bay and anchored in the shelter of Rio's encircling mountains on 9 November 1823. The news of Cochrane's liberation of the northern provinces had been received in the capital with an outburst of public celebrations. Buildings had been decorated and illuminated, and there had been gala performances at the theatre. The emperor now came out to greet Cochrane on his flagship and to reward him with a grand title and other honours: he was created Marquis of Maranhão, given the Grand Cross of Brazil, and made a member of the Privy Council. Reunited with his wife and family after an absence of nearly two years he must have expected and hoped for a rest from his exertions. Like Nelson at Naples after the Battle of the Nile, he was a hero in a distant land, laden with honours in a foreign court. But within days of his return he was involved in the political turmoil which engulfed the city and, as in Chile, embarked on a long-running campaign to secure the pay and the huge sums of prize money which he reckoned were owing to him and his crews for their seizures of ships, cargoes and property.

While Cochrane had been away, the ruling Assembly had split into two factions. Both sides continued to back independence but one faction was in favour of an anti-Portuguese line while the other wanted the restoration of friendly relations with Portugal. The Chief Minister, José Bonifácio, had been forced to resign and debates on a new constitution had become increasingly acrimonious. On 12 November, three days after Cochrane's return to Rio, Emperor Pedro surrounded the Assembly building with troops and ordered the delegates to disperse. He appointed a new government and drew up a new constitution which was in many respects more liberal and closer to Cochrane's ideals than the previous one. But although Cochrane's relations with the young emperor continued to be friendly, he did not get on well with the new ministers, particularly the Minister of Marine. Francisco Villela Barbosa was a university-trained mathematician who would prove an exceedingly capable administrator but his cold and calculating temperament was at odds with Cochrane's high-handed demands on behalf of himself and his men, his passionate belief in the justice of his cause and his somewhat careless approach to facts and figures.

During the naval campaign in the north the Brazilian squadron had taken three warships, eight gunboats, seventy-eight merchant vessels and a prodigious amount of public and private property. The total value was estimated at £252,000 (nearly £6 million in today's terms). As commander-in-chief Cochrane expected the prize courts to award him one-eighth of the value of the captured vessels and goods. The government, however, was intent on a policy of peace and reconciliation which meant that Portuguese property was to be restored to its

owners. Those merchant vessels seized in port or within two leagues
of the coast were to be released; claims on public property taken in
Maranhão and Para were dismissed on the grounds that these
provinces were not enemy territory but were Brazilian and had only
been under temporary Portuguese rule; and the captured warships
were judged to be the property of the crown. Irregularities in the
paperwork and the handling of some of the prizes caused further
problems. The lawyers' deliberations took many weeks but the result
was that in February 1824 the Superior Prize Court dismissed almost
all the squadron's claims. Cochrane was outraged and, unable to see
the reasoning behind the decision, he imagined sinister forces at work,
blaming the pro-Portuguese faction for plotting to weaken the navy
and undermine his authority. He wrote to the emperor to protest at his
treatment and offered his resignation. To add to his troubles his wife
and daughter had been laid low by the intense heat of the Brazilian
summer and Kate had decided that she must return to England. 'Lady
Cochrane embarks this day 16th February for England for the
recovery of her health,' he wrote to his brother William, 'she having
been ill ever since her arrival in this cursed hot place; and the little girl
has only been saved by the utmost attention and skill of a Dr Williams
who is now going home with Lady Cochrane.' He added, 'I am battling
the watch here with the same kind of people I left on the other side –
an ignorant obstinate narrow-minded gang; the Emperor however is
my friend, and I shall, indeed, I have beaten all the intriguers who have
attempted to annoy me.'[21]

For the next two months he carried on with the usual administrative duties involved in being commander-in-chief of the navy (ship
movements, victualling, promotions, transfers, punishments, pay and
pensions) and he bombarded the Minister of Marine with complaints
about the state of the ships and their need for repairs, the arrears of
pay owed to the seamen, the looting of prizes and the withholding of
the prize money due to himself and his men. During this time he
became increasingly depressed and withdrawn. When Captain Kotzebue of the Russian navy met him he found him to be very different
from the heroic figure he had expected. He described him as a man

whose 'appearance and manners are off-putting, and who in conversation never does more than express himself in monosyllables, so that it
is difficult to detect the intelligence and experience beneath . . . Tall,
thin and round shouldered, his eyes are always downcast; he never
looks to the front or at the person to which he is speaking.'[22]

The situation took a more ominous turn in May 1824 when Captain
Grenfell returned to Rio after his successful liberation of the province
of Para. In addition to seizing a number of vessels in the harbour of
Belem he had taken possession of a new 50-gun frigate which he had
renamed the *Imperatriz* and it was in this ship that he returned to Rio.
Instead of rewarding him for his actions the authorities seized the ship
and his personal possessions, confiscated the prize money which he
had on board, and charged him with failing to carry out his orders
correctly. He was acquitted, but a few weeks later Cochrane received a
warning that the authorities were planning to remove a large sum of
prize money which he had brought back from Maranhão and hidden
on board the *Pedro Primiero*. This prompted Cochrane to ride out to
the emperor's palace, to wake him during the night and obtain his
assurance that the prize money would not be touched.

It was the news of a rebellion in the north and reports from Europe
that Portugal was planning to reconquer Brazil which resolved some
of the problems of pay and prize money. It was agreed that an
expeditionary force must be despatched to crush the rebellion and
it must be escorted by a squadron led by Cochrane. To prevent further
desertions from the navy and to pacify those already in service the
Minister of Marine raised the pay of officers and men and paid out
£40,000 (200 contos) as an advance on the prize money due to the
squadron. On 2 August 1824 the expedition set sail and headed for the
rebellious province of Pernambuco. The troops went ashore at Ala-
goas and marched northwards while Cochrane took his squadron to
Recife where he threatened to bombard the town. The leader of the
rebellion, Manuel de Carvalho, offered him a massive bribe of £80,000
to change sides which Cochrane indignantly refused, pointing out that,
'it did not follow that, because the Brazilian ministers were unjust and
hostile to me, I should accept a bribe from a traitor to follow his

example'.[23] Leaving some of his ships to blockade the port, Cochrane sailed on to Bahia and while he was away the Brazilian army attacked Recife from the landward side while a naval force under Captain Norton captured the forts guarding the harbour and took possession of the shipping in the port. De Carvalho fled and the town was recaptured from the rebels.

Having taken no part in the final action at Recife, Cochrane sailed on to São Luis, the capital of Maranhão, where he intended to secure payment of the prize money which he believed was owing to him following his capture of the town in 1823. He arrived to find the province gripped by civil war and the town in a state bordering on anarchy. It took him nearly two months to restore order and set up a new administration. Having done so he wrote a formal letter to the Provincial President on 11 January 1825 demanding that the sum of £21,000 (106 contos) owing in prize money be paid within thirty days.[24] On 5 February a new Provincial President, who had been appointed by the authorities in Rio, arrived at São Luis, and when it became clear that he was going to oppose the payment of prize money Cochrane had him shipped along the coast to Belem. Within two days the junta had handed over £6,600 and in two months had raised the entire sum demanded. Cochrane's secretary, William Jackson, arranged the distribution of the prize money to the crews of those ships of the squadron which were anchored at São Luis, but the crews of the ships at Rio never received their share. Cochrane received his pay and his one-eighth share of prize money which enabled him to buy £28,000-worth of cotton and ship it back to England in four merchant ships.[25]

After six months of grappling with the intrigues of local politics and attempting to keep the peace by martial law, Cochrane had had enough. He had written to the emperor in January offering his resignation and informing him 'I have now accomplished all that can be expected from me', but his offer to resign had been rejected. Letters from Maria Graham, who had returned to Rio to take up her position as governess to the princess, warned him that his enemies were plotting against him and there was talk of dismissing the navy's

British officers. He made his preparations for leaving São Luis. He would later explain in his autobiography that the stress of dealing with internal wars, anarchy and revolution 'began to make serious inroads on my health; whilst that of the officers and men, in consequence of the great heat and pestilential exhalations of the climate, and the double duty which they had to perform afloat and ashore, was even less satisfactory'.[26] He shifted his flag into the frigate *Piranga* and sent the *Pedro Primiero* back to Rio. 'I resolved upon a short run into a more bracing northerly atmosphere, which would answer the double purpose of restoring our health and of giving us a clear offing for our subsequent voyage to the capital.'[27] He explained that his intention had been to sail towards the latitude of the Azores and then pick up the trade winds and head south-west to Rio. Instead he headed for England.

He had collected a substantial amount of his prize money and, since he was clearly disillusioned by the events of his past year in Brazil, it is reasonable to suppose that he never had any intention of returning to Rio. However, in his autobiography he maintains that his decision to head for home was determined by problems encountered during the voyage. He had put to sea on 18 May 1825 and a succession of easterly winds swept them across the Atlantic. On 11 June they passed to the northward of the Azores island of São Miguel when, 'strong gales coming on, we made the unpleasant discovery that the frigate's main-topmast was sprung, and, when putting her about, the main and main-topsail yards were discovered to be unserviceable'.[28] The running rigging was as rotten as the masts, and they were low on provisions. He consulted his officers and it was agreed that a direct return to Rio, which was more than 4,000 miles away, was out of the question. 'It was therefore absolutely necessary to seek some nearer harbour.' He would not be welcome in Portugal or Spain, and France had not yet recognised the independence of Brazil. So they sailed up the English Channel and on 26 June they dropped anchor at Spithead.

While Cochrane had been away the British government had passed a Foreign Enlistment Act which was designed to prevent British seamen joining the navies of foreign powers. There was therefore a risk that Cochrane himself and most of his crew (all his officers and many of his men were British) might be prosecuted under the act. There was also the problem of explaining to his Brazilian masters what he was doing sailing one of their finest frigates across the Atlantic to Britain. In the circumstances it might have been tactful to slip into the anchorage quietly. The arrival of another ship among the lines of anchored warships and merchantmen in the Solent would scarcely have been noticed, and Cochrane could have gone ashore and made discreet enquiries about the legality of his position. Typically and defiantly he decided to arrive in style. With an immense Brazilian ensign flying at the stern, and the flag of an admiral of the Brazilian navy at the mainmast, the *Piranga* attracted considerable attention. One observer thought the frigate had 'a very showy appearance'.[29] Cochrane's first act was to signal the *Victory*, the flagship of the port admiral, and find out whether his salute would be answered by the same number of guns. On receiving an affirmative answer the *Piranga* fired a fifteen-gun salute to the flag of Admiral Sir George Martin and raised the Union flag to her fore topgallant masthead. In return the guns of the Portsmouth forts thundered out an answering salute of fifteen guns. This was the first time the flag of independent Brazil had been formally saluted by a European state, and it was also an acknowledgement of Cochrane's rank as an admiral. Two days later Sir George Martin received a letter from the First Lord of the Admiralty advising him that 'the arrival of a Brazilian frigate with Lord Cochrane's flag on board places the Government in rather an awkward predicament'.[30] Sir George was admonished for returning Cochrane's salute; he was reminded that Cochrane and his officers were liable to penalties under the Foreign Enlistment Act; and he was informed that the Attorney General was looking into the numerous actions being brought against Cochrane by the owners of British ships and goods 'which were seized by him in a manner wholly unauthorised by the law of nations'.[31]

The newspapers published a detailed account of Cochrane's arrival. We learn that he was rowed ashore and around ten o'clock he landed at the King's Sally Port where a crowd which had gathered on the waterfront gave him three cheers which he acknowledged with a polite bow. He walked up the High Street to the George Hotel dressed in a blue undress military coat with a forage cap with gold band and was accompanied by a number of his officers and staff. 'Time and the elements seem to have had some effect on his Lordship's person,' noted *The Times* correspondent, who thought that he seemed to stoop in his gait and was looking rather pale.[32] A number of naval and military officers called to see Cochrane at his hotel which led to rumours that he might be reinstated. 'It is conjectured by the naval circles that his Lordship's visit may have connexion with his restoration to the British naval service, of which he was once, and it is hoped again may be, a brilliant ornament.'[33] The next morning Cochrane paid a brief visit to London, was reunited with Lady Cochrane and returned with her to Tunbridge Wells where she had been staying with her relations, Mr and Mrs Simpson, since her return from Brazil four months earlier.

Surprisingly little had changed on the political scene during the seven years that Cochrane had been away. Lord Liverpool was still Prime Minister, George Canning had replaced Castlereagh as Foreign Secretary and Lord Melville was still First Lord of the Admiralty.[34] The Duke of Wellington (no friend of Cochrane or the new South American republics) was a member of the Cabinet as Master-General of the Ordnance. King George III had died at Windsor in 1820, almost forgotten since his periodic bouts of insanity had confined him to his royal residences and all his powers had been transferred to his dissolute son. The little-loved and much-derided Prince Regent (who had stripped Cochrane of the Order of the Bath) was now ruling as King George IV. Another five years would pass before Britain had a monarch and a Cabinet sympathetic to Cochrane personally and more in tune with the views of his radical friends like Sir Francis Burdett. Of the admirals who had played a part in his life, Lord St Vincent and Lord Keith had died, Gambier was in his seventies and retired and his uncle Admiral Sir Alexander Cochrane was commander-in-chief at Plymouth.

Little might have changed on the political scene but in the arts and sciences there had been an extraordinary burst of creative activity during Cochrane's absence. Keats and Shelley had produced their finest work during those years but both had died tragically young: Keats in 1821 of consumption while staying in lodgings in Rome, and Shelley had drowned in 1822 while sailing off the Italian coast near Leghorn. William Hazlitt, Charles Lamb and his friend Coleridge were notably productive during this period. The Waverley novels of Walter Scott were proving hugely popular: *Ivanhoe* was published in 1819. Jane Austen (born within a few days of Cochrane, it will be recalled) had died at Winchester in 1817, aged forty-one, but her work was now recognised by her fellow writers and by an increasingly wide readership as a major contribution to English literature: *Northanger Abbey* and *Persuasion*, her novel in which naval officers feature prominently, were both published in 1818. J.M.W. Turner had continued to dazzle his contemporaries with his luminous landscapes but the period also saw the emergence from obscurity of John Constable: *The Hay Wain* of 1820 and *View on the Stour* of 1821 had caused a sensation in the Paris Salon of 1824 and earned him a gold medal.

Of more significance to Cochrane were recent developments on the scientific front. In 1819 the steamship *Savannah* arrived in Liverpool having made the crossing from America in twenty-six days. It would be seventy or eighty years before steam finally ousted sail for cargo and passenger-carrying ships across the oceans but the *Savannah* was a sign of things to come. The early 1820s saw a regular steamboat service operating on the Thames between London and Margate, and steam tugboats were an increasingly familiar sight in British harbours. 1825, the year of Cochrane's return, also witnessed the opening of the Stockton to Darlington railway with the world's first passenger steam train hauled by George Stephenson's *Locomotion No. 1*. In a few years time Cochrane would design a rotary steam engine and would borrow Stephenson's most famous locomotive, the *Rocket*, for trials with his engine. He would also embark on a long-running battle with the Admiralty to convince their Lordships that steam-driven warships were the navy's future.

NINETEEN

A Greek Fiasco

1825–1828

After spending a few weeks in Tunbridge Wells with his wife's relations, Cochrane took Kate on an extended visit to Scotland. Although he had seen very little of his native land since he had joined the navy and, when not at sea, had spent most of his time in London or Hampshire, he always regarded Scotland as his home. Many years later Kate would recall, 'He gloried in being a Scotchman; he said it was the pride of his life, and he used after his dinner, when he was drinking his wine, and so on, always to bring in something about Scotland – his dear Scotland – the days of his youth . . .'[1]

They followed the route they had taken thirteen years before. The horses were changed at Carlisle and as their carriage passed through the village of Annan he turned to Kate and said, 'My love, this is the place where we plighted our troth. This is where we were married. Where you were mine.'[2] They did not stop in the village but headed for Fife and the friends and relations he had not seen for so many years. 'I was most kindly received by them all, by Sir Robert Preston, and by all the friends and relations,' Kate remembered fondly. 'Great hospitality was shown us, and the greatest kindness.'[3] They stayed for a while with Sir Robert Preston who had bought Culross Abbey from Cochrane's father and who lived at Valleyfield on the adjoining estate. There is no doubt that one of the driving forces behind Cochrane's

pursuance of prize money and his determination to make a fortune in
South America was his hope that he would one day be able to buy back
his childhood home at Culross or, failing that, to acquire a fine house
or castle in the Scottish lowlands. According to Kate he particularly
had his eye on Blair Castle, the magnificent home of the Dukes of
Atholl: 'He said that with the first money he could save in South
America he would buy Blair Castle.'[4] But Blair Castle was out of his
reach and Sir Robert was not prepared to sell Culross. It was left to a
later generation of the Dundonald family to acquire a family seat in
Scotland.

    They remained in Scotland for nearly three months. They saw Lord
and Lady Napier, and Lady Maxwell, visited Castle Craig and stayed
for a while at a hotel in Edinburgh.[5] In October they attended the
theatre and received a standing ovation from the audience when a
reference was made to South America. Walter Scott was present and
was so impressed by the occasion that he was inspired to write a poem
which was largely devoted to praising the beauty of Lady Cochrane.
He described her pure brow and her dark locks and praised her for the
love, strength and constancy she had shown during the wars she had
lived through.

> Even now, as through the air the plaudits rung,
> I marked the smiles that in her features came;
> She caught the word that fell from every tongue,
> And her eye brightened at her Cochrane's name;
> And brighter yet became her bright eyes' blaze;
> It was his country, and she felt the praise.[6]

    During this period in Scotland Cochrane was also engaged in more
prosaic matters. In particular he carried on a lengthy correspondence
with Manuel Gameiro Pessoa, the Brazilian agent in London. The
crew of the *Piranga* needed to be paid and the agent arranged for their
pay and prize money to be settled. Less easily solved was Cochrane's
position as First Admiral of the Brazilian navy. Was he planning to
return to Rio de Janeiro with the *Piranga* and, if so, when? Cochrane

prevaricated, sending a number of polite but evasive replies to the agent's increasingly urgent letters. He was reluctant to resign his Brazilian post because he did not wish to lose the payment of his salary or his pension, but he was now under increasing pressure from the Greek Committee in London to take command of the Greek navy and help in the liberation of Greece from Turkish rule. After several months of correspondence the Minister of Marine in Rio de Janeiro had no alternative but to dismiss him from the Brazilian navy.

Cochrane had received unofficial overtures to help the Greek cause while he was still in Chile and it had been one of the reasons why he had been doubtful of offering his services to Brazil. In his letter accepting the post of Admiral of the Brazilian navy he had written, 'I confess however that I had not hitherto directed my attention to the Brazils; considering that the struggle for the liberties of Greece – the most oppressed of modern states – afforded the fairest opportunity for enterprise and exertion.'[7] The movement for Greek independence had attracted the support of liberal-minded people throughout western Europe, and committees had been set up to raise money for the Greek cause in London, Paris, Vienna and elsewhere. Prominent on the London Committee were Sir Francis Burdett and John Cam Hobhouse, who had succeeded Cochrane as Member of Parliament for Westminster. Hobhouse was a close friend of Lord Byron who had been a passionate advocate of Greek independence for many years. Byron had travelled to Greece in January 1824 and was preparing to take part in the fighting when he contracted fever. His death in April 1824 attracted widespread attention and gained more adherents for the cause.

The Greek War of Independence, like so much in the history of the Balkans, was riven by local conflicts and ethnic and religious hatreds, and it was marked by numerous atrocities. Underground protests against the oppressive Turkish rule had come out into the open in March 1821 when Bishop Germanos of Patras had hoisted the Greek flag over the monastery of Agias Lavras. Fighting had broken out in the Peloponnese with bands of freedom fighters attacking Turkish garrisons and the homes of Turks. This culminated in the massacre at

Tripolitsa (Tripolis) when more than 8,000 Turkish men, women and children were killed. On 13 January 1822 Greek independence was proclaimed at Epidaurus. The Turks retaliated in April with the notorious massacre of Chios when Turkish soldiers slaughtered some 25,000 inhabitants of the island, raped thousands of women and enslaved those women and children who escaped the slaughter. In the words of a contemporary historian of the conflict, 'The massacre of Chios excited just indignation in all the Christian countries. It also opened the eyes of statesmen to the fact that the struggle between the Turks and the Greeks was a war of extermination.'[8] But although most of Britain's ruling class had received a classical education and had a natural sympathy for the nation which had produced Aristotle, Plato and Pericles, the British government was determined to remain neutral in the conflict. Canning, the Foreign Secretary, was aware that Russia had a long-standing interest in the Balkans, and was particularly anxious to maintain the balance of power in Europe.

Sultan Mahmoud, the ruler of the Turkish empire, had called on the help of Mohamed Ali, Pasha of Egypt. The Arabs, led by Mohamed Ali's son Ibrahim Pasha, had assembled a fleet and invaded the Peloponnese in February 1825. By the autumn of that year many of the Greek strongholds had fallen and Athens was under threat. It was at this stage that Cochrane was formally invited by the Greek National Assembly to take up the command of the Greek navy.[9] Just as in Chile and Brazil there was a realisation that seapower would play a key role in the outcome of the war. Captain Frank Hastings, a naval officer who had fought at Trafalgar and was now in active service in Greek waters, had told Byron in 1823 that 'Greece cannot obtain any decisive advantage over the Turks without a decided maritime superiority; for it is necessary to prevent them from relieving their fortresses and supplying their armies by sea'.[10]

Cochrane put a high price on his services. He demanded a salary of £57,000 of which £37,000 was to be paid in advance and the remaining £20,000 when Greece was freed. He also wanted a fleet of steam warships. The original idea for using steamships had come from Captain Hastings who had gone to Greece in April 1822 as a volunteer. He realised that in the tideless and relatively sheltered waters of the Greek islands, steam-powered vessels could be extremely effective against sailing vessels becalmed in light airs. Cochrane was enthusiastic but while Hastings thought it would be quicker to buy and adapt existing steam vessels Cochrane insisted that new ships should be specially constructed. It was eventually agreed that six armed steamships were to be built in England by Gordon and Brent at a cost of £25,000 each, and fitted with engines by Alexander Galloway; and two heavy sailing frigates were to be built in the United States at a cost of £75,000 each.[11] Cochrane's mistake was to entrust the construction of the steam engines to Galloway who had already proved his incompetence over the construction of the *Rising Star*. Moreover, his son was in the employment of the enemy, Mohamed Ali of Egypt, so he had every reason to delay the contract. The outcome was a fiasco. One steamship, the *Perseverance*, which had been ordered by Captain Hastings back in March 1825, eventually reached the Mediterranean in the summer of 1826, when her boilers burst. Following repairs she arrived at the ancient port of Nafplion on the south-east coast of Greece on 14 September 1826. The other five vessels were meant to be fitted out with steam engines in two and half months after the order had been placed in August 1825. One vessel, the *Enterprise*, took fourteen months to complete, produced endless problems during sea trials, and did not arrive in Greece until September 1827, too late to be of any use to Cochrane. Of the remaining steam vessels, two of them reached Greece in the autumn of 1828 after the naval war was over; the other two were never completed. The construction of the two heavy frigates in America was a saga of corruption and delays: costs escalated to such an extent that one of the vessels had to be sold to the United States navy in order to pay for the other vessel which, against all the odds, did reach Greece in time to be of some service.[12]

Having insisted that the steamships were essential to his campaign, Cochrane did not intend to arrive in Greece without them. However, he could not remain in England to hurry along their construction because he received ominous news from his lawyer friend, Henry Brougham. On 8 November 1825, Cochrane wrote to Sir Francis Burdett to inform him, 'My life is rendered so inquiet by the constant fear of prosecution under the Foreign Enlistment Act which Brougham has given his opinion may be put in force against me, even for my services in Brazil, that I have resolved to place myself on the other side of the water without delay, and tomorrow morning I make the attempt by steamboat from the Tower.'[13] He sailed to Boulogne where he was joined a week later by Kate and their four-year-old daughter Lizzie and Arthur, the latest addition to the family, who was just over a year old. The eldest boys, Tom and Horace, were at school and followed some time later.

In the period between her return from Brazil and her departure to France, Kate had become friendly with George Eden, who had inherited the title of Lord Auckland in 1810 when his eldest brother, William, had drowned in the Thames. Kate had met him during her visits to London in 1824 while Cochrane was still in Brazil. Her occasional letters to him during that period are friendly but formal, thanking him for his kindness, and giving him news of her family and their future plans.[14] But on 16 November 1825, shortly before leaving for France, she dashed off an anguished letter to him which indicates that he had become rather more than a friend.

'I have only a moment to say God bless you,' she wrote. She told him that she was leaving, perhaps for ever.

> My heart is almost broken. However when the Greeks are free, think of my glory and forget all the anguish you have seen me suffer. I ask you to write to me sometimes and to look with kind feeling on the little remembrance you have of me. The ring shall be a happiness to me, I will always love you for what has passed, but I cannot expect you to continue the same feeling for me for I shall be too long absent and too far distant. Yet I should grieve to know another had my place.
>
> Farewell dearest may you be more happy than
> your wretched unhappy
> but affectionate Katherine.[15]

After spending six weeks in France, Cochrane and Kate and their family had to leave the country because the French government intended to prosecute Cochrane for the seizure of a French brig in the Pacific while he was commanding the Chilean navy. On 23 December they travelled to Brussels where they took up residence. From Brussels, on 17 April 1826, Kate wrote another letter to Lord Auckland: 'If thinking of you could convince you of my unchanged affection I can assure you, you have not been absent from my thoughts for one single instant since I last parted from you in Brook Street, how long, how painfully long it has been since I heard from you.' She told him that she was leaving Brussels soon to go to Switzerland for a few months; 'That done I proceed to Florence and then to Genoa and after that God alone can tell. I would make any sacrifice to see you again but I fear it is next to impossible.'[16]

A few days later, on 22 April, Cochrane wrote to Auckland explaining that he would be proceeding on his mission in a few days but, because he was worried about the nature of the service, 'I have felt it right to make some arrangements relative to Lady Cochrane and my children which you will greatly oblige us if you will see fulfilled. Lady Cochrane had strengthened this hope by reading to me part of your last very friendly letter, in which you offer to render any service in your power.'[17] Kate's next letter to Auckland makes it clear that he has agreed to become a trustee for the children in the event of anything happening to Cochrane – who is evidently far more concerned about the outcome of the Greek campaign than he has been before embarking on similar exploits in the past.

'My husband left me last Saturday morning,' Kate wrote, 'and was more uneasy than I ever before knew him to be – I love the little buttons you sent me, and I always wear them night and day; and until I die I shall continue to do so – I hope to hear from you whenever you have an idle moment and you will tell me about yourself – and not about commercial speculations all that is very good but you are dearer to me than all the commerce in the world. You may blush at my folly but you cannot blame me if I speak the truth.'[18]

This is the last of the seven letters from Kate to Lord Auckland written around this time. There can be no doubt that she fell in love with him but we do not have his letters to her, and although his gifts indicate that he was very fond of her we cannot be certain that they had a physical love affair. What is certain is that Kate remained loyal to Cochrane. She stayed with him for another twelve years, and bore him two more children.[19] Lord Auckland was nine years younger than Cochrane. He was good looking and had been educated at Eton and Christ Church, Oxford, before becoming a barrister and then an MP. On the death of his father in 1814 he had moved to the House of Lords. He was, however, a reluctant politician, being shy and reserved and a notably poor speaker. He never married but lived with two of his eight sisters.[20] Whether Cochrane ever knew or suspected his wife's feelings for Auckland is not known but the two men remained on good terms. Many years later, when Auckland was First Lord of the Admiralty, he was directly responsible for appointing Cochrane to the command of a British squadron.

For fourteen frustrating months Cochrane waited for his fleet to be assembled. To enable him to have freedom of movement the Greek Committee in London supplied him with a yacht, the schooner *Unicorn* of 158 tons. This enabled him to sail from Flushing on 8 May 1826 and cross the Channel to Weymouth. He made a secret visit to Galloway's yard at Greenwich on Sunday 16 May to find that the *Perseverance* was apparently completed but the other two vessels 'were filled with pieces of the high-pressure engines, all unfixed, and scattered about in the engine-room and on deck'.[21] He boarded the *Unicorn* at Dartford on 20 May and headed back down the Channel to Falmouth to await the arrival of the *Perseverance*. When she failed to appear he sailed across the Irish Sea to Bantry Bay to avoid any possibility of the authorities arresting him under the Foreign Enlistment Act. On hearing that Captain Hastings was at last on his way in the *Perseverance*, Cochrane set a course for the Mediterranean. The *Unicorn* passed through the Straits of Gibraltar on 26 June and on 12 July dropped anchor in the Sicilian harbour of Messina. Again Cochrane waited in vain. After a visit to Malta he sailed to Marseilles where he met Hobhouse who had the welcome news that one of the

American frigates was on its way. He also met Dr Louis-André Gosse, a Swiss member of the French Committee which was supporting the Greek cause. On hearing of Cochrane's problems Gosse arranged for the brig-of-war *Sauveur* to be purchased and made available.

The situation in Greece had been steadily deteriorating. The Turks had taken Missolonghi in April 1826, sacked the town, embarked on an orgy of atrocities, and enslaved thousands of woman and young boys. The fishing port had no particular military significance but it had a symbolic importance because of its association with Lord Byron who had spent the last four months of his life there. He had given large sums of money to the Greek cause and raised a brigade of freedom fighters before dying of fever in April 1824. Of greater significance for the Greek cause was the fall of Athens to the Turks in June 1826. Only the Acropolis on its lofty plateau above the city held out. Some of the Greek inhabitants had taken refuge on the heights among the ruins of the Parthenon and the adjoining temples, and they were bravely defended by a force of 570 soldiers led by a veteran French commander, Colonel Charles Fabvier. What made things worse was that the Greeks were divided among themselves. Sir Richard Church, who had received an invitation from one of the Greek factions to take command of the Greek forces, wrote to Cochrane to warn him, 'This unhappy country is now divided by absurd and criminal dissensions. I hope, however, that your Lordship's arrival will have a happy effect, and that they will do everything in their power to be worthy of such a leader.'[22]

Not till 17 March 1827 did Cochrane finally sail into the Greek harbour of Poros with two sailing vessels: the *Sauveur* and the yacht *Unicorn*. Of his promised fleet only three other vessels were waiting for him: the American-built frigate *Hellas* of 60 guns; the *Hydra*, a small corvette; and the steamship *Perseverance* (now named the *Karteria*) under the command of Captain Hastings. This was not the sort of fleet he had been hoping for but his presence alone was worth a great deal. Indeed, his arrival seems to have had an extraordinary effect on the unruly and warring Greek parties. George Finlay, who was serving as a volunteer on the staff of General Thomas Gordon, and later wrote *The History of the Greek Revolution*, was much impressed by the way in which Cochrane assessed the situation and took command. 'His influence became suddenly unbounded, and faction was for a moment silenced. All parties agreed to think only of the nation's interests.'[23] On 7 April the leaders of the various Greek parties met in a lemon grove at Damala, a village on the mainland opposite Poros town. Count John Capodistrias (Ioannis Kapodistrias) was elected as President of the National Assembly. Although born in Corfu he had been out of the country for many years and had served as foreign minister of Russia under Tsar Alexander. According to Finlay the early meetings of the National Assembly were tumultuous but 'the authority of Lord Cochrane over all parties prevented an open rupture'. On 18 April the Assembly formally agreed to the appointment of Sir Richard Church as commanding general of the Greek army, and the appointment of Cochrane as commanding admiral of the Greek navy. The current naval commander, Admiral Miaoulis, a brave but elderly sea captain from Hydra who had achieved some success in local naval actions, was happy to serve under Cochrane.[24]

The first and most urgent task was to relieve the garrison on the Acropolis which was under siege by an army of some 7,000 Turkish soldiers and was rapidly running out of provisions. The Greek forces were gathered around the harbour of Piraeus a few miles south-west of Athens. They could see the distant Acropolis but their path to the summit was blocked by a contingent of Turkish troops who were occupying the monastery of Saint Spiridion. Cochrane may have lacked a classical education but he had been lent a great number of books on Greek history by Hobhouse and during the long wait for his steam fleet there had been plenty of opportunity to read them. He now issued a series of stirring proclamations, quoting Demosthenes, and calling on the Greeks to rise up against the enemy. He produced a large flag of his own devising which depicted the owl of the goddess Athena set against a blue and white background and let it be known among the soldiers in the Greek camps that whoever raised the flag on the summit of the Acropolis would receive $1,000 as a reward for his bravery.

On the night of 24 April a force of marines, augmented by a thousand men who had been recruited on the island of Hydra, were landed on the shore where they were in a position to attack the monastery from the rear. Thirty more soldiers under the supervision of Cochrane were landed the next day. The watching Turks, seeing an opportunity to drive the landing party back into the sea, left the monastery and the earthworks they had thrown up around its walls, and began advancing down the hillside. Cochrane was quick to take advantage of the situation. 'He observed a moment when a daring charge would ensure victory to the Greeks, and, cheering on the troops near him, he led them to the attack with nothing but his telescope in his hand. All eyes had been watching his movements, and when he was seen to advance, a shout ran through the Greek army, and a general attack was made simultaneously on all the positions occupied by the Turks . . .'[25] Such was the fury of the attack that the Turks abandoned their earthworks and fled. Three hundred of them took refuge in the monastery and the rest headed towards Athens. The Greeks had lost eight men during the fighting, the Turks sixty.

Cochrane now ordered the *Hellas*, which was anchored in the Bay of Phalerum, to open fire on the monastery. The 32-pounders of the powerful frigate flashed and boomed and sent clouds of gun smoke swirling across the bay, and once the range had been established the walls of the monastery began to crumble. The Turks held out for three days but on 28 April they negotiated a surrender. The last successful action of Cochrane's career as a naval and military commander was marred by what he later described as 'the most horrid scene I ever beheld'. Karaiskakes, one of the Greek commanders, had agreed that the Turks should be allowed to retire from the monastery with their arms and baggage and return to their own army. Cochrane had returned to his yacht and was standing on the deck with Gordon and Finlay watching the proceedings through a telescope. As the Turks emerged and made their way through the dense crowd of armed men, Finlay realised what was going to happen.

'All those men will be murdered,' he said and they watched in horror as the Greeks opened fire. In the massacre which followed two hundred men lost their lives and fewer than seventy escaped to the safety of the Turkish lines. Worse was to follow. Cochrane was determined to follow up the attack on the monastery and rescue the beleaguered soldiers and civilians under siege on the Acropolis. General Church and most of the Greek commanders were reluctant to proceed, knowing only too well the indifferent fighting qualities of their men when faced with Turkish artillery and mounted soldiers armed with scimitars. Impatiently Cochrane bombarded Church with letters: 'Pray let me know if the army <u>will</u> or <u>will not</u> advance,' he wrote, and threatened to leave if the men were not embarked and ordered to proceed to Athens. Against his better judgement Church at length agreed to Cochrane's plan which was to land 3,000 troops at night near Cape Colios, due south of Athens. Under cover of darkness they would cross the open plain which lay between the coast and the city and capture the heights on which stood the Temple of Zeus. This was close to the Acropolis and was a strong position from which to relieve the besieged garrison. The rest of the Greek army were to advance on Athens by a different route and cause a diversion.

At midnight on 6 May the Greek troops were landed on the shore 'in a clear moonlight and in the most perfect order,' according to Dr Gosse who was acting as Commissary-General of the Greek navy. The *Hellas* was anchored nearby to provide covering fire if necessary. An advance party of picked men crossed the plain unopposed and reached the planned rendezvous but, instead of following them, the remainder proceeded to dig themselves in near the shore. When Gosse went to find out why the soldiers providing the diversion were not moving he came across one commander who was smoking his pipe on the beach and refused to move until he was paid. At dawn the Turkish cavalry appeared. They cut down the advance party who had begun to retreat and then swept across the plain towards the men on the beach who fled in panic towards the water. At least seven hundred men were killed in the resulting slaughter, 240 were taken prisoner and the remainder of the Greek army fled as the Turkish artillery in the foothills opened fire on the plain. Cochrane managed to wade out to where Gosse was waiting in a boat and, grabbing the oars, he rowed them back to the *Hellas.* The guns of the frigate were directed at the Turkish artillery and the boats were sent ashore to evacuate the

ritish sailors boarding a man-of-war. A lieutenant leads the boarding party, followed by sailors
randishing cutlasses and red-coated marines firing their muskets. Coloured aquatint published
1815, after a picture by John Atkinson.

he Rock of Lisbon, a watercolour by the marine artist J. C. Schetky. This view is typical of
uch of the rocky coast of Spain and Portugal, and the crew of the *Imperieuse* spent weeks
iling past similar coastlines as they hunted for enemy shipping.

Crowds gathered around the hustings at Covent Garden for the election of the parliamentary candidates for Westminster. Engraving after the drawing by Pugin and Rowlandson from Ackermann's *Microcosm of London*, published in 1808.

Lord Cochrane, the naval hero. Engraving after the portrait by Stroehling which was published in the *Naval Chronicle* in 1809.

Lord Cochrane, the Radical politician. This is one of a series of portraits by Adam Buck.

A watercolour by Lieutenant William Innes Pocock identifying seven types of Mediterranean vessel. From left to right: a xebec, a polacre ship, a trabacolo, a secca leva, a sciabecca, a courier and a gunboat settee.

Sir Francis Burdett, the wealthy aristocrat who was the leading spokesman for the Radicals in the House of Commons. Watercolour by Adam Buck.

William Cobbett, writer, journalist and fearless campaigner against corruption in politics and public life. Portrait attributed to George Cooke.

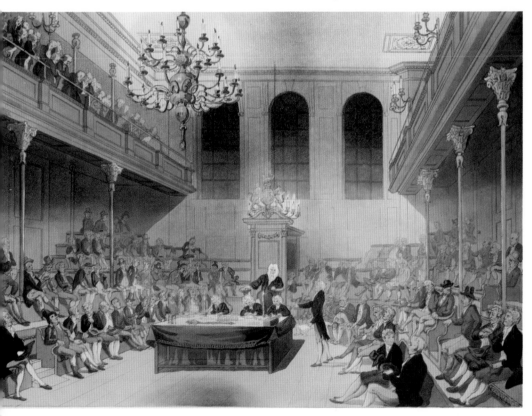

The House of Commons as it would have looked in Cochrane's day. Engraving after the drawing by Pugin and Rowlandson from Ackermann's *Microcosm of London*, published in 1808.

Cochrane's wife Kate with their daughter Elisabeth on horseback in the Italian mountains. Painted by Sir George Hayter in 1830 during the period when the family were living in Italy following Cochrane's return from his campaigns in Greece.

Portrait by Sir Thomas Lawrence of Maria Graham, who was a friend and admirer of Cochrane in South America.

General Bernardo O'Higgins, who became Supreme Director of Chile following the overthrow of Spanish rule in 1817.

A view of the Bay of Guanabara, Brazil, showing the forts at the entrance, the Sugar Loaf mountain, and on the right the city of Rio de Janeiro. Aquatint after the drawing by George L. Hall, 1860.

A fine portrait of Cochrane in his fifties by Sir George Hayter. A romantic view of the liberator of oppressed nations, probably painted when he returned from Greece in 1830.

survivors but the overall result was a disastrous and costly defeat which many blamed on Cochrane.[26] A month later, on 5 June, the garrison on the Acropolis surrendered to the Turks.

Increasingly disillusioned by the Greek troops and by the failure of his efforts on land, Cochrane decided to concentrate on naval actions. He had sent Captain Hastings with the steamship *Karteria* and five smaller vessels to intercept and capture the ships which were supplying the Turkish army, and Hastings had proved conspicuously successful at this, but when Cochrane set sail in the *Hellas* he failed dismally. His first attempt to capture two Turkish frigates was frustrated by his largely Greek crew who either ignored his commands or proved hopelessly ineffective at gunnery. After a few weeks of cruising he noted that, 'the frequent mutinies or resistance to authority, and the numerous instances in which I have been obliged to return to port, or abstain from going to sea, are recorded in the logbook of the *Hellas*, together with the disgraceful conduct of the crew in stripping and robbing prisoners, and their want of coolness in the presence of the enemy . . .'.[27]

The next failure was on a grand scale and was a parody of his heroic action at Basque Roads. On 11 June 1827 he gathered an assortment of ships off Cape Saint Antonio on the south-east coast of the Peloponnese with the aim of launching a fireship attack on the harbour of Alexandria. The Egyptian port was the base for the fleet of Ibrahim Pasha and was the principal source of all supplies to the Turkish forces operating in Greece. Cochrane had at his disposal the frigate *Hellas*, the corvette *Sauveur*, eight vessels converted into fireships and fourteen armed brigs – many of which were manned by crews more accustomed to making piratical attacks on unarmed merchantmen than confronting an armed enemy. After a slow crossing they sighted the distant towers of Alexandria at five o'clock on the morning of 15 June. In an attempt to inspire his men Cochrane issued another of his rousing proclamations, which began, 'Brave officers and seamen, one decisive blow and Greece is free . . .'[28] Unfortunately only enough volunteers could be found to man two of the fireships. On the night of 16 June, with the *Hellas* and *Sauveur* flying Austrian flags, Cochrane led his squadron towards the entrance of the port. One of the fireships was successfully manoeuvred alongside an Egyptian warship and set it alight. This so alarmed the remaining ships in the harbour that they hastily weighed anchor and headed for the open sea. The sight of the enemy fleet advancing towards them caused such panic among the ships of the Greek squadron that most of them fled. Cochrane abandoned his intention of seizing the port and set off in pursuit of the enemy but after eighty miles he gave up the chase.

For the next three months the *Hellas* cruised on her own along the western coast of the Greek mainland, intercepting the occasional merchantman or pirate and making an unsuccessful attempt to capture a coastal fort. Meanwhile, the governments of Britain, France and Russia had belatedly decided to intervene in the conflict. Representatives of the three countries met in London in July 1827 and signed a treaty, the short-term aim of which was to secure an armistice in the war. The long-term aim was to ensure that Greece achieved independence and internal self-government but under the nominal sovereignty of Turkey. A deadline of one month was set for the armistice and to make sure that it was enforced the three powers despatched squadrons to Greece.

The combined Turkish and Egyptian fleets were now anchored in the great bay of Navarino on the west coast of Greece and in October the three allied fleets gathered outside the narrow entrance to the bay. The British squadron was commanded by Vice-Admiral Sir Edward Codrington who had instructions to enforce the armistice and prevent reinforcements reaching the enemy. Realising that a lengthy blockade was not practical he decided to enter the bay and by midday on 20 October the two opposing fleets were facing each other. It was an impressive sight. The allies had twenty-six warships between them, including twelve ships of the line and eight frigates; the enemy had sixty-five warships with seven ships of the line and fifteen frigates. Codrington had no instructions to secure the armistice by force and there was some attempt to parley but it only needed a minor incident to provoke a full-scale battle. At 2.30 p.m. a boat from HMS *Dartmouth* was fired on, and soon a general engagement was under way. For three hours there was a murderous bombardment at close range. The superior gunnery of the allies reduced the enemy to a tangled and smoking mass of dismasted, burning and sinking ships. By dawn the next day only fifteen enemy ships remained afloat. Turkish and Egyptian casualties were reckoned at between 4,000 and 8,000 dead and wounded.[29]

The news of the Battle of Navarino, the last major fleet action to be fought under sail, was received with mixed reactions in Britain where it was memorably described as 'an untoward event' by sources within the Cabinet. Prince William, the king's sailor brother, considered it a splendid victory and insisted that Codrington be awarded the Order of the Bath, but the government was concerned about the likely reper-cussions of the unplanned act of aggression. In fact the destruction of the Turkish and Egyptian fleets hastened the end of the Balkan conflict and, although there were to be many disagreements about territorial boundaries, Britain, France and Russia agreed to recognise the independence of Greece in February 1830.

Cochrane had been in Poros on the other side of the mainland when the crucial sea battle took place and some days later he wrote to Dr Gosse, 'If you have heard the result of the battle of Navarino pray inform us, we are quite ignorant of everything but that a terrible fight did take place.'[30] On 27 October he sailed to Chios in order to provide support to a Greek force which was planning to recapture the island from the Turks, but on 2 November he received a letter signed by the three allied commanders demanding a cessation of all hostilities. The letter warned that all Greek vessels, armed for war, found beyond twelve miles from the shores of continental Greece, would be de-stroyed.[31] The British government had never approved of Cochrane's presence in Greece and it was now clear that he and his ships were regarded as pirates and a threat to the peace of the region. His protests were in vain and were not helped by the fact that most of the captains and crews of the ships which had briefly formed the Greek navy had returned to their usual occupation of preying on defenceless merchant ships. He wrote a long letter to Capodistrias, the Greek president, complaining about the conduct of his Greek crews and informing him that he was returning to England to recruit seamen: 'Sober, steady men can be obtained from the northern nations, who will do their duty, and, since precept is useless, teach the Greeks by example. Then piracy may cease and commerce may flourish.'[32]

He handed over command of the *Hellas* to Admiral Miaoulis and on 10 January 1828 he left Poros in the schooner *Unicorn*. He arrived at Portsmouth on 11 February but when he met the members of the Greek Committee in London he found them disillusioned by the internal quarrels and unpatriotic conduct of the Greeks. The Foreign Enlistment Act prevented him recruiting seamen and his attempts to bypass this proved fruitless. The remaining steam vessels in which he had placed such faith were still in an unfinished state in Galloway's yard. He travelled to Paris to meet up with his wife and family, and had an unsatisfactory meeting with the French Philhellenic Committee. His position was becoming impossible and was affecting his health. 'I am very low, and do not feel at all well,' he wrote on 24 March. 'I cannot free myself from the oppression of spirits occasioned by seeing everything in the lamentable state in which all must continue in Greece, unless some effectual steps are taken to put an end to the intrigues and rivalships headed by unprincipled chiefs and backed by their savage followers.'[33] To make matters worse Sir Francis Burdett forwarded a letter to him written by one of the Greek deputies who had originally recruited him in London. He was informed that by leaving Greece he had broken his contract and he must repay the sum of £37,000, a demand he indignantly rejected.

By the end of September he was back in Greece but he was coldly received. He no longer had a role to play and he had to suffer ten miserable weeks of being treated with contemptuous indifference by those in power while his naval accounts were scrutinised. On 26 November he wrote to Count Capodistrias offering his resignation. He asked that the sum of £20,000, which was due to be paid to him when Greece achieved independence, should be used for the relief of wounded seamen and the families of those who had died during the conflict.[34] His resignation was accepted and he received a gracious reply thanking him for his services on behalf of Greece. 'You have taken part in her restoration and she will reckon you, with sentiments of profound gratitude, among her first and generous defenders.'[35]

He was grudgingly lent the brig *Proserpine* to take him home but was treated with such calculated rudeness by her captain that he lodged a formal complaint. Fortunately his reputation still remained high among naval men and Admiral Heyden, who had commanded the Russian fleet at Navarino, offered to give him a passage on the Russian corvette *Grimachi* as proof of his esteem. He further promised to 'receive him with the honours due to his rank and with musical honours; and at his departure I will man the yards'.[36] The corvette left Poros on 20 December and took him to Malta where he was warmly welcomed by Admiral Sir Pulteney Malcolm who had commanded the 74-gun ship *Donegal* at Basque Roads and had been one of the few captains to come out in support of Cochrane at Lord Gambier's court martial in 1809. Malcolm arranged for him to travel to Naples on HMS *Racer* and from there he made his way to Paris to rejoin his family. His active life as a naval commander in battle and an admiral in the service of foreign powers was over.

TWENTY

The Fightback

1828–1851

During his last months in Greece and the early months of 1829, Cochrane was more depressed than he had been at any time since his imprisonment following the Stock Exchange trial. So much had been expected of him by the Greeks and by the supporters of the Greek cause throughout Europe that his evident failure to influence the course of the war was humiliating and bitterly disappointing. When Captain Grenfell, who had proved such a capable commander in Brazil, learnt that Cochrane had returned from Greece, he wrote from Rio de Janeiro, urging him to rehoist his flag and resume command of the Brazilian navy. Cochrane refused the offer and told him, 'The mental fever I contracted in Greece has not yet subsided, nor will it probably for some months to come.'[1] There seems little doubt that he had suffered a nervous breakdown and it is not hard to see why his usually indomitable character was finally brought low. Apart from the troubles he had endured with his men and his ships, and the intrigues, rivalries and needless slaughter he had witnessed, he had found himself ostracised by the British government, side-lined by the Royal Navy, and was now unable to return to Britain for fear of prosecution under the Foreign Enlistment Act.

The year 1829 was also marked by family tragedies. On 6 August his youngest brother, Archibald, died at the age of forty-seven leaving a wife and young children. They had served together in the navy in the early days and, when Archibald had retired with the rank of captain, Cochrane had suggested that he come out and join him in South America. Later in the year Kate gave birth to a stillborn child after suffering what were described as 'dreadful puerperal convulsions'. This did not quench her lively and spirited nature but in later years Cochrane always blamed her difficulties on this unhappy event.

During his brief visit to England during the summer of 1828, Cochrane had addressed a lengthy petition to the Duke of Clarence asserting his innocence of the Stock Exchange fraud and asking him to persuade his brother, King George IV, to reinstate him 'in that rank and station in the Royal Navy which he previously held'.[2] The document was passed to the Cabinet and was predictably rejected by the Duke of Wellington who was now Prime Minister. However, events in England soon began to turn in Cochrane's favour, coinciding with the lifting of his depression and the recovery of his old energy and determination. In the spring of 1830 he was staying in Florence with his family and met Charles Greville, the diarist and associate of Palmerston and other members of the Tory Cabinet. They talked at length about the political situation in England where the movement for parliamentary reform was gathering momentum. Greville recorded in his diary a conversation with Cochrane: 'I thought things would explode at last in England, which he concurred in, and seemed to like the idea of it, in which we differ, owing probably to the difference of our positions.' A few days later Greville rode out to Cochrane's villa, 'where we found them under a matted tent in the garden, going to dinner. He talks of going to Algiers to see the French attack it. He had made £100,000 by the Greek bonds. It is a pity he ever committed a robbery; he is such a fine fellow, and so shrewd and good humoured.'[3] Cochrane had invested his £37,000 salary advance in Greek funds which had apparently made an enormous profit and would enable him to live in some style when he returned to London later in the year.

The two events which cleared the path for Cochrane's return were the death of the king and the fall of the Tory government. King George IV died in June 1830 and was succeeded by the Duke of

Clarence who became William IV. The new king had spent his early years in the navy and was known to be an admirer of Cochrane. In November the Duke of Wellington's Tory government fell and was replaced by a Whig government led by Lord Grey, with Lord Melbourne as Home Secretary, and Cochrane's friend Lord Brougham as Lord Chancellor. The first task of the new government was to steer through Parliament the Reform Bill which incorporated many of the measures which Cochrane and his radical friends Sir Francis Burdett, Henry Hunt and William Cobbett had been fighting for since the days of the Westminster election of 1807.

While he had been out of the country Cochrane had prepared a comprehensive review of his case. When he and his family arrived in London in the autumn of 1830 he had several copies printed and on 10 December one copy was forwarded through Lord Melbourne to the king, accompanied by a brief petition in which Cochrane stressed that he 'had no participation in, and no knowledge, not even the most indistinct or remote, of the crime under the imputation of which I have been so variously and so unceasingly punished. It is this alone which impels me to approach your Majesty . . .'[4] Other copies of the review were sent to Cabinet ministers. There were sympathetic replies from Lord Grey and Lord Melbourne but Lord Brougham warned that there was opposition from some ministers and sixteen months were to pass before Cochrane learnt the results of his petition.

One reason for the delay was that the controversial Reform Bill was causing uproar in Parliament and each time the bill was rejected there were riots and angry public meetings throughout the country. It was observed by enemies of reform that there were popular disturbances wherever William Cobbett or other radical speakers appeared in the country districts. In April 1831 Parliament was dissolved and in May the Whigs were returned with an increased majority. Lord Grey and his ministers spent much of the rest of the year endeavouring to get the bill, with amendments, through the House of Commons and the House of Lords.

On 1 July, Cochrane's father died at his lodgings in Paris at the age of eighty-three. He had fallen out with his eldest son at the time of the

Stock Exchange trial and they had had little contact since. The old earl's third wife had died nine years before and he had spent the last years of his life in poverty.[5] The fifty-five-year-old Lord Cochrane now became the tenth Earl of Dundonald. But although he inherited the title and the name borne by a long line of Scottish ancestors, he still had to clear that name of the crime for which he had been fined, imprisoned, stripped of the Order of the Bath and struck off the Navy List. On 27 November he succeeded in obtaining a personal interview with King William at the Royal Pavilion in Brighton. The king was sympathetic to his cause and promised to see that his case was examined by the appropriate authorities.[6] Kate, now Lady Dundonald, had several meetings with Lord Grey, the Prime Minister, who assured her that he would do all he could to help, and friends such as Sir Francis Burdett continued to lobby on his behalf in Parliament. At last, at a meeting of the Privy Council on 2 May 1832, a free pardon was granted and the same day he was reinstated as an officer of the Royal Navy. The *London Gazette* published the announcement from the Admiralty Office: 'This day, in pursuance of His Majesty's pleasure, the Earl of Dundonald was promoted to be Rear-Admiral

Hanover Lodge, the home of Cochrane and his family in the 1830s. The house was one of several villas in Regents Park, London, designed by Decimus Burton.

of the Blue, taking rank next after the Hon George Heneage Lawrence Dundas.'[7] It was in the uniform of a rear-admiral that Cochrane (as we shall continue to call him) was presented to the king at a royal levee held at St James's Palace on 9 May.

Soon after returning to England from Italy, Cochrane had bought Hanover Lodge, a handsome villa situated on land to the north of the John Nash terraces in Regents Park. He had asked his brother William to look for a suitable property and on 3 November 1829 William had written to him to say that he and their naval uncle Alexander had been to see an excellent house in the park, 'with two acres of land, with three drawing rooms, a dining room and a library on the ground floor and eight bedrooms above with standing for two carriages and stabling for eight horses'.[8] The house had been designed by Decimus Burton for Colonel Sir Robert Arbuthnot, a hero of the Napoleonic campaigns.[9] Cochrane purchased the property for £12,000 from Lady Arbuthnot and for a few years it was the family home. For most of her adult life Kate had lived and brought up her children in lodgings, or had stayed for months at a time with relations, or had lived in what must always have seemed temporary accommodation in Valparaiso, Santiago, Lima, Rio de Janeiro, Boulogne, Brussels, Paris and Florence. She was now able to live and entertain in a manner which suited her outgoing temperament and her place in society. Hanover Lodge had spacious tree-lined grounds bordering the Regents Park Canal. After overseeing extensive improvements to the interior of the house, Kate filled the reception rooms with classical busts and statues, Chinese vases and portraits and paintings 'of the gallant Admiral's achievements, by sea and land'. The household included three men servants, a lady's maid, a cook, a nursery maid, a house maid, a scullery maid and a governess for the two younger children – Lizzie was aged ten when they moved into the house; Arthur was eight. In the summer of 1832 when all the improvements had been completed, Kate held a *fête-champêtre* – a magnificent reception with the grounds lit by a variety of lamps, dinner in a marquee adjoining the house and dancing till midnight. The guest list included the

Prince of Canino, the Duke and Duchess of Padua and a glittering gathering of British aristocracy, naval and military officers and people of note in London society.[10]

With the ending of the long war against Napoleonic France in 1815 the Admiralty had drastically reduced the numbers of men and ships in service. There was therefore no reason for Cochrane to expect to be given a command. However, he ruled himself out of the running anyway by making it known that he would not accept an appointment unless he was restored to the Order of the Bath and fourteen years were to pass before this was achieved. He spent these years industriously working on scientific projects and inventions. This was not a new departure, of course. He had been one of the first naval officers to use Congreve rockets; the explosion ships at Basque Roads had been of his own devising; and he had used kites to distribute propaganda leaflets on the coast of France in 1805.[11] The convoy lamp on which he was working at the time of the Stock Exchange trial had failed to interest the Admiralty but a few years later he won the £50 prize by entering the lamp under the name of another person. In 1812, following his discovery of the sulphur mines in Sicily, he had worked out a method for using poison gas as a deadly weapon against enemy naval bases and he had submitted the details in his 'Secret War Plans' which were considered by a high-level committee but subsequently rejected.[12] And he had shown himself to be years ahead of most of his contemporaries by his recognition that steam power would replace sail as the propulsion for ships. He had demonstrated his faith in this by ordering the *Rising Star* for the Chilean navy and then insisting that steam-powered warships be built for the Greek navy.

On his return from Italy in 1830 he became involved in the construction of the tunnel which was being built under the Thames from Rotherhithe to Wapping under the direction of Marc Brunel, the French-born engineer and father of Isambard Kingdom Brunel.[13] Progress had been hampered by the influx of mud and Cochrane devised and patented a method of using compressed air to assist in the excavations. He continued to correspond with Marc Brunel and in 1833 they were discussing ways of improving steam engines. Cochrane had invented a steam-powered rotary engine which theoretically had a number of advantages over the reciprocating steam engine which used pistons and connecting rods to convert the steam power into a circular motion to drive the wheels of a locomotive or the paddle wheels of a ship. The rotary engine was lighter and smoother running and had fewer moving parts. 'There are no beams, cranks, side rods, connecting rods, parallel motions, levers, slide valves, excentrics,' Cochrane wrote of his rotary engine. 'As the moving parts of the Revolving Engine pursue their course in perfect circles (without stop or hindrance) this Engine is capable of progressive acceleration, until the work performed equals the pressure of steam on the vacuum, or on the atmosphere: – an advantage which the Reciprocating Engine does not possess.'[14]

Initially he used his rotary engine to drive a small boat on the Thames. His experiments were sufficiently successful to persuade the directors of the Liverpool and Manchester Railway to come down to London to examine his prototype model and they subsequently allowed him to use George Stephenson's *Rocket* for further experiments.[15] The famous locomotive had been withdrawn from service after mechanical problems but when trials were held in October 1834 using Cochrane's rotary engine to drive the *Rocket* the results were disappointing. However, in December the directors of the London and Greenwich Railway offered to build two of his rotary engines. They were concerned about the jarring vibrations of reciprocating engines on the elevated viaducts of the railway and thought that the smooth-running rotary engine would be more suitable. Trials of the first locomotive driven by rotary engines were held on 24 June 1835 and proved more satisfactory than those carried out with the *Rocket*, but serious defects soon developed and by the end of the year the engine had completely broken down. Another engine was built, but problems continued, leading to a dispute and legal proceedings between Cochrane and the railway company. By the time he withdrew from the venture in October 1838 he had spent at least £4,000 of his own money on the project.

Unlike his father who had tended to abandon his experiments when they went wrong and move on to other projects, Cochrane refused to admit failure. He was certain that the problems encountered with his

LIVERPOOL PRIZE ENGINES.

THE ROCKET.

The Rocket, designed by George and Robert Stephenson.
The famous locomotive, which had won the Rainhill trials in 1829, was lent
to Cochrane five years later for experiments with his rotary steam engine.

rotary engine could be overcome and his next move was to persuade the Admiralty to carry out tests with his engine at Portsmouth dockyard. These were so successful that in due course the navy paid for his engine to replace the unsatisfactory engines in the small steam vessel *Firefly*. Throughout the many years that he worked on his rotary engine Cochrane remained convinced that it would prove a commercial success and make his fortune. This is confirmed in a letter he wrote in 1839 to his old friend James Guthrie, the surgeon, who had retired to Scotland and was living in a small village in Fife overlooking the Firth of Tay. The letter was written in a reflective mood from Hanover Lodge and is worth quoting at some length:

Dear Guthrie,

This is the sixth of May, and thirty eight years have now passed since the affair of the Gamo, when we were together in the little Speedy. How many things have passed; how many acquaintances have departed since that day, leaving scarcely a trace to recall them to mind! I have often, however,

thought of you, though I have not written now for a long time. The truth is
I have had an absorbing pursuit, that of perfecting the Rotary or Revolving
Engine which I am glad to tell you has been crowned with the most
complete success and will shortly realise a fortune. The most talented
engineers have examined the engine made for the Admiralty which are
now setting up in Portsmouth Yard, and they have at last given up their
opposition.

He went on to give Guthrie news of his family: his eldest son,
Thomas, was with his regiment in Canada; his second son, Horace,
was with the army at Malta; his third son, Arthur, had just joined
HMS *Benbow*; and his daughter

is with my youngest son Ernest, with Lady Dundonald at Boulogne; who
resides there for her health, which is by no means good – nor has it so been
for many years. I am as grey as a badger, but on the whole wear pretty
well, considering the rough kind of usage I have had in my time. Pray how
are you, and how is Mary Guthrie, to whom I must pay my respects
whenever I get to the north. I have now made up my mind to sell this nice
pretty place, for two reasons; first Lady Dundonald has not resided here
for years; and secondly it is a costly place to keep up, and inconvenient to
me in that respect, seeing that my sons are now drawing bills, and wanting
promotion, and that my engine has cost money and not yet returned any –
though I hope it will soon do so.[16]

Cochrane's description of his wife and family plays down the
troubles they had gone through since they settled back in London.
The marriage, which had survived the long absences every seaman's
family had to endure, came under increasing strain now that they were
living under the same roof for longer than a few months at a time.
Cochrane, who was sixty-four in 1839, was no longer the glamorous
naval hero who had swept Kate off her feet when she was a girl in her
teens. He had put on weight and seems to have lost the charisma which
had impressed Maria Graham in Chile. The writer and journalist
Cyrus Redding, who had met Cochrane in Plymouth when he was in

his prime as a successful frigate captain, recalled seeing him more recently at the Temple Bar: 'Alas! What ravage time had made in his once handsome and active figure. Such changes tell painfully in the history of our fleeting humanity . . .'

Kate, who was twenty years younger, was still a good-looking woman who enjoyed society life and shone in company. Her love for Lord Auckland must have put a strain on the marriage but his work and her travels had kept them apart. Any hopes she may have had of resuming their relationship were ended when, in 1835, he went abroad for six years as Governor-General of India. Meanwhile, she was increasingly exasperated by Cochrane's obsession with steam engines and was concerned that his inventions were draining the family finances. Their financial problems were exacerbated by the extravagant behaviour of their children. While serving in the army in Canada, Tom had run up huge bills, obtained money on false pretences and returned in 1836 with debts of more than £5,000. Cochrane agreed to settle his debts and arranged for him to take up a five-year posting with the army in Hong Kong. Horace had been forced to resign his army commission after embarking on a life of gambling and riotous living which had forced him to borrow large sums from a moneylender. He was now living under an assumed name to escape his creditors. Lizzie made an unsuitable marriage in 1840 which would soon lead to her abandoning her husband and fleeing to France with another man.

Whether it was the difference in their ages and their interests, their financial problems, Kate's ill health or her disillusionment with Cochrane and her resentment at the time and money he was spending on his scientific projects, the strains proved too much. Towards the end of the 1830s they separated and Kate moved to France, initially taking up residence at Boulogne but later moving to Paris. He offered her a generous financial settlement and they continued to see each other at regular intervals but they never lived under the same roof again. Hanover Lodge was eventually sold in 1845.

Cochrane worked harder than ever on his inventions and in January 1843 a patent was granted to him for important modifications he had made to the boilers used for steam engines, and for his improved version of the screw propeller for ships. The Admiralty was sufficiently convinced by the experiments on the *Firefly* to order the construction of the *Janus*, a steam frigate which was designed by Cochrane and was to be fitted with his rotary engine and his improved boilers. The ship was built at Chatham dockyard and by 10 July 1844 he was writing, 'The Janus is now completing – that is, being coppered – and having the part of her deck laid down which was left off for the purpose of getting the boilers on board.'[17] On 24 October he reported that the First Lord of the Admiralty Sir George Cockburn, accompanied by Sir John Barrow, the Admiralty Secretary, and Lord Brougham, had seen his engine, 'all of whom were well pleased with my explanation of its principles'.[18] During a nine-day trial towards the end of 1845 the *Janus* performed successfully in calm water. 'Nothing can exceed the beauty of her passage through the water, without even a ripple, far less the wave which ordinary steamboats occasion.'[19] But a serious miscalculation in her design caused her to lie too low in the water, making her dangerously unseaworthy in bad weather. Other faults developed and work on the vessel was abandoned amidst complaints from some quarters about the waste of public money.

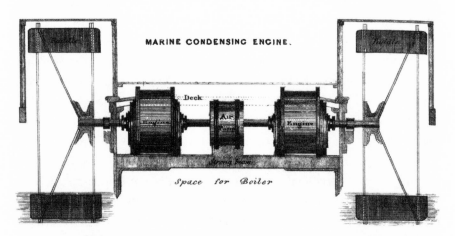

A diagram showing Cochrane's rotary steam engines driving two paddle wheels.
An illustration from 'The steam engine simplified', by the Earl of Dundonald.

Cochrane, meanwhile, continued to keep up unrelenting pressure on those in power to restore him to the Order of the Bath. He had put his case in letters to a succession of prime ministers, presidents of the Privy Council and his friends in government. To add further ammunition to his cause, in April 1847 he published a remarkable document which he entitled 'Observations on Naval Affairs, and some Collateral Subjects including Instances of Injustice experienced by the Author with a summary of his Navy Service and a copious appendix'. This was the forerunner of his later autobiographies – a selective and strongly argued defence of his naval and parliamentary career designed to show himself in the best possible light at the expense of those he regarded as his enemies. The document also included details of the sums of money which he believed he was still owed by Chile and Brazil, the legal expenses he had incurred for the Stock Exchange trial, his claim on the Royal Navy for eighteen years' back pay, the loss of Culross Abbey and estate valued at £50,000, and the sum of £15,000 which he had spent on scientific research and inventions and for which he expected to be reimbursed.[20] In spite of the controversial nature of much of the contents the document was generally well received. 'I hear from all quarters that the pamphlet has made, and is making, a great impression and I have every hope that all will end well.'[21]

The timing was right for the final rehabilitation of the man Anthony Trollope would later describe as 'that indefatigable old hero Lord Dundonald'. He had outlived most of his opponents and, thanks to the support of friends in high places, and the writings of Captain Marryat, Maria Graham and others, he was now widely regarded as a brave liberator of oppressed nations and a heroic survivor of the Nelson era who had been unjustly treated by his country. The Tory government of Robert Peel had recently been replaced by a Whig administration led by the reforming and liberal-minded Lord John Russell. Two of Cochrane's friends were in the Cabinet – Lord Lansdowne was President of the Council and Lord Auckland was First Lord of the Admiralty. And crucial for Cochrane's cause was the fact that the young Queen Victoria was on his side. She told Lord Lansdowne on 6 May that, with or without the approval of her Privy Counsellors, she would confer on Lord

Dundonald the next vacant Order of the Bath. On 25 May the announcement appeared in the *London Gazette* that 'The Queen has been pleased to
appoint Vice-Admiral the Earl of Dundonald to be a Knight Grand Cross
of the most Hon. Order of the Bath.'[22] Prince Albert, who was Grand
Master of the Order, arranged for him to wear the insignia at the
birthday drawing room of the Queen on 27 May.

'Today there was a grand muster at the palace of all the Knights
Grand Crosses, and many inferior Crosses,' Cochrane wrote on 12
July, 'and I was installed. Lord Ellenborough was one of my sponsors,
and the Duke of Wellington shook hands with me, and expressed his
satisfaction at my restoration to the Order.'[23] That the son of the judge
who had sent Cochrane to prison should have been one of his sponsors
was a sign of the times, although the grandson of the judge would
insist that this unexpected gesture had no particular significance.

Six months later Cochrane received a letter from Lord Auckland
inviting him to become commander-in-chief for the North American
and West Indian stations. 'I am satisfied that your nomination will be
agreeable to her Majesty, as it will be to the country – particularly to
the Navy.'[24] On 17 March 1848 Cochrane had the satisfaction of
hoisting his flag on the foremast of the 74-gun ship HMS *Wellesley.* He
was now a Vice-Admiral of the Red and was able to appoint his son
Arthur as his flag lieutenant. They set sail with a squadron of ships
from Plymouth on 25 March and reached Bermuda on 3 May. From
there they sailed north to Halifax, Nova Scotia. From the naval bases
of Bermuda and Halifax they made extensive cruises and during the
course of the next three years they visited the West Indian islands of
Barbados, Trinidad, St Lucia, Antigua and Jamaica, as well as Louisbourg, Nova Scotia and St John's, Newfoundland.[25] After his miserable
experiences in Greece it was good to be back on a British ship among
British sailors, and the men much appreciated his easy style of
command. Thomas Branton, who was a member of the crew of the
admiral's galley (the boat used for taking him ashore) later wrote,

I was never tired of hearing of the fine old fellow's exploits when, as young
Lord Cochrane, he fought the French and Spaniards in Nelson's days. He

was a fine old man with typical Scottish features. He was an ideal officer, and was so beloved by the men that his name on the lower deck was 'Dad'. He would not allow flogging, greatly to the disgust of some of the other officers, who considered that leniency was bad for discipline. When he was in the galley he would talk to the coxwain and the crew as though we were his equals.[26]

Cochrane took extensive notes wherever he went and sent back detailed reports to Lord Auckland. He recorded the decline of the Newfoundland fisheries; he was impressed by the civil administration in Bermuda but thought conditions in Kingston, Jamaica, were lamentable; he recommended a number of improvements for the naval hospital at Port Royal; and he took samples of bitumen from the famous lake of pitch at Trinidad and experimented with a mixture of bitumen and coal as fuel for the steam vessel *Scourge* which was part of his squadron. The overseas posting ended in April 1851 and Sir George Seymour was appointed to succeed him. As so often in the small world of the navy the two men had served together in the past. While in command of the 16-gun *Kingfisher* in 1806 Seymour had come to Cochrane's aid when the *Pallas* had been severely damaged in her action with the *Minerve* off the Ile d'Aix. Seymour had later commanded the *Pallas* during the fireship attack at Basque Roads and had been openly critical of the delay in sending in the fleet when he gave evidence at Lord Gambier's court martial. Cochrane and his squadron set sail from Halifax, Nova Scotia, on 14 May 1851 and arrived at Portsmouth on 10 June. The following day his flag was hauled down and for the last time he disembarked from a British warship as a serving officer. He was seventy-five years old.

TWENTY-ONE

The Last Years

1851–1860

On 1 May 1851, a few weeks before Cochrane stepped ashore at Portsmouth, Queen Victoria opened the Great Exhibition in Hyde Park. The exhibition, the brainchild of Prince Albert, was an astonishing display of the latest achievements in engineering, manufacturing and the fine and decorative arts. It was housed in a soaring structure of iron and glass which was three times the length of St Paul's Cathedral and tall enough to house three of the park's large elm trees. Designed by Joseph Paxton, the friend and former gardener of the Duke of Devonshire, it was initially derided by *The Times* as a 'monstrous greenhouse' but proved as great an attraction as the displays and became known as the Crystal Palace. The exhibits ranged from the Koh-i-noor diamond and the finest products of the Wedgwood pottery to a thirty-one-ton steam locomotive and the hydraulic presses used to build the supports of the railway bridge over the Menai Straits – an engineering marvel designed by George Stephenson's son Robert which had been completed the previous year.

The Great Exhibition attracted six million visitors during the five months that it was open and was a showcase for Britain's technical ingenuity and manufacturing prowess. There is no record in his letters or journals of Cochrane visiting the exhibition in Hyde Park but he did pay a visit to the Crystal Palace a few years later after it had been moved and re-erected in Sydenham. In April 1857 he told Arthur that he proposed to take his brother William and his wife, 'down to the neighbourhood of the Crystal Palace, where there are so many objects to divert attention, and stay there for a month or more . . .'[1] His activities on his return to London certainly show him to have been very much in tune with the spirit of the times. He continued to work on his steam engine and his improved boiler and between 1851 and 1853 he took out a series of patents for using the bitumen from Trinidad in the construction of sewers and tunnels; for laying pipes below ground; for insulating wire; and for use as a waterproofing building material in an enlightened scheme to construct an embankment along the Thames.[2] He also published the observations he had made during his Atlantic cruise in a paper entitled 'Notes on the Mineralogy, Government and Conditions of the British West India Islands, and the North-American Maritime Colonies'.

On the outbreak of the Crimean War in 1854 he revived his 'Secret War Plans' and wrote to Sir James Graham, who had succeeded Lord Auckland as the First Lord of the Admiralty, urging him to consider the use of smoke screens and poison gas against the Russian forces and ships at Sebastopol and Kronstadt. At one stage the Admiralty seriously considered appointing Cochrane as commander-in-chief of the Baltic Fleet but he was now seventy-nine and it was decided that 'though his energies and faculties are unbroken, and though, with his accustomed courage, he volunteers for the Service, yet, on the whole, there is reason to apprehend that he might deeply commit the Force under his command in some desperate enterprise, where the chance of success would not countervail the risk of failure and of the fatal consequences, which might ensue'.[3] However, his plans for the use of poison gas were carefully considered by a secret committee chaired by Admiral Sir Thomas Byam Martin. The committee sought advice from the eminent scientist Michael Faraday who agreed that burning sulphur would yield deadly fumes that could incapacitate or kill men but he was doubtful whether it would prove practicable on the scale which was proposed. He pointed out that the fumes from 400 tons of burning sulphur 'being heavier than air, would descend and move along over the surface of the water . . .'. He reckoned that the height of the poisonous fumes would be anything between ten and fifteen feet at first, and the width would be less than a mile, but the water 'would tend continually to take part of the noxious vapour out of it'. He suspected that much larger quantities would be required than was proposed and he pointed out that if the enemy had sufficient warning of the attack they could be supplied with respirators to resist the effects of the sulphur fumes.[4] Although Cochrane's plans were turned down he continued to argue his case with Sir James Graham and then with Lord Palmerston who was tempted to let Cochrane go out to the Crimea and superintend the scheme and take the blame if it failed, but in the end the plans were shelved.

On his return from his Atlantic cruise Cochrane stayed with his brother William for a while and then moved into lodgings at 2 Belgrave Road in Pimlico.[5] He paid a visit to France in August 1851 to help Kate move from Paris back to Boulogne but reported to Arthur, 'Poor Mama is no better in health than she was.' As for his children, three of them were doing well and two of them seemed to be beyond redemption. His eldest son, Tom, had returned from Hong Kong a reformed character. He had married Louisa, the daughter of William Mackinnon, a Scottish MP and head of the Mackinnon clan, and was now living a respectable life in the remote but fashionable Scottish coastal resort of Banff.[6] But the debts of Horace had now risen to £8,000 and Cochrane believed him to be irretrievably ruined. 'I have been so tortured by Horace,' he wrote on 20 July, 'who, if caught will undoubtedly be transported . . .'[7] The situation of his daughter was equally worrying. 'Poor Liz is lost, incurably gone. She is living at Florence in the society of young men, not one but in the plural number, the females, though virtue is there not much prized, having cut her.'[8] However, he could take consolation in the naval careers of Arthur and his youngest son, Ernest. They both took part in the attack on the Russian fortress of Bomarsund during the Crimean War and served with distinction; Arthur was promoted to post-captain following the fall of Bomarsund and Ernest was promoted to lieutenant.[9]

Cochrane in his eighties had become an admired and much-revered figure, laden with so many honours that photographs taken of him in his admiral's uniform around this time show him weighed down by medals, ribbons and gold braid. In addition to the Order of the Bath he had a number of medals which had been presented to him by the Chilean government; the Emperor Pedro had, as we have seen, bestowed on him the Grand Cross of Brazil and created him Marquis of Maranhão; and in 1835 King Otho of Greece had conferred on him the insignia of Grand Commander of the Order of the Saviour of Greece. He had now risen to the rank of Admiral of the Red in the British navy, and had been given the additional honorary title of Rear-Admiral of the United Kingdom. In 1854, at the invitation of Prince Albert, he had become an Elder Brother of Trinity House and in 1856 he was persuaded by his old colleague George Seymour, now a vice-admiral, to become an honorary member of the United Services Club in Pall Mall. An article describing his achievements was published in the *Illustrated Times* around this time and included a memorable description of his appearance:

'Fancy to your self a broad-built Scotchman, rather seared than conquered by age, with hair of a snowy white, and a face in which intellect still beams through traces of struggle and sorrow, and the marks of eighty years of active life. A slight stoop takes away from a height that is almost commanding. Add to these a vision of good old-fashioned courtesy colouring the whole man, his gestures and his speech, and you have some idea of the Earl of Dundonald in this present June, 1855.'[10] In contrast to this sympathetic description are the critical observations of his wife which are recorded in numerous letters to their sons: 'Your father is becoming very shaking in his mind and memory,' she wrote in 1856, 'and indeed I think through his terrible deafness that he will lose all power of business powers . . .'[11] She continued to be resentful of the way in which he had squandered the large sums of money which had come his way from prize money, and from his naval service as a commander of the navies of Chile, Brazil and Greece. 'I hope, my dearest Arthur, that you will not imbue your hands in that hateful Pitch and dirt. For forty years and more I have been your Father's wife and I have seen two noble fortunes spent, and not one penny of money spent ever returned . . .' She reckoned that £70,000 had been spent on the two earliest parliamentary elections, £10,000 had gone on the convoy lamp experiments, and the steam engines and the pitch experiments had caused further ruination. She recalled that Hanover Lodge had been sold at a loss 'to pay for the outlays on that hateful Janus'.[12]

In 1857 Cochrane began work on the first of his autobiographies. This was devoted to his exploits in South America and seems to have been prompted by a request from official sources in Chile for 'a biographical sketch' of his eventful life.[13] He used the opportunity to set down and justify the demands for prize money and back pay which he believed he was still owed by the governments of Chile and Brazil. The book was published in 1859 in two volumes under the title *Narrative of Services in the Liberation of Chili, Peru, and Brazil from Spanish and Portuguese Domination.* Although it was written in the first person – and the accounts of most of the actions and many minor incidents are clearly based on his reminiscences – Cochrane entrusted the writing of the book to George Butler Earp, a professional author who had recently published *A History of the Crimean War.* As Cochrane's memory of events which had taken place more than thirty years before was far from perfect, Earp took much of the material from those documents and copies of letters which Cochrane's secretary, William Jackson, had saved and brought back from South America. He was also able to draw on the published memoirs and biographies of Cochrane's associates in South America, notably John Miers, Captain Hall, Maria Graham, Major Miller and William Bennet Stevenson who had spent twenty years in South America and had acted as Cochrane's Spanish language secretary. *Narrative of Services* contains some graphic accounts of the most spectacular of the naval actions, but a disproportionate amount of space is devoted to arguments about pay and prize money and the book is heavily biased in Cochrane's favour at the expense of men like San Martin, Zenteno, Villela Barbosa and Captain Guise who had incurred his displeasure.

By the time the book was published many of Cochrane's financial

demands had been settled. The Chileans had rejected his more out-
rageous claims but did agree to pay him £6,000. And during the
course of 1857 the Brazilian government remitted bills of exchange
worth £34,000 to cover his claims for back pay and half-pay.[14]
Cochrane used some of the money to pay off the debts of his son
Horace, and some of it he put towards the purchase of a London house
for his eldest son, Tom. Writing to Arthur from a villa in Nice where
she had been staying, Kate recorded that Tom 'has bought a house in
Albert Road . . . Your father has given him four thousand five hundred
pounds out of his Brazilian money.'[15] The actual address of the house
was 12 Prince Albert Road but a few years later the road was renamed
Queens Gate (it lies parallel with Exhibition Road and runs from the
Natural History Museum towards the Royal Albert Hall). Around
1858 Cochrane moved into the house and most of his later letters are
addressed from 12 Queens Gate, South Kensington.

In the summer of 1859 he paid a visit to his wife in Boulogne and
then spent six weeks on the south coast at Deal working on *The
Autobiography of a Seaman*, the book which would reinforce his
reputation as the most brilliant naval officer of his generation. On
20 July he wrote to Tom from the Royal Hotel, Deal, 'I am here with
Mr Earp getting on with the book, notwithstanding the cruel heat
that even here at the sea side, and within ten yards of the beach,
pervades the atmosphere . . .'[16] A few days later he moved into
lodgings at 89 Beach Street, Deal, where he stayed until the first
week of September. *The Autobiography of a Seaman* was published in
two volumes: the first covered his career in the Royal Navy up to the
fireship attack at Basque Roads; the second volume began with Lord
Gambier's court martial and concluded with a description of the Stock
Exchange trial. Again the book was written by George Earp with
material supplied by William Jackson, but they had at their disposal
far more material than had been available for *Narrative of Services*.
Cochrane had kept copies of most of his letters and there were his
logbooks and occasional journals as well as parliamentary reports,
newspaper cuttings, naval histories and recent biographies such as
Raikes' life of Jahleel Brenton. According to George Earp, 'My general

practice in writing that book was to write it from his documents, not from his words, because I frequently found his memory fail of late years.' As with the South American volumes there was a hidden agenda and in this case it was to exonerate Cochrane from complicity in the Stock Exchange fraud and to show that at several key moments of his life he had been the victim of enemies in the Admiralty or in the political establishment. As Earp made clear in a letter to Jackson, 'My object is to clear Lord Dundonald's character.'[17]

Considering that Cochrane was an ailing eighty-four, and that Jackson and Earp were both elderly and ill, it is surprising that between them they were able to produce a book that would become a classic of naval literature. Of course the dramatic nature of so much of Cochrane's life provided the basis for an extraordinary adventure story while his personal grievances and vendettas only added to the image of a great man surrounded by jealous and scheming enemies. The book was received with widespread acclaim but even Cochrane was aware of its shortcomings. 'The book now requires another edition,' he told Jackson in January 1860. 'I wish the text was correct for even with your improvements I have found a dozen blunders. If you have any more errors pray send them to me.'[18]

The compiling of the biography inevitably revived many unhappy memories and Cochrane became particularly depressed by his recollections of Lord Gambier's court martial. He was more than ever convinced that Gambier's followers had fabricated the charts on which so much of the court's judgement hinged and he devoted considerable space in the second volume to the action and the aftermath. However, he was now suffering increasing pain from an illness which was diagnosed as stones in his kidneys. On 19 March 1860 he wrote to Jackson, 'my hand shakes so much I can hardly write legibly – but I daresay you will make it out. I am a little better than I have been and the Doctor says I will get over it.'[19] But a few days later he was writing, 'I am far from being well, and fear that this is the beginning of the end.' On 4 April he had an operation which was carried out while he was anaesthetised with chloral, 'which takes off all sense of pain both at the time and – in my case – after, has relieved me, so that I have hope of getting better'.[20] After the operation he was still obsessed by the forged charts and falsehoods surrounding the court martial but was cheered by the news that his youngest son, Ernest, was returning from his most recent tour of duty.

On 12 April Arthur wrote to Kate in Boulogne, 'I think my Father's state of health precarious to the last degree. He underwent another operation yesterday under Bruce Jones, Lee and others and a large quantity of stone was brought away. He may or may not have the power to rally . . .'[21] Cochrane did rally and from his bedroom in Queens Gate he continued to work with Earp and Jackson on the second volume of his book, correcting proofs and suggesting improvements. He lived on through the summer but towards the end of October he had to undergo an emergency operation from which he failed to recover. He died on 31 October 1860, a few weeks short of his eighty-fifth birthday.

The funeral was held a fortnight later on 14 November and was, in the words of one observer, 'most solemn and impressive'. There were no military bands, or battalions of infantry or mounted Horse Guards and Life Guards as there had been for the funeral of the Duke of Wellington in 1852, and no representatives of the government or royal family attended the service, but Cochrane's family and friends ensured that his passing was marked with a ceremony worthy of the old hero. It took an hour and a half for the long line of horses and carriages to travel from the house in Kensington, along Piccadilly, St James's Street, Pall Mall and Parliament Street to Westminster Abbey. The funeral procession was led by a hearse drawn by six black horses and arrived at the doors of the abbey at exactly one o'clock. A large crowd had gathered outside but 'everything connected with the external and internal arrangements was so complete that no unseemly pressure or confusion took place'.[22] Slabs of stone had been removed in the centre of the nave so that the grave could be dug, and the nave itself was filled with those mourners who had tickets for the funeral service. The coffin was met at the cloister entrance by the Dean of Westminster accompanied by the High Constable of Westminster, a reminder of Cochrane's past service as Westminster's

Member of Parliament. The pallbearers accompanying the coffin were Admiral Sir George Seymour, Admiral Pascoe Grenfell, who had played a key role in the Brazilian campaign, Admiral Collier, Captain Goldsmith (Cochrane's flag captain on the *Wellesley*), Captain Hay, Captain Nolloth, Captain Schomberg, and his Excellency the Brazilian Ambassador. The choir, wearing black scarves over their surplices, joined the procession as it moved up the south aisle towards the west end of the nave while the organ played William Croft's funeral anthem 'I am the resurrection and the life . . .'. The psalms were sung to the music of Henry Purcell and were followed by an anthem celebrating Cochrane's life which had been specially composed for the occasion by John Goss, composer to the queen and organist of St Paul's Cathedral. After the coffin had been lowered into the grave and prayers had been read by the Dean, the service was concluded with Handel's moving anthem 'His body is buried in peace, but his memory shall live for ever'.

Most of the men and women who had featured in Cochrane's early life in the navy and Parliament had died many years before. William Cobbett had died on his farm in Surrey in 1835, and the 1840s had seen the deaths of Maria Graham, Sir Francis Burdett, Captain Marryat and Jahleel Brenton, the latter ending his days with a knighthood and the rank of vice-admiral. But Lord Brougham travelled from Cannes to attend the funeral. When the service was concluded he went across to shake hands with Cochrane's eldest son, Tom, now the Earl of Dundonald, and it was observed that he was evidently labouring under deep emotion. Shortly before his death Cochrane had sent a copy of the second volume of *The Autobiography of a Seaman* to Brougham with an accompanying letter. Brougham had replied from Paris reminding Cochrane of the impression he had made when they had paid a visit to the palace of the Tuileries. When Cochrane's name was mentioned there had been 'a general start and shudder' among the assembled company. 'I remember saying, as we drove away, that it ought to satisfy you as to your disappointment at Basque Roads; and you answered that you would rather have had the ships.'[23]

One of Cochrane's long-standing grievances was that the banner and regalia of the Order of the Bath, which he had been awarded for his role in leading the fireship attack at Basque Roads, was still missing from Westminster Abbey. On 26 May 1856 he had written to the Prime Minister, Lord Palmerston, asking for the banner to be replaced in King Henry VII's Chapel. He had also asked for the repayment of the fine that had been imposed on him, and the restoration of his half-pay during the period he had been suspended from the navy. 'Unless these be done,' he wrote, 'I shall descend to my grave with the consciousness, not only that justice has not fully been done to me, but under the painful conviction that its omission will be construed to the injury of my character in the estimation of posterity.'[24] Palmerston was not prepared to accede to any of these demands but on the day before the funeral, the banner and regalia (which had apparently been found in a junk shop) were restored to their former place in the abbey by command of Queen Victoria and Prince Albert.

Cochrane's wife had not attended the funeral.[25] Kate had suffered from poor health for many years and most people would have accepted this as the reason why she was not able to be present. However, she had no difficulty in crossing the Channel a year later to appear before a committee of the House of Lords and it seems more likely that there were other other reasons for her failure to appear at Westminster. We know that she had had ambivalent feelings about Cochrane for many years. The letters she wrote to her favourite son, Arthur, during Cochrane's declining years frequently describe her husband in contemptous terms. In her view he was a deaf, miserable and senile old man and she continued to blame him for squandering the family fortune on his ruinous inventions.[26] On learning of his habit of taking evening strolls in Regents Park with his housekeeper she had even accused him of having an affair with the woman – which is possible but seems unlikely in view of his age and infirmities and his lifelong devotion to his wife. Kate had also fallen out with her son Tom and she may have been reluctant to face him, as well as all Cochrane's friends and admirers, at the public ceremony in London.[27]

Like Cochrane's father, Kate spent the last years of her life in

France. Unlike the ninth Earl of Dundonald who had ended his days in humiliating poverty, Kate was well provided for and was visited at regular intervals by her children. She outlived Cochrane by less than five years and died at Boulogne on 25 January 1865 at the age of sixty-nine.

EPILOGUE

The obituaries of Cochrane were unusual. They listed his exploits at considerable length and drew attention to his audacity and bravery but they were also surprisingly emotional. There was a deep-felt sympathy for a man who, it was widely believed, had been wronged by his country and had suffered considerably as a consequence. There was also a sense of loss and regret at what he might have achieved for his country if he had not been dismissed from the Royal Navy and forced to seek employment overseas. *The Times* described him as one of the great characters of the past generation and a man of outstanding achievements but pointed out, 'Nothing can exceed the audacity of his designs or the singularity of his successes although, owing to the jealousy or spite of his superiors, his exploits were usually confined to spheres comparatively unimportant or remote.'[1] The *Illustrated London News* described him as a very remarkable man, 'for so many years known as the daring, the indefatigable, the persecuted Lord Cochrane'.[2] Tom Taylor, the writer and journalist and later the editor of *Punch*, published a lengthy eulogy in the form of a poem which began:

> Ashes to Ashes! Lay the hero down
> Within the grey old Abbey's glorious shade.
> In our Valhalla ne'er was worthier laid
> Since martyr first won palm, or victor crown.

The poem depicted Cochrane as a caged lion, a 'heroic soul, branded with a felon's doom' and denounced his enemies as 'crawling worms that in corruption breed'. It described how he sought service in other seas and returned to England to eat out his heart in 'weary, wishful days' until he was eventually restored to honour.[3]

This image of a man unjustly accused and deeply wronged owed much to the recently published *Autobiography of a Seaman* but it was given added weight by the staunch support Cochrane had always received from his friends such as Cobbett, Burdett, Lord Auckland and Lord Brougham, and by a number of publications by his admirers during his lifetime and in the years following his death – in particular the novels and memoirs of Captain Marryat, the memoirs of Jahleel Brenton and General Miller, the travel books of Maria Graham, and the accounts of his exploits in the *Naval Chronicle*. None of his supporters seem to have doubted his innocence of the Stock Exchange fraud. Were they all mistaken? Did his gallant record as a seaman, his mild and unassuming manner and his steadfast protestations of his innocence blind them to his participation in the scandal which turned his life upside down? William Napier, who had been one of Cochrane's bravest officers, wrote to James Guthrie when he heard the result of the trial, 'I can hardly bring myself to believe that he could have been concerned in so foul a transaction.'[4] And this was the opinion of all who knew him well. His wife never doubted his innocence and launched a passionate defence of his character when she was cross-examined by the House of Lords Committee which was set up in 1861 to examine the claims of Cochrane's younger son Arthur to inherit the earldom on the grounds that the earlier marriage was illegal. Interrogated by an august group of lawyers including the Lord Chancellor and the Attorney General, she became exasperated by their polite but persistent insinuations:

'I cannot bear to be sitting here to vindicate the honour of such a man. It is too much not to speak and tell my feelings, it would be impossible. He was a glorious man. He was incapable of deception such as is imputed to him by the world, I know . . . Such a God of a man! A man who could have ruled the world upon the sea!'[5]

Cochrane's attacks on Lord Ellenborough in his autobiography, and a number subsequent publications which proclaimed his innocence of the Stock Exchange fraud, provoked the Ellenborough family to come to the defence of their ancestor. *The Trial of Lord Cochrane before Lord Ellenborough* by J.B. Atlay not only examined the evidence presented at the trial but also included a sober account of Cochrane's naval and parliamentary career. The book was intended to clear Lord Ellenborough's name but left the reader in little doubt that the author believed Cochrane guilty of participating in the Stock Exchange fraud. This was followed by a book written by Ellenborough's grandson entitled *The Guilt of Lord Cochrane in 1814* which underlined Atlay's conclusions and accused Cochrane of having 'an utter disregard for truth and . . . an unwholesome greed for gold'.[6]

Two more recent publications have also found Cochrane guilty of the Stock Exchange fraud. In 1965 Henry Cecil, a judge and the author of a string of novels with a legal theme, published *A Matter of Speculation: The Case of Lord Cochrane* which examined the evidence presented at the trial, challenged the findings of Lord Campbell and other lawyers who had come out in Cochrane's favour, and set out his reasons for believing the guilty verdict to have been correct.[7] A biography by Brian Vale, published in 2004, has a particularly damning account of Cochrane's financial dealings in South America and is based on extensive research in the archives in Chile, Peru and Brazil. Vale has no doubt that Cochrane was an active participant in the Stock Exchange fraud. John Sugden, whose critical study of Cochrane's life up to and including the Stock Exchange trial is a model of historical research, concluded, 'Although much has been written to vindicate or accuse the captain, the question of his guilt cannot satisfactorily be resolved.'[8] The naval historian Christopher Lloyd, who had reservations about aspects of Cochrane's character (his personal prejudices, his obsession with money) thought that his innocence or guilt of the fraud could never be determined for certain owing to the conflicting and incomplete nature of the evidence, but concluded, 'Personally, I believe that he was innocent, but for reasons which are not the sort acceptable in a court of law.'[9]

My own opinion, after reviewing the material for and against Cochrane and after consulting the views of a distinguished judge on the evidence presented at the trial, is that Cochrane was innocent of any involvement in the planning and executing of the fraud. It seems possible that he may have suspected that something was amiss when De Berenger came to his house but that he decided to stand by his uncle Cochrane-Johnstone, not realising that to do so would lead to his being found guilty by association. There is no doubt that Cochrane was taken aback by the verdict and shocked by the sentence. Even by the standards of the day the sentence of imprisonment, a fine of £1,000 and the pillory was severe and must surely have been politically motivated. For forty-five years Cochrane carried on a single-minded crusade to overturn the verdict of the court. This could be seen as the bloody-mindedness of an arrogant man determined to get his own back on the world, but it seems more likely to have been driven by the natural desire of an innocent man to clear the stain on his character and on the Dundonald family name.

Whatever the differing opinions on the Stock Exchange trial, most of the critics of Cochrane are agreed that he was a remarkable man. Henry Cecil described him as 'a man of immense courage and almost fantastic determination'[10] and Brian Vale summed him up as 'a master of naval warfare, the scourge of the French, the liberator of South America, a talented inventor and a fearless fighter for radical causes'.[11] As a naval commander Cochrane was bold and resourceful; brave but cool in action; and a master of the ruse and stratagem. His men were devoted to him and he went out of his way to ensure their safety by his careful reconnaissance and detailed preparations before any action. During his lifetime and in the years following his death he was frequently compared with Nelson but such a comparison does him no favours. Their backgrounds were very different; their naval careers had little in common; and their achievements were not remotely comparable. Nelson had the good fortune to be born at the right time so that he was in a position of relatively high command when the opportunities arose; in addition to his personal courage and his qualities as a bold tactician and an inspirational leader, he was the supreme exponent of pitched battles between fleets. Cochrane never commanded a squadron let alone a fleet until he arrived in South America and the circumstances and conditions there bore little resemblance to those which faced Nelson in Europe. A more mean-ingful comparison would be with those seamen who excelled at coastal raids like Sir Francis Drake and Sir Henry Morgan – or John Paul Jones, a fellow Scot who became an American hero, made his name with some spectacular single-ship actions but ended his career fight-ing for the Russian navy.

Apart from the numerous biographies and what might be called his literary legacy (his autobiography, the novels by Captain Marryat, G. A. Henty, C. S. Forester, Patrick O'Brian and others) it is surprising how little there is to show today for such an extraordinary life. There is the memorial tablet in Westminster Abbey, a few pictures of his naval actions, some caricatures and engravings, and the family por-traits. But unlike Drake, Anson, Hawke, Rodney, Hood, St Vincent, Collingwood, Nelson and a dozen other naval heroes who were the subjects of commemorative pottery, and have had ships and streets and pubs named after them, Cochrane has not made much of a mark in Britain, and his reputation among naval historians has suffered a steady decline. It is only in South America that he receives the recognition which might have been expected of such a heroic figure. Dozens of streets, and a small town, are named after him in Chile. There is a magnificent statue of him on the waterfront of Valparaiso and several rooms of the maritime museum are devoted to him. And in the house of the Nobel prize-winning poet Pablo Neruda there is a framed copy of the moving poem he wrote to commemorate Cochra-ne's contribution to the liberation of his country which begins, 'Lord of the sea come to us . . .'

It was Cochrane's fate as a naval commander to spend most of his career operating on the margins of naval history and, apart from the controversial action at Basque Roads, he never had the opportunity to distinguish himself in a famous sea battle. It is interesting to speculate what sort of posthumous reputation he might have enjoyed if he had died at the age of thirty-four during or immediately after the fireship attack on the French fleet. The court martial of Lord Gambier would not have taken place and Basque Roads would have been seen as a glorious victory and not a wasted opportunity. His exploits in the

Speedy, the *Pallas* and the *Imperieuse* would have been recalled, as they were in a celebratory article in the *Naval Chronicle* in 1809, and he would have been hailed as the boldest and best of a generation of brilliant frigate captains. The words of one of these captains, who observed Cochrane's operations along the coast of Spain in the autumn of 1808, provide a memorable summary of his talents as a seaman: 'The conduct of Lord Cochrane during this service is far above my praise,' Jahleel Brenton reported to Admiral Collingwood. 'It was throughout a most animating example of intrepidity, zeal, professional skill and resources which I trust will be treasured up in the memory of all who witnessed it.'

APPENDIX

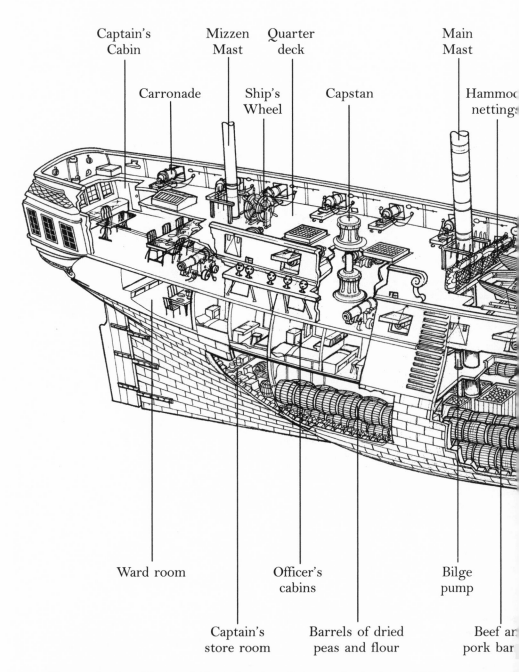

Captain's
Cabin

Mizzen
Mast

Quarter
deck

Main
Mast

Carronade

Ship's
Wheel

Capstan

Hammock
nettings

Ward room

Officer's
cabins

Bilge
pump

Captain's
store room

Barrels of dried
peas and flour

Beef and
pork barrels

Cutaway drawing of Cochrane's frigate *Imperieuse* of 38 guns, showing internal fittings and stores. Drawn by John Batchelor and based on the plans in the National Maritime Museum.

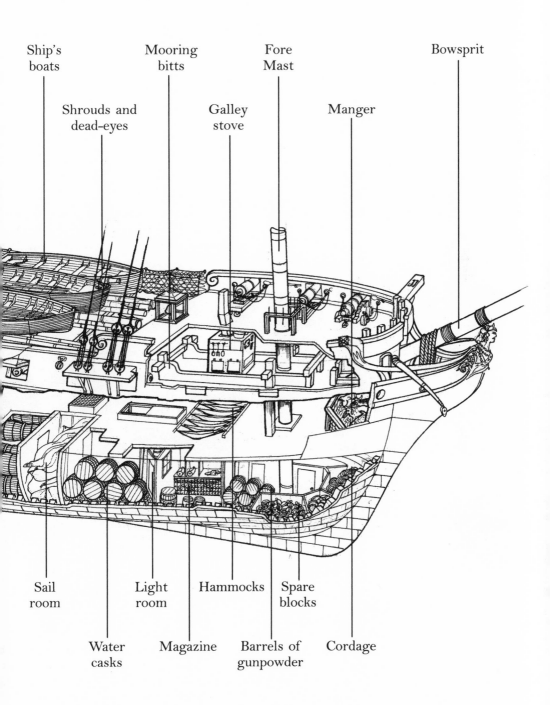

Ship's
boats

Shrouds and
dead-eyes

Mooring
bitts

Galley
stove

Fore
Mast

Manger

Bowsprit

Sail
room

Light
room

Hammocks

Spare
blocks

Water
casks

Magazine

Barrels of
gunpowder

Cordage

GLOSSARY

aft, after Situated at the back or stern part of a vessel.

block A pulley containing one, two or more sheaves, used to increase the power applied to ropes.

block and tackle An arrangement of pulleys and ropes used to raise heavy loads, and to increase the purchase on ropes used for the running rigging.

boatswain, or bosun The warrant officer in charge of sails, rigging, anchors and associated gear.

bomb, bomb vessel A warship which carried one or two heavy mortars for shore bombardment.

bombarde French term for a bomb vessel.

bowsprit A heavy spar pointing forward from the stem or front of the vessel.

brace A rope used to control the horizontal movement of a square-sailed yard.

brig A two-masted vessel, fully square-rigged on both masts, with a fore-and-aft sail on the lower part of the mainmast.

brigantine A two-masted vessel having a fully square-rigged foremast and a fore-and-aft rigged mainmast with squaresails on the main topmast.

broadside The simultaneous firing of all the guns on one side of a ship.

bulkhead A vertical partition inside a ship.

bumboat A small boat used to bring out and sell fruit, vegetables and other produce to the sailors on ships anchored some distance from the shore.

cable A measure of distance, 100 fathoms (200 yards). Also refers to any large rope such as the rope used for anchoring a ship.

caulk To seal the gaps between the planks with oakum and pitch.

collier A sturdy, flat-bottomed sailing vessel for carrying coal.

colours The flags worn by a vessel to show her nationality.

companionway The staircase or ladder down to a cabin or the lower deck; or the cover or protection built over the head of the staircase or ladder leading below.

corvette A type of French warship, usually a small ship of 20 to 24 guns or a ship sloop of 14 to 18 guns.

cutter A small, one-masted vessel rigged with a fore-and-aft mainsail, foresail and jib. In the eighteenth century a cutter usually had a square topsail as well.

deadeye A round wooden block with three holes for extending the shrouds.

East Indiaman A large ship engaged in trade with the East Indies.

ensign The national flag usually flown by ships at or near the stern of the vessel.

fathom A measure of six feet, used to describe the depth of water.

felucca A small, two-masted vessel of the Mediterranean with lateen sails on both masts.

flagship A ship commanded by an admiral and flying the admiral's distinguishing flag.

flag captain The captain of a ship carrying an admiral and flying his flag. (Captain Hardy was Nelson's flag captain on board HMS *Victory* at the Battle of Trafalgar).

fore Situated in front; the front part of a vessel at the bow.

fore-and-aft At bow and stern; backwards and forwards or along the length of the ship.

fore-and-aft rig Having mainly fore-and-aft sails, i.e. sails set lengthwise (and not at right-angles to the ship's hull, as is the case with square-rigged sails).

Forecastle/fo'c's'le The short deck built over the fore part of the main deck; the forward part of a ship where the sailors lived.

foremast The mast at the front of the vessel.

foretop A platform at the head of the lower foremast serving to spread the topmast rigging and provide a place for sailors working aloft.

frigate A fast cruising warship, less heavily armed than a ship of the line. Most frigates were fifth and sixth rates with between 40 and 20 guns.

galley 1. The ship's kitchen. 2. A notably fast type of boat under oar and sail, originally used by smugglers and later adopted for anti-smuggling patrols. Was also used as a ship's boat for raiding parties on enemy coasts.

galliot A small trading vessel, usually sprit-rigged.

gig A light, clinker-built boat carried by a warship and often favoured by captains for their own use.

grape, grapeshot Anti-personnel shot made up of small balls secured in a cylindrical canvas bag which flew apart on firing, scattering the shot over a wide area.

gunwale The upper planking along the sides of the vessel.

halyard A rope for raising and lowering a sail or yard.

heave to (past tense: hove to) To check the course of a vessel and bring her to a standstill by heading her into the wind and backing some of the sails.

hawser A large rope or a small cable.

helm   The tiller or wheel which controls the rudder and enables a vessel to be steered.

hulk   An old ship taken out of service and moored in harbour. Hulks were used as prison ships, convict ships, hospitals, floating barracks and receiving ships for pressed men.

jury rig   A makeshift arrangement of masts, yards and sails used to replace those damaged by storm or enemy action.

lateen sail   A triangular sail attached to a long yard with the foot of the sail made fast on deck and the middle of the yard hoisted so that it is at a slanting, oblique angle to the mast.

larboard   An old word for *port* (the left side of a vessel facing forward) which was preferred for helm orders. It was abandoned in 1844.

league   A measure of distance: 5 km (3 miles).

lee   The side or direction away from the wind, or downwind.

lee shore   The shore on to which the wind is blowing; a hazardous shore for a sailing vessel particularly in strong or gale-force winds.

log, logbook   A journal or diary which recorded the ship's position, speed and course, with notes on the wind direction, weather, sail changes, flag signals and other vessels met en route. The official log-book in a British warship was kept by the ship's master (navigator) but the captain and lieutenants also kept log-books and so did the midshipmen.

longboat   The largest and heaviest boat carried by a warship and used for laying out anchors and carrying water casks and other heavy loads.

lugger   A vessel rigged with one or more fore-and-aft lugsails. Each sail is set on a yard, of which about one-third is on the fore side of the mast.

mainmast   1. The mast at the centre of the ship or vessel, always the largest in square-rigged ships. 2. The name of the first and lowest section of the mainmast in a square-rigged ship; the others are the maintopmast, maintopgallant mast and main royalmast.

mainsheet   The rope at the lower corner of the mainsail for regulating its position.

man-of-war   An armed ship belonging to the navy of a country.

mizzenmast   The mast at the stern or back of a vessel.

muster book   A book containing the names of the ship's company.

pendant   (pronounced 'pennant')   The term can be used for any long tapering flag. The commissioning pendant of a naval ship was a very long flag like a streamer flown from the main masthead and it distinguished a warship in commission from a merchant ship.

pennant   *see* **pendant**

polacre   A three-masted vessel with square sails on the main and mizzen masts and a large lateen sail on the foremast.

poop deck   The aftermost and highest deck of a ship.

port   The left side of a vessel facing forward.

press gang   A group of men led by an officer who were employed to round up men for service in the Royal Navy.

privateer   A privately owned warship licensed by a letter of marque to capture enemy shipping for profit.

prize   A ship or smaller vessel captured from the enemy in time of war.

quarter   The side of a ship towards the stern.

quarterdeck   A deck above the main deck which stretched from the stern to about halfway along the length of the ship. It was from this deck that the captain and officers controlled the ship.

quarter gallery   A covered gallery with windows that projected from the side of the ship at the stern, used as a lavatory or toilet by the captain and officers.

rate (as in first-rate, second-rate, etc.)   Warships were grouped into six different categories according to the number of guns they carried. In the eighteenth century a first-rate ship had 100 guns, a second-rate ship had 90 guns, a third-rate had 80, 74 or 64 guns, a fourth-rate had between 64 and 50 guns, a fifth-rate had between 44 and 32 guns, and a sixth-rate had between 28 and 20 guns.

reef   To reduce the area of a sail by rolling it up or bundling part of it and securing that part with short lines called reef-points.

road, roadstead   An open anchorage.

running rigging   Ropes which run through blocks or are moved in any way to operate the sails and gear of a vessel – as distinct from **standing rigging.**

schooner   A two-masted vessel, fore-and-aft rigged on both masts. Some vessels had square topsails on the foremast or on both topmasts.

scuppers   Holes in a ship's side through which water could drain off from the deck.

settee   A small sailing vessel, usually single-masted, with a settee sail which was similar to the triangular lateen sail but with a short luff at the forward end of the sail.

sheet   A rope made fast to the lower corner or corners of a sail to control its position.

sheer hulk   A vessel, usually an old ship, fitted with a pair of sheer legs (two large spars forming an 'A frame') to hoist masts in and out of vessels; a floating crane.

ship   1. A vessel with three or more masts and fully square-rigged throughout. 2. The term is also used to describe any large sea-going vessel.

ship of the line   A warship large enough to take her place in the line of battle. In the late eighteenth century this usually ranged from third-rate ships of between 64 and 80 guns up to first-rate ships of 100 guns or more.

shrouds   The set of ropes forming part of the standing rigging and supporting the mast or topmast.

sloop 1. A vessel having one fore-and-aft rigged mast with mainsail and a single foresail. 2. In the Royal Navy any ship or vessel commanded by an officer with the rank of master and commander, usually rigged as a ship or brig with 16 to 18 guns.

spar A stout wooden pole used for the mast or yard of a sailing vessel.

spring A rope or hawser used on an anchored ship to enable her to swing round and bring her broadside to bear on an enemy. The rope led from the capstan out of the stern of the ship and was made fast some way along the anchor cable.

square-rigged The principal sails set at right angles to the length of the ship and extended by horizontal yards slung to the mast (as opposed to fore-and-aft rigged).

standing rigging That part of the rigging which supports the masts and spars and which is not moved when operating the vessel, as distinct from **running rigging.**

starboard The right side of a vessel facing forward.

studding sail A light sail set outboard of a square sail and used in light airs.

supernumerary A person borne on the ship's books surplus to the established complement.

tack To change the direction of a sailing vessel's course by turning her bows into the wind until the wind blows on her other side.

tender A vessel attending a larger vessel and used to supply stores or convey passengers.

three-decker The largest class of warship, with upwards of 90 guns on three gundecks.

top (as in foretop, maintop, mizzentop) A platform built at the head of the lower mast serving to spread the topmast rigging and provide a place for sailors working aloft.

topgallant, topgallant sail A square sail set on the topgallant mast which was usually the highest of a ship's masts, and was set above the topmast and the lower or mainmast.

topmen The sailors who went aloft to raise or lower the sails.

topsail A sail set on the topmast.

transport (noun) A vessel for carrying troops, usually a hired merchant ship converted for the purpose.

two-decker A ship of the line having two complete gun-decks.

van The foremost or leading ships of a fleet.

warp (noun) A rope used in towing or warping.

warp (verb) In calms or contrary winds it was often necessary to warp a vessel in and out of harbour or along a river. This was done by taking a rope or ropes from the ship to a fixed point ashore, or to a heavy post or pile driven into the river bed alongside the channel, and then heaving in the rope to haul the ship along.

warrant officers   These ranked below the commissioned officers (the captain and lieutenants) and included the master, purser, surgeon, gunner, boatswain, carpenter and cook.

wear (as in 'to wear ship')   o change the direction of a sailing vessel's course by turning her bows away from the wind until the wind blows on her other side (the opposite manoeuvre from tacking when the bows are turned into the wind).

weather (adjective)   The side facing the wind. The weather column of a fleet is the column to windward or nearest the direction from which the wind is blowing.

weigh   To pull up the anchor.

xebec   A three-masted vessel with lateen sails found along the coasts of Spain, Portugal and the Barbary States.

yard   A long spar suspended from the mast of a vessel to extend the sails.

yardarm   Either end of a yard.

BIBLIOGRAPHY

Cochrane has been the subject of a great number of books and articles. Under the list of published material I have included only those books which I found most useful. I have not included relevant articles in the *Naval Chronicle*, the *Mariners Mirror* or similar journals, nor have I included newspaper references. These will be found in the notes to the individual chapters. A useful list of publications relating to Cochrane and South America will be found in *The Audacious Admiral Cochrane* by Brian Vale.

UNPUBLISHED MATERIAL

The Dundonald papers in the National Archives of Scotland, Edinburgh: GD.233. This is a vast archive which includes correspondence and printed papers concerning Cochrane's naval career, the Gambier court martial, the Stock Exchange trial, his time in South America, his work on his autobiography, as well as family letters, maps, plans and newspaper cuttings. There is a summary index of these papers in the National Archives at Kew: NRA.8150.

The National Library of Scotland, Edinburgh, also has a number of letters to and from Cochrane, although most of this collection concerns other members of the family.

The papers of Captain Frederick Marryat in the National Maritime Museum, London, including letters, a private log with intermittent entries from 1806 to 1825, and a number of his drawings and watercolours: MRY/2, MRY/6, MRY/11 and 12.

The papers of Dr James Guthrie in the National Maritime Museum, London, including correspondence between Guthrie and Cochrane: JOD/55 and 56.

The papers of Admiral Collingwood in the British Library, London: Add.MSS 14276; 14278; 14279; 14280.

Minutes of Evidence given before the House of Lords Committee of Privileges in 1861, 1862, 1863. British Library (Social Sciences Dept): BS.96/51.

The papers of Lord Auckland in the British Library: Add.MSS. 34,459.

In the National Archives at the Public Record Office, Kew, London: Cochrane's letters to
   the Admiralty; the logs and muster books of Cochrane's ships (except for the log of the
   Speedy, which is in the National Archives of Scotland) and other ships associated with his
   career in the British Navy; the transcripts of court martials; minutes of Admiralty
   Board meetings; etc.
David J. Cubitt, *Lord Cochrane and the Chilean Navy* (Edinburgh University, PhD thesis,
   1974).
John Sugden, *Lord Cochrane, Naval Commander, Radical, Inventor: a study of his early career,
   1775–1818* (University of Sheffield, PhD thesis, 1981).

PUBLISHED MATERIAL

Atlay, J. B., *The Trial of Lord Cochrane before Lord Ellenborough* (London, 1897)
Bamford, Samuel, *The Autobiography of Samuel Bamford: Passages in the Life of a Radical*,
   edited by W. H. Chaloner (London, 1841; edition cited, 1967)
Blake, Nicholas and Lawrence, Richard, *The Illustrated Companion to Nelson's Navy*
   (London, 1999)
Bonner-Smith, David, ed., *Letters of Admiral of the Fleet the Earl of St Vincent, 1801–1804*
   (Navy Records Society, volumes 55 and 61, 1922–7)
Campbell, Lord John, *The Lives of the Chief Justices of England* (London, 1858)
Cecil, Henry, *A Matter of Speculation: the Case of Lord Cochrane* (London, 1965)
Chatterton, Lady Georgiana, ed., *Memorials Personal and Historical of Admiral Lord
   Gambier* (London, 1861)
Cochrane, Alexander, *The Fighting Cochranes: a Scottish Clan over six hundred years of naval
   and military history* (London, 1983)
Cochrane, Archibald, 9th Earl of Dundonald, *Description of the Estate and Abbey of Culross*
   (Edinburgh, 1793)
Cochrane, Thomas, 10th Earl of Dundonald, *The Autobiography of a Seaman* (first
   published as two volumes in 1860. The edition cited was published by Chatham
   Publishing in 2000 with an introduction by Richard Woodman)
Cochrane, Thomas, 10th Earl of Dundonald, *Observations on Naval Affairs . . . Including
   Instances of Injustice experienced by the author* (London, 1847)
Cochrane, Thomas, 10th Earl of Dundonald, *Narrative of Services in the Liberation of Chili,
   Peru, and Brazil from Spanish and Portuguese Domination* (London, 1859)
Cochrane, Thomas Barnes, 11th Earl of Dundonald and Bourne, H. R. Fox, *The Life of
   Thomas, Lord Cochrane, 10th Earl of Dundonald* (London, 1869)
Congreve, Major-General Sir W., *A Treatise on the general principles, powers and facility of
   application of the Congreve Rocket System* (London, 1827)
Dale, Richard, *'Napoleon is dead': Lord Cochrane and the great Stock Exchange scandal* (Stroud,
   Glos., 2006)
Ellenborough, Lord, *The Guilt of Lord Cochrane in 1814: a Criticism* (London, 1914)

Finlay, George, *History of the Greek Revolution* (London, 1861)

Gardiner, Robert, *Frigates of the Napoleonic Wars* (London, 2000)

—*The First Frigates: Nine-pounder and twelve-pounder frigates 1748–1815* (London, 1992)

Graham, Maria, (Lady Callcott) *Journal of a Residence in Chile during the year 1822, and a Voyage from Chile to Brazil in 1823* (London, 1824)

—*Journal of a Voyage to Brazil and residence there during the years 1821, 1822, 1823* (London, 1824)

Grimble, Ian, *The Sea Wolf: the life of Admiral Cochrane* (London, 1978; edition cited, 2000)

Gurney, W. B., *Minutes of a Court Martial . . . on the Trial of the Right Honourable James Lord Gambier* (Portsmouth, 1809)

—*The Trial of Charles Random de Berenger, Sir Thomas Cochrane, commonly called Lord Cochrane . . . for a Conspiracy in the Court of King's Bench, Guildhall on Wednesday 8th and Thursday 9th June 1814* (London, 1814)

Hall, Basil, *Extracts from a Journal written on the Coasts of Chile, Peru, and Mexico in the Years 1820, 1821 and 1822* (Edinburgh, 1824)

Hill, Richard, *The Prizes of War: the naval prize system in the Napoleonic Wars 1793–1815* (Stroud, Glos., 1998)

Hughes, Edward, ed., *The private correspondence of Admiral Lord Collingwood* (Navy Records Society, volume 98, 1957)

Ingrams, Richard, *The Life and Adventures of William Cobbett* (London, 2005)

James, William, *The Naval History of Great Britain* (London, 6 volumes, 1878 edition)

Knight, Roger, *The Pursuit of Victory: the Life and Achievements of Horatio Nelson* (London, 2005)

Lambert, Andrew, compiler of the entry on Cochrane in *The Oxford Dictionary of National Biography* (Oxford, 2004)

Lavery, Brian, *Nelson's Navy: the Ships, Men and Organisation, 1793–1815* (London, 1989)

—*The Arming and Fitting of English Ships of War, 1600–1815* (London, 1987)

Lloyd, Christopher, *Lord Cochrane: Seaman, Radical, Liberator* (London, 1947)

Mackesy, Piers, *The war in the Mediterranean, 1803–1810* (London, 1957)

Markham, Sir Clements, ed., *Selections from the Letters of Admiral John Markham* (Navy Records Society, volume 28, 1904)

Marryat, Captain Frederick, *Frank Mildmay, or the Naval Officer* (London, 1829)

—*Peter Simple* (London, 1834)

—*Mr Midshipman Easy* (London, 1839)

Marryat, Florence, *Life and Letters of Captain Marryat* (London, 1872)

Miers, John, *Travels in Chile and La Plata* (London, 1826)

John Miller, ed., *Memoirs of General Miller in the service of the Republic of Peru* (London, 1829)

Mitford, Mary Russell, *Recollections of a Literary Life, or Books, Places and People,* (London, 1852)

Newnham Collingwood, G. L., *A Selection from the Public and Private Correspondence of Vice-Admiral Lord Collingwood* (London, 1829)

Oman, Carola, *A History of the Peninsular War* (London, 1902)

Patterson, M. W., *Sir Francis Burdett and his Times* (London, 1931)

Pocock, Tom, *Captain Marryat, Seaman, Writer and Adventurer* (London, 2000)

Raikes, Henry, ed., *Memoir of Vice-Admiral Sir Jahleel Brenton* (London, 1855)

Redding, Cyrus, *Fifty Years Recollections, Literary and Personal* (London, 1858)

Richardson, William, *A Mariner of England* (London, 1908)

Rodger, N. A. M., *The Command of the Ocean: A Naval History of Britain, 1649–1815,* (London, 2004)

Smyth, W. H., *The Life and Services of Captain Philip Beaver* (London, 1829)

Spater, George, *William Cobbett: the Poor Man's Friend* (Cambridge, 1982)

Stephenson, Charles, *The Admiral's secret weapon: Lord Dundonald and the origins of chemical warfare* (Woodbridge, Suffolk, 2006)

Stevenson, W. B., *A Historical and Descriptive Narrative of Twenty Years Residence in South America* (London, 1825)

Thomas, Donald, *Cochrane: Britannia's Sea Wolf* (London, 1978)

Twitchett, E. G., *Life of a Seaman: Thomas Cochrane, 10th Earl of Dundonald* (London, 1931)

Vale, Brian, *The Audacious Admiral Cochrane: the true life of a naval legend* (London, 2004)

Woodman, Richard, *The Victory of Seapower: Winning the Napoleonic War 1806–1814* (London, 1998)

—*The Sea Warriors: Fighting Captains and Frigate Warfare in the Age of Nelson* (London, 2001)

NOTES

List of Abbreviations

BL   British Library
Oxford DNB   The new Oxford Dictionary of National Biography
NA   National Archives
NAS   National Archives of Scotland
NLS   National Library of Scotland
NMM   National Maritime Museum, Greenwich, London
PRO   Public Record Office, Kew, London

Prologue

1. *The Times,* Friday 2 November 1860.
2. Quoted by Ian Grimble, *The Sea Wolf: The Life of Admiral Cochrane* (first published 1978; cited paperback edition, Edinburgh, 2000), p. 193.
3. Georgiana, Lady Chatterton, *Memorials, Personal and Historical of Admiral Lord Gambier* (London, 1861).
4. J. B. Atlay, *The Trial of Lord Cochrane before Lord Ellenborough* (London, 1897), p. 327.
5. Lord Ellenborough, *The Guilt of Lord Cochrane in 1814* (London, 1914), p. ix.
6. Mary Russell Mitford, *Recollections of a Literary Life, or Books, Places, and People* (London, 1852), vol. 2, p. 24.
7. Cyrus Redding, *Fifty Years Recollections, Literary and Personal with observations on persons and things* (London, 1858), vol. 1, p. 148.
8. Maria Graham, Lady Callcott, *Journal of a Residence in Chile during the year 1822, and a Voyage from Chile to Brazil in 1823* (London, 1824), p. 188.
9. Samuel Bamford, *The Autobiography of Samuel Bamford: Passages in the Life of a Radical,* edited by W. H. Chaloner (London 1841, cited 1967 edition), vol. 2, p. 20.
10. Quoted by E. G. Twitchett in *Life of a Seaman: Thomas Cochrane, 10th Earl of Dundonald* (London, 1931), p. 279.

Chapter 1

1. The details about Culross, the abbey and Culross Abbey House are taken from: Samuel Lewis, *A Topographical Dictionary of Scotland* (London, MDCCCXLVI), vol. 1, p. 246; *Ordnance Gazetteer of Scotland: A Survey of Scottish Topography, Statistical, Biographical and Historical,* ed. Francis Groome (Edinburgh, 1884), vol. 1, p. 323; the entry for Culross in *Royal Commission on the Ancient and Historical Monuments of Scotland;* and *Culross: A Short History of the Royal Burgh,* National Trust for Scotland (Edinburgh 2003).

2. Oxford DNB; G. E. Cockayne, *The Complete Peerage of England, Scotland, Ireland,* vol. IV, p. 526 (cited London, 1916, edition); Alexander Cochrane, *The Fighting Cochranes: A Scottish Clan Over Six Hundred years of Naval and Military History* (London, 1983), pp. 58–71.

3. For the life of Archibald, ninth Earl of Dundonald, see Oxford DNB; Thomas Cochrane, *The Autobiography of a Seaman* (hereafter abbreviated to *Autobiography*); John Sugden, *Lord Cochrane, Naval Commander, Radical, Inventor: A Study of his Early Life* (University of Sheffield, Ph.D. thesis, 1981) (hereafter cited as *Lord Cochrane*); Cockayne, *Complete Peerage,* vol. IV, pp. 528–9; Donald Thomas, *Cochrane: Britannia's Sea Wolf* (London, 1978); Christopher Lloyd, *Lord Cochrane: Seaman, Radical, Liberator* (London, 1947).

4. From a private collection.

5. J. Cochrane to Rev. Robert Rolland, 16 November 1784, NAS, Edinburgh: GD233/105/A7.

6. Some of these letters are reproduced in Alexander Cochrane, *The Fighting Cochranes,* pp. 229–33.

7. *Autobiography,* p. 6.

8. Dundonald to Mrs Gilchrist, 22 November 1784, NAS, Edinburgh: GD233/105/A8.

9. *Minutes of Evidence: The petition of the Earl of Dundonald; evidence given before the House of Lords Committee of Privileges in 1861, 1862, 1863,* BL: BS.96/51, p. 65.

10. *Autobiography,* p. 5.

11. The Culross Abbey estate was sold in July 1798 for £17,000. Initially purchased by Mr Glenny, it then passed to Sir Robert Preston, who owned the adjoining estate of Valleyfield. See William Hamilton to Lord Dundonald, 5 July 1798, NAS, Edinburgh: GD233/105/B21; and Dundonald to Lord Dundas, 12 July 1798, NAS, Edinburgh: GD233/105/B22.

12. Earl of Dundonald, *Description of the Estate and Abbey of Culross* (Edinburgh, 1793), p. 23.

13. Quoted by Thomas, *Cochrane: Britannia's Sea Wolf,* p. 24.

14. NLS, Edinburgh: MS.5379 (British Tar Company), pp. 3–7.

15. *Autobiography,* p. 7.

16. NLS, Edinburgh: MS.5379 (British Tar Company), pp. 16–18.

17. Quoted by Twitchett, *Life of a Seaman,* p. 10.
18. Quoted by Sugden, *Lord Cochrane,* p. 33.
19. *Autobiography,* p. 10.
20. Ibid., p. 10.
21. Dundonald, *Description of the Estate and Abbey of Culross,* p. 7.
22. Admiral Sir Alexander Forrester Inglis Cochrane was born on 22 April 1758. He was made lieutenant in 1778, post-captain in 1782. In 1809 he captured Guadeloupe and was subsequently made governor of the island. He was in command of the North American station during the War of 1812. His final rank was Admiral of the White, and his last appointment was as commander-in-chief at Plymouth in 1821. He died in Paris on 26 January 1832. See Oxford DNB; Alexander Cochrane, *The Fighting Cochranes.*
23. Log of *Hind,* PRO: ADM.51/452.

Chapter 2

1. According to Cochrane's *Autobiography* he joined the ship at Sheerness on 27 June 1793. His memory was at fault because the log of the *Hind* shows that she was sailing off Ushant at that time. Cochrane later describes a cruise to Norway in the *Hind* but he never put to sea in the *Hind* and the Norway cruise was made in the *Thetis.* See the log of the *Hind,* PRO: ADM.51/452. The log of the *Thetis* is with the Dundonald Papers at NAS, Edinburgh, GD233/81/81C.
2. *Autobiography,* p. 11.
3. Log of *Thetis,* NAS, Edinburgh: GD233/81/81C.
4. *Autobiography,* p. 17.
5. Ibid., p. 13.
6. In 1794 the system was changed by an Order in Council and a new class of 'Volunteers Class 1' was created for boys intending to be officers. For a detailed description of the ways in which boys entered the navy see Brian Lavery, *Nelson's Navy* (London 1990), p. 88; and N.A.M. Rodger, *The Command of the Ocean* (London, 2004), pp. 507–8.
7. I am greatly indebted to John Sugden's Ph.D. thesis on the early life of Cochrane for much of the correspondence quoted in this chapter.
8. Muster book of the *Hind,* PRO: ADM.36/11153.
9. Muster books of *Caroline* and *Hind,* PRO: ADM.36/9762 and ADM.36/9869. See also certificates of service in NAS, Edinburgh: GD233/78/16.
10. Spencer to Coutts, March 1795, NLS, Edinburgh: 2264, f. 11.
11. Coutts to Captain Cochrane, 16 November 1793, NLS, Edinburgh: 2264, f. 4.
12. The muster book of the *Africa* shows that Cochrane joined the ship by order of Admiral Murray and then transferred to the *Lynx* on 18 May 1795. See PRO: ADM.36/11423 and log of *Africa,* PRO: ADM.51/1134.

13. Spencer to Coutts, 30 July 1795, NLS, Edinburgh: 2264, ff. 17–19.

14. Jane Dundonald to Captain Cochrane, 12 July 1795, NLS, Edinburgh: 2264, f. 15.

15. Lieutenant's commission, 27 May 1766, in *Minutes of Evidence*, p. 11.

16. Coutts to Captain Cochrane, 5 April 1797, NLS, Edinburgh: 2254, ff. 30–31.

17. *Autobiography*, p. 24.

18. Cochrane to Dundonald, January 1798, NAS, Edinburgh: GD233/105/A22

19. Ibid.

20. Ibid.

21. Brian Lavery, 'George Keith Elphinstone, Lord Keith' in *Precursors of Nelson: British Admirals of the Eighteenth Century*, eds P. le Fevre and R. Harding (London, 2000); Oxford DNB; *The Keith Papers* (3 vols, Navy Records Society, 1927, 1950, 1955).

22. Cochrane to Dundonald, November 1798, NAS, Edinburgh: GD233/105/A22.

23. W. H. Smyth, *The Life and Services of Captain Philip Beaver*, (London 1829), p. 124

24. Court martial held on *Barfleur* in Tetouan Bay on 18 February 1799. PRO: ADM.1/5348.

25. Minutes of the court martial, PRO: ADM.1/5348.

26. Keith to Captain Cochrane, 29 August 1801, NLS, Edinburgh: 2569, ff. 197–8.

27. *Autobiography*, p. 32.

28. Ibid., p. 36.

29. Spencer to Cochrane, 22 August 1799, NLS, Edinburgh: 2568, f. 76.

30. Quoted by Roger Knight, *The Pursuit of Victory: The Life and Achievements of Horatio Nelson* (London, 2005), p. 335. Knight provides an authoritative account of Nelson's controversial actions at Naples in June 1799 and the subsequent months he spent at Palermo, pp. 321–7, 330–39.

31. *Autobiography*, p. 37.

32. For an account of the capture of the *Généreux* by Nelson's squadron see Knight, *The Pursuit of Victory*, pp. 335–6.

33. Keith to Cochrane, 20 February 1800; and T. Maude to Nepean, 27 March 1800. PRO: ADM.1/1629.

34. Keith to Cochrane, 21 February 1800. PRO: ADM.1/1629.

35. Muster book of the *Généreux*, PRO: ADM.36/14328.

36. Log of the *Généreux*, PRO: ADM.51/2067.

37. In his *Autobiography*, p. 40, Cochrane suggests that he received his promotion and appointment to the *Speedy* because Lord Keith 'was so well satisfied with my conduct of the Genereux' but Keith had appointed him commander of the *Speedy* before he set sail in the *Généreux*. See Keith to Cochrane, 20 February 1800, PRO: ADM.1/1629.

38. Lavery in *Precursors of Nelson*, p. 389.

39. Log of the *Speedy*, NAS, Edinburgh: GD233/80/78.

Chapter 3

1. Strictly speaking Cochrane was 'commander' of the *Speedy* and not 'master and commander' because the word 'master' had been dropped from the name of the rank in 1794. From the late seventeenth century onwards the term 'master and commander' had been applied to captains of vessels which were thought too small to require a master as well as a captain. One man therefore carried out the duties of both captain and master. The term 'master and commander' has a fine ring about it which was no doubt why it was used by Patrick O'Brian as the title of his first book in the Aubrey/Maturin novels. It was subsequently used as the title of the film based on his books.

2. The *Speedy* was one of two brig sloops built by King of Dover; the other was the *Flirt*. In addition to her fourteen 4-pounder guns she had twelve swivel guns. For further details see David Lyon, *The Sailing Navy List* (London, 1993), p. 98, and the plans in the NMM.

3. The brig sloop *Childers*, 14 guns, was one of six vessels of the Childers class designed by Williams. She was built at the private yard of Menetone and Son on the Thames, and was launched in 1778. She measured seventy-eight feet seven inches on her upper deck and her breadth was twenty-five feet. Lyon, *The Sailing Navy List*, p. 98, and plans in the NMM.

4. Henry Raikes, *Memoir of Vice Admiral Sir Jahleel Brenton* (London, 1855), p. 28.

5. Brenton's despatch, 21 August 1799, quoted in Raikes, *Memoir*, p. 40.

6. Brenton's despatch to Admiral Duckworth, 21 November 1799, quoted in Raikes, *Memoir*, pp. 46–7.

7. Cochrane's commission is quoted in full in *Minutes of Evidence*, BL: BS.96/51.

8. The details of the *Speedy*'s cruises in this chapter are based primarily on the *Speedy*'s log, NAS, Edinburgh: GD233/80/78, augmented by Guthrie's letter to Earp, NAS, Edinburgh: GD233/83/95; the court martial on the loss of the *Speedy*, PRO: ADM.1/5357; accounts in the *Naval Chronicle*, vol. VI, (1801) pp. 151, and 320–21; William James, *Naval History*, vol. III, pp. 132–5; and Cochrane's *Autobiography*.

9. *Autobiography*, p. 41.

10. Alexandre Dumas, *The Count of Monte Cristo* (first published 1844–5, cited Penguin Classics edition, 2006), p. 187. It is tempting to see some parallels with Cochrane's life in Dumas' tale of a sailor who was wrongfully imprisoned, and on his release sought to clear his name and revenge himself on his enemies, but Dumas based his novel on the true story of a young Frenchman, François Picaud, who suffered that fate in 1807.

11. NAS, Edinburgh: GD233/83/95.

12. NMM: JOD/55, 56.

13. There is an obvious parallel here with the friendship of Jack Aubrey and Stephen Maturin in Patrick O'Brian's novels but although O'Brian would have noted the part played by the ship's doctor in the *Gamo* incident as recounted in Cochrane's

Autobiography, it is unlikely that he was aware of how closely fact followed fiction in this case.

14. NAS, Edinburgh: GD233/83/95. Many accounts of this incident suggest that the Spanish frigate was the *Gamo*. Guthrie's letter contradicts this, and Cochrane, recalling the incident years later, wrote, 'It has been stated by some naval writers that this frigate was the *Gamo*, which we subsequently captured. To the best of my knowledge this is an error'. *Autobiography*, p. 48.

15. Ibid.

16. Ibid.

17. In his official despatch to Captain Manley Dixon, written on 6 May, the day of the action, Cochrane described the *Gamo* as 'a Spanish xebec frigate, of 32 guns, twenty-two long twelve-pounders, eight nines, and two heavy carronades, named the Gamo, commanded by Don Francisco de Torris, manned by 319 naval officers, seamen, supernumeraries, and marines'. There has been some discussion among naval historians about the appearance and rig of the *Gamo* and whether she was a xebec frigate, a polacre frigate or just a Mediterranean xebec. See Robert Gardiner, 'Cochrane and the Speedy' in *Nelson against Napoleon* (London, 1997), pp. 94–5; Michael Bouquet, 'The Speedy and the Gamo' in *Mariners Mirror*, vol. LV (1969), p. 210; James Henderson, *Sloops and Brigs* (London, 1972), pp. 59–61; Richard Woodman, *The Sea Warriors* (London, 2001, cited paperback edition, 2002), pp. 154–6.

18. Cochrane to Dixon, 6 May 1801, PRO: ADM.1/404, f. 147.

19. There was a brief mention of the action between the *Speedy* and *El Gamo* in *The Times*, 5 August 1801, following an account of the battle off Gibraltar between the squadron commanded by Saumarez and the French squadron under Linois.

20. Pocock had sailed to Leghorn via Minorca in 1770 as captain of the merchant ship *Betsey* so he had some knowledge of Mediterranean sailing craft. Since he always went to considerable lengths to ensure the accuracy of his pictures of sea battles, we may assume that his picture of the *Speedy* and *El Gamo* is a realistic portrayal of the ships and the action.

21. Pulling to Keith, 10 June 1801, PRO: ADM.1/404, f. 188.

22. Ibid.

23. Keith to Nepean, 10 July 1801, PRO: ADM.1/404, f. 188.

24. When captured by the *Desaix*, Cochrane was told by Captain Christy-Pallière that the French squadron had special instructions to look out for the *Speedy*. *Autobiography*, p. 67. According to Michael Bouquet the *Gamo* was especially fitted out by the merchants of Barcelona in order to capture the *Speedy*. See M. Bouquet, 'The Speedy and the Gamo' in *Mariners Mirror*, vol. LV (1969), p. 210.

25. Named *Saint Pierre* by the French the former *Speedy* was renamed *San Pietro* on receipt by the Pope. M. Bouquet, *Mariners Mirror*, vol. LV, p. 210.

Chapter 4

1. Court martial of Lord Cochrane and his officers for the loss of the *Speedy*, 18 July 1801, PRO: ADM.1/5357.

2. Ibid.

3. Lord Cochrane's name appears in the muster book of the *Spider* as a supernumerary, PRO: ADM.36/14267. The relevant logbook of the *Spider* is ADM.51/4503.

4. In a letter to St Vincent of 23 September 1801 Lord Dundonald writes, 'in behalf of my son, Lord Cochrane, who is now in Scotland . . .'. *Autobiography*, p. 77.

5. *The Times*, 1 August and 3 August 1801.

6. For a detailed account of the attacks on Boulogne see Knight, *The Pursuit of Victory*, pp. 405–13. See also *Nelson against Napoleon*, ed. Robert Gardiner (London, 1997), pp. 138–9.

7. C. S. Forester, *Lieutenant Hornblower* (first published 1952).

8. Earl of Dundonald to St Vincent, 23 September 1801. *Autobiography*, pp. 77–8.

9. St Vincent to Earl of Dundonald, 24 September 1801, *Letters of Admiral of the Fleet the Earl of St Vincent, 1801–1804*, ed. David Bonner Smith (Navy Records Society, 1921), vol. 1, p. 353.

10. For a shrewd assessment of St Vincent's character and his disastrous spell as First Lord of the Admiralty see N.A.M. Rodger, *The Command of the Ocean*, pp. 464–5, 476–9.

11. St Vincent to Lord Keith, 4 September 1801, *Letters of Lord St Vincent*, (Navy Records Society, 1921), vol. 1, p. 222.

12. St Vincent to Markham, 14 April 1806, *Letters of Admiral Markham*, ed. Sir Clements Markham (Navy Records Society, 1904), vol. 28, pp. 47–48.

13. *The Times*, Saturday 1 May 1802.

14. *The Letters of Charles and Mary Lamb*, ed. Edwin Marrs (London, 1976), p. 54.

15. Ibid., p. 60.

16. *Diary and Letters of Madame D'Arblay*, ed. Charlotte Barrett (London, 1891), vol. IV, p. 168.

17. *Autobiography*, p. 87.

18. J. M. Thompson, *Napoleon Bonaparte* (Oxford 1988, edition cited 2002), p. 221.

19. St Vincent to Douglas, 18 May 1803, *Letters of Lord St Vincent* (Navy Records Society, 1921), vol. 2, p. 337.

20. St Vincent to Dundonald, 5 July 1803, *Letters of Lord St Vincent* (Navy Records Society, 1921), vol. 2, p. 344.

21. *Letters of Admiral Markham*, (Navy Records Society, 1904), vol. 28, p. 366.

22. *Autobiography*, p. 88.

23. Muster book of *Arab*, PRO: ADM.36/16946.

24. The details of the *Arab*'s cruises are taken from the captain's log, PRO: ADM.51/1504.

25. Cochrane to Marsden, 24 January 1804, PRO: ADM.1/1639, f. 420.

26. Keith to Markham, 23 January 1804, PRO: *Letters of Admiral Markham*, (Navy Records Society, 1904), vol. 28, p. 141.

27. Cochrane to Keith, 24 January 1804, PRO: ADM.1/1639.

28. Cochrane to Marsden at Admiralty, 8 February 1804. PRO: ADM.1/1639.

29. *Letters of Admiral Markham*, (Navy Records Society, 1904), vol. 28, p. 153.

30. Cochrane to Marsden at the Admiralty, 27 November 1804, PRO: ADM.1/1639.

31. Henry Dundas, first Viscount Melville, was distantly related to the Cochrane family. He had married the half-sister of the Earl of Hopetoun whose daughter had married Cochrane's uncle Andrew Cochrane-Johnstone. Melville was also on friendly terms with Jane, the Countess Dowager of Dundonald. See Sugden, *Lord Cochrane*, p. 71.

32. Rodger, *The Command of the Ocean*, p. 511.

Chapter 5

1. See Robert Gardiner, *The First Frigates: Nine-pounder and Twelve-pounder Frigates 1748–1815* (London, 1992), pp. 55–7. For an illuminating description of St Vincent's attempts to reform naval administration and root out corruption in the royal dockyards see Rodger, *The Command of the Ocean*, pp. 476–80.

2. For detailed information on carronades see Brian Lavery, *The Arming and Fitting of English Ships of War 1600–1815*, pp. 104–9, 130–34.

3. Quoted by Nicholas Blake and Richard Lawrence *The Illustrated Companion to Nelson's Navy* (London 1999), p. 141.

4. Cochrane to Melville, 30 November 1804, NA, Kew: ADM.1/1639.

5. One of the Spanish ships captured was the *Medea*, which was renamed the *Imperieuse* and became Cochrane's next command. For a detailed description of the action off Cadiz see *The Campaign of Trafalgar*, ed. Robert Gardiner (London, 1997), pp. 110–11; and for the background to the incident see Rodger, *The Command of the Ocean*, pp. 531–2.

6. Orders from Vice-Admiral Young to Lord Cochrane, issued at Plymouth 17 January 1805. The orders directed Cochrane to proceed to 'the Western Islands' which was the British navy's term for the islands of the Azores, NAS, Edinburgh: GD233/65/7.

7. The Admiralty solicitor was Charles Bicknell who was instructed to prosecute the Mayor of Plymouth. For further details of the ensuing case see Bicknell to Marsden, 16 January, 19 January, 16 March 1805, PRO: ADM.1/3691, and Bicknell to Marsden 22 July 1806, PRO: ADM.1/3692.

8. The details of the cruises of the *Pallas* and her various actions are taken from: the log of the *Pallas*, PRO: ADM.51/1554; the muster book of the *Pallas*, PRO: ADM.36/16835; Cochrane's correspondence with the Admiralty, PRO ADM.1/1643, and ADM.1/1645; *The Royal Cornwall Gazette, Falmouth Packet and Plymouth Journal*, Saturday 7 June 1806; *Naval Chronicle*, vol. XIII (1805), p. 329; vol. XV (1806), pp.

347–8; vol. XVI (1806), pp. 75–6; William James, *Naval History*, vol. IV, pp. 138–42; *Autobiography*; Richard Woodman, *The Victory of Seapower: Winning the Napoleonic War 1806–1814* (London, 1998), pp. 34–5.

9. Young to Cochrane, 17 January 1805, NAS, Edinburgh: GD233/65/7.

10. *Autobiography*, pp. 96–97.

11. Reports in the *Naval Chronicle*, based on newspaper reports, give the figure of 432,000 dollars (£130,000) for the gold and silver on board *La Fortuna*. Cochrane confirms this in his *Autobiography*. There is no mention of the value in money terms of the rich cargoes on the other three Spanish ships captured. Assuming that the two ships with cargoes of treasure and dollars were worth a minimum of £15,000 each, the total value of the prizes must have been at least £160,000 (£4 million in today's terms). Cochrane's two-eights share would therefore have been in excess of £40,000 (£1 million today). *Naval Chronicle*, vol. XIII (1805), pp. 243, 328–9, 357–8; vol. XXII (1809), p. 9; *Autobiography*, pp. 94–5.

12. Young to Cochrane, 17 January 1805, NAS, Edinburgh: GD233/65/7.

13. Alexander Cochrane to Melville, 20 February 1805, NLS, Edinburgh: 3841, ff. 24–5.

14. For a more detailed account of the prize money system see Brian Lavery, *Nelson's Navy*, pp. 116, 131; Richard Hill, *The Prizes of War: The Naval Prize System in the Napoleonic Wars 1793–1815* (Stroud, 1998).

15. Rodger, *The Wooden World*, p. 257.

16. Hill, *The Prizes of War*, pp. 14, 16; and Rodger, *The Command of the Ocean*, p. 523.

17. For further details of the events preceding Nelson's funeral and the funeral itself see Knight, *The Pursuit of Victory*, pp. 529–35; and Colin White, 'Nelson's Funeral' in Robert Gardiner (ed.), *The Campaign of Trafalgar*, pp. 180–83.

18. *Autobiography*, p. 103.

19. See Robert Gardiner, *Frigates of the Napoleonic Wars* (London, 2000), p. 108, 'Lord Cochrane had a galley designed for the quarter davits of the *Imperieuse* that so impressed the Admiralty that they ordered the lines taken off.' See Cochrane's reference to the galley in his *Autobiography*, p. 103. In PRO: ADM.106/2093 (Abstract of Admiralty Orders 1 Jan. to 31 Dec. 1809) the entry for 30 June 1809 reads: 'Quarter Galley belonging to Lord Cochrane/Lines to be taken off'.

20. See Gardiner, *Frigates of the Napoleonic Wars*, pp. 107–9; and Brian Lavery, *The Arming and Fitting of English Ships of War 1600–1815*, pp. 207–37. Although there were formal boat establishments for ships of the line, frigates and smaller warships, individual captains were allowed some licence in the boats which they carried. Experience often led captains to request particular types of boat because they were faster, or lighter, or more seaworthy.

21. *The Macmillan Reeds Nautical Almanac* (2001), p. 850.

22. *Autobiography*, p. 105.

23. *Naval Chronicle*, vol. XV (1806), pp. 347–8.

24. Cochrane to Thornborough, 25 April 1806, NAS, Edinburgh, GD233/65/7.

25. *Naval Chronicle*, vol. XVI (1806), p. 76.

26. Raikes, *Memoir of Vice Admiral Sir Jahleel Brenton*, p. 339.

27. Edward Brenton, *The Naval History of Great Britain* (London, 1837), vol. 2, p. 125.

Chapter 6

1. *The Royal Cornwall Gazette, Falmouth Packet and Plymouth Journal*, Saturday 7 June 1806.

2. *Cobbett's Weekly Political Register*, 28 June 1806.

3. Ibid.

4. Mitford, *Recollections of a Literary Life*, vol. 2, p. 25.

5. Quoted by John Sugden in his article entitled 'The Honiton Elections of 1806 and the Genesis of Parliamentary Reform' in *The Devon Historian*, vol. 31, October 1985, p. 6.

6. *Western Flying Post*, 23 June 1806.

7. Cochrane gives 67 Harley Street as his London address in his letters to the Admiralty of 25 August 1806, 14 and 27 March 1807, 7 April 1807, PRO: ADM.1/1648.

8. Cochrane's commission dated 23 August 1806 is included among his other appointments in the *Minutes of Evidence*, p. 14. BL: BS.96/51.

9. For details of the action see *The Campaign of Trafalgar*, ed. Robert Gardiner, pp. 110–11. For details of the *Imperieuse* see the plans in the NMM; and David Lyon, *The Sailing Navy List*, p. 271; and Robert Gardiner, *Frigates of the Napoleonic Wars*, p. 179.

10. Cochrane to Marsden, 30 September 1806, PRO: ADM.1/1645.

11. See *Trewman's Exeter Flying Post*, 23 October 1806, and *Western Flying Post*, 27 October 1806.

12. Quoted by Sugden from a letter from A. Cochrane to Thomas John Cochrane, 17 November 1806, NLS, Edinburgh: MS. 2264:70.

13. Hansard's *Parliamentary Debates*, 29 January 1817, vol. XXXV, p. 92.

14. The muster table for the period ending 31 December 1806, when the *Imperieuse* was at sea, shows her official complement as 284 but the actual number of men and boys borne and mustered was 268 (ship's company 210; volunteers and boys 19; marines 39). PRO: ADM.37/1457.

15. There were three classes of boy on board naval ships of this period and the first class was reserved for young gentlemen intended to become officers. In 1794 the Admiralty had abolished the old rating of 'captain's servant' and by an Order in Council had created three classes of 'boy'. The second and third class were divided according to age and were intended to become topmen but, according to Rodger, 'many of them were acting as domestics and were not encouraged or even allowed to go aloft'. See Rodger, *The Command of the Ocean*, p. 499; see also Lavery, *Nelson's Navy*, p. 88.

16. Tom Pocock, *Captain Marryat*, (London 2000) p. 165.

17. Florence Marryat, *The Life and Letters of Captain Marryat* (London, 1872), vol. 1, p. 19.

18. Captain Marryat, *Frank Mildmay*, p. 27.

Chapter 7

1. Cochrane to Marsden, 3 April 1807, PRO: ADM.1/1648.
2. Enclosure in letter from Cochrane to Marsden, 4 April 1807, PRO: ADM.1/1648.
3. Florence Marryat, *Life and Letters*, vol. 1, p. 23.
4. For a more detailed account of the British constitution and election procedures at this period see: Asa Briggs, *The Age of Improvement, 1783–1867* (London, 1959, revised edition 1963); J. Stephen Watson, *The Reign of George III* (Oxford, 1960, revised edition 1985), in the Oxford History of England series.
5. For further details of the radical movement see: S. MacCoby, *The English Radical Tradition, 1763–1914* (London, 1952), book 5 of the series The British Political Tradition, eds Alan Bullock and F. W. Deakin; and 'The making of a political radical', eds Noel Thompson and David Eastwood, vol. 4 of The *Collected Social and Political Writings of William Cobbett* (London, 1998).
6. Admiral Lord Samuel Hood (1724–1816) is not to be confused with Sir Samuel Hood (1762–1814) who fought with Nelson at the Battle of the Nile.
7. *The Times*, Monday 4 May 1807.
8. Ibid., Saturday 2 May 2 1807.
9. The details of Cochrane's election campaign are taken from: Francis Place's papers in the British Museum, Add.MS.27,838; *The Times*; Christopher Lloyd, *Lord Cochrane*; Donald Thomas, *Cochrane*; Cochrane's *Autobiography*.
10. Quoted by Thomas, *Cochrane*, p. 111.
11. *The Times*, Friday 8 May 1807.
12. *Cobbett's Weekly Political Register*, 30 May 1807.
13. *Autobiography*, p. 126.
14. *The Autobiography of Samuel Bamford* (London, 1841, edition cited 1967) ed. W. H. Chaloner, vol. 2, p. 27.
15. Cochrane's very long speech on naval abuses was recorded in Hansard's *Parliamentary Debates*, vol. IX, and is also reproduced in Cochrane's *Observations of Naval Affairs* (1847), pp. 99–105.
16. The naval officers present were Rear-Admiral Eliab Harvey, Admiral Lord Samuel Hood and Rear-Admiral John Markham.

Chapter 8

1. Florence Marryat, *The Life and Letters of Captain Marryat*, vol. 1, p. 23.
2. The Hon. William Napier (1786–1834) was the eldest son of Lord Napier of Merchistoun. He entered the navy in 1803 and joined the crew of the *Imperieuse* in November 1806. In 1816 he married Elizabeth, the only daughter of Andrew Cochrane-Johnstone. On the death of his father in 1823 he succeeded to the peerage. In 1833 he travelled to China to take up a post as chief superintendent of trade but his

mission was unsuccessful. Within a year of his arrival he went down with fever and died and was buried in Macao.

3. Florence Marryat, *Life and Letters*, vol. 1, pp. 25–6.

4. Cochrane to Collingwood, 14 November 1807. Reproduced in Cochrane's *Autobiography*, p. 128.

5. Florence Marryat, *Life and Letters*, vol. 1, pp. 27–8.

6. *Memorial of Lord Cochrane to the Right Honourable the Lords of the Admiralty*, 28 April 1809. The Admiralty forwarded it to Sir William Scott, Judge of the Admiralty Court, PRO: ADM.1/1652.

7. Cuthbert Collingwood (1750–1810) had served in the West Indies as a lieutenant, and later played a distinguished role in the the the battles of the Glorious First of June, Cape St Vincent, and Trafalgar. He was commander-in-chief of the Mediterranean fleet from 1805 until his death at sea in 1810.

8. Collingwood to Cochrane, 16 November 1807 and 19 November 1807. BL: Add.MSS.14276, f. 91, f. 93.

9. Patrick Campbell (1773–1841) was an energetic and successful frigate captain but it was known that he made a habit of selling prizes locally instead of sending them to the Prize Court at Malta, as well as other dubious practices. However, he went on to become a vice-admiral and was made KCB in 1836. Cochrane's allegations are discussed in Piers Mackesy, 'Lord Cochrane on abuses in the Adriatic', *Mariners Mirror*, vol. XL, no. 3 (August 1954), pp. 230–33; and in greater detail in John Sugden's thesis, *Lord Cochrane*, pp. 97–8.

10. The details of the attack at Almeria are taken from the *Imperieuse* log, PRO: ADM.51/2462, part 3; Cochrane's despatch to Collingwood, 23 February 1808, PRO: ADM.1/414; Florence Marryat, *Life and Letters*; and Captain Marryat, *Frank Mildmay*.

11. Florence Marryat, *Life and Letters*, vol. 1, p. 44.

12. Captain Marryat, *Frank Mildmay*, p. 65.

13. Florence Marryat, *Life and Letters*, vol. 1, p. 45.

14. Cochrane's despatch to Collingwood, PRO: ADM.1/414.

15. Collingwood to Cochrane, 26 April 1808. BL: Add.MSS.14278, f. 133.

16. The details in this paragraph are taken from the *Imperieuse* log, PRO: ADM.51/2462, and the relevant passage in Marryat's *Peter Simple* (Macmillan edition, London, 1925), p. 120.

17. Collingwood to Pole, HMS *Ocean* off Cadiz, 11 June 1808. PRO: ADM.1/414, f. 127.

Chapter 9

1. Collingwood to Martin, 20 June 1808. BL: Add.MSS.14278, f. 182.

2. Collingwood to Cochrane, given on board HMS *Ocean* off Cadiz, 21 June 1808. BL: Add.MSS.14276, f. 202.

3. Much first-hand detail of the coastal raids of the *Imperieuse*, including the careful preparations for boat attacks, will be found in Marryat's novels especially *Frank Mildmay*, *Peter Simple* and *Mr Midshipman Easy*.

4. Captain Marryat, *Frank Mildmay*, p. 91; *Autobiography*, p. 146; *Imperieuse* log, PRO: ADM.51/2462, part 4.

5. Cochrane to Collingwood, 31 July 1808. BL: Add.MSS.14279, f.117.

6. Collingwood to Pole, 27 August 1808, PRO: ADM.1/414, f. 195.

7. Piers Mackesy, *The War in the Mediterranean, 1803–1810* (London, 1957), pp. 283–4; Carola Oman, *A History of the Peninsular War* (1902), vol. I, pp. 314–18; *Autobiography*, p. 150.

8. Cochrane to Collingwood, 28 September 1808. BL: Add.MSS.14279, f. 177.

9. The first signal had been sent at 6.00 a.m. on 30 September and gave warning of the presence of the *Imperieuse*: 'The enemy is at anchor and is a frigate she is E by N 4 leagues distant the enemy hoists out his boats and debarks . . .' Cochrane to Pole, 17 October 1808, PRO: ADM.1/1651.

10. Collingwood to Thornborough, 21 June 1808. BL: Add.MSS.14278, f. 98.

11. Thornborough to Collingwood, 9 September 1808. BL: Add.MSS.14279, f. 69.

12. *A Treatise on the general principles, powers and facility of application of the Congreve Rocket System*, by Major-Gen. Sir W. Congreve, Bart (London, 1827), p. 6.

13. *The Times*, Saturday 18 October 1806.

14. Raikes, *Memoir of Vice Admiral Sir Jahleel Brenton*, p. 236.

15. Raikes, *Memoir*, p. 235.

16. Brenton to Thornborough, 16 September 1808. BL: Add.MSS.14279, f. 132.

17. *Autobiography*, p. 170.

Chapter 10

1. For the background to the situation in Spain at this period see Carola Oman, *A History of the Peninsular War* and Piers Mackesy, *The War in the Mediterranean, 1803–1810*.

2. Cochrane to Collingwood, 5 December 1808. *Autobiography*, p. 188.

3. The events in this chapter are taken from: the log of the *Imperieuse*, PRO: ADM.51/2462, part 4; Collingwood Papers, BL: Add.MSS.14276 and 14279; Florence Marryat, *The Life and Letters of Captain Marryat*, vol. 1, pp. 52–8; Captain Marryat, *Frank Mildmay*, pp. 83–90; Sugden, *Lord Cochrane*, pp. 104–9; *Autobiography*, pp. 170–90.

4. *Autobiography*, p. 177.

5. PRO: ADM.51/2462

6. Captain Marryat, *Frank Mildmay*, p. 85.

7. Quoted by Sugden, *Lord Cochrane*, p. 106, from Bennett to Collingwood, 22 November–4 December 1808, PRO: ADM.1/414.

8. *Autobiography*, pp. 178–9.

9. Captain Marryat, *Frank Mildmay*, p. 86.

10. Florence Marryat, *Life and Letters*, vol. 1, p. 56.

11. Ibid., p. 57. The incident is also mentioned by Cochrane in his *Autobiography*, p. 184. See also *Imperieuse* log, PRO: ADM.51/2462, part 4, entry for 4 December 1808.

12. PRO: ADM.51/2462, part 4, entry for 5 December 1808.

13. Mackesy, *The War in the Mediterranean*, p. 296.

14. Collingwood to Pole, 7 January 1809. This letter and Cochrane's despatch of 5 December 1808 are quoted in *Autobiography*, pp. 187–9.

15. Florence Marryat, *Life and Letters*, vol. 1, p. 63.

Chapter 11

1. Allemand had recently replaced Rear-Admiral Willaumez who had led the break-out of the French fleet from Brest but had failed to capitalise on this.

2. Gambier to Mulgrave, 11 March 1809. *Autobiography*, p. 205; and William James, *Naval History*, vol. IV, p. 396.

3. Cochrane to Thornborough, 25 April 1806, NAS, Edinburgh: GD233/65/7. In a letter to the Admiralty, 23 April 1807, Captain Richard Goodwin Keats had also recommended an attack on the anchorage by the Ile d' Aix with 'bombs, fireships, and rockets, covered and protected by a squadron'. His letter is quoted in the minutes of the court martial of Gambier, p. 18.

4. Hope to Cochrane, 21 March 1809. NAS, Edinburgh: GD233/82/84, and *Autobiography*, p. 202.

5. The details for the account of the action at Basque Roads are taken from: the logs of the *Imperieuse, Caledonia, Etna, Emerald, Beagle* and *Mediator*; W. B. Gurney, *Minutes of a Court Martial . . . on the trial of the Right Honourable James, Lord Gambier* (Portsmouth, 1809); James, *Naval History*, vol. IV, pp. 394–431; *Naval Chronicle*, vol. XXI (1809), pp. 344–414; William Richardson, *A Mariner of England* (London, 1908), pp. 243–4; Captain Marryat, *Frank Mildmay*, pp. 132–7; *Autobiography*, pp. 202–44; various charts and documents in the Dundonald Papers NAS, Edinburgh, especially GD233/71/35, GD233/78/35, GD233/81/82, GD233/81/84, GD233/83/93 and GD233/12183–7; see also 'Basque Roads, 1809' in *The Victory of Seapower*, ed. Robert Gardiner (London, 1998), pp. 44–7; and a detailed account in John Sugden's thesis, pp. 112–43.

6. Admiralty Board minutes, 15 March 1809, PRO: ADM.3/167.

7. Cochrane to Mulgrave, 25 March 1809. NAS, Edinburgh: GD233/65/7; and *Autobiography*, p. 209.

8. Gambier to Pole, 26 March 1809. The letter is quoted in *Autobiography*, pp. 211–12, and James, *Naval History*, vol. IV, p. 398, and Minutes of court martial of Gambier.

9. Pole to Gambier, 25 March 1809. *Autobiography*, p. 215

10. Court martial of Admiral Harvey, 22 May 1809, PRO: ADM.1/5396.

11. Ibid.

12. Ibid.

13. Ibid.
14. Gurney, *Minutes of a Court Martial*, p. 58.
15. Richardson, *A Mariner of England*, pp. 243–4.
16. *Autobiography*, p. 224.
17. Richardson, *A Mariner of England*, p. 244.
18. Log of the *Beagle*, PRO: ADM.51/1932.
19. The *Mediator* had left Plymouth on 24 March loaded with bullocks, vegetables and other provisions for Gambier's fleet. She arrived at Basque Roads on 3 April, PRO: ADM.51/1864.
20. Admiral Allemand's report of 12 April 1809 to the Minister of Marine. This was reproduced in *Le Moniteur* of 23 April and a translation published in the *Naval Chronicle*, vol. XXI (1809), p. 373.
21. Log of *Aetna*, PRO: ADM.51/1887.
22. *Autobiography*, p. 229.
23. Captain Marryat, *Frank Mildmay*, p. 133.
24. Ibid., p. 134.
25. Richardson, *A Mariner of England*, p. 247.
26. *Naval Chronicle*, vol. XXI (1809), p. 403.
27. The fire signals seen by Allemand were those displayed by the *Redpole* and the *Lyra* and not by the advanced frigates. *Naval Chronicle*, vol. XXI (1809), p. 373.
28. Ibid.
29. James, *Naval History*, vol. V, p. 109.

Chapter 12

1. Log of *Caledonia*, PRO: ADM.51/1981.
2. All Cochrane's signals are recorded under the heading 'Signals made 12th April 1809' in the *Caledonia*'s log, PRO: ADM.51/1981.
3. Gambier's despatch to the Admiralty, *The Times*, 22 April 1809, and *Naval Chronicle*, vol. XXI (1809), p. 345.
4. Gordon to the eleventh Earl of Dundonald, 12 April 1861, NAS, Edinburgh: GD33/74/3–4.
5. *Autobiography*, p. 235
6. Ibid.
7. James, *Naval History*, vol. IV, p. 394.
8. Maitland, a Scot, had already distinguished himself as a daring frigate captain. He made his name in 1815 when he returned to Basque Roads in the 74-gun ship *Bellerophon*, received the surrender of Napoleon, and brought him back to England.
9. *Autobiography*, p. 237.
10. Captain Marryat, *Frank Mildmay*, p. 136. The details of the killed and wounded appear in Lord Gambier's despatch of 14 April.

11. Log of *Imperieuse*, PRO: ADM.51/2462, part 5.

12. *Naval Chronicle*, vol. XXI (1809), p. 405.

13. Richardson, *A Mariner of England*, p. 248.

14. Ibid., p. 249.

15. *Autobiography*, p. 239; the log of the *Imperieuse* records that the French captain died of his wounds at 1.00 a.m. on 13 April; the incident is also noted by Richardson, *A Mariner of England*, p. 251; Captain Marryat, *Frank Mildmay*, p. 137; and a report under the heading 'Lord Cochrane's Victory', *The Times*, 27 April 1809.

16. An officer of the *Revenge* wrote from Rochefort, 13 April 1809, 'Lord Cochrane behaved most gallantly; he is now in a bomb, firing away at a three-decker that is on shore, which I hope he will be able to destroy.' *Naval Chronicle*, vol. XXI (1809), p. 399.

17. Quoted by John Sugden, *Lord Cochrane*, p. 137.

18. Gambier to Cochrane, 13 April 1809. Gurney, *Minutes of a Court Martial*, p. 53.

19. Cochrane to Gambier, 13 April 1809. Gurney, *Minutes of a Court Martial*, p. 53.

20. Gambier to Cochrane, 13 April 1809. Gurney, *Minutes of a Court Martial*, p. 54.

21. *Autobiography*, p. 243.

22. Ibid.

23. Gurney, *Minutes of a Court Martial*, p. 179.

24. James, *Naval History*, vol. IV, p. 422.

25. Sugden, *Lord Cochrane*, p. 138.

26. *Naval Chronicle*, vol. XXI (1809), p. 407.

27. Barry O'Meara, *Napoleon in Exile, or a Voice from St Helena* (London, 1822), vol. II, pp. 292–3.

Chapter 13

1. *The Times*, Saturday 22 April 1809.

2. Quoted by Christopher Lloyd in *Lord Cochrane*, p. 66.

3. *The Times*, Tuesday 2 May 1809.

4. List of promotions, PRO: ADM.1/141.

5. Wordsworth to Thomas de Quincey, 5 May 1809, in *The Letters of William and Dorothy Wordsworth: the Middle Years*, edited by Ernest de Selincourt (Oxford 1937), vol. I, p. 299.

6. Court martial of Harvey, PRO: ADM.1/5396.

7. Gurney, *Minutes of a Court Martial.* p. 2.

8. See James, *Naval History*, vol. IV, p. 425; Lloyd, *Lord Cochrane*, p. 68.

9. Ibid., p. 47.

10. Sugden, *Lord Cochrane*, note 25, p. 121.

11. Gurney, *Minutes of a Court Martial*, pp. 218–20.

12. Ibid., p. 138.

13. Ibid., p. 231.

14. *Autobiography,* p. 254.

15. Georgiana, Lady Chatterton, *Memorials of Admiral Lord Gambier,* vol. II, p. 334.

16. Ibid., vol. II, p. 328.

17. Ibid, p. 342.

18. Details of Holly Hill are given in the *Minutes of Evidence* on pp. 62, 65, 66, 75, 76. Katherine says he bought the house from his uncle, the Hon. Mr Cochrane, in 1810 or 1811, before she knew Cochrane.

19. Mitford, *Recollections of a Literary Life,* vol. 2, p. 24. There is no indication of the date of Mary Mitford's visit, but the evidence indicates it must have been either the summer of 1809 or the summer of 1810.

20. See Richard Ingrams, *The Life and Adventures of William Cobbett* (London, 2005), p. 93.

21. See Richard Woodman, 'Walcheren, 1809 – the lost opportunity' in *The Victory of Seapower,* pp. 136–9.

22. Christopher Lloyd, *Captain Marryat and the Old Navy* (London, 1939), p. 118.

23. Cochrane to Guthrie, 14 December 1809. NMM: AGC/38/1.

24. William James, in his *Naval History of Great Britain,* published in 1822–4, was particularly damning about Gambier's actions at Basque Roads. Lady Chatterton, in her *Memorials of Admiral Lord Gambier,* challenged James's conclusions and pointed out the errors and inconsistencies in Cochrane's account of the action in his *Autobiography.* The majority of Cochrane's biographers have unsurprisingly backed his version of the proceedings.

25. Admiral Sir Francis Austen to Lord Dundonald, 1 March 1860, NAS, Edinburgh: GD233/83/95.

Chapter 14

1. See M. W. Patterson, *Sir Francis Burdett and his Times* (London, 1931), pp. 242–69; and *The Times.*

2. Henry Hunt, *Memoirs of Henry Hunt* (London, 1820), vol. II, p. 391.

3. Hansard's *Parliamentary Debates,* 11 May 1810, vol. XVI, pp. 1006–11.

4. Grimble, *The Sea Wolf,* p. 133.

5. The correspondence between Cochrane and Yorke in June 1810 is in the Dundonald Papers, NAS, Edinburgh: GD 233/65/7.

6. Presumably this is '*La Julie,* lugger, 5 guns, 4 swivels, 44 men' that he reported capturing in a letter sent to Collingwood from Caldagues, 2 January 1809. *Autobiography,* p. 196.

7. Cochrane to Stuart, 11 February 1811, NAS, Edinburgh: GD 233/82/85.

8. First-hand detail about Cochrane's adventures in Malta, including the diary he kept at the time and several relevant letters, are among the Dundonald Papers in Edinburgh, GD.233/65/9; see also *Naval Chronicle,* vol. XXV (1811), pp. 299–302; John Sugden's

thesis on Lord Cochrane, pp. 201–4; and the chapter 'The Cochranes and the Courts' in Hill, *The Prizes of War*, pp. 106–17.

9. For detail on the workings of the prize courts, see Hill, *The Prizes of War*.

10. The relevant act was 45th Geo. III, c 72 which Cochrane kept quoting passages from when he was arrested and taken to court.

11. G. L. Collingwood, *Correspondence and Memoir of Lord Collingwood* (London, 1829), p. 285.

12. There is some confusion over which room the table of fees was in, Cochrane's account suggesting it was on the door of the judge's privy. See *Autobiography*, p. 297; Lloyd, *Lord Cochrane*, p.102; Vale, *Audacious Admiral Cochrane*, p.67; Hill, *Prizes of War*, p. 111

13. Scott to Croker, 30 May 1811, NA, Kew: ADM.1/3900

14. See Hill, *The Prizes of War*; PRO: ADM.1/3900 and ADM.1/3901.

15. Grimble, *The Sea Wolf*, p. 143.

16. Ibid, p. 144.

17. His 'Secret War Plans' for chemical warfare are discussed with his other inventions in Chapter 20.

18. Quoted by Grimble, *The Sea Wolf*, p. 171, from a letter of 14 October 1814 in the Dundonald Papers, NAS. Edinburgh.

19. For Katherine's correspondence with Lord Auckland see: Auckland Papers, BL: Add.MSS.34,459, ff.397, 399, 401, 430, 432, 439 and 443.

20. *Minutes of Evidence*. BL:, BS.96/51, p. 58.

21. In the *Minutes of Evidence* Kate says her parents died in her infancy and she did not know either of them. In Cochrane's *Autobiography* she is described as 'the orphan daughter of a family of honourable standing in the Midland Counties' who had been placed 'under the guardianship of her first cousin, Mr John Simpson of Portland Place and also of Fairlorn House in the County of Kent, of which county he was then High Sheriff'. Her name is given as 'Miss Katherine Corbett Barnes' in Cochrane's *Autobiography* p. 317; and as 'Katherine Frances Corbett, daughter of Thomas Barnes' in G. E. Cockayne, *The Complete Peerage*, p. 530; but appears as 'Catherine Corbett' and 'Catherine Corbet Barnes' in *Minutes of Evidence*, pp. 56, 73, 82. See Cochrane's entry in G. E. Cockayne, *The Complete Peerage*, vol. IV, p. 530.

22. Searches at the Essex Record Office and elsewhere have so far failed to reveal the birth or baptism certificate of Kate.

23. Captain Nathaniel Day Cochrane was five years younger than Cochrane. He entered the navy in 1794 and became a lieutenant in 1800 and a post-captain in 1806. He finished his naval career as a Rear-Admiral of the Blue.

24. *Minutes of Evidence*, p. 58.

25. Ibid.

26. Ibid., pp. 82–3.

Chapter 15

1. Quoted by J. M. Thompson, *Napoleon Bonaparte*, p. 340.
2. Quoted in Blake and Lawrence, *The Illustrated Companion to Nelson's Navy*, p. 191.
3. Cochrane arrived at Chatham on 9 February 1814 and took over command of the *Tonnant*, but on 16 March he was superseded by Captain Johnson who sailed the ship to Spithead. Captain Alexander Skene superseded Johnson on 5 April and on 7 April the *Tonnant* and her convoy sailed for Bermuda. Log of *Tonnant*, PRO. ADM.51/2901.
4. Dundonald to Cochrane, 13 May 1814, BL: Add.MSS.38257, ff. 249–51.
5. Oxford DNB.
6. A. Cochrane to Basil Cochrane, 18 October 1808; 2 November 1808; 26 February 1809; NLS, Edinburgh: 2572, ff. 172–3.
7. De Berenger's full name was Baron Charles Random De Berenger. He had originally traded in engravings but claimed to have lost £7,000 in trying to establish a fund for the dependants of artists. He had entered the Duke of Cumberland's Sharpshooter Volunteers in 1804. In May 1813 he met Andrew Cochrane-Johnstone who used him to prepare drawings for improvements in a property. I am grateful to John Sugden for this information and for many of the references to family papers used in this chapter.
8. *Autobiography*, p. 330.
9. The prime sources for the events leading up to the Stock Exchange fraud and the subsequent trial are: the transcript of the trial proceedings taken down in shorthand by W. B. Gurney and subsequently published under the title *The Trial of Charles Random de Berenger, Sir Thomas Cochrane, commonly called Lord Cochrane, the Hon. Andrew Cochrane Johnstone . . . for a Conspiracy in the Court of King's Bench, Guildhall on Wednesday 8th and Thursday 9th June 1814* (London, 1814); trial documents held by Farrer & Co., Cochrane's solicitors, NAS, Edinburgh: GD233/199; *Report of the sub-committee of the Stock Exchange relative to the late fraud* (London 1814); and J. B. Atlay, *The Trial of Lord Cochrane before Lord Ellenborough*; see also Lord John Campbell, *The Lives of the Chief Justices of England*, 3 vols (London, 1858); Lord Ellenborough, *The Guilt of Lord Cochrane in 1814: a Criticism* (London, 1914); Henry Cecil, *A Matter of Speculation: The Case of Lord Cochrane* (London, 1965).
10. William C. Townsend, *Modern State Trials* (1850), vol. II, p. 29.
11. These figures are taken from Gurney, *The Trial*, pp. 23–4.
12. Log of the *Tonnant*, PRO: ADM.51/2901.
13. *Minutes of Evidence*. BL: BS96/51, p. 63.
14. Ibid.
15. Gurney, *The Trial*, p. 8.
16. *Autobiography*, p. 341.
17. Campbell, *The Lives of the Chief Justices of England* (London, 1858), vol. III, p. 243.
18. Gurney, *The Trial*, p. 254.
19. This Lord Melville (the second Viscount) was Robert Dundas (1771–1851) and he

was the son of Henry Dundas, first Viscount Melville, who was the friend of the Cochrane family. Confusingly, both held the office of First Lord of the Admiralty.

20. Gurney, *The Trial*, p. 255

21. Ibid.

22. Ibid.

23. Ibid., p. 275.

24. Quoted in the Law Report in *The Times* of 10 June 1814. This neatly summarised Lord Ellenborough's lengthy summing-up which is quoted in full by Atlay, *The Trial of Lord Cochrane before Lord Ellenborough*, pp. 411–72.

25. Sugden, *Lord Cochrane*, p. 221.

26. Gurney, *The Trial*, p. 555.

27. Ibid., p. 563.

28. From the diary of Henry Crabb Robinson, a young barrister who attended the trial. Quoted by Cecil, *A Matter of Speculation*, p. 169.

29. Cochrane to Elizabeth Cochrane-Johnstone, 25 June 1814, NAS, Edinburgh: GD 233/177/103.

30. *Letters and Papers of Sir Thomas Byam Martin*, edited by R. V. Hamilton (Navy Records Society, 1903) vol. III, pp. 198–9.

31. Hansard, *Commons Journals*, 5 July 1814, vol. LXIX, pp. 427–33.

32. A. G. l'Estrange, *The Life of Mary Russell Mitford* (1870), vol. I, p. 271.

33. *The Times*, 12 August 1814. The expulsion from the Order of the Bath followed a resolution of a meeting of the Order and was carried out with a warrant from Lord Sidmouth, the Home Secretary in Lord Liverpool's administration.

34. *Autobiography*, p. 338.

35. Sugden, *Lord Cochrane*, pp. 222–46.

36. I am grateful to the Rt Hon. Sir Anthony Evans, PC, former Judge of the High Court of Justice and a former Lord Justice of Appeal, for examining all the relevant books and papers of the Stock Exchange trial of 1814 and giving me his opinions on the conduct of the case and the verdict.

37. Quoted by Grimble, *The Sea Wolf*, p. 166.

38. Ibid., pp. 164–5.

39. Ibid.

40. Elizabeth Cochrane-Johnstone (Lady Napier) to Dundonald (Cochrane), Christmas 1859, NAS, Edinburgh: GD233/177/103.

41. Vincent Cronin, *Napoleon*, London 1971, edition cited 1994 p. 365.

Chapter 16

1. Sugden, *Lord Cochrane*, p. 245.

2. *Autobiography*, p. 319.

3. Cochrane to Kate, 14 October 1814. Quoted by Grimble, *The Sea Wolf*, p. 171.

4. *The Trial of Lord Cochrane at Guildford, August 17, 1816, for an escape from the Kings bench Prison* (London, 1816), p. 10.

5. Dundonald and Bourne, *Life of Lord Cochrane*, vol. 1, pp. 55, 56.

6. Report of William Jones to the Committee of Privileges, 23 March 1815. *Minutes of Evidence*, p. 19.

7. Report by Mr Bennet, MP, quoted by Grimble, *The Sea Wolf*, p. 174.

8. *Cobbett's Weekly Political Register*, vol. 31, nos VIII and IX, Saturday 31 August 1816, p. 180.

9. Dundonald and Bourne, *Life of Lord Cochrane*, vol. 1, pp. 72–3.

10. Cochrane to Guthrie, 12 October 1815. Guthrie Papers, NMM, JOD/55, 56 (AGC/ 38).

11. Cochrane to Guthrie, 19 January 1816. NMM: JOD/55, 56

12. Dundonald and Bourne, *Life of Lord Cochrane*, vol. 1, p. 86.

13. Cochrane to Guthrie, 28 November 1816. NMM: JOD/55, 56

14. Quoted by Richard Ingrams, *The Life and Adventures of William Cobbett*, p. 125.

15. Samuel Bamford, *Passages in the Life of a Radical*, vol. 2, p. 7.

16. Grimble, *The Sea Wolf*, p. 180.

17. Bamford, *Passages in the Life of a Radical*, vol. 1, p. 20.

18. Ibid.

19. In her evidence to the House of Lords Committee of Privileges, Kate said that Holly Hill 'was sold after the terrible conspiracy of that time', and of the two houses in Hampshire (at Warsash and Holly Hill), 'They were sold to pay lawyers' debts, and all sorts of bothers and miseries.' *Minutes of Evidence*, p. 65.

20. Quoted by Ingrams, *The Life and Adventures of William Cobbett*, p. 133.

21. Alvarez to Zenteno, 12 January 1818. Luiz Uribe Orrego, *Nuestra Marina Milita* (Valparaíso, 1910), p. 174.

22. Andrew Lambert, *Steam, Steel and Shellfire* (London 2001), p. 19. There is an engraved illustration of the *Rising Star* in the National Maritime Museum which is reproduced by Ian Grimble in *The Sea Wolf*.

23. Dundonald and Bourne, *Life of Lord Cochrane*, vol. 1, pp. 133–5.

Chapter 17

1. Quoted from information in the Museo Naval y Maritimo, Valparaiso, Chile.

2. *Memoirs of General Miller*, ed. John Miller (London, 1829), vol. 1, p. 425.

3. Maria Graham, Lady Callcott, *Journal of a Residence in Chile during the year 1822, and a Voyage from Chile to Brazil in 1823* (London, 1824), p. 43.

4. W.G.D. Worthington to John Quincy Adams, 26 January 1819. William R. Manning, *Diplomatic Correspondence of the United States concerning the independence of the Latin-American nations.* (New York 1925), vol. II, p. 1027.

5. Ibid, p. 1028.

6. Thomas, Earl of Dundonald, *Narrative of Services in the Liberation of Chili, Peru, and Brazil* (London, 1859), vol. 1, p. 3.

7. Zenteno to Cochrane, 7 January 1819, NAS, Edinburgh: Dundonald Papers, GD233/39/261.

8. Bowles to Croker 28 November 1817, quoted in Graham and Humphreys, eds, *The Navy and South America* (Navy Records Society), vol. 104.

9. See Dundonald and Bourne, *Life of Lord Cochrane*, vol. 1, pp. 152–3; Grimble, *The Sea Wolf*, p. 196; Thomas, *Cochrane*, p. 249.

10. The frigates were the *O'Higgins*, 50 guns, the *San Martin*, 56 guns, and the *Lautaro*, 44 guns; the brigs were the *Chacabuco*, 20 guns, the *Galvarino*, 18 guns, and the *Araucano*, 16 guns; and the sloop was the 14-gun *Puyrredon*. For further detail on the ships, and the composition of the crews (and invaluable information on all Cochrane's operations in Chile) see David Cubitt, *Lord Cochrane and the Chilean Navy, 1818–1823* (Edinburgh University Ph.D. thesis, 1974).

11. Dundonald, *Narrative of Services*, vol. 1, p. 4.

12. Vale, *The Audacious Admiral Cochrane*, p. 93. I am indebted to Brian Vale for his pioneering research into Cochrane's life in South America and am grateful to him for helpful discussions and for generously making available to me some of his unpublished material.

13. William Miller (1795–1861) became a general in the army of Peru after the country had been liberated, and in 1843 became the British consul-general in the Pacific. He died at Callao.

14. Diary entry for 20 July 1835, quoted in *Charles Darwin's Diary of the Voyage of HMS Beagle*, ed. Nora Barlow (Cambridge, 1933), p. 330.

15. Dundonald, *Narrative of Services*, vol. 1, p. 10.

16. Miller, ed., *Memoirs of General Miller* (London, 1829), vol. 1, p. 215.

17. Quoted by Grimble, *The Sea Wolf*, p. 198.

18. See Vale, *The Audacious Admiral Cochrane*, p. 99, and note 12 on p. 222. In fact the net annual pay (excluding table money) of a British vice-admiral in 1815 was £1,186 11s 4d, and his annual table money was £364 0s 0d.

19. The armed vessels captured were the *Aguila* and *Begona*. Miller, ed., *Memoirs of General Miller*, vol. 1, p. 239, and Dundonald and Bourne, *Life of Lord Cochrane*, vol. 1, p. 165.

20. Cubitt, *Lord Cochrane and the Chilean Navy*, pp. 143–4.

21. Dundonald, *Narrative of Services*, vol. 1, p. 36.

22. John Miers, *Travels in Chile and La Plata* (London, 1826), vol. 1, p.. 489.

23. Miller, ed., *Memoirs of General Miller*, vol. 1, p. 243

24. Dundonald, *Narrative of Services*, vol. 1, p. 38.

25. Cochrane to Zenteno, 6 February 1820. Quoted by Grimble, p. 208.

26. Quoted by Grimble, *The Sea Wolf*, p. 209.

27. Maria Graham, Lady Callcott, *Journal of a Residence in Chile during the year 1822, and a Voyage from Chile to Brazil in 1823*, p. 43.

28. W. B. Stevenson, *A Historical and Descriptive Narrative of Twenty Years Residence in South America* (London 1825) vol. III, pp. 247–8.

29. Grimble, *The Sea Wolf*, p. 211.

30. Ibid. p. 219.

31. Dundonald, *Narrative of Services*, vol. 1, p. 83.

32. Cubitt, *Lord Cochrane and the Chilean Navy*, p. 120.

33. Dundonald, *Narrative of Services*, vol. 1, p. 85.

34. Ibid., p. 86.

35. Searle to Sir Thomas Hardy, 8 November 1820. Quoted by Vale, *The Audacious Admiral Cochrane*, p. 116, from Graham and Humphreys, eds, *The Navy and South America* (Navy Records Society), vol. 104.

36. Basil Hall, *Extracts from a Journal written on the Coasts of Chile, Peru, and Mexico in the Years 1820, 1821 and 1822* (Edinburgh, 1824), vol. 2, p. 77.

37. San Martin to Cochrane, 10 November 1820. Quoted in Dundonald, *Narrative of Services*, vol. 1, p. 92.

38. San Martin to O'Higgins, 1 December 1820. Dundonald, *Narrative of Services*, vol. 1, p. 93.

39. Lady Cochrane to Cochrane, 6 November 1820, NAS, Edinburgh: GD233/13.

40. See *The Times*, 5, 6, 7 and 11 September and 23 October 1821 for reports complaining about Cochrane's actions. Sir Thomas Hardy, who was in command of the British squadron in the area, made it clear that he considered Cochrane's blockade to be illegal.

41. Grimble, *The Sea Wolf*, p. 233,

42. General José de San Martin (1778–1850) was Protector of Peru for no more than fourteen months. He resigned in September 1822. He told O'Higgins that he decided to abdicate because of bad health and because he was tired of being called a tyrant. He returned to Chile, travelled on to his native Argentina but finding the country in political turmoil he decided to emigrate to France, where he spent the rest of his life. See Michael J. Jost, *The Cochrane–San Martin Conflict (1818–1823)*, Ph.D. thesis, Texas, 1973.

43. This sum was made up of $150,000 in arrears of pay; $110,000 in prize money for the *Esmeralda*; a gratuity of $50,000 for capturing the frigate; and $110,000 which had been promised on the fall of Lima. See Vale, *The Audacious Admiral Cochrane*, p. 122.

44. He sent $40,000 back to Valparaiso, distributed $111,382 for future expenses, and distributed $131,618 as pay and prize money. On 14 September he shipped home $13,507 (£2,700) in coin and bullion in HMS *Superb*. See Vale, *The Audacious Admiral Cochrane*, p. 124.

45. Dundonald, *Narrative of Services*, vol. 1, p. 188.

Chapter 18

1. Maria Graham, *Journal of a Residence in Chile*, p. 146.

2. Zenteno to Cochrane, 22 February 1820. NAS. Edinburgh: GD233/39/262.

3. Maria Graham (1785–1842) was born near Cockermouth, Cumbria, the daughter of George Dundas, a naval officer. She spent her early years in Oxford, London and Edinburgh, and travelled to India in 1808 when her father was posted to Bombay. She met Lieutenant Thomas Graham on the voyage out and married him in Bombay in 1809. Following her adventures in South America she returned to England and married Sir Augustus Wall Callcott in 1827. They lived at The Mall, Kensington Gravel Pits, and their house was a notable gathering place for writers and artists.

4. Graham, *Journal of a Residence in Chile*, p. 146.

5. Ibid., p. 150.

6. Brian Vale has shown that after the capture of the schooner *Sacramento* in September 1821 Cochrane shipped home $13,507 (£2,700) in HMS *Superb*. On his return to Valparaiso in June 1822 he shipped home $16,997 (£3,360) in the British warships *Alacrity* and *Doris*; and when he left Chile for Brazil in the *Colonel Allen* he took with him boxes of gold bullion worth £10,400. See Brian Vale, *The Audacious Admiral Cochrane*, pp. 123–4, 129 and 134; and NAS, Edinburgh: GD233/39/261, GD233/20/450.

7. Graham, entry for July 7, 1822, *Journal of a Residence in Chile*, p. 173.

8. Ibid., p. 188.

9. Ibid., p. 335.

10. Maria Graham, *Journal of a Voyage to Brazil* (London, 1824), p. 218.

11. Vale, *The Audacious Admiral Cochrane*, pp. 139–40.

12. Graham, *Journal of a Voyage to Brazil*, p. 222.

13. For a detailed description of the ships, the battle and Cochrane's subsequent exploits while in command of the Brazilian navy, see Brian Vale, 'Lord Cochrane in Brazil: the Naval War of Independence, 1823', in *Mariners Mirror*, vol. LVII (1971), no. 4, pp. 415–42.

14. Dundonald, *Narrative of Services*, vol. 2, p. 31.

15. According to Cochrane's account in the *Narrative of Services*, the *Pedro Primiero* entered the bay alone, but Brazilian sources make it clear that the flagship was accompanied by the *Maria da Gloria* and the *Real Carolina*. See Brian Vale 'Lord Cochrane in Brazil', *Mariners Mirror*, vol. LVII (1971), no. 4, p. 427.

16. Dundonald, *Narrative of Services*, vol. 2, p. 56.

17. In his *Narrative of Services*, vol. 2, p. 60, Cochrane describes sailing towards São Luis flying Portuguese colours but all contemporary observers agree that the ship flew the British flag. See Vale, p. 147, and Note 6 on p. 225.

18. *Narrative of Services*, vol. 2, p. 61–2.

19. Grimble, *The Sea Wolf*, p. 265.

20. Graham, *Journal of a Voyage to Brazil*, p. 321.

21. Cochrane to Major William Cochrane, April 1824, NAS, Edinburgh: GD233/26/186.

22. Quoted by Vale, p. 226, from 'Kotzebue e o Rio de Janeiro em 1824', *Revista fo Instituto Historico Brasileiro*, 80 (1918), p. 517.

23. Dundonald, *Narrative of Services*, vol. 2, p. 162.

24. This was a part payment. Cochrane reckoned the full amount owed in prize money was £85,000 (424 contos). See Vale, *The Audacious Admiral Cochrane*, p. 163, and Dundonald, *Narrative of Services*, vol. 1, pp. 219–23.

25. Vale, *The Audacious Admiral Cochrane*, p. 164. Information from William Jackson's diary, NAS, Edinburgh: GD233/31/237.

26. Dundonald, *Narrative of Services*, vol. 2, p. 247.

27. Ibid.

28. Ibid., p. 248.

29. A report from Portsmouth, 27 June, headed 'Arrival of Lord Cochrane at Portsmouth', published in *The Times*, 29 June 1825.

30. Lord Melville to Sir George Martin, 28 June 1825, NLS, Edinburgh: 2618, f. 223.

31. Ibid.

32. *The Times*, 29 June 1825.

33. Report from 'A private correspondent', Portsmouth, 27 June, also published in *The Times*, 29 June 1825.

34. Robert Dundas, second Viscount Melville (1771–1851), held the office of First Lord of the Admiralty from 1812 to 1827.

Chapter 19

1. *Minutes of Evidence*, p. 65.

2. Ibid., p. 68.

3. Ibid., p. 78.

4. *Minutes of Evidence*, p. 79.

5. In *Minutes of Evidence*, p. 78, Kate says that Cochrane used to stay at Douglas's Hotel in St Andrews Square, Edinburgh. His last letter to Guthrie is from the George Hotel.

6. Scott's poem was published in the *Morning Post* on 19 October 1825. The full six verses are reproduced in Dundonald and Bourne, *Life of Lord Cochrane*, vol. 1, p. 326.

7. Dundonald, *Narrative of Services*, vol. 2, p. 8.

8. George Finlay, *History of the Greek Revolution* (London, 1861), vol. 1, p. 320.

9. Cochrane received a formal letter of invitation by Alexander Mavrocordatos, Secretary of the Greek National Assembly, in September 1825. See Vale, *The Audacious Admiral Cochrane*, p. 170.

10. Quoted by Lloyd, *Lord Cochrane*, p. 175.

11. The original order was for three large and three small steamships. The large steamships (length 150 feet, breadth 25 feet) were the *Perseverance* (renamed *Karteria*), *Enterprise* (renamed *Epicheiresis*) and *Irresistible* (renamed *Hermes*). The small steamships (length 100 feet, breadth 16 feet) were the *Alert, Lasher* and *Mercury*. The *Mercury* arrived in Greece in December 1828. The *Alert* and *Lasher* were never completed. See Douglas Dakin, 'Lord Cochrane's Greek steam fleet' in *Mariners Mirror*, vol. 39, (1953), pp. 211–19.

12. The two sailing warships built in America were heavy 60-gun frigates. The *Hellas* played a part in the Greek war but the second frigate, which was sold to the American navy, became the USS *Hudson*. See Howard I. Chapelle, *The American Sailing Navy* (New York, 1949), pp. 351–2, 362.

13. Grimble, *The Sea Wolf*, p. 294.

14. Auckland Papers, BL: Add. MSS.34,459, ff. 397, 399, 401.

15. Ibid., f. 430.

16. Ibid., f. 439.

17. Cochrane to Auckland, 22 April 1826. Ibid., f. 441.

18. Katherine Cochrane to Auckland, 8 May 1826. Ibid., f. 443.

19. The fourth surviving child of Katherine and Cochrane, christened Arthur Auckland Leopold Pedro, was born in September 1824 before Katherine's friendship with Lord Auckland had developed into a love affair. The fifth child of Katherine and Cochrane died in childbirth in 1829. Their sixth child, Ernest Gray Lambton, was born in 1834.

20. George Eden, Earl of Auckland (1784–1849), was born in Beckenham, Kent, the son of William Eden, first Baron Auckland. He was President of the Board of Trade 1830–34; First Lord of the Admiralty 1835; Governor-General of India 1835–41; First Lord of the Admiralty 1846 until his death in 1849. See Oxford DNB.

21. Dundonald and Bourne, *Life of Lord Cochrane*, vol. 2, p. 356.

22. Quoted by Finlay, *History of the Greek Revolution*, vol. 2, p. 19.

23. Finlay, *History of the Greek Revolution*, vol. 2, p. 138.

24. Admiral Miaoulis had written to Cochrane from Poros on 23 February 1827 expressing his pleasure 'at the honour you do me in associating me with your important operations. I shall be happy, my admiral, if in serving you I can do my duty'. Dundonald and Bourne, *Life of Lord Cochrane*, vol. 2, p. 386.

25. Finlay, *History of the Greek Revolution*, vol. 2, p. 144.

26. General Gordon, disillusioned by the behaviour of the Greeks, had left for England a few weeks before, and when he came to write his *History of the Greek Revolution* he called Cochrane's strategy for 6 May 'an insane scheme' and other historians, including Finlay, were equally critical.

27. Quoted by Lloyd, *Lord Cochrane*, p. 184,

28. Dundonald and Bourne, *Life of Lord Cochrane*, vol. 2, p. 93.

29. For further details of the battle see: C. M. Woodhouse, *The Battle of Navarino* (London, 1965) and Michael Sanderson, *Sea Battles: A Reference Guide* (Newton Abbot, 1975), pp. 126–8.

30. Quoted by Lloyd, *Lord Cochrane*, p. 188.

31. Dundonald and Bourne, *Life of Lord Cochrane*, vol. 2, pp. 136, 156.

32. Ibid., p. 156.

33. Cochrane to Monsieur Eynard, quoted by Dundonald and Bourne, *Life of Lord Cochrane*, vol. 2, p. 169.

34. See his letter of 26 November to Capodistrias, quoted by Dundonald and Bourne, *Life of Lord Cochrane*, vol. 2, pp. 177–8.

35. Capodistrias to Cochrane, 4 December 1828. Dundonald and Bourne, *Life of Lord Cochrane*, vol. 2, p. 179.

36. Grimble, *The Sea Wolf*, p. 316.

Chapter 20

1. Quoted by Grimble, *The Sea Wolf*, p. 316.

2. Memorial of 4 June 1818 to Duke of Clarence, Lord High Admiral. Quoted in full in Dundonald and Bourne, *Life of Lord Cochrane*, vol. 2, pp. 202–6.

3. *The Greville Memoirs* (1938), vol. 1, eds Lytton Strachey and Roger Fulford, pp. 398–9. The attack on Algiers was led by Count de Ghaisnes de Beaumont, Marshal of France, and was a pretext to begin the conquest of Algeria.

4. Dundonald and Bourne, *Life of Lord Cochrane*, vol. 2, p. 209.

5. Cochrane's father, the 9th earl, had married his third wife, Anna Maria Plowden, in 1819 but she died in 1822.

6. Dundonald and Bourne, *Life of Lord Cochrane*, vol. 2, pp. 214–5.

7. *The Times*, 9 May 1832. The order was issued from the Admiralty Office on 2 May and published in the *London Gazette* on 8 May.

8. William Cochrane to Lord Cochrane, 3 November 1829, NAS, Edinburgh: GD233/180.

9. Hanover Lodge was built in 1827 and was one of several villas in Regents Park which were designed by Decimus Burton (1800–81), a leading architect of the Greek Revival and the designer of the Athenaeum Club, London, the Palm House at Kew and the screen at Hyde Park Corner.

10. Grimble, *The Sea Wolf*, p. 324.

11. *Autobiography*, p. 115. Cochrane had also experimented with giant kites to increase the speed of the *Pallas*, rather in the manner of the modern spinnaker or cruising chute.

12. Cochrane had visited the sulphur mines in Sicily in 1811, and in April 1812 he submitted a Memorial to the Prince Regent setting out his plans for using sulphur dioxide as a weapon to destroy the French fleet at Toulon. The Memorial was considered by a committee which included the Duke of York, Lord Keith and William Congreve, but his proposals were not taken up. For further details see 'The Secret War Plan of Lord Dundonald', a postscript in Grimble, *The Sea Wolf*, pp. 384–417 and Charles Stephenson, *The Admiral's Secret Weapon: Lord Dundonald and the origins of chemical warfare*, (Woodbridge 2006).

13. The civil engineer Sir Marc Isambard Brunel (1769–1849) was born in Normandy and served in the French navy for six years. He came to England in 1799 to patent his machinery for making ships' blocks. The Thames Tunnel, the first to be built under a navigable river, was opened in 1843. It is now part of the London Underground system (the East London line from Whitechapel to New Cross).

14. From 'The Steam Engine Simplified' by the Earl of Dundonald in *Letters to R. Stephenson Senior, 1818–1836*. BL: Add.MS.38,781, ff. 68–9. See also John Bourne, *A Treatise on the Steam Engine* (London, 1861).

15. In 1829 the *Rocket*, designed by George and Robert Stephenson, had triumphantly beaten the opposition at the trials held at Rainhill near Liverpool for the best steam engine and won the £500 prize offered by the directors of the Liverpool to Manchester Railway.

16. Cochrane to James Guthrie, MD, 6 May 1839. NMM: JOD/55, 56 (AGC/38). According to Guthrie's service record in the National Archives (*Surgeons for Service*, PRO: ADM.104/12) his address from 1815 to his death in 1862 was Wester Drumhead, Newburgh, Fife.

17. Dundonald and Bourne, *Life of Lord Cochrane*, vol. 2, p. 240.

18. Ibid., p. 241.

19. Ibid., p. 243.

20. Earl of Dundonald, *Observations on Naval Affairs and on some Collateral Subjects; including Instances of Injustice experienced by the Author: with a Summary of his Naval Service; and a Copious Index* (London, 1847). See also Christopher Lloyd's observations in *Lord Cochrane*, p. 194.

21. Letter of 27 April 1847 quoted in Dundonald and Bourne, *Life of Lord Cochrane*, vol. 2, p. 283.

22. The announcement was published in *The Times* on Wednesday 26 May 1847.

23. Dundonald and Bourne, *Life of Lord Cochrane*, vol. 2, p. 285.

24. Auckland to Dundonald, 27 December 1847. Quoted by Dundonald and Bourne, *Life of Lord Cochrane*, vol. 2, p. 290.

25. See log of HMS *Wellesley*, NA, Kew: ADM.51/3703.

26. Quoted by Grimble, *The Sea Wolf*, p. 351.

Chapter 21

1. Quoted by Grimble, *The Sea Wolf*, p. 370. The Crystal Palace was re-opened by Queen Victoria at Sydenham on 10 June 1854.

2. See Dundonald and Bourne, *Life of Lord Cochrane*, vol. 2, footnote on p. 334, which gives details of the patents and the years in which each was taken out.

3. A. C. Benton and Viscount Esher, eds, *The Letters of Queen Victoria, 1837–1861* (London, 1908), vol. 2, p. 9.

4. For more detail see Charles Stevenson, 'To the Imperial Mind: The Secret War Plan of Lord Dundonald', in N. Tracy and M. Robson, eds, *The Age of Sail*, vol. 1 (London, 2002). The same article appears as a Postscript in Grimble, *The Sea Wolf*, pp. 384–417.

5. Grimble, *The Sea Wolf*, p. 358.

6. In 1861 William Alexander Mackinnon, MP, gave evidence before the House of Lords Committee of Privileges. *Minutes of Evidence*, p. 38.

7. Grimble, *The Sea Wolf*, p. 358.

8. Ibid., p. 359.

9. Arthur Cochrane (1824–1905) later saw action in the Far East and ended his career with a Knighthood and the rank of admiral. Ernest was promoted to post-captain and commanded a ship off West Africa before marrying the daughter of the Governor of Sierra Leone. He retired to Ireland and became High Sheriff of Donegal.

10. *Illustrated Times*, 9 June 1855

11. Grimble, *The Sea Wolf*, p. 364.

12. Ibid., p. 365.

13. Robert Simpson to Dundonald, 15 May 1857. Simpson told Cochrane that the Government of Chile were giving him a medal for his past services, and added, 'I have been requested to procure a biographical sketch of your Lordship's eventful life in order to its publication in this country . . .' Quoted by Grimble, *The Sea Wolf*, p. 370.

14. See Brian Vale, *Audacious Admiral Cochrane*, pp. 202–7, for a detailed account of Cochrane's extravagant demands for back pay, prize money and other payments from the Chilean and Brazilian governments.

15. Grimble, *The Sea Wolf*, p. 371.

16. Cochrane to Thomas Cochrane, 20 July 1859. NAS, Edinburgh: GD 233/14.

17. *Minutes of Evidence*, p. 41.

18. Cochrane to Jackson, 1 January 1860. NAS. Edinburgh, GD 233/29/217.

19. Grimble, *The Sea Wolf*, p. 376.

20. Ibid.

21. Ibid., p. 377.

22. *The Times*, Thursday 15 November 1860.

23. Brougham to Dundonald, 31 October 1860. Quoted by Dundonald and Bourne, *Life of Lord Cochrane*, vol. 2, pp. 360–61.

24. Ibid., p. 357.

25. According to the report of the funeral in *The Times* of 15 November, 'In the first carriage were the chief mourners, the new Earl of Dundonald and his three brothers; the second and third carriages contained the pall-bearers, the others being occupied by mourners immediately related to the family.'

26. Many of Kate's later letters are in the Dundonald archives in Edinburgh and several are quoted by Grimble, *The Sea Wolf*, pp. 363–74.

27. Cochrane wrote to his son Tom from the Royal Hotel, Deal, on 3 August 1859, 'I shall be deeply, deeply grieved if the apparent difference between your Mamma and you increases to dislike, or to a break . . .', NAS, Edinburgh: GD233/14.

Epilogue

1. *The Times*, 2 November 1860.

2. *Illustrated London News*, 3 November 1860 (no. 1058, vol. XXXVII), p. 413.

3. *Punch*, 24 November 1860 (vol. XXXIX), p. 203.

4. Napier to Guthrie, 12 March 1814, Guthrie Papers, NMM.

5. *Minutes of Evidence*. BL: BS.96/51, p.58

6. Lord Ellenborough, *The Guilt of Lord Cochrane in 1814: a Criticism* (London, 1914), p. vi.

7. Lord John Campbell, *The Lives of the Chief Justices of England* (London, 1858).

8. Sugden, *Lord Cochrane*, p. 222.

9. Lloyd, *Lord Cochrane* p. 190.

10. Cecil, *A Matter of Speculation*, p. 11.

11. Vale, *The Audacious Admiral Cochrane*, p. 213.

INDEX

A NOTE ON THE TYPE

The text of this book is set in Bell. Originally cut for John Bell in 1788, this type was used in Bell's newspaper, *The Oracle*. It was regarded as the first English Modern typeface. This version was designed by Monotype in 1932.